Two Hundred Years of American Educational Thought

D1243920

Two Hundred Years of American Educational Thought

Henry J. Perkinson

New York University

David
McKay
Company,
Inc.
New
York

Two Hundred Years of American Educational Thought

MANUFACTURED IN THE UNITED STATES OF AMERICA

Developmental Editor: Nicole Benevento
Interior Design: Gloria Gentile
Cover Design: Jane Sterrett
Manufacturing and Production Supervisor: Donald W. Strauss
Composition: Colonial Press Inc.
Printing and Binding: Haddon Craftsmen

Library of Congress Cataloging in Publication Data

Perkinson, Henry J
  Two hundred years of American educational thought.

  (Educational policy, planning, and theory)
  Includes index.
  1. Education—United States—History. 2. Education
—Philosophy. I. Title.
LA205.P45   370.1'0973   75–43907
ISBN 0–679–30305–7

To my mother, and the memory of my father.

Preface

What are schools for? What's worth knowing? Who can be educated? These are the perennial questions of education. This book contains some of the answers Americans have given to them over the last two hundred years.

The educational theories put forth during the past two centuries underlie many of the arrangements that exist in our schools today. Thus, one purpose of this book is to help readers understand what's going on in American education. But these educational theories are not perfect—fallible men created them. So I urge readers to approach them critically, raising arguments against them, entering into the continuing dialogue on these perennial questions of education. Critical confrontations with different theories can help us gain a better understanding of our own theories and assumptions. Because this is so, the second purpose of this book is to help readers—especially educators and educators-to-be—articulate, clarify, criticize, and perhaps improve their own theories of education.

A word on the historical method used in the book. My concern throughout was to discover the problem, or problems, that launched each of these figures into the realm of educational theory. I base my interpretation of the development of their theories on my reading of their own books and articles. In some instances I have greatly benefited from recent biographies.

A number of friends and colleagues read one or more parts, in one or more drafts, of this book. I am grateful to them for their help: Don Adams, Thomas Colwell, Stephenie Edgerton, Maxine Greene, Robert Heslep, Paul Mattingly, Jonathan Messerli, Neil Postman, Jennings Waggoner.

Atlantic Highlands, N.J.

Henry J. Perkinson

vii

Acknowledgments

The author wishes to thank these publishers for their kind permission to reprint the following:

Pages 312–29 are from the book *How Children Fail* by John Holt. Copyright © 1964 by Pitman Publishing Corporation. Reprinted by permission of Pitman Publishing Corp.

Pages 16–40 are from *The Papers of Benjamin Franklin, Volume 3*, by Leonard W. Labaree, ed. Reprinted by permission of Yale University Press.

Pages 220–35 are from *Schools of Tomorrow* by John and Evelyn Dewey. Copyright 1915 by E. P. Dutton & Co.; renewal, 1943 by John Dewey and Evelyn Dewey. Reprinted by permission of the publishers, E. P. Dutton & Co., Inc.

Pages 329–52, "Why We Must Disestablish School," are from *Deschooling Society* by Ivan Illich. Volume Forty-four of World Perspective Series, planned and edited by Ruth Nanda Anshen. Copyright © 1970 by Ivan Illich. Reprinted by permission of Harper & Row, Publishers, Inc.

Pages 49–58 are from *The Papers of Thomas Jefferson, Volume 2, January 1777 to June 1779*, by Julian P. Boyd, ed. Copyright 1950 by Princeton University Press. Reprinted by permission of Princeton University Press.

Pages 261–81 are from the book *The Child, the Parent, and the State* by James Bryant Conant. Cambridge: Harvard University Press. Copyright © 1959 by the President and Fellows of Harvard College.

Pages 119–33 are from *The Early Lectures of Ralph Waldo Emerson*, Volume 3, edited by R. E. Spiller and W. E. Williams. Cambridge: The Belknap Press of Harvard University Press. Copyright © 1972 by the President and Fellows of Harvard College.

Contents

Two
Hundred
Years
of
American
Educational
Thought

1
Benjamin Franklin

In the early pages of his *Autobiography*, Benjamin Franklin reports that as a child he read his father's copy of Cotton Mather's *Essays to Do Good*. This book, he confesses, "gave me a turn of thinking that had an influence on some of the principal future events of my life."

This is surprising coming from the worldly Franklin, all the more so when one looks at Cotton Mather's book. Written in the language of a Puritan theologian and minister, Mather's tract is full of references to the Devil ("the great destroyer") and "the Blessed Jesus and the Glorious Christ"—neither of whom figured prominently in the writings of Benjamin Franklin. Nor did Franklin ever write about Mather's favorite topics: the worth of the Bible, prayer, or spiritual meditation. Yet Franklin, near the end of his life, wrote to Cotton Mather's son reaffirming his debt to the *Essays to Do Good*. That book, he claimed, had "an influence on my conduct through life, for I·have always set a greater value on the character of a doer of good than on any other kind of reputation; and if I have been, as you seem to think, a useful citizen, the public owes the advantage of it to that book." So Franklin must have meant it. The *Essays to Do Good* did influence him. But how?

Mather's book has the puritan ethic as its central theme: a virtuous life signals personal salvation. Although no one could guarantee the salvation of another, each could help "save" others by "doing good"—reminding them of their Christian duties, and leading them back to the path of righteousness. Mather lists ways husbands and wives can do good to their neighbors; how ministers, schoolteachers, magistrates, and physicians all have opportunities to do good. For all, the task is the same: to restore others to the proper spiritual life. To the physician, for example, he says: "And what should hinder you from considering the *Souls* of your *Patients, Interior* State; their *Spiritual Health;* what they *have done,* and what they have to do, that they may be on *Good Terms with Heaven?*

Franklin was born into a household imbued with this kind of stern piety—his militant nonconformist father had left England after the Restoration of Charles II. Yet, from early youth on, Benjamin accepted only the substance and rejected the form of his father's strict Calvinism. Benjamin had no worries about the devil, nor fear of the Lord; spent no time praising God, nor offering supplication to him. Late in life he privately revealed his religious beliefs to Ezra Stiles, the president of Yale: "Here is my Creed. I believe in one God, Creator of the Universe. That he governs it by his Providence. That he ought to be worshipped. That the most acceptable service we render to him is doing good to his other Children. That the soul of Man is immortal, and will be treated with Justice in another Life respecting its Conduct in this. These I take to be the fundamental Principles of all sound Religion."

The most revealing phrase here is Franklin's explanation of how men can render "service" (the choice of word is significant) to God: by "doing good to his other children." This was Cotton Mather's message. But in Franklin's hands, that mission to do good became secularized. "Doing good" for him meant helping to make people happy here and now. And happiness, he sagely noted in his *Autobiography*, consists of little things, the elimination of small but concrete evils that afflict us: "Human felicity is produced not so much by great pieces of good fortune that seldom happen, as by little advantages that occur every day."

Many were the little advantages that Franklin himself conferred on his fellow men. There were advantages like clean and safe streets: in Philadelphia Franklin initiated the creation of regular fire, police, and sanitation departments; and he got many streets paved and lighted. He invented bifocals, the folding step stool, and the gadget still used by grocers to take items from high shelves. He devised a stove that heated houses without filling them with smoke. He refused to take out a patent on the stove, giving the model to a friend who manufactured stoves and became quite wealthy. To contribute to the happiness of others was a duty. Franklin observed: "As we enjoy great advantages from the inventions of others, we shall be glad of ours; and this we should do freely and generously."

The invention of the lightning rod brought Franklin world renown. It moved the philosopher Immanuel Kant to declare that Franklin was "a new Prometheus" who had stolen fire from heaven—releasing men from the historic dread of lightning.

In addition to his many ingenious inventions Franklin contributed to the public good through services rendered in the many public offices he held. For a time he was postmaster general of North America—developing our present postal system. Later he became a colonial agent in England, representing the colonies of Pennsylvania, Massachusetts, and Georgia. During the Revolutionary War he was minister to France, securing much needed support for the American cause. Following the war he helped formulate the Articles of Confederation and, later, the federal constitution. Perhaps no one man has ever done so much to improve the quality of life of his fellow men. Franklin was, as Carl Van Doren put it, "a syndicate of men."

❉

Of all the many roles Franklin played in his efforts to do good, none was more lasting or more pervasive than his role as educator. Before retiring from business in 1748, Franklin had his own printing establishment where he published, among other things, *Poor Richard's Almanack* and a newspaper, the *Pennsylvania Gazette.* In his *Autobiography* he tells us that he viewed both publications as educational ventures: "I considered it [the almanac] as a proper vehicle for conveying instruction among the common people, who bought scarcely any books . . . I considered my newspaper also as another means of communicating instruction." This "instruction" consisted of exhortations to moral virtue. The message was simply that moral virtue produced wealth. He reports that he filled all the spaces in the almanac with "proverbial sentences, chiefly such as inculcated industry and frugality, as the means of preserving wealth." Here is one of his most famous quotes from *Poor Richard's Almanack*:

> The way to wealth is as plain as the way to market. It depends chiefly on two words, industry and frugality; that is, waste neither time nor money, but make the best of both. Without industry and frugality nothing will do, and with them everything.

Franklin's role as an educator reached the pinnacle in his *Autobiography*. Here he became the quintessential educator, taking on the task of instructing the entire human race, presenting his own life as a model for emulation. In the introductory paragraphs of this work he makes his educational purpose quite clear: "Having emerged from the poverty and obscurity in which I was born and bred, to a state of affluence and some degree of reputation in the world, and having gone so far through life with a considerable share of felicity, the conducing means I made use of, which with the blessing of God, so well succeeded, my posterity may like to know, as they may find some of them suitable to their own situations, and therefore fit to be imitated."

One of the most famous sections of the *Autobiography* is Franklin's attempt to instruct others in the art of virtue. He supplies the reader with the very scheme he himself used as a youth in a "bold and arduous project of arriving at moral perfection." The scheme consisted of a list of thirteen basic virtues (Temperance, Silence, Order, Resolution, Frugality, Industry, Sincerity, Justice, Moderation, Cleanliness, Tranquility, Charity, and Humility), and a scorecard for keeping a daily record of progress. Franklin confessed that he had never arrived at perfection, but the endeavor itself made him "a better and happier man." Temperance led to a long life with good health; Industry and Frugality brought him his wealth and reputation; Sincerity and Justice obtained the confidence of his country; while the remaining virtues secured evenness of temper and cheerfulness in conversation, which made his company sought for and agreeable.

It is these attempts to do good by instructing people in moral virtue that so infuriate his critics, such as D. H. Lawrence who finds Franklin a self-righteous, priggish, pedantic defender of American materialism—someone who would limit men to a barbed-wire corral of moral virtues. "A snuff-colored little man," Lawrence concludes.

Lawrence is correct. Franklin *is* a self-righteous moralizer. And this results directly from his secularization of the Christian injunction to do good. As long as the primary and almost sole concern was salvation, no one could ever claim with certainty that his acts of "doing good" would actually secure that goal—one meekly and humbly followed God's commands, and prayerfully awaited the administration of Divine Justice. Nor were Puritan ministers self-righteous moralizers; a minister could never hold himself up as an example for others to imitate. He, like them, was a miserable sinner, not an exemplar. He served simply as a messenger of God—someone to remind his miserable fellow creatures of their religious duties.

But once happiness in this life became man's goal, there was a way of knowing what acts led to it: Experience. Whether or not Industry and Frugality brought Wealth and Reputation is not a matter of speculation or faith—it is a matter of experience. Franklin had tried it; it worked. His own experience proved that he knew the way to wealth. But when he sought to instruct others in this way to wealth—when he tried to do good—*citing his own experience as authoritative,* he emerged as a moralizing elitist, an exemplar for the people to imitate.

*

The elitism inherent in Franklin's secularized version of the mission to do good springs forth in Franklin's attempts to promote new educational institutions. If "doing good" consists of acts that contribute to the physical and social well-being of others, then, obviously, this limits the opportunity to do good to those with ability, those talented enough to contribute some significant benefit to humanity. As an educator

Franklin wanted to locate the people with ability, develop their talents, and channel them appropriately. Just as the earliest colonists in Massachusetts had created Harvard college to train clergymen because they feared to have none when their "present ministers should lie in the dust," so now Franklin called for new educational institutions to replenish the elite. In a letter to Samuel Johnson, he revealed his conception of what educational institutions are for: "I think with you, that nothing is of more importance for the public weal, than to form and train up youth in wisdom and virtue. . . . And though the culture bestowed on *many* should be successful only with a few, yet the influence of those few and the service in their power may be very great." Franklin construed educational institutions as *nets* to catch those few who had ability, and as *instruments* to channel those abilities to do good.

More than simply a journalist-educator self-righteously instructing the common people how to be truly happy, Franklin was also an educational promoter—perhaps the greatest promoter of educational institutions in the history of American education. The Philadelphia Library, the Junto, the American Philosophical Society, the Philadelphia Academy—Franklin created all of them; each was an institution to help the talented few do good for the people.

Franklin's earliest efforts as an educational promoter centered on institutions to encourage self-education. Just as each man has to save his own soul—no one can save another—so Franklin thought each man responsible for his own education. After all, his own experience confirmed this. No more phenomenal autodidactic ever lived!

Franklin had a scant two years of formal schooling in his entire life—a year in the Boston Latin School, and another under the tutelege of a scrivener, one Mr. George Brownell, who taught him to write, but failed to teach him arithmetic. The rest of his education Franklin secured on his own, including the basics: he taught himself to read (he reports he does not remember ever not being able to read); he taught himself foreign languages—French, Italian, Spanish, and Latin; and he taught himself the arithmetic Mr. Brownell could not—along with "a little geometry."

The most extraordinary account of Franklin's prodigious feats of self-education is his description of how—at the age of fourteen or fifteen—he learned to be a writer. Impressed with the excellence of the writing in the British newspaper *The Spectator*, Franklin took it as an exemplar to be imitated. "I took some of the papers, and making short hints of the sentiment in each sentence, laid them by a few days, and then without looking at the book, try'd to compleat the papers again, by expressing each hinted sentiment at length, and as fully as it had been expressed before, in any suitable words that should come to hand. Then I compared my *Spectator* with the original, discovered some of my faults, and corrected them." Next, to increase his vocabulary, he took some of the tales and turned them into verse; and, after a time, "when I had pretty well forgotten the prose, turned them back again." To teach himself organization and structure, he reports, "I sometimes jumbled my collections of hints into confusion, and after some weeks endeavored to reduce them into the best order, before I began to form the full sentences and compleat the paper."

Franklin rapidly developed a remarkably lucid prose style. By the age of sixteen he regularly published articles in his brother's newspaper, under the apt pseudonym of Silence Dogood—a widow of a New England minister with "a natural inclination to observe and reprove the faults of others."

Understandably then, Franklin's own highly successful experience led him initially to promote institutions that would facilitate self-education. In 1728 he formed some of his "most ingenious acquaintances" in Philadelphia into a club for mutual improvement, called the Junto. At weekly meetings each member produced one or more queries on any point of morals, politics, or natural philosophy, to be discussed by the company, and once in three months produced and read an essay of his own writing on any subject he pleased.

The Junto had a long list of standing queries that the members took up at each meeting. These queries, which Franklin drew up, indicate the ways these young men were to channel their talents to do good. Here are some examples:

1. Have you met with anything in the author you last read remarkable, or suitable to be communicated to the Junto? particularly in history, morality, poetry, physic, travels, mechanic arts, or other parts of knowledge?

9. Have you or any of your acquaintances been lately sick or
wounded? If so, what remedies were used, and what were their
effects?

11. Do you think of anything at present, in which the Junto may
be serviceable to *mankind?* to their country, to their friends, or
to themselves?

13. Do you know of any deserving young beginner lately set up,
whom it lies in the power of the Junto any way to encourage?

With the Junto, Franklin revealed his astute understanding of
educational organization. For when the club became more widely
known, many people sought to join. He convinced the other
members to restrict the membership to twelve, but to have each of
them create *another* club of twelve members, federated to the
parent body. In this way he preserved the seminarlike size of the
club, ensuring its continued educational worth and at the same
time expanding the Junto in a way that allowed each branch to
profit from the experience of the initial group. The club lasted some
forty years, and was, Franklin said, "the best school of philosophy,
and politics that then existed in the province."

One of the difficulties Franklin had encountered in his
self-education was the securing of books. As a young boy, after
having read all the books in his father's library he began to
purchase his own. He would buy a book, read it, sell it, and use the
money to buy another book. When he reached the age of twelve his
father apprenticed him to his older brother, a printer. This opened
new opportunities to get books. One way he found was to borrow
them from the apprentices of booksellers he met. "Often," he
admits, "I sat up in my room reading the greater part of the night,
when the book was borrowed in the evening and to be returned
early in the morning, lest it should be missed or wanted." As an
apprentice Franklin devised an ingenious way to secure additional
funds to buy books. After reading a book on it, he became a
vegetarian and proposed to board himself if his brother would give
him weekly half the money he paid for Ben's board. The brother
agreed, and the frugal Franklin was able to save *half* what his
brother paid him. This, he records, "was an additional fund for
buying books."

In light of his own struggles to secure books for his education, it is not surprising that Franklin initiated a plan for a subscription library. Established in Philadelphia in 1732, it was the first library in the colonies. Other communities soon imitated Philadelphia in setting up such a useful institution. As a result, Franklin wrote in his *Autobiography,* "reading became fashionable; and our people, having no public amusements to divert their attention from study, became better acquainted with books, and in a few years were observed by strangers to be better instructed and more intelligent than people of the same rank generally are in other countries."

The most imaginative and neoteric educational institution Franklin promoted to enroll men of talent in the mission to do good was the American Philosophical Society. He first put forth the plan in 1743 in "A Proposal for Promoting Useful Knowledge Among the British Plantations in America." Now that the first drudgery of settling new colonies was over, he argued, men have leisure "to cultivate the finer arts and improve the commonstock of knowledge." The observations, speculations, and experiments to be made, he continued, "might produce discoveries to the advantage of some or all of the British Plantations or to the benefit of mankind in general." But such persons as might advance knowledge were separated far distances from one another, so they did not communicate. The result, Franklin concluded, is "a loss of valuable knowledge, or even a loss of encouragement to pursue the advancement of knowledge." He proposed to unite all these ingenious men into one group, the American Philosophical Society, through which all could maintain a constant correspondence. Through its members, representing a variety of fields, the society was to gather and disseminate information on all research conducted in America (postage-free dissemination—Franklin was postmaster general). In addition, according to Franklin's scheme, the society provided an answering service for all scientific and technical queries, published abstracts, and offered grants for research.

The program of research Franklin proposed makes quite clear that he saw this society as a means to do good. The society was to report

> all new-discovered plants, herbs, trees, roots, their virtues, uses, etc.; methods of propagating them, and making such as are

useful, but particular to some plantations, more general; improvements of vegetable juices, as ciders, wines, etc.; new methods of curing or preventing diseases; all new-discovered fossils in different countries, as mines, minerals, and quarries; new and useful improvements in any branch of mathematics; new discoveries in chemistry, such as improvements in distillation, brewing, and assaying of ores; new mechanical inventions for saving labor, as mills and carriages, and for raising and conveying of water, draining of meadows, etc.; all new arts, trades, and manufactures that may be proposed or thought of; surveys, maps, and charts of particular parts of the sea-coasts or inland countries; course and junction of rivers and great roads, situation of lakes and mountains, nature of the soil and productions; new methods of improving the breed of useful animals; introducing other sorts from foreign countries; new improvements in planting, gardening, and clearing land; and all philosophical experiments that let light into the nature of things, tend to increase the power of man over matter and multiply the conveniences or pleasures of life.

❋

The most famous educational institution Franklin ever promoted was the Academy of Philadelphia. Intending to supplant, or at least supplement, existing educational institutions, he proposed the Academy as a school to catch and channel youths of talent. "Thus instructed," he claimed, "youth will come out of this school fitted for learning any business, calling or profession . . . [with] such a foundation of knowledge and ability as, properly improved, may qualify them to pass through and execute the several offices of civil life, with advantage and reputation to themselves and country."

The traditional educational institutions in America had emerged in the previous century. They functioned primarily to supply the churches with trained ministers. There were the colleges—Harvard, Yale, William and Mary—and the grammar schools that prepared students for entry into them. No educational institutions existed for preparing young people to take up other professions, callings, or businesses, except for some private schools that had sprung up in cities like Boston, New York, and Philadelphia. Here the "school" usually consisted of one man who taught practical subjects such as bookkeeping, navigation, foreign languages, composition, and whatever else he knew of use. But these schools were ephemeral creations that disappeared if the instructor died, moved, or found more lucrative employment.

After discussing the need for a permanent educational institution with his friends over a period of years, Franklin began his campaign to create the Academy with the publication in 1749 of his "Proposals Related to the Education of Youth in Pennsylvania." "It has long been regretted as a misfortune to the youth of this province," the proposal began, "that we have no ACADEMY, in which they might receive the Accomplishments of a regular Education." Continuing his argument, he wrote: "The good Education of Youth has been esteemed by Wise Men in all Ages, as the surest Foundation of the Happiness both of private Families and of Commonwealths. Almost all Governments have therefore made it a principal Object of their attention, to establish and endow with proper Revenues, such Seminaries of Learning as might supply the succeeding Age with Men qualified to serve the Public with Honor to themselves and to their country." Franklin proposed that some persons of public spirit incorporate themselves in order to create and govern an academy. He then went on to describe the curriculum for such a school, ending with a succinct statement of how the school will contribute to the common good: "The Idea of what is *true Merit,* should also be often presented to Youth, explained and impress'd on their Minds, as consisting in an *Inclination* join'd with an *Ability* to serve Mankind, one's Country, Friends and Family; which *Ability* is (with the Blessing of God) to be acquired or greatly increas'd by *true Learning;* and should indeed be the great *Aim* and *End* of all Learning."

Franklin followed up his proposal with a fund drive—after which the twenty-four principal subscribers became trustees. They promptly appointed Franklin to draw up a plan and a constitution for the new institution. Then they hired a house, engaged teachers, and opened the school—all within a year.

In the course of studies he proposed for the Academy, Franklin tried to explode the myth that the study of Latin classics constituted the only *real* education a school could offer. "As to their STUDIES, it would be well if they could be taught *every Thing* that is useful, and *every Thing* that is ornamental: But Art is long, and their Time is short. It is therefore proposed that they learn those things that are likely to be *most useful* and *most ornamental.* Regard being had to the several Professions for which they are intended."

Quite early in life Franklin had concluded that the classical education in the ancient languages offered by the grammar schools and the colleges was of little use—it did not develop the skills appropriate for attaining success and doing good in this world. His father had originally planned to send him to Harvard, enrolling him in the Boston Latin School when he was ten years of age. But he removed him after a year; he realized that with a family of seventeen children he really could not afford to send Benjamin, his fifteenth, to college—which was all a grammar school education would prepare him for. Besides, he told some friends, in his son's hearing, many college graduates have trouble making a living.

Later, when he began publishing the Silence Dogood papers in his brother's newspaper, young Benjamin often ridiculed parents who sent their sons to Harvard, "the Temple of Learning, where for want of a suitable Genius, they learn little more than how to carry themselves handsomly, and enter a room genteely, (which might as well be acquired at a Dancing-School,) and from whence they return, after Abundance of Trouble and Charge, as great Blockheads as ever, only more proud and self-conceited."

In Franklin's experience the most useful studies he had pursued were those that gave him his mastery of his own language. And this is what he would have the students of the Academy learn: to write clearly, speak effectively, and read with understanding. In addition, he wanted them to study the practical parts of mathematics—arithmetic, accounts, mechanical drawing, and the use of the globes.

When the Academy opened in January 1750 there was to be one English tutor, one in mathematics, and one in Latin. Franklin had to agree to the inclusion of the last since few of the trustees could fathom a reputable school not providing instruction in Latin, the learned language. But right from the start the English studies were devalued. By vote of a majority of the trustees the Latin teacher became rector, received two hundred pounds a year, and had to teach only twenty boys. The English master got *one* hundred pounds and had to teach *forty* boys. Moreover, in the initial ordering of supplies, the trustees allotted one hundred pounds to buy Latin and Greek books and supplies for the Latin master; no funds were allotted for English books or for supplies for the English teacher. As if to ensure the lack of parity between the two courses of study, the trustees did not hire the English teacher until a year after the Academy had opened. They had to add fifty pounds to the original low salary to secure the services of one Mr. Dove—who still thought the pay "too scanty." Mr. Dove proved to be an excellent teacher and in a short time had over ninety students. But the low salary forced him to resign after two years. A less able teacher replaced him; enrollment declined, and the English school never again revived its reputation.

In the meantime the trustees increased the number of Latin teachers (although enrollments never exceeded sixty students) and augmented their salaries. Then, in 1755, the trustees started a college and grafted it on to the Academy. The Latin master, William Smith, formerly rector of the Academy, became the provost of the College and Academy of Philadelphia. A few years later the college became the University of Pennsylvania—the very kind of institution Franklin had originally rejected as a suitable educational institution!

After launching his unique educational institutions in 1749, Franklin's many political responsibilities in the colonies and abroad prevented him from maintaining a guiding influence over it. Finally in 1789, Franklin, at the age of eighty-three, wrote a long memorandum to the trustees, excoriating them for their continual discrimination against the English studies and their departure from the original plan of the Academy. In the memorandum Franklin admits that there is an "unaccountable Prejudice in mankind in favor of ancient Customs and Habitudes—a prejudice that inclines people to continue them long after they are useful. Hats, for example, were once useful, but with the coming into use of wigs and dressed hair people stopped wearing them. But they still continued carrying them—under the arm: a *chapeau bras.*" Latin, Franklin concludes, is the *chapeau bras* of modern education. It is useless. It does not provide the right kind of education "for such a country as ours."

＊

Franklin, as one would expect, had definite ideas about how teachers should go about the task of educating others.

In spite of its continual use since the Middle Ages as a way of teaching, Franklin eschewed the pedagogical method of disputation. Early in life he discovered you could not teach someone by contradicting him—this merely makes him extremely disagreeable. Disputation spoils conversation, produces disgust, makes enemies, and subverts any basis for friendship. Persons of good sense, Franklin concluded, seldom fall into it, "except lawyers, university men, and men of all sorts that have been bred at Edinborough."

Along with the traditional scholastic method of disputation, Franklin also rejected the Socratic approach to pedagogy—although he confesses that, for a time, he was enamored of it. Acknowledging that as a young man he grew very "artful" and expert in drawing people into concessions, the consequences of which they did not foresee, entangling them in difficulties out of which they could not extricate themselves, he nevertheless came to see that this Socratic method embarrassed and frustrated people. Thus it could not really be educative.

Nor did Franklin think a straightforward didactic approach effective, either. A positive, assuming manner, he says, disquiets people, creates opposition, and subverts communication. When sensible people meet with someone firmly fixed in his opinions, they avoid or ignore him.

After rejecting didacticism, disputation, and the Socratic method, Franklin lets us in on his pedagogical secret. He tells us how he so successfully educated others: he used the art of persuasion. Never dogmatic, always self-effacing, he constantly expressed himself "in terms of modest diffidence." Avoiding words like "certainly" or "undoubtedly," he presented his thoughts by saying: I conceive or apprehend a thing to be so and so for such and such reasons; or I imagine it to be so; or it is so, if I am not mistaken. This approach worked; anyone wishing to teach others should adopt it—or so it seemed to him.

❀

Benjamin Franklin is in many ways the prototypical American educator. Down to the present most Americans, particularly those who are educators, continue to share his educational ideas and beliefs. For one thing most hold on to his faith in the power of education—they still see education as the panacea for all ills, both private and public. This faith is indeed commendable. It has provided stability to the society by channeling agitation for change into movements for educational reform. As Lawrence Cremin has noted: "Instead of political revolution we have had curricular reforms."

But this American faith in education leads to escapism. By placing the burden for improvement on the schools, Americans can avoid directly confronting serious social, political, and economic ills, and so escape the sometimes painful structural and institutional reforms necessary to cure them. At the same time, this dodge provides the public with a scapegoat, someone to blame, when the schools fail, inevitably, to solve the problems foisted upon them.

Most Americans also continue to share Franklin's pragmatic construction of schooling. This emphasis on desirable practical outcomes has cast the American school as society's lever to promote the fortunes of individuals and the entire nation. Most Americans who have "made it" readily credit their success to their education; most attribute much of the economic and technical hegemony of the United States to its educational system.

But this pragmatic construction of education also produces a narrowness, a one-dimensionality of educational expectations. When the only worthy education is that which successfully leads to some predetermined, practical goal, people pay no heed to the intrinsic worth of what is learned, or to the worth of other, unanticipated consequences of learning, or the worth of the process itself. This almost exclusive emphasis on the cash values of schooling has led, in our time, to the "credential society," where an education is prized solely for the degree, diploma, or certificate it yields. The substance, the process, all other consequences of learning, count for nothing.

Finally, most educators continue to employ Franklin's persuasive approach to instruction. This persuasive approach has undoubtedly resulted in blessing America with more than its share of warm, friendly, and benign educators. Anyone familiar with European education, where teachers have largely followed the traditions of didacticism and disputation, will readily attest to this.

And yet, the fact that most American teachers are kindly about it, does not negate the fact that they, like Franklin, construe the educational process as one of manipulation of the young; the persuasive approach simply serves to mask educational authoritarianism. This is not to say that Franklin's ideas about instruction instigated authoritarianism into educational practice—it goes back much, much farther in educational history. It is to say that Franklin's ideas have made it more difficult to uncover and combat it.

WORKS AND COMMENTARY

The complete works of Franklin are being published by Yale University under the editorship of Leonard W. Labaree and others, *The Papers of Benjamin Franklin* (New Haven, 1959 et seq.). Four volumes have appeared so far. Earlier editions are ten volumes edited by Albert Henry Smyth (New York, 1905–7), and the ten volumes edited by John Bigelow (New York, 1887–88). The *Autobiography* has been published in many editions, including paperback.

Thomas Woody's *Educational Views of Benjamin Franklin* (New York: 1931) is an anthology of Franklin's major educational writings. A more broadly conceived anthology with a perceptive, critical essay and commentary is John H. Best's *Benjamin Franklin on Education* (New York: Teachers College Bureau of Publications, 1962).

The selection that follows is from volume 3 of *The Papers of Benjamin Franklin,* pages 397–421.

Proposals Relating to the Education of Youth in Pennsylvania

Proposals Relating to the Education of Youth in Pensilvania. Philadelphia: Printed in the Year, M,DCC,XLIX. (Yale University Library)

Advertisement to the Reader

It has long been regretted as a Misfortune to the Youth of this Province, that we have no ACADEMY, in which they might receive the Accomplishments of a regular Education.

The following Paper of *Hints* towards forming a Plan for that purpose, is so far approv'd by some publick-spirited Gentlemen, to whom it has been privately communicated, that they have directed a Number of Copies to be made by the Press, and properly distributed, in order to obtain the Sentiments and Advice of Men of Learning, Understanding, and Experience in these Matters; and have determin'd to use their Interest and best Endeavours, to have the Scheme, when compleated, carried gradually into Execution; in which they have Reason to believe they shall have the hearty Concurrence and Assistance of many who are Wellwishers to their Country.

Those who incline to favour the Design with their Advice, either as to the Parts of Learning to be taught, the Order of Study, the Method of Teaching, the Oeconomy of the School, or any other Matter of Importance to the Success of the Undertaking, are desired to communicate their Sentiments as soon as may be, by Letter directed to B. Franklin, Printer, in Philadelphia.

Authors Quoted in This Paper

1. The famous Milton, whose Learning and Abilities are well known and who had practised some Time the Education of Youth, so could speak from Experience.

2. The great Mr. Locke, who wrote a Treatise on Education, well known, and much esteemed, being translated into most of the modern Languages of Europe.

3. *Dialogues on Education,* 2 Vols. Octavo, that are much esteem'd, having had two Editions in 3 Years. Suppos'd to be

wrote by the ingenious Mr. Hutcheson (Author of *A Treatise on the Passions,* and another on the *Ideas of Beauty and Virtue*) who has had much Experience in Educating of Youth, being a Professor in the College at Glasgow, &c.

4. The learned Mr. Obadiah Walker, who had been many Years a Tutor to young Noblemen, and wrote a Treatise *on the Education of a young Gentleman;* of which the Fifth Edition was printed 1687.

5. The much admired Mons. Rollin, whose whole Life was spent in a College; and wrote 4 Vols. on Education, under the Title of, *The Method of Teaching and Studying the Belles Lettres;* which are translated into English, Italian, and most of the modern Languages.

6. The learned and ingenious Dr. George Turnbull, Chaplain to the present Prince of Wales; who has had much Experience in the Educating of Youth, and publish'd a Book, Octavo, intituled, *Observations on Liberal Education, in all its Branches,* 1742.

With some others.

Proposals, &c.

The good Education of Youth has been esteemed by wise Men in all Ages, as the surest Foundation of the Happiness both of private Families and of Common-wealths.[1] Almost all Gov-

---

1. As some Things here propos'd may be found to differ a little from the Forms of Education in common Use, the following Quotations are to shew the Opinions of several learned Men, who have carefully considered and wrote expresly on the Subject; such as Milton, Locke, Rollin, Turnbull, and others. They generally complain, that the *old Method* is in many Respects wrong; but long settled Forms are not easily changed. For us, who are now to make a Beginning, 'tis, at least, as easy to set out right as wrong; and therefore their Sentiments are on this Occasion well worth our Consideration.

   Mr. Rollin says (*Belles Lett.* [IV] p. 249. speaking of the Manner of Educating Youth) "Though it be generally a very wise and judicious Rule to avoid all Singularity, and to follow the received Customs, yet I question whether, in the Point we now treat of, this Principle does

ernments have therefore made it a principal Object of their Attention, to establish and endow with proper Revenues, such Seminaries of Learning, as might supply the succeeding Age with Men qualified to serve the Publick with Honour to themselves, and to their Country.

Many of the first Settlers of these Provinces, were Men who had received a good Education in Europe, and to their Wisdom and good Management we owe much of our present Prosperity. But their Hands were full, and they could not do all Things. The present Race are not thought to be generally of equal Ability: For though the American Youth are allow'd not to want Capacity; yet the best Capacities require Cultivation, it being truly with them, as with the best Ground, which unless well tilled and sowed with profitable Seed, produces only ranker Weeds.

That we may obtain the Advantages arising from an Increase of Knowledge, and prevent as much as may be the mischievous Consequences that would attend a general Ignorance among us, the following *Hints* are offered towards forming a Plan for the Education of the Youth of Pennsylvania, viz.

It is propos'd,

THAT some Persons of Leisure and publick Spirit, apply for a CHARTER, by which they may be incorporated, with Power to erect an ACADEMY for the Education of Youth, to govern the same, provide Masters, make Rules, receive Donations, purchase Lands, &c. and to add to their Number, from Time to Time such other Persons as they shall judge suitable.

---

not admit of some Exception, and whether we ought not to apprehend the Dangers and Inconveniencies of blindly following the Footsteps of those who have gone before us, so as to consult *Custom* more than *Reason,* and the governing our Actions rather by what others *do,* than by what they *should do;* from whence it often happens, that an Error once established is handed down from Age to Age, and becomes almost a certain Law, from a Notion, that we ought to act like the rest of Mankind, and follow the Example of the greatest Number. But human Nature is not so happy as to have the greatest Number always make the best Choice, and we too frequently observe the contrary."

That the Members of the Corporation make it their Pleasure, and in some Degree their Business, to visit the Academy often, encourage and countenance[2] the Youth, countenance and assist the Masters, and by all Means in their Power advance the Usefulness and Reputation of the Design; that they look on the Students as in some Sort their Children, treat them with Familiarity and Affection, and when they have behav'd well, and gone through their Studies, and are to enter the World, zealously unite, and make all the Interest that can be made to establish them,[3] whether in Business, Offices, Marriages, or any other Thing for their Advantage, preferably to all other Persons whatsoever even of equal Merit.

And if Men may, and frequently do, catch such a Taste for cultivating Flowers, for Planting, Grafting, Inoculating, and the like, as to despise all other Amusements for their Sake, why may not we expect they should acquire a Relish for that *more useful* Culture of young Minds. Thompson says,

> 'Tis Joy to see the human Blossoms blow,
> When infant Reason grows apace, and calls
> For the kind Hand of an assiduous Care;
> Delightful Task! to rear the tender Thought,
> To teach the young Idea how to shoot,
> To pour the fresh Instruction o'er the Mind,
> To breathe th' enliv'ning Spirit, and to fix
> The generous Purpose in the glowing Breast.

2. Rollin, Vol. 2. p. 371. mentions a French Gentleman, Mons. Hersan, who, "at his own Expence, built a School for the Use of poor Children, one of the finest in the Kingdom; and left a Stipend for the Master. That he himself taught them very often, and generally had some of them at his Table. He clothed several of them; and distributed Rewards among them from Time to Time, in order to encourage them to study."

3. Something seems wanting in America to incite and stimulate Youth to Study. In Europe the Encouragements to Learning are of themselves much greater than can be given here. Whoever distinguishes himself there, in either of the three learned Professions, gains Fame, and often Wealth and Power: A poor Man's Son has a Chance, if he studies hard, to rise, either in the Law or the Church, to gainful Offices or Benefices; to an extraordinary Pitch of Grandeur; to have a

That a House be provided for the ACADEMY, if not in the Town, not many Miles from it; the Situation high and dry, and if it may be, not far from a River, having a Garden, Orchard, Meadow, and a Field or two.

That the House be furnished with a Library (if in the Country, if in the Town, the Town Libraries[4] may serve) with Maps of all Countries, Globes, some mathematical Instruments, an Apparatus for Experiments in Natural Philosophy, and for

Voice in Parliament, a Seat among the Peers; as a Statesman or first Minister to govern Nations, and even to mix his Blood with Princes.

4. Besides the English Library begun and carried on by Subscription in Philadelphia, we may expect the Benefit of another much more valuable in the Learned Languages, which has been many Years collecting with the greatest Care, by a Gentleman distinguish'd for his universal Knowledge, no less than for his Judgment in Books. It contains many hundred Volumes of the best Authors in the best Editions, among which are the Polyglot Bible, and Castel's Lexicon on it, in 8 large Vols. Aldus's Septuagint, Apocrypha and New Testament, in Greek, and some other Editions of the same; most of the Fathers; almost all the Greek Authors from Homer himself, in divers Editions (and one of them in that of Rome, with Eustathius's Commentaries, in 4 Vols.) to near the End of the 4th Century, with divers later, as Photius, Suidas, divers of the Byzantine Historians; all the old Mathematicians, as Archimedes, Apollonius, Euclid, Ptolomy's Geography and Almagest, with Theon's Commentaries and Diophantus, in the whole above 100 Vols. in Greek Folio's. All the old Roman Classics without Exception, and some of them in several Editions (as all Tully's Works in four Editions). All Graevius, Gronovius, Salengre's and Poleni's Collections of Roman and Greek Antiquities, containing above Five Hundred distinct Discourses in 33 Tomes, with some Hundreds of late Authors in Latin, as Vossius, Lipsius, Grotius, &c. A good Collection of Mathematical Pieces, as Newton in all the three Editions, Wallis, Huygens, Tacquet, Dechales, &c. in near 100 Vols. in all Sizes, with some Orientals, French and Italian Authors, and many more English, &c. A handsome Building above 60 Feet in front, is now erected in this City, at the private Expence of that Gentleman, for the Reception of this Library, where it is soon to be deposited, and remain for the publick Use, with a valuable yearly Income duly to enlarge it; and I have his Permission to mention it as an Encouragement to the propos'd Academy; to which this noble Benefaction will doubtless be of the greatest Advantage, as not only the Students, but even the Masters themselves, may very much improve by it.

Mechanics; Prints, of all Kinds, Prospects, Buildings, Machines, &c.[5]

That the RECTOR be a Man of good Understanding, good Morals, diligent and patient, learn'd in the Languages and Sciences, and a correct pure Speaker and Writer of the English Tongue; to have such Tutors under him as shall be necessary.

That the boarding Scholars diet[6] together, plainly, temperately, and frugally.

That to keep them in Health, and to strengthen and render active their Bodies, they be frequently exercis'd[7] in Running, Leaping, Wrestling, and Swimming,[8] &c.

That they have peculiar Habits to distinguish them from

5. See in Turnbull, p. 415. the Description of the Furniture of the School called the Instituto at Bologna, procur'd by the Care and Direction of Count Marsigli, and originally at his private Expence.

6. Perhaps it would be best if none of the Scholars were to diet abroad. Milton is of that Opinion *(Tractate of Education)* for that much Time would else be lost, and many ill Habits got.

7. Milton proposes, that an Hour and Half before Dinner should be allow'd for Exercise, and recommends among other Exercises, the handling of Arms, but perhaps this may not be thought necessary here. Turnbull, p. 318. says, "Corporal Exercise invigorates the Soul as well as the Body; let one be kept closely to Reading, without allowing him any Respite from Thinking, or any Exercise to his Body, and were it possible to preserve long, by such a Method, his Liking to Study and Knowledge, yet we should soon find such an one become no less soft in his Mind than in his outward Man. Both Mind and Body would thus become gradually too relaxed, too much unbraced for the Fatigues and Duties of active Life. Such is the Union between Soul and Body, that the same Exercises which are conducive, when rightly managed, to consolidate or strengthen the former, are likewise equally necessary and fit to produce Courage, Firmness, and manly Vigour, in the latter. For this, and other Reasons, certain hardy Exercises were reckoned by the Antients an essential Part in the Formation of a liberal Character; and ought to have their Place in Schools where Youth are taught the Languages and Sciences." See p. 318 to 323.

8. 'Tis suppos'd that every Parent would be glad to have their Children skill'd in *Swimming*, if it might be learnt in a Place chosen for its Safety, and under the Eye of a careful Person. Mr. Locke says, p. 9. in his *Treatise of Education;* " 'Tis that saves many a Man's Life; and the Romans thought it so necessary, that they rank'd it with Letters; and it was the common Phrase to mark one ill educated, and good for

other Youth, if the Academy be in or near the Town; for this, among other Reasons, that their Behavior may be the better observed.

As to their STUDIES, it would be well if they could be taught *every Thing* that is useful, and *every Thing* that is ornamental: But Art is long, and their Time is short. It is therefore propos'd that they learn those Things that are likely to be *most useful* and *most ornamental,* Regard being had to the several Professions for which they are intended.

All should be taught to write a *fair Hand,* and swift, as that is useful to All. And with it may be learnt something of *Drawing,*[9] by Imitation of Prints, and some of the first Principles of Perspective.

---

nothing, that he had neither learnt to read nor to swim; *Nec Literas didicit nec Natare.* But besides the gaining a Skill which may serve him at Need, the Advantages to Health by often Bathing in cold Water during the Heat of the Summer, are so many, that I think nothing need be said to encourage it."

'Tis some Advantage besides, to be free from the slavish Terrors many of those feel who cannot swim, when they are oblig'd to be on the Water even in crossing a Ferry.

Mr. Hutchinson [i.e., Fordyce], in his *Dialogues concerning Education,* 2 Vols. Octavo, lately publish'd, says, Vol. 2. p. 297. "I would have the Youth accustomed to such Exercises as will harden their Constitution, as Riding, Running, Swimming, Shooting, and the like."

Charlemagne, Founder of the German Empire, brought up his Sons hardily, and even his Daughters were inur'd to Industry. Henry the Great of France, saith Mons. Rhodez, "was not permitted by his Grandfather to be brought up with Delicacy, who well knew that *seldom lodgeth other than a mean and feeble Spirit in an effeminate and tender Body.* He commanded that the Boy should be accustomed to run, to leap, to climb the Rocks and Mountains; that by such Means he might be inured to Labour, &c. His ordinary Food also was of coarse Bread, Beef, Cheese and Garlick; his Cloathing plain and coarse, and often he went barefoot and bareheaded." Walker *of Education,* p. 17, 18.

9. *Drawing* is a kind of Universal Language, understood by all Nations. A Man may often express his Ideas, even to his own Countrymen, more clearly with a Lead Pencil, or Bit of Chalk, than with his Tongue. And many can understand a Figure, that do not comprehend a Description in Words, tho' ever so properly chosen. All Boys

Arithmetick,[10] *Accounts,* and some of the first Principles of
Geometry and *Astronomy.*

---

have an early Inclination to this Improvement, and begin to make
Figures of Animals, Ships, Machines, &c. as soon as they can use a
Pen: but for want of a little Instruction at that Time, generally are
discouraged, and quit the Pursuit.

Mr. Locke says, p. 234. "When your Son can write well and
quick, I think it may be convenient not only to continue the Exercise
of his Hand in Writing, but also to improve the Use of it further in
Drawing; a Thing very useful to a Gentleman on several Occasions;
but especially if he travel; as that which helps a Man often to express
in a *few Lines* well put together, what a *whole Sheet of Paper in
Writing* would not be able to represent and make intelligible. How
many Buildings may a Man see, how many *Machines* and Habits
meet with, the Ideas whereof would be easily retain'd, and communicated by a little Skill in Drawing; which being committed to
Words, are in Danger to be lost, or at best but ill retained in the most
exact Descriptions? I do not mean that I would have him a perfect
Painter; to be that to any tolerable Degree, will require more Time
than he can spare from his other Improvements of greater Moment.
But so much Insight into Perspective and Skill in Drawing, as will
enable him to represent tolerably on Paper any Thing he sees, except
Faces, may, I think, be got in a little Time."

Drawing is no less useful to a *Mechanic* than to a Gentleman.
Several Handicrafts seem to require it; as the Carpenter's, Ship-
wright's, Engraver's, Painter's, Carver's, Cabinet-maker's, Gardiner's,
and other Businesses. By a little Skill of this kind, the Workman may
perfect his own Idea of the Thing to be done, before he begins to
work; and show a Draft for the Encouragement and Satisfaction of
his Employer.

10. Mr. Locke is of Opinion, p. 269. that a Child should be early enter'd
in Arithmetick, Geography, Chronology, History and Geometry.
"Merchants Accounts, he says, if it is not necessary to help a
Gentleman to *get* an Estate, yet there is nothing of more Use and
Efficacy to make him *preserve* the Estate he has. 'Tis seldom observ'd
that he who keeps an Account of his Income and Expences, and
thereby has constantly under View the Course of his Domestic
Affairs, lets them run to Ruin: And I doubt not but many a Man gets
behind-hand before he is aware, or runs farther on when he is once
in, for want of this Care, or the Skill to do it. I would therefore advise
all Gentlemen to learn perfectly *Merchants Accounts;* and not to
think 'tis a Skill that belongs not to them, because it has received its
Name, and has been chiefly practis'd by Men of Traffick." p. 316.

Not only the *Skill,* but the *Habit* of keeping Accounts, should be
acquir'd by all, as being necessary to all.

The English Language[11] might be taught by Grammar; in which some of our best Writers, as Tillotson, Addison, Pope,

11. Mr. Locke, speaking of *Grammar,* p. 252. says, "That to those the greatest Part of whose Business in this World is to be done with their Tongues, and with their Pens, it is convenient, if not necessary, that they should speak properly and correctly, whereby they may let their Thoughts into other Mens Minds the more easily, and with the greater Impression. Upon this Account it is, that any sort of Speaking, so as will make him be understood, is not thought enough for a Gentleman. He ought to study *Grammar,* among the other Helps of Speaking well, but it *must be* THE GRAMMAR OF HIS OWN TONGUE, of the Language he uses, that he may understand his own Country Speech nicely, and speak it properly, without shocking the Ears of those it is addressed to with Solecisms and offensive Irregularities. And to this Purpose *Grammar is necessary;* but it is the Grammar *only* of *their own proper Tongues,* and to those who would take Pains in cultivating their Language, and perfecting their Stiles. Whether all Gentlemen should not do this, I leave to be considered, since the Want of Propriety and Grammatical Exactness is thought very misbecoming one of that Rank, and usually draws on one guilty of such Faults, the Imputation of having had a lower Breeding and worse Company than suits with his Quality. If this be so (as I suppose it is) it will be Matter of Wonder, why young Gentlemen are forc'd to learn the Grammars of foreign and dead Languages, and are never once told of the Grammar of their own Tongues. They do not so much as know there is any such Thing, much less is it made their Business to be instructed in it. Nor is their own Language ever propos'd to them as worthy their Care and Cultivating, tho' they have *daily Use* of it, and are not seldom, in the future Course of their Lives, judg'd of by their handsome or awkward Way of expressing themselves in it. Whereas the Languages whose Grammars they have been so much employed in, are such as probably they shall scarce ever speak or write; of if upon Occasion this should happen, they should be excused for the Mistakes and Faults they make in it. Would not a Chinese, who took Notice of this Way of Breeding, be apt to imagine, that all our young Gentlemen were designed to be Teachers and Professors of the dead Languages of foreign Countries, and not to be Men of Business in their own." Page 255. the same Author adds, "That if Grammar ought to be taught at any Time, it must be to one that can speak the Language already; how else can he be taught the Grammar of it? This at least is evident from the Practice of the wise and learned Nations among the Antients. They made it a *Part of Education* to cultivate *their own,* not foreign Tongues. The Greeks counted all other Nations barbarous, and had a Contempt for their Languages. And though the Greek

Algernon Sidney, Cato's Letters, &c. should be Classicks: The *Stiles* principally to be cultivated, being the *clear* and the *concise*. Reading should also be taught, and pronouncing,

---

Learning grew in Credit amongst the Romans towards the End of their Commonwealth, yet it was the Roman Tongue that was made the Study of their Youth: *Their own* Language they were to make Use of, and therefore it was *their own* Language they were *instructed* and *exercised* in." And p. 281. "There can scarce be a greater Defect (says he) in a Gentleman, than not to express himself well either in Writing or Speaking. But yet I think I may ask the Reader, whether he doth not know a great many, who live upon their Estates, and so, with the Name, should have the Qualities of Gentlemen, who cannot so much as tell a Story as they should, much less speak clearly and persuasively in any Business. This I think not to be so much their Fault as the *Fault of their Education.*" Thus far Locke.

Mons. Rollin, reckons the Neglect of Teaching their own Tongue a great Fault in the French Universities. He spends great Part of his first Vol. of *Belles Lettres*, on that Subject; and lays down some excellent Rules or Methods of Teaching French to Frenchmen grammatically, and making them Masters therein, which are very applicable to our Language, but too long to be inserted here. He practis'd them on the Youth under his Care with great Success.

Mr. Hutchinson, *Dial.* [II] p. 297. says, "To perfect them in the Knowledge of their Mother Tongue, they should learn it in the Grammatical Way, that they may not only speak it purely, but be able both to correct their own Idiom, and afterwards enrich the Language on the same Foundation."

Dr. Turnbull, in his *Observations on a liberal Education*, says, p. 262. "The Greeks, perhaps, made more early Advances in the most useful Sciences than any Youth have done since, chiefly on this Account, that they studied no other Language but their own. This no Doubt saved them very much Time; but they *applied themselves carefully* to the Study of *their own* Language, and were *early* able to speak and write it in *the greatest Perfection*. The Roman Youth, though they learned the Greek, did not neglect their own Tongue, but studied it more carefully than we now do Greek and Latin, without giving ourselves any Trouble about our own Tongue."

Mons. Simon, in an elegant Discourse of his among the Memoirs of the Academy of Belles Lettres at Paris, speaking of the Stress the Romans laid on Purity of Language and graceful Pronunciation, adds, "May I here make a Reflection on the Education we commonly give our Children? It is very remote from the Precepts I have mentioned. Hath the Child arrived to six or seven Years of Age, he mixes with a Herd of ill-bred Boys at School, where under the Pretext of Teaching

properly, distinctly, emphatically; not with an even Tone, which *under-does,* nor a theatrical, which *over-does* Nature.

To form their Stile, they should be put on Writing Letters[12]

---

him *Latin,* no Regard is had to his *Mother Tongue.* And what happens? What we see every Day. A young Gentleman of eighteen, who has had this Education, CANNOT READ. For to articulate the Words, and join them together, I do not call *Reading,* unless one can pronounce well, observe all the proper Stops, vary the Voice, express the Sentiments, and read with a delicate Intelligence. Nor can he speak a Jot better. A Proof of this is, that he cannot write ten Lines without committing gross Faults; and because he did not learn his own Language well in his early Years, he will never know it well. I except a few, who being afterwards engaged by their Profession, or their natural Taste, cultivate their Minds by Study. And yet even they, if they attempt to write, will find by the *Labour* Composition costs them, what a *Loss it is,* not to have learned their Language in the proper Season. Education among the Romans was upon a quite different Footing. Masters of Rhetoric taught them early the Principles, the Difficulties, the Beauties, the Subtleties, the Depths, the Riches of their own Language. When they went from these Schools, they were perfect Masters of it, they were never at a Loss for proper Expressions; and I am much deceived if it was not owing to this, that they produced such excellent Works with so *marvellous Facility.*"

Pliny, in his Letter to a Lady on chusing a Tutor for her Son, speaks of it as the most material Thing in his Education, that he should have a good Latin Master of Rhetoric, and recommends Julius Genitor for his *eloquent, open and plain Faculty of Speaking.* He does not advise her to a Greek Master of Rhetoric, tho' the Greeks were famous for that Science; but to a Latin Master, because Latin was the Boy's Mother Tongue. In the above Quotation from Mons. Simon, we see what was the Office and Duty of the Master of Rhetoric.

12. This Mr. Locke recommends, *Educ.* p. 284. and says, "The Writing of Letters has so much to do in all the Occurrences of human Life, that no Gentleman can avoid shewing himself in this Kind of Writing. Occasions will daily force him to make this Use of his Pen, which, besides the Consequences that, in his Affairs, the well or ill managing it often draws after it, always lays him open to a severer Examination of his Breeding, Sense and Abilities, than oral Discourses, whose transient Faults dying for the most Part with the Sound that gives them Life, and so not subject to a strict Review, more easily escape Observation and Censure." He adds,

"Had the Methods of Education been directed to their right End, one would have thought this so necessary a Part could not have been neglected, whilst Themes and Verses in Latin, of no Use at all,

to each other, making Abstracts of what they read; or writing the same Things in their own Words; telling or writing Stories lately read, in their own Expressions. All to be revis'd and

---

were so constantly every where pressed, to the Racking of Childrens Inventions beyond their Strength, and hindring their chearful Progress by unnatural Difficulties. But Custom has so ordained it, and who dares disobey? And would it not be very unreasonable to require of a learned Country Schoolmaster (who has all the Tropes and Figures in Farnaby's Rhetorick at his Finger's Ends) to teach his Scholar to express himself handsomely in English, when it appears to be so little his Business or Thought, that the Boy's Mother (despised, 'tis like, as illiterate for not having read a System of Logic or Rhetoric) outdoes him in it?

"To speak and write correctly, gives a Grace, and gains a favourable Attention to what one has to say: And since 'tis English that an Englishman will have constant Use of, that is the Language he should chiefly cultivate, and wherein most Care should be taken to polish and perfect his Stile. To speak or write better Latin than English, may make a Man be talk'd of, but he will find it more to his Purpose to express himself well in his own Tongue, that he uses every Moment, than to have the vain Commendation of others for a very insignificant Quality. This I find universally neglected, nor no Care taken any where to improve young Men in their own Language, that they may thoroughly understand and be Masters of it. If any one among us have a Facility or Purity more than ordinary in his Mother Tongue, it is owing to Chance, or his Genius, or any Thing, rather than to his Education, or any Care of his Teacher. To mind what English his Pupil speaks or writes, is below the Dignity of one bred up among Greek and Latin, tho' he have but little of them himself. These are the Learned Languages, fit only for Learned Men to meddle with and teach: English is the Language of the illiterate Vulgar. Though the Great Men among the Romans were daily exercising themselves in their own Language; and we find yet upon Record the Names of Orators who taught some of their Emperors Latin, tho' it were their Mother Tongue. 'Tis plain the Greeks were yet more nice in theirs. All other Speech was barbarous to them but their own, and no foreign Language appears to have been studied or valued amongst that learned and acute People; tho' it be past Doubt, that they borrowed their Learning and Philosophy from abroad.

"I am not here speaking against Greek and Latin. I think Latin at least ought to be well understood by every Gentleman. But whatever foreign Languages a young Man meddles with, that which he should critically study, and labour to get a Facility, Clearness and Elegancy to express himself in, should be *his own;* and to this purpose *he should daily be* EXERCISED in it."

corrected by the Tutor, who should give his Reasons, explain the Force and Import of Words, &c.

To form their Pronunciation,[13] they may be put on making Declamations, repeating Speeches, delivering Orations, &c. The

---

To the same Purpose writes a Person of eminent Learning in a Letter to Dr. Turnbull: "Nothing certainly (says he) can be of more Service to Mankind than a right Method of Educating the Youth, and I should be glad to hear ———— ———— to give an Example of the great Advantage it would be to the *rising Age,* and to our Nation. When our publick Schools were first establish'd, the Knowledge of Latin was thought Learning; and he that had a tolerable Skill in two or three Languages, tho' his Mind was not enlightened by any *real Knowledge,* was a profound Scholar. But it is not so at present; and People confess, that Men may have obtained a Perfection in these, and yet continue *deeply ignorant.* The Greek Education was of another Kind [which he describes in several Particulars, and adds] They studied to write their *own Tongue* more accurately than we do Latin and Greek. But where is English taught at present? Who thinks it of Use to study correctly *that Language* which he is to use *every Day* in his Life, be his Station ever so high, or ever so insignificant. It is in *this* the Nobility and Gentry defend their Country, and serve their Prince in Parliament; in *this* the Lawyers plead, the Divines instruct, and all Ranks of People write their Letters, and transact all their Affairs; and yet who thinks it worth his learning to write *this* even accurately, not to say politely? Every one is suffer'd to form his Stile by Chance; to imitate the first wretched Model which falls in his Way, before he knows what is faulty, or can relish the Beauties of a just Simplicity. Few think their Children qualified for a Trade till they have been whipt at a Latin School for five or six Years, to learn a little of that which they are oblig'd to forget; when in those Years right Education would have improv'd their Minds, and taught them to acquire Habits of Writing *their own Language* easily under right Direction; and this would have been useful to them as long as they lived." *Introd.* p. 3, 4, 5.

Since Mr. Locke's Time, several good Grammars have been wrote and publish'd for the Use of Schools; as Brightland's, Greenwood's, &c.

13. By Pronunciation is here meant, the proper Modulation of the Voice, to suit the Subject with due Emphasis, Action, &c. In delivering a Discourse in Publick, design'd to persuade, the *Manner,* perhaps, contributes more to Success, than either the *Matter* or *Method.* Yet the two latter seem to engross the Attention of most Preachers and other Publick Speakers, and the former to be almost totally neglected.

Tutor assisting at the Rehearsals, teaching, advising, correcting their Accent, &c.

But if HISTORY[14] be made a constant Part of their Reading, such as the Translations of the Greek and Roman Historians, and the modern Histories of antient Greece and Rome, &c. may not almost all Kinds of useful Knowledge be that Way introduc'd to Advantage, and with Pleasure to the Student? As

GEOGRAPHY, by reading with Maps, and being required to point out the Places *where* the greatest Actions were done, to give their old and new Names, with the Bounds, Situation, Extent of the Countries concern'd, &c.

CHRONOLOGY, by the Help of Helvicus or some other Writer of the Kind, who will enable them to tell *when* those Events happened; what Princes were Cotemporaries, what States or famous Men flourish'd about that Time, &c. The several principal Epochas to be first well fix'd in their Memories.

ANTIENT CUSTOMS, religious and civil, being frequently mentioned in History, will give Occasion for explaining them; in which the Prints[15] of Medals, Basso Relievo's, and antient Monuments will greatly assist.

14. As nothing *teaches* (saith Mr. Locke) so nothing *delights* more than HISTORY. The first of these recommends it to the Study of grown Men, the latter makes me think it the *fittest* for a young Lad, who as soon as he is instructed in Chronology, and acquainted with the several Epochas in Use in this Part of the World, and can reduce them to the Julian Period, should then have some History put into his Hand. *Educ.* p. 276.

Mons. Rollin complains, that the College Education in France is defective in Teaching *History;* which he thinks may be made of great Advantage to Youth. This he demonstrates largely in his *Belles Lettres,* to the Satisfaction of all that read the Book. He lays down the following Rules for Studying History, viz. 1. To reduce the Study to Order and Method. 2. To observe what relates to Usages and Customs. 3. To enquire particularly, and above all Things, after the Truth. 4. To endeavour to find out the Causes of the Rise and Fall of States, of the Gaining or Losing of Battles, and other Events of Importance. 5. To study the Character of the Nations and great Men mentioned in History. 6. To be attentive to such Instructions as concern MORAL EXCELLENCY and the CONDUCT OF LIFE. 7. Carefully to note every Thing that relates to RELIGION. Vol. 3. p. 146.

15. Plenty of these are to be met with in Montfaucon; and other Books of Antiquities.

MORALITY,[16] by descanting and making continual Observations on the Causes of the Rise or Fall of any Man's Character, Fortune, Power, &c. mention'd in History; the Advantages of Temperance, Order, Frugality, Industry, Perseverance, &c. &c.[17] Indeed the general natural Tendency of Reading good History, must be, to fix in the Minds of Youth deep Impressions of the Beauty and Usefulness of Virtue of all Kinds, Publick Spirit, Fortitude, &c.

History will show the wonderful Effects of ORATORY, in governing, turning and leading great Bodies of Mankind, Armies, Cities, Nations. When the Minds of Youth are struck with Admiration at this,[18] then is the Time to give them the Principles of that Art, which they will study with Taste and Application. Then they may be made acquainted with the best Models among the Antients, their Beauties being particularly

16. For the Importance and Necessity of moral Instructions to Youth, see the latter Notes.

17. Dr. Turnbull, *Liberal Education*, p. 371, says, "That the useful Lessons which ought to be inculcated upon Youth, are much better taught and enforced from *Characters, Actions,* and *Events,* developing the inward Springs of human Conduct, and the different Consequences of Actions, whether with Respect to private or publick Good, than by abstract Philosophical Lectures. History points out in Examples, as in a Glass, all the Passions of the human Heart, and all their various Workings in different Circumstances, all the Virtues and all the Vices human Nature is capable of; all the Snares, all the Temptations, all the Vicissitudes and Incidents of human Life; and gives Occasion for Explaining all the Rules of Prudence, Decency, Justice and Integrity, in private Oeconomy, and in short all the Laws of natural Reason."

18. "Rules are best understood, when Examples that confirm them, and point out their Fitness or Necessity, naturally lead one, as it were by the Hand, to take Notice of them. One who is persuaded and moved by a Speech, and heartily admires its Force and Beauty, will with Pleasure enter into a critical Examination of its Excellencies; and willingly lay up in his Mind the Rules of Rhetoric such an Example of Eloquence plainly suggests. But to teach Rules abstractly, or without Examples, and before the agreeable Effects the Observance of them tends to produce (which are in Reality their Reason or Foundation) have been felt, *is exceedingly preposterous.*" Turnbull, p. 410.

"I have seldom or never observed any one to get the Skill of Speaking handsomely, by Studying the Rules which pretend to teach Rhetoric." Locke, p. 279.

pointed out to them. Modern Political Oratory being chiefly performed by the Pen and Press, its Advantages over the Antient in some Respects are to be shown; as that its Effects are more extensive, more lasting, &c.

History will also afford frequent Opportunities of showing the Necessity of a *Publick Religion,* from its Usefulness to the Publick; the Advantage of a Religious Character among private Persons; the Mischiefs of Superstition, &c. and the Excellency of the CHRISTIAN RELIGION above all others antient or modern.[19]

History will also give Occasion to expatiate on the Advantage of Civil Orders and Constitutions, how Men and their Properties are protected by joining in Societies and establishing Government; their Industry encouraged and rewarded, Arts invented, and Life made more comfortable: The Advantages of *Liberty,* Mischiefs of *Licentiousness,* Benefits arising from good Laws and a due Execution of Justice, &c. Thus may the first Principles of sound *Politicks*[20] be fix'd in the Minds of Youth.

On *Historical* Occasions, Questions of Right and Wrong, Justice and Injustice, will naturally arise, and may be put to Youth, which they may debate in Conversation and in Writing.[21] When they ardently desire Victory, for the

19. See Turnbull on this Head, from p. 386 to 390. very much to the Purpose, but too long to be transcribed here.
20. Thus, as Milton says, *Educ.* p. 381. should they be instructed in the Beginning, End and Reasons of political Societies; that they may not, in a dangerous Fit of the Commonwealth, be such poor, shaken, uncertain Reeds, of such a tottering Conscience, as many of our great Councellors have lately shewn themselves, but stedfast Pillars of the State.
21. "After this, they are to dive into the Grounds of Law and legal Justice; deliver'd first and with best Warrant by Moses; and as far as human Prudence can be trusted, in those celebrated Remains of the antient Grecian and Roman Lawgivers, &c." [Milton,] p. 382.

"When he has pretty well digested Tully's Offices, says Mr. Locke, p. 277. and added to it Puffendorff *de Officio Hominis & Civis,* it may be seasonable to set him upon Grotius, *de Jure Belli & Pacis,* or which perhaps is the better of the two, Puffendorff *de Jure naturali [naturae] & Gentium;* wherein he will be instructed in the natural Rights of Men, and the Original and Foundations of Society, and the Duties resulting from thence. This *general Part of Civil Law* and History are Studies which a Gentleman should not barely touch

Sake of the Praise attending it, they will begin to feel the Want, and be sensible of the Use of *Logic,* or the Art of Reasoning to *discover* Truth, and of Arguing to *defend* it, and *convince* Adversaries. This would be the Time to acquaint them with the Principles of that Art. Grotius, Puffendorff, and some other Writers of the same Kind, may be used on these Occasions to decide their Disputes. Publick Disputes[22] warm the Imagination, whet the Industry, and strengthen the natural Abilities.

When Youth are told, that the Great Men whose Lives and Actions they read in History, spoke two of the best Languages

---

at, but constantly dwell upon, and never have done with. A virtuous and well-behaved young Man, that is well versed in the *general Part of the Civil Law* (which concerns not the Chicane of private Cases, but the Affairs and Intercourse of civilized Nations in general, grounded upon Principles of Reason) understands Latin well, and can write a good Hand, one may turn loose into the World, with great Assurance that he will find Employment and Esteem every where."

22. Mr. Walker, in his excellent Treatise of the Education of young Gentlemen, speaking of *Publick and open Argumentation pro and con,* says p. 124, 125. "'"This is it* which brings a Question to a Point, and discovers the very Center and Knot of the Difficulty. *This* warms and *activates* the Spirit in the Search of Truth, excites Notions, and by replying and frequent Beating upon it, *cleanseth* it from the Ashes, and makes it shine and flame out the clearer. Besides, it puts them upon a continual *Stretch* of their Wits to defend their Cause, it makes them quick in Replies, intentive upon their Subject; where the *Opponent* useth all Means to drive his Adversary from his Hold; and the *Answerer* defends himself *sometimes* with the Force of Truth, *sometimes* with the Subtilty of his Wit; and *sometimes* also he escapes in a Mist of Words, and the Doubles of a Distinction, whilst he seeks all Holes and Recesses to shelter his persecuted Opinion and Reputation. This properly belongeth to the Disputations which are Exercises of young Students, who are by these Velitations and in this Palaestra brought up to a more serious Search of Truth. And in them I think it not a Fault *to dispute for Victory,* and to endeavour to save their Reputation; nor that their Questions and Subjects are concerning Things of small Moment and little Reality; yea, I have known some Governors that have absolutely forbidden such Questions, where the Truth was of Concernment, on purpose that the Youth might have the Liberty of exerting their Parts to the uttermost, and that there might be no Stint to their Emulation."

that ever were, the most expressive, copious, beautiful; and that
the finest Writings, the most correct Compositions, the most
perfect Productions of human Wit and Wisdom, are in those
Languages, which have endured Ages, and will endure while
there are Men; that no Translation can do them Justice, or give
the Pleasure found in Reading the Originals; that those Languages contain all Science; that one of them is become almost
universal, being the Language of Learned Men in all Countries;
that to understand them is a distinguishing Ornament, &c. they
may be thereby made desirous of learning those Languages, and
their Industry sharpen'd in the Acquisition of them. All intended for Divinity should be taught the Latin and Greek; for
Physick, the Latin, Greek and French; for Law, the Latin and
French; Merchants, the French, German, and Spanish: And
though all should not be compell'd to learn Latin, Greek, or the
modern foreign Languages; yet none that have an ardent Desire
to learn them should be refused; their English, Arithmetick, and
other Studies absolutely necessary, being at the same Time not
neglected.

    If the new *Universal History* were also read, it would give a
connected Idea of human Affairs, so far as it goes, which should
be follow'd by the best modern Histories, particularly of our
Mother Country; then of these Colonies; which should be
accompanied with Observations on their Rise, Encrease, Use to
Great-Britain, Encouragements, Discouragements, &c. the
Means to make them flourish, secure their Liberties, &c.

    With the History of Men, Times and Nations, should be
read at proper Hours or Days, some of the best *Histories of
Nature*,[23] which would not only be delightful to Youth, and

---

   23. Rollin, Vol. 4. p. 211. speaking of *Natural Philosophy*, says, "That
    much of it falls within the Capacity of all Sorts of Persons, even of
    Children. It consists in attending to the Objects with which Nature
    presents us, in considering them with Care, and admiring their
    different Beauties, &c. Searching out their secret Causes indeed
    more properly belongs to the Learned.

    "I say that even Children are capable of Studying Nature, for
    they have Eyes, and don't want Curiosity; they ask Questions, and
    love to be informed; and here we need only awaken and keep up in
    them the Desire of Learning and Knowing, which is natural to all

furnish them with Matter for their Letters, &c. as well as other History; but afterwards of great Use to them, whether they are Merchants, Handicrafts, or Divines; enabling the first the better to understand many Commodities, Drugs, &c. the second to improve his Trade or Handicraft by new Mixtures, Materials, &c. and the last to adorn his Discourses by beautiful Comparisons, and strengthen them by new Proofs of Divine Providence. The Conversation of all will be improved by it, as Occasions

---

Mankind. Besides this Study, if it is to be called a Study, instead of being painful and tedious, is pleasant and agreeable; it may be used as a Recreation, and should usually be made a Diversion. It is inconceivable, how many Things Children are capable of, if all the Opportunities of Instructing them were laid hold of, with which they themselves supply us.

"A Garden, a Country, a Plantation, are all so many Books which lie open to them; but they must have been taught and accustomed to read in them. Nothing is more common amongst us than the Use of Bread and Linnen. How seldom do Children know how either of them are prepared, through how many Operations and Hands the Corn and Flax must pass, before they are turned into Bread and Linnen? The same may be said of Cloth, which bears no Resemblance to the Wool whereof it is formed, any more than Paper to the Rags which are picked up in the Streets: And why should not Children be instructed in these wonderful Works of Nature and Art which they every Day make Use of without reflecting upon them?"

He adds, that "a careful Master may in this Way enrich the Mind of his Disciple with a great Number of useful and agreeable Ideas, and by a proper Mixture of short Reflections, will at the same Time take Care to form his Heart, and lead him by Nature to Religion."

Milton also recommends the Study of *Natural Philosophy* to Youth, *Educ.* p. 380. "In this," says he, "they may proceed leisurely from the History of Meteors, Minerals, Plants and living Creatures, as far as Anatomy; Then also in Course might be read to them out of some not tedious Writer, the Institution of Physick; that they may know the Tempers, the Humours, the Seasons, and how to manage a Crudity; which he who can wisely and timely do, is not only a great Physician to himself, and to his Friends, but also may at some Time or other save an Army by this frugal and expenseless Means only; and not let the healthy and stout Bodies of young Men rot away under him for want of this Discipline, which is a great Pity, and no less a Shame to the Commander."

Proper Books may be, Ray's *Wisdom of God in the Creation*, Derham's *Physico-Theology, Spectacle de la Nature*, &c.

frequently occur of making Natural Observations, which are instructive, agreeable, and entertaining in almost all Companies. *Natural History* will also afford Opportunities of introducing many Observations, relating to the Preservation of Health, which may be afterwards of great Use. Arbuthnot on Air and Aliment, Sanctorius on Perspiration, Lemery on Foods, and some others, may now be read, and a very little Explanation will make them sufficiently intelligible to Youth.

While they are reading Natural History, might not a little *Gardening, Planting, Grafting, Inoculating,* &c. be taught and practised; and now and then Excursions made to the neighbouring Plantations of the best Farmers, their Methods observ'd and reason'd upon for the Information of Youth. The Improvement of Agriculture being useful to all,[24] and Skill in it no Disparagement to any.

The History of *Commerce,* of the Invention of Arts, Rise of Manufactures, Progress of Trade, Change of its Seats, with the Reasons, Causes, &c. may also be made entertaining to Youth, and will be useful to all. And this, with the Accounts in other History of the prodigious Force and Effect of Engines and Machines used in War, will naturally introduce a Desire to be

---

24. Milton would have the Latin Authors on Agriculture taught at School, as Cato, Varro and Columella; "for the Matter," says he, "is most easy, and if the Language be difficult, yet it may be master'd. And here will be an Occasion of *inciting* and *enabling* them hereafter to improve the Tillage of their Country, to recover the bad Soil, and to remedy the Waste that is made of Good; for this was one of Hercules' Praises." *Educ.* p. 379.

Hutcheson [i.e., Fordyce] (*Dialogues on Educ.* 303, 2d Vol.) says, "Nor should I think it below the Dignity or Regard of an University, to descend even to the general Precepts of *Agriculture* and *Gardening.* Virgil, Varro, and others eminent in Learning, tho't it not below their Pen——and why should we think meanly of that Art, which was the Mother of Heroes, and of the Masters of the World."

Locke also recommends the Study of Husbandry and Gardening, as well as gaining an Insight in several of the manual Arts; *Educ.* p. 309, 314, 315. It would be a Pleasure and Diversion to Boys to be led now and then to the Shops of Artificers, and suffer'd to spend some Time there in observing their Manner of Working. For the Usefulness of Mechanic Skill, even to Gentlemen, see the Pages above cited, to which much might be added.

instructed in *Mechanicks*,[25] and to be inform'd of the Principles of that Art by which weak Men perform such Wonders, Labour is sav'd, Manufactures expedited, &c. &c. This will be the Time to show them Prints of antient and modern Machines, to explain them, to let them be copied,[26] and to give Lectures in Mechanical Philosophy.

With the whole should be constantly inculcated and cultivated, that *Benignity of Mind*,[27] which shows itself in *searching for* and *seizing* every Opportunity *to serve* and *to oblige;* and is the Foundation of what is called GOOD BREEDING; highly useful to the Possessor, and most agreeable to all.[28]

25. How many Mills are built and Machines constructed, at great and fruitless Expence, which a little Knowledge in the Principles of Mechanics would have prevented?

26. We are often told in the Journals of Travellers, that such and such Things are done in foreign Countries, by which Labour is sav'd, and Manufactures expedited, &c. but their Description of the Machines or Instruments used, are quite unintelligible for want of good Drafts. Copying Prints of Machines is of Use to fix the Attention on the several Parts, their Proportions, Reasons, Effects, &c. A Man that has been us'd to this Practice, is not only better able to make a Draft when the Machine is before him, but takes so much better Notice of its Appearance, that he can carry it off by Memory when he has not the Opportunity of Drawing it on the Spot. Thus may a Traveller bring home Things of great Use to his Country.

27. "Upon this excellent Disposition (says Turnbull, p. 326.) it will be *easy to build* that amiable Quality commonly called GOOD BREEDING, and upon *no other Foundation* can it be raised. For whence else can it spring, but from a general Good-will and Regard for all People, deeply rooted in the Heart, which makes any one that has it, careful not to shew in his Carriage, any Contempt, Disrespect, or Neglect of them, but to express a Value and Respect for them according to their Rank and Condition, suitable to the Fashion and Way of their Country? 'Tis a Disposition to make all we converse with easy and well pleased."

28. "It is this lovely Quality which gives true Beauty to all other Accomplishments, or renders them useful to their Possessor, in procuring him the Esteem and Good-will of all that he comes near. Without it, his other Qualities, however good in themselves, make him but pass for proud, conceited, vain or foolish. Courage, says an excellent Writer, in an ill-bred Man has the Air, and escapes not the Opinion of Brutality; Learning becomes Pedantry; Wit, Buffoonery; Plainness, Rusticity; and there cannot be a good Quality in him

The Idea of what is *true Merit,* should also be often presented to Youth, explain'd and impress'd on their Minds, as consisting in an *Inclination* join'd with an *Ability* to serve Mankind, one's Country, Friends and Family; which *Ability* is (with the Blessing of God) to be acquir'd or greatly encreas'd by *true Learning;* and should indeed be the great *Aim* and *End*[29] of all Learning.

---

which Ill-breeding will not warp and disfigure to his Disadvantage." Turnbull, p. 327.

29. To have in View the *Glory* and *Service of God,* as some express themselves, is only the same Thing in other Words. For *Doing Good to Men* is the *only Service of God* in our Power; and to *imitate his Beneficence* is to *glorify him.* Hence Milton says, "The *End* of Learning is to repair the Ruins of our first Parents, by regaining to *know God aright,* and out of that Knowledge to *love him,* to *imitate him,* to be *like him,* as we may the nearest by possessing our Souls of true Virtue." *Educ.* p. 373. Mr. Hutcheson [i.e., Fordyce] says, *Dial.* v. 2. p. 97. "The *principal End* of Education is, to *form us wise and good Creatures, useful to others and happy ourselves.* The whole Art of Education lies within a narrow Compass, and is reducible to a very simple Practice; namely, *To assist in unfolding those Natural and Moral Powers with which Man is endowed, by presenting proper Objects and Occasions; to watch their Growth that they be not diverted from their End, or disturbed in their Operation by any foreign Violence; and gently to conduct and apply them to all the Purposes of private and of public Life."* And Mr. Locke (p. 84. *Educ.*) says, " 'Tis VIRTUE, then, direct VIRTUE, which is to be *aim'd at* in Education. All other Considerations and Accomplishments are nothing in Comparison to this. This is the *solid* and *substantial* Good, which Tutors should not only read Lectures and talk of, but the *Labour* and *Art of Education* should furnish the Mind with, and *fasten* there, and never cease till the young Man had a true Relish of it, and plac'd his *Strength,* his *Glory,* and his *Pleasure,* in it." And Mons. Rollin, *Belles Lettres,* Vol. 4. p. 249. to the same Purpose, "If we consult our Reason ever so little, it is easy to discern that the END which Masters should have in View, is not barely to teach their Scholars Greek and Latin, to learn them to make Exercises and Verses, to charge their Memory with Facts and historical Dates, to draw up Syllogisms in Form, or to trace Lines and Figures upon Paper. These Branches of Learning I own are useful and valuable, but as *Means,* and not as the *End;* when they conduct us to other Things, and not when we stop at them; when they serve us as Preparatives and Instruments for better Knowledge, without which the rest would

be useless. Youth would have Cause to complain, if they were condemned to spend eight or ten of the best Years of their Life in learning, at a great Expence, and with incredible Pains, one or two Languages, and some other Matters of a like Nature, which perhaps they would seldom have Occasion to use. The end of Masters, in the long Course of their Studies, is to habituate their Scholars to serious Application of Mind, to make them love and value the Sciences, and to cultivate in them such a Taste, as shall make them thirst after them when they are gone from School; to point out the Method of attaining them; and make them thoroughly sensible of their Use and Value; and by that Means dispose them for the different Employments to which it shall please God to call them. Besides this, the *End* of Masters should be, *to improve their Hearts* and Understandings, to protect their Innocence, to *inspire* them with Principles of *Honour* and *Probity,* to train them up to good Habits; to correct and subdue in them by gentle Means, the ill Inclinations they shall be observed to have, such as Pride, Insolence, and high Opinion of themselves, and a saucy Vanity continually employed in lessening others; a blind Self-love solely attentive to its own Advantage; a Spirit of Raillery which is pleased with offending and insulting others; and Indolence and Sloth, which renders all the good Qualities of the Mind useless."

Dr. Turnbull has the same Sentiments, with which we shall conclude this Note. "If," says he, "there be any such Thing as DUTY, or any such Thing as HAPPINESS; if there be any Difference between right and wrong Conduct; any Distinction between Virtue and Vice, or Wisdom and Folly; in fine, if there be any such Thing as Perfection or Imperfection belonging to the rational Powers which constitute moral Agents; or if Enjoyments and Pursuits admit of Comparison; *Good Education* must of Necessity be acknowledged to mean, *proper Care* to instruct early in the Science of Happiness and Duty, or in the Art of Judging and *Acting aright* in Life. Whatever else one may have learned, if he comes into the World from his Schooling and Masters, quite unacquainted with the Nature, Rank and Condition, of Mankind, and the *Duties of human life* (in its more ordinary Circumstances at least) he hath lost his Time; *he is not educated;* he is not prepared for the World; he is not qualified for Society; he is not fitted for discharging the *proper Business of Man.* The Way therefore to judge whether Education be on a right Footing or not, is to compare it with the END; or to consider what it does in order to accomplish Youth for choosing and *behaving well* in the various Conditions, *Relations* and Incidents, of Life. If Education be calculated and adapted to furnish young Minds betimes with proper Knowledge for their Guidance and Direction in the chief Affairs of the World, and in the principal Vicissitudes to which human

Concerns are subject, then it is indeed *proper or right Education.* But if *such Instruction* be not the *principal Scope* to which all other Lessons are rendered subservient in what is called the *Institution of Youth,* either *the Art of Living and Acting well* is not Man's *most important* Business, or what ought to be the CHIEF END of Education is neglected, and sacrificed to something of *far inferior* Moment. *Observations on Liberal Education,* p. 175, 176.

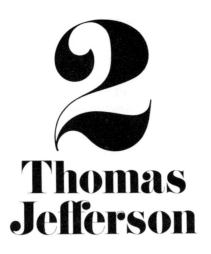

Thomas Jefferson

"**I** have sworn upon the altar of God eternal hostility against every form of tyranny over the mind of man." However pompous this may sound to us today, probably no statement from Jefferson more fully explains his public career. Sensitive to the many different forms tyranny could take, he spent most of his adult life unmasking it to his fellow men. And it was for this work he asked to be remembered.

From among the many spectacular accomplishments of his life he selected but three "testimonials" for inscription on his tombstone. Each of these reveal his continual "hostility against every form of tyranny." As author of the Declaration of Independence— his most famous "testimonial"—Jefferson unmasked the tyranny of the British monarch, who had let loose a "long train of abuses and usurpations" designed to place the American colonists "under absolute Despotism."

A second accomplishment he asked for his epitaph was that he had authored the statutes for religious freedom in Virginia. He saw this, too, as a battle against tyranny over the mind of man. Organized religion he regarded as a form of potential tyranny, actualized whenever the power of the church in some way joined hands with the power of the state. His "Bill for Establishing Religious Freedom," passed by the Virginia House of Burgesses in 1786, prohibited the state from establishing any religion as the official one, guaranteed the free exercise of all religious beliefs, and proscribed any and all religious tests for holding political office.

Early in his public life Jefferson saw that, young as America was, various forms of institutionalized tyranny had already become accepted as a way of life. In his native Virginia, for example, a powerful landed aristocracy had emerged, an aristocracy that threatened the liberty of the rest. While still a relative newcomer to the Virginia legislature, Jefferson introduced bills that abolished both primogeniture and entail—the two pillars that maintained the power of the landed gentry. In the matter of slavery—the most blatant form of tyranny in the South—Jefferson was less forthright. Fearful, like most southerners, of slave revolt and racial warfare, he never advocated abolition. But he did perceive slavery as tyranny —"I tremble for my country when I reflect that God is just"—and advocated in various ways and at various times a scheme of gradual emancipation and expatriation of the blacks. His proposed constitution for Virginia in the 1770s prohibited holding in slavery any person henceforth coming into the country. (The assembly would not go this far, but in 1778 it prohibited foreign slave trade.)

Jefferson's lifelong battle against tyranny led him to what can be called a protectionist theory of government. According to this theory the sole function of government is to protect the people— their lives, liberties, property, and their right to pursue happiness. Most of his public life Jefferson devoted to developing and refining the various political and governmental arrangements that would protect these rights of his countrymen. In Virginia he was first a member of the assembly, then governor during the formative years of statehood. At the national level he served as member of the Continental Congress, minister to France, secretary of state, vice-president, and President of the United States.

The doctrine that the sole function of the government is protection of the people contains, as Jefferson clearly saw, a dilemma. For in its efforts to protect the people, the government may become so powerful it winds up oppressing the people. For this reason Jefferson, in all his governmental roles, favored a "weak" government; he was not, he wrote, "a friend to a very energetic government." And yet if the government was really going to protect the people, it sometimes had to become "energetic." Thus Jefferson himself, as President, with seeming arbitrariness purchased Louisiana from France. This was an act to protect the people against the threat of a foreign power proximate to our borders, and against the tyranny that results from land scarcity.

Could the dilemma be resolved? Could the government effectively protect people *without* becoming itself the most dangerous and oppressive tyrant of all? Any solution, Jefferson saw, had to be an institutional one—specific checks and restraints built into the processes of government. As one of the "founding fathers," Jefferson helped to institutionalize these checks and restraints into the national government. The resulting American Constitution separates the powers of government into three distinct branches—Legislative, Executive, and Judiciary; spells out and limits the sphere of responsibility of each branch; and makes the acts of each branch subject to a check or veto from one of the other branches.

In a letter to Madison in 1787, Jefferson, who was then serving as minister to France, wrote approvingly of all these features in the proposed constitution. He made two additional recommendations. First, he insisted that the constitution must contain a "bill of rights" to protect the people from arbitrary and tyrannical actions by the government: "A bill of rights is what the people are entitled to against every government on earth, general or particular, and what no just government should refuse or rest on inference." Second, he approved the institution of frequent elections as a superb device to check the power of government, but he wanted rotation in office, particularly in the case of the President, who might become "an officer for life." Jefferson was unsuccessful in his bid to limit the reelection of the President, although Americans finally recognized the wisdom of this and put it into law in the twentieth century.

These institutionalized checks and restraints on government only partially solved the problem of protection against the protectors. For, as Jefferson noted, "experience hath shown, that even under the best forms, those entrusted with power have, in time, and by slow operation, perverted it into tyranny." Institutions are like fortresses. They can protect us only if they are maintained and well manned. The maintenance and use of these institutionalized checks and balances is up to the people themselves. "It is an axiom of my mind," Jefferson wrote to Washington, "that our liberty can never be safe but in the hands of the people themselves" adding: "and that, too, of the people with a certain degree of instruction."

For Jefferson, then, education is the ultimate safeguard of liberty—only an educated people can maintain and use the institutions designed to protect them against tyranny. Education is so basic to the preservation of freedom that the state itself must see to it that all its children receive an education. In 1779 Jefferson introduced to the Virginia assembly his "Bill for the More General Diffusion of Knowledge." This bill provided for universal education in Virginia. It called for the establishment of one elementary school in each "hundred," or ward, throughout the state. There all free children—male and female—would receive three years of education *without charge.* During these three years all children were to learn how to read, write, and calculate. In addition they would study history so that "possessed thereby of the experience of other ages and countries, they may be enabled to know ambition under all its shapes and prompt to exert their material powers to defeat its purposes."

Literacy, and some knowledge of history, Jefferson thought, was sufficient to enable men to protect themselves, as long as newspapers were available. "When the press is free, and every man able to read," Jefferson wrote, "all is safe." Universal education of the people was only part of Jefferson's educational scheme. Those who actually wielded the power, those who held government office, had to receive an appropriate education. Rulers should be men of character—upright, responsible, and virtuous—members of what Jefferson termed "a natural aristocracy." Jefferson distinguished this natural aristocracy founded on virtue and intellectual talents from an artificial aristocracy founded on wealth and birth.

And virtue and talent, where did they come from? Unlike most of his contemporaries, Jefferson did not see Christianity as the basis for moral virtue. A rationalist from youth onward, he maintained that conscience aided by reason was the cornerstone of morality. Moreover, each man could promote the happiness of others through the exercise of his reason—reason directed him to act in ways that neither harmed nor hurt others.

Since men of conscience and reason were virtuous, the best

candidates for governmental office, then we should encourage such talent wherever we may find it. Ability did not reside only among the wealthy and well born (although many among that artificial aristocracy were indeed natural aristocrats, e.g., Thomas Jefferson), it was ubiquitous. Here, then, was another task for a state system of education: it would separate "the gems from the rubbish." Jefferson's "Bill for the Diffusion of Knowledge" did more than simply provide three years of elementary education for all. Above these elementary schools were to be twenty secondary schools, called grammar schools. Here parents had to pay tuition. However, state scholarships existed for "promising geniuses from poor families." Each elementary school could send one deserving student to a grammar school. These hundred "public foundationers" got two years of free education. At this point each grammar school selected one of the scholarship students to continue for four more years of education. "By this means," Jefferson wrote, "twenty of the best geniuses will be raked from the rubbish annually, and be instructed, at the public expense, so far as grammar schools go."

At the top of the proposed educational pyramid stood the College of William and Mary. Every year each grammar school would choose and send to the college ten "of the best learning and most hopeful geniuses and disposition"; these to be "educated, boarded, and clothed, three years" at public expense.

William and Mary, of course, was an Anglican college. But it was an institution of such great importance to the commonwealth, Jefferson argued in 1779, that the legislature should transform it into a state university. William and Mary, he reminded his colleagues, "was the only seminary in which those who are to be the future guardians of the rights and liberties of their country may be endowed with science and virtue, to watch and preserve the sacred deposit." His "Bill for Amending the Constitution of the College of William and Mary," also introduced in 1778, proposed to replace the Anglican board of trustees with a secular board appointed by the General Assembly. The same bill proposed to restructure the faculty and eliminate the teaching of religion and languages in favor of science.

The assembly did not pass Jefferson's "Bill for the More General Diffusion of Knowledge." Too expensive and too impracticable, reported James Madison. Nor did the assembly pass his

"Bill for Amending the Constitution of the College of William and Mary." Too radical.

Some years later, Jefferson—after having abandoned all hope of reforming his alma mater—began to consider the creation of a wholly new university in his native state. He discussed this with his friends Joseph Priestley and Pierre Samuel Dupont de Nemours, who each obliged him with educational plans. In 1805 Jefferson himself drew up a sketch for a university. Already Georgia, North Carolina, South Carolina, and Tennessee had established state universities. Virginia, Jefferson thought, could not be indifferent to this need. But once more the Virginia legislature disappointed him. Then, in December 1806, in his second term as President, he recommended that the U.S. Congress create a national university. Again, nothing came of this.

Five years after his "retirement" from public life, Jefferson once again took up the battle for a state university. In 1814 some friends had asked him to serve on the board of a new private secondary school, Albemarle Academy, in Charlottesville. He accepted and promptly set about to transform the fledgling academy into his longed-for university. Within a year he had drafted and helped secure the passage of a bill that converted Albemarle Academy into Central College.

Jefferson, of course, sought a complete statewide educational system—with the state university as the capstone. In 1815 he revised and published his original 1779 plan. Using this as a basis, he prepared a new bill to establish three levels of education in Virginia—elementary schools, grammar schools (now called "colleges"), and the state university. Once again his plan met with the old arguments: it was not the responsibility of the state to finance a statewide system of education; the colony was too sparsely settled to execute such a system.

Instead of Jefferson's total educational system, the legislature passed an act to provide appropriations for the education of the poor in "charity schools"—should any county set up such schools. It made no provisions for district colleges. However, Jefferson did get his state university: an appropriation for $15,000 annually and an order to create a commission to choose a site and develop an educational plan for a state university.

Appointed to this commission in 1818, Jefferson convinced the other members to choose Central College in Charlottesville as the site for the new university. He also got them to adopt, as their final report, his already written plan for its educational development into a university.

Appointed rector of the proposed university, Jefferson worked tirelessly in recruiting faculty, securing books for the library, designing all the buildings and supervising their construction. Most grueling of all were his efforts to secure additional funds from the state.

The University of Virginia opened its doors in 1825. The long-standing dream had come true! Yet the creation of the University of Virginia realized only half of Jefferson's dream of a total educational system. The system of charity schools created in 1817 proved totally inadequate. "The present plan," Jefferson wrote in 1820, "has appropriated to the primary schools $45,000 for three years, making $135,000. I should be glad to know if this sum has educated one hundred and thirty-five poor children? I doubt it much." Jefferson's commitment to the need for primary schools was even stronger than that to the state university. At least this is what he told Joseph Cabell in a letter of 1823: "Were it necessary to give up either the Primaries or the University, I would rather abandon the last, because it is safer to have a whole people respectably enlightened than a few in a high state of science and the many in ignorance. This last is the most dangerous state in which a nation can be. The nations and governments of Europe are so many proofs of it."

But it was not to be. Virginia got her state university, but neither Virginia nor any other state created a system of free education in the early years of the Republic.

Almost all the founding fathers agreed with Jefferson that universal education was necessary in order for men to be able to protect their liberties—Washington and Madison, Jay and Clinton, Rush and Knox, and Adams, too, all followed this line when discussing education. Many of the state constitutions constructed at this time reflect this theory. Massachusetts' 1789 Constitution put it this way: "Wisdom and knowledge as well as virtue, diffused generally among the body of the people, being necessary for the preservation of their rights and liberties . . . it shall be the duty of legislatures and magistrates, in all future periods of this commonwealth, to cherish the interests of literature and the sciences, and all seminaries of them."

Yet for all the rhetorical claims that universal education is necessary to preserve freedom, why did no systems of universal education come into being during this period? Granted the real and quite severe shortage of public funds; granted, too, the impracticability of systems of education in the sparsely settled states; granted, furthermore, the popular prejudice against free instruction—granted all this, not one gets to the root of the failure of Jefferson's theory of instruction.

The failure, I think, emerges from the contradiction inherent in the theory itself. For if the function of the free schools was to educate people so they can protect themselves against governmental abuse of power, then it is contradictory—or at least foolish—for the government to establish such schools. In so acting the government would become more powerful, hence a greater threat than before to the very liberties its action was supposed to protect. Understandably the legislators balked at passing a law to grant the state government power to compel the creation of schools throughout the state. They took a compromise path, appropriating public money to support free education established by voluntary agencies.

Only when the theory of universal education changed, only when people came to construe it as a way of socializing the masses—socializing them in order *to protect society against* them or their excesses—only then would the state begin to move into the business of setting up systems of education. Even then, as we shall see in the next chapter, grass-roots support for a free educational system sprang up only when leaders construed it as a means to advancement.

Jefferson never abandoned his conviction that only educated citizens could protect their freedoms, or did he ever overcome the contradiction in his theory of education that subverted his plans to set up a system to diffuse education to all. He failed to become the father of universal education. Yet he had tried—and he knew it. The third testimonial he chose for his epitaph reads simply: "Father of the University of Virginia."

WORKS AND COMMENTARY

Not all of the projected fifty volumes of *The Papers of Thomas Jefferson*, edited by Julian P. Boyd and others (Princeton, N.J.: Princeton University Press, 1950 et seq.), have yet appeared. There are two earlier published collections, both called *The Writings of Thomas Jefferson*; one of ten volumes edited by Paul L. Ford (New York, 1892–99), the other of twenty volumes edited by A. A. Lipscomb and A. E. Bergh (Washington, 1903).

Two helpful collections of Jefferson's writings on education along with commentaries on them are those of Gordon C. Lee, *Crusade Against Ignorance* (New York: Teachers College Bureau of Publications, 1961) and Roy J. Honeywell, *The Educational Work of Thomas Jefferson* (Cambridge: Harvard University Press, 1931).

A good recent biography is that by Merrill D. Peterson, *Thomas Jefferson and the New Nation* (New York: Oxford University Press, 1970). Robert Heslep's *Thomas Jefferson and Education* (New York: Random House, 1969) is an excellent analysis of Jefferson's educational thought.

The selection that follows is from volume 2 of *The Papers of Thomas Jefferson*, pages 526–33.

A Bill for the More General Diffusion of Knowledge

Whereas it appeareth that however certain forms of government are better calculated than others to protect individuals in the free exercise of their natural rights, and are at the same time themselves better guarded against degeneracy, yet experience hath shewn, that even under the best forms, those entrusted with power have, in time, and by slow operations, perverted it into tyranny; and it is believed that the most effectual means of preventing this would be, to illuminate, as far as practicable, the minds of the people at large, and more especially to give them knowledge of those facts, which history exhibiteth, that, possessed thereby of the experience of other ages and countries, they may be enabled to know ambition under all its shapes, and prompt to exert their natural powers to defeat its purposes; And whereas it is generally true that people will be happiest whose laws are best, and are best administered, and that laws will be wisely formed, and honestly administered, in proportion as those who form and administer them are wise and honest; whence it becomes expedient for promoting the publick happiness that those persons, whom nature hath endowed with genius and virtue, should be rendered by liberal education worthy to receive, and able to guard the sacred deposit of the rights and liberties of their fellow citizens, and that they should be called to that charge without regard to wealth, birth or other accidental condition or circumstance; but the indigence of the greater number disabling them from so educating, at their own expence, those of their children whom nature hath fitly formed and disposed to become useful instruments for the public, it is better that such should be sought for and educated at the common expence of all, than that the happiness of all should be confided to the weak or wicked:

Be it therefore enacted by the General Assembly, that in every county within this commonwealth, there shall be chosen annually, by the electors qualified to vote for Delegates, three of the most honest and able men of their county, to be called the Aldermen of the county; and that the election of the said Aldermen shall be held at the same time and place, before the same persons, and notified and conducted in the same manner as by law is directed for the annual election of Delegates for the county.

The person before whom such election is holden shall certify to the court of the said county the names of the Aldermen chosen, in order that the same may be entered of record, and shall give notice of their election to the said Aldermen within a fortnight after such election.

The said Aldermen on the first Monday in October, if it be fair, and if not, then on the next fair day, excluding Sunday, shall meet at the court-house of their county, and proceed to divide their said county into hundreds, bounding the same by water courses, mountains, or limits, to be run and marked, if they think necessary, by the county surveyor, and at the county expence, regulating the size of the said hundreds, according to the best of their discretion, so as that they may contain a convenient number of children to make up a school, and be of such convenient size that all the children within each hundred may daily attend the school to be established therein, distinguishing each hundred by a particular name; which division, with the names of the several hundreds, shall be returned to the court of the county and be entered of record, and shall remain unaltered until the increase or decrease of inhabitants shall render an alteration necessary, in the opinion of any succeeding Aldermen, and also in the opinion of the court of the county.

The electors aforesaid residing within every hundred shall meet on the third Monday in October after the first election of Aldermen, at such place, within their hundred, as the said Aldermen shall direct, notice thereof being previously given to them by such person residing within the hundred as the said Aldermen shall require who is hereby enjoined to obey such requisition, on pain of being punished by amercement and imprisonment. The electors being so assembled shall choose the most convenient place within their hundred for building a school-house. If two or more places, having a greater number of votes than any others, shall yet be equal between themselves, the Aldermen, or such of them as are not of the same hundred, on information thereof, shall decide between them. The said Aldermen shall forthwith proceed to have a school-house built at the said place, and shall see that the same be kept in repair, and, when necessary, that it be rebuilt; but whenever they shall think necessary that it be rebuilt, they shall give notice as before directed, to the electors of the hundred to meet at the said school-house, on such day as they shall appoint, to determine by vote, in the manner before directed, whether it shall be rebuilt at the same, or what other place in the hundred.

At every of these schools shall be taught reading, writing, and common arithmetick, and the books which shall be used therein for instructing the children to read shall be such as will at the same time make them acquainted with Græcian, Roman, English, and American history. At these schools all the free children, male and female, resident within the respective hundred, shall be intitled to receive tuition gratis, for the term of three years, and as much longer, at their private expence, as their parents, guardians or friends, shall think proper.

Over every ten of these schools (or such other number nearest thereto, as the number of hundreds in the county will admit, without fractional divisions) an overseer shall be appointed annually by the Aldermen at their first meeting, eminent for his learning, integrity, and fidelity to the commonwealth, whose business and duty it shall be, from time to time, to appoint a teacher to each school, who shall give assurance of fidelity to the commonwealth, and to remove him as he shall see cause; to visit every school once in every half year at the least; to examine the schollars; see that any general plan of reading and instruction recommended by the visiters of William and Mary College shall be observed; and to superintend the conduct of the teacher in every thing relative to his school.

Every teacher shall receive a salary of _____ by the year, which, with the expences of building and repairing the schoolhouses, shall be provided in such manner as other county expences are by law directed to be provided and shall also have his diet, lodging, and washing found him, to be levied in like manner, save only that such levy shall be on the inhabitants of each hundred for the board of their own teacher only.

And in order that grammar schools may be rendered convenient to the youth in every part of the commonwealth, Be it farther enacted, that on the first Monday in November, after the first appointment of overseers for the hundred schools, if fair, and if not, then on the next fair day, excluding Sunday, after the hour of one in the afternoon, the said overseers appointed for the schools in the counties of Princess Ann, Norfolk, Nansemond and Isle-of-Wight, shall meet at Nansemond court house; those for the counties of Southampton, Sussex, Surry and Prince George, shall meet at Sussex courthouse; those for the counties of Brunswick, Mecklenburg and Lunenburg, shall meet at Lunenburg court-house; those for the counties of Dinwiddie, Amelia and Chesterfield, shall meet at Chesterfield court-house; those for the counties of Powhatan, Cumberland, Goochland, Henrico and Hanover, shall meet at Henrico court-house; those for the counties of Prince Edward, Charlotte and Halifax, shall meet at Charlotte court-house;

those for the counties of Henry, Pittsylvania and Bedford, shall meet at Pittsylvania court-house; those for the counties of Buckingham, Amherst, Albemarle and Flubanna, shall meet at Albermarle court-house; those for the counties of Botetourt, Rockbridge, Montgomery, Washington and Kentucky, shall meet at Botetourt court-house; those for the counties of Augusta, Rockingham and Greenbrier, shall meet at Augusta court-house; those for the counties of Accomack and North-ampton, shall meet at Accomack court-house; those for the counties of Elizabeth City, Warwick, York, Gloucester, James City, Charles City and New-Kent, shall meet at James City court-house; those for the counties of Middlesex, Essex, King and Queen, King William and Caroline, shall meet at King and Queen court-house; those for the counties of Lancaster, North-umberland, Richmond and Westmoreland, shall meet at Rich-mond court-house; those for the counties of King George, Stafford, Spotsylvania, Prince William and Fairfax, shall meet at Spotsylvania court-house; those for the counties of Loudoun and Fauquier, shall meet at Loudoun court-house; those for the counties of Culpeper, Orange and Louisa, shall meet at Orange court-house; those for the counties of Shenandoah and Freder-ick, shall meet at Frederick court-house; those for the counties of Hampshire and Berkeley, shall meet at Berkeley court-house; and those for the counties of Yohogania, Monongalia and Ohio, shall meet at Monongalia court-house; and shall fix on such place in some one of the counties in their district as shall be most proper for situating a grammar school-house, endeavour-ing that the situation be as central as may be to the inhabitants of the said counties, that it be furnished with good water, convenient to plentiful supplies of provision and fuel, and more than all things that it be healthy. And if a majority of the overseers present should not concur in their choice of any one place proposed, the method of determining shall be as follows: If two places only were proposed, and the votes be divided, they shall decide between them by fair and equal lot; if more than two places were proposed, the question shall be put on those two which on the first division had the greater number of votes; or if no two places had a greater number of votes than the others, as where the votes shall have been equal between one or both of them and some other or others, then it shall be decided by fair and equal lot (unless it can be agreed by a majority of votes) which of the places having equal numbers shall be thrown out of the competition, so that the question shall be put on the remaining two, and if on this ultimate question the votes shall be equally divided, it shall then be decided finally by lot.

The said overseers having determined the place at which the grammar school for their district shall be built, shall forthwith (unless they can otherwise agree with the proprietors of the circumjacent lands as to location and price) make application to the clerk of the county in which the said house is to be situated, who shall thereupon issue a writ, in the nature of a writ of ad quod damnum, directed to the sheriff of the said county commanding him to summon and impannel twelve fit persons to meet at the place, so destined for the grammar school house, on a certain day, to be named in the said writ, not less than five, nor more than ten, days from the date thereof; and also to give notice of the same to the proprietors and tenants of the lands to be viewed, if they be to be found within the county, and if not, then to their agents therein if any they have. Which freeholders shall be charged by the said sheriff impartially, and to the best of their skill and judgment to view the lands round about the said place, and to locate and circumscribe, by certain metes and bounds, one hundred acres thereof, having regard therein principally to the benefit and convenience of the said school, but respecting in some measure also the convenience of the said proprietors, and to value and appraise the same in so many several and distinct parcels as shall be owned or held by several and distinct owners or tenants, and according to their respective interests and estates therein. And after such location and appraisement so made, the said sheriff shall forthwith return the same under the hands and seals of the said jurors, together with the writ, to the clerk's office of the said county and the right and property of the said proprietors and tenants in the said lands so circumscribed shall be immediately devested and be transferred to the commonwealth for the use of the said grammar school, in full and absolute dominion, any want of consent or disability to consent in the said owners or tenants notwithstanding. But it shall not be lawful for the said overseers so to situate the said grammar school-house, nor to the said jurors so to locate the said lands, as to include the mansion-house of the proprietor of the lands, nor the offices, curtilage, or garden, thereunto immediately belonging.

The said overseers shall forthwith proceed to have a house of brick or stone, for the said grammar school, with necessary offices, built on the said lands, which grammar school-house shall contain a room for the school, a hall to dine in, four rooms for a master and usher, and ten or twelve lodging rooms for the scholars.

To each of the said grammar schools shall be allowed out of the public treasury, the sum of   pounds, out of which shall be paid by the Treasurer, on warrant from the Auditors, to the proprietors or tenants of the lands located, the value of their several interests as fixed by the jury, and the balance thereof shall be delivered to the said overseers to defray the expence of the said buildings.

In these grammar schools shall be taught the Latin and Greek languages, English grammar, geography, and the higher part of numerical arithmetick, to wit, vulgar and decimal fractions, and the extraction of the square and cube roots.

A visiter from each county constituting the district shall be appointed, by the overseers, for the county, in the month of October annually, either from their own body or from their county at large, which visiters or the greater part of them, meeting together at the said grammar school on the first Monday in November, if fair, and if not, then on the next fair day, excluding Sunday, shall have power to choose their own Rector, who shall call and preside at future meetings, to employ from time to time a master, and if necessary, an usher, for the said school, to remove them at their will, and to settle the price of tuition to be paid by the scholars. They shall also visit the school twice in every year at the least, either together or separately at their discretion, examine the scholars, and see that any general plan of instruction recommended by the visiters of

William and Mary College shall be observed. The said masters and ushers, before they enter on the execution of their office, shall give assurance of fidelity to the commonwealth.

A steward shall be employed, and removed at will by the master, on such wages as the visiters shall direct; which steward shall see to the procuring provisions, fuel, servants for cooking, waiting, house cleaning, washing, mending, and gardening on the most reasonable terms; the expence of which, together with the steward's wages, shall be divided equally among all the scholars boarding either on the public or private expence. And the part of those who are on private expence, and also the price of their tuitions due to the master or usher, shall be paid quarterly by the respective scholars, their parents, or guardians, and shall be recoverable, if withheld, together with costs, on motion in any Court of Record, ten days notice thereof being previously given to the party, and a jury impannelled to try the issue joined, or enquire of the damages. The said steward shall also, under the direction of the visiters, see that the houses be kept in repair, and necessary enclosures be made and repaired, the accounts for which, shall, from time to time, be submitted to the Auditors, and on their warrant paid by the Treasurer.

Every overseer of the hundred schools shall, in the month of September annually, after the most diligent and impartial examination and enquiry, appoint from among the boys who shall have been two years at the least at some one of the schools under his superintendance, and whose parents are too poore to give them farther education, some one of the best and most promising genius and disposition, to proceed to the grammar school of his district; which appointment shall be made in the court-house of the county, on the court day for that month if fair, and if not, then on the next fair day, excluding Sunday, in the presence of the Aldermen, or two of them at the least, assembled on the bench for that purpose, the said overseer being previously sworn by them to make such appointment, without favor or affection, according to the best of his skill and judgment, and being interrogated by the said Aldermen, either on their own motion, or on suggestions from the parents, guardians, friends, or teachers of the children, competitors for such appointment; which teachers shall attend for the information of the Aldermen. On which interregatories the said Aldermen, if they be not satisfied with the appointment proposed, shall have right to negative it; whereupon the said visiter may proceed to make a new appointment, and the said Aldermen again to interrogate and negative, and so toties quoties until an appointment be approved.

Every boy so appointed shall be authorised to proceed to the grammar school of his district, there to be educated and boarded during such time as is hereafter limited; and his quota of the expences of the house together with a compensation to the master or usher for his tuition, at the rate of twenty dollars by the year, shall be paid by the Treasurer quarterly on warrant from the Auditors.

A visitation shall be held, for the purpose of probation, annually at the said grammar school on the last Monday in September, if fair, and if not, then on the next fair day, excluding Sunday, at which one third of the boys sent thither by appointment of the said overseers, and who shall have been there one year only, shall be discontinued as public foundationers, being those who, on the most diligent examination and enquiry, shall be thought to be of the least promising genius and disposition; and of those who shall have been there two years, all shall be discontinued, save one only the best in genius and disposition, who shall be at liberty to continue there four years longer on the public foundation, and shall thence forward be deemed a senior.

The visiters for the districts which, or any part of which, be southward and westward of James river, as known by that name, or by the names of Fluvanna and Jackson's river, in every other year, to wit, at the probation meetings held in the years, distinguished in the Christian computation by odd numbers, and the visiters for all the other districts at their said meetings to be held in those years, distinguished by even numbers, after diligent examination and enquiry as before directed, shall chuse one among the said seniors, of the best learning and most hopeful genius and disposition, who shall be authorised by them to proceed to William and Mary College, there to be educated, boarded, and clothed, three years; the expence of which annually shall be paid by the Treasurer on warrant from the Auditors.

3

Horace Mann

"This institution is the greatest discovery ever made by man: we repeat it, *the common school is the greatest discovery ever made by man.*" Horace Mann, the "father of the common school," wrote these words in 1840, during a period when all he had worked for as secretary of the State Board of Education of Massachusetts had come under sharp attack. This ringing affirmation was no mere immodest boast from a proud parent. The attacks had forced him to look deeply into the springs of public action in America. There he discovered the liberal roots of the common school. This discovery in 1840 marked a turning point in the history of popular education in America; now Mann could—and did—firmly plant the common school as an indispensable institution in American society.

＊

Early in the nineteenth century the American ideal of weak government had to give way to economic reality. Although many of the founding fathers had believed that the sole task for the government was the protection of all citizens' rights to life, liberty, and the pursuit of happiness, those who now manned the government felt that they had to expand the notion of "protection." The government had to protect the fledgling economy. Manufacturers demanded tariffs on imports; investors sought regulation of the currency; everyone wanted improved transportation—roads, canals, and, soon, railroads.

To protect the general welfare the government granted corporate charters, donated lands, and supplied funds; it imposed tariffs and issued currency. Inevitably, these actions made some men rich and, ofttimes, diminished the wealth of others. Understandably, then, the matter of corruption in government loomed larger and larger in the minds of people, especially those people who had not profited from the actions of the government. It dominated political debates, erupting most vociferously in the 1820s when Andrew Jackson battled for the Presidency.

Elected in 1828, Jackson represented the "triumph of the mob" or, depending upon one's angle of vision, the "emergence of democracy." Now the common people expected to get their share. Through the principle of rotation in office—"the spoils system"—Jackson opened all public offices, elective and appointive, to "men of intelligence," whatever their social rank. When he vetoed the bill to renew the charter of the Bank of the United States—thus destroying "the monster"—Jackson lambasted those governmental laws that "make the rich richer and the potent more powerful." The government, he declared, should "shower its favors alike on the high and the low, the rich and the poor."

The scramble to secure economic gain through governmental help rampaged through the state houses of government, too. State legislators spent long hours working up schemes to promote roads and bridges, canals and railroads, all of which would protect the general welfare and at the same time enlarge the private wealth of some. Some politicians sought to restrict existing "privileges"; others fought to combat existing privileges—which they called "monopolies"—often trying to secure new privileges for their own backers. As the politicians vied with each other, rhetoric about the "rights of private property" clashed with solemn pleas to "consider the public interest."

By the late 1830s, this rapacious greed rampant in the chambers of government had begun to disillusion many, none more than the president of the Massachusetts senate, Horace Mann. True, just a few years earlier, when a representative from Dedham, he had enthusiastically sought and supported legislation for railroads and internal improvements—for the general welfare. But now, in 1837, his enthusiasms for such projects had waned. The tragic death of his wife, five years before, had forced him to restructure completely his outlook on life. Anguish and desolate grief had emaciated his body, turned his hair white, and brought him to the brink of despair. Reconciliation to his fate came only after he concluded that God had taken his beloved Charlotte in order to punish him for his inordinate ambition. At that point he announced that all desire for "worldly distinction" died away. In his journal he wrote, "Nothing but the stern mandate of duty urges me forward."

When he again took up his political life as the senator from Boston (where anxious friends had persuaded him to live), Horace Mann discovered that his rigorous moral outlook on affairs was out of place. Much as he tried to convince his fellow senators to abandon the vainglorious pursuit of the transient goals of power and wealth, he failed. "My ideas produced no effect," he complained to his friends the Peabody sisters.

In pursuing their own selfish interests, he saw his ambitious colleagues subverting their responsibility to be "the parents of the state." Instead of promoting a cohesive and harmonious community, they were dividing it, tearing it asunder. The masses, left without guidance, without worthy examples to imitate, had descended to uncivility, violence, and anarchy. Mann himself directly experienced this social chaos in the spring of 1837, when a gang of incendiaries set fire to his office building. Two weeks later he witnessed a spontaneous and senseless riot in the streets of Boston that resulted in massive looting and injury to dozens of people. Such national outbursts simply reinforced his conviction that the "educated, the wealthy, the intelligent," had abandoned their responsibility to guide, to direct, to educate the people.

Here Horace Mann found himself in agreement with many others who concurred that the people were a threat to the harmony of society. They had to be controlled and restrained. Not by force or power—that was not the American way—but by education. As his friend William Ellery Channing confided, education could turn the energy of the people into the right channel. What was needed, however, was a means, a vehicle, an agency to carry out this task of socialization. Some, like his fellow legislator James Carter, thought that the existing common schools could be renewed and reconstructed for this purpose.

The people of Massachusetts traced their common schools back to the earliest colonial times when the general court had required every town to provide a school to educate the young. But by the second quarter of the nineteenth century, that two-hundred-year tradition was in danger of disappearing. Carter blamed the decline of the common schools on decentralization. Through a law passed in 1789 the responsibility for maintaining schools had shifted from the towns to districts within each town. Without adequate control or supervision the people in the districts, especially in the more rural districts, had become apathetic about the common schools. Those who could afford it abandoned these schools completely and sent their children to the growing number of academies and private schools that had come into being during the period. If this dual system of education continued, Carter warned, it would threaten the stability of society: "Then will the several classes, being educated differently and without a knowledge of each other, imbibe mutual prejudices and hatreds, and entail them upon posterity from generation to generation."

Carter had written essays on the decline of popular education in the 1820s. But his proposals to revive the common schools had come to nothing. Obviously the state had to enter to exert pressure on the districts. He proposed a bill to establish a state board of education, and after an initial defeat, finally succeeded in securing its passage in 1837.

The board, appointed by the governor, was to gather and diffuse information about public education in the state. It was to function in an advisory capacity; it was not a board of control. To facilitate this work, the law empowered the board to hire a permanent executive secretary. For this position, the board recommended, and Governor Everett appointed, Horace Mann.

Here indeed was an opportunity for the president of the Senate to demonstrate that he really had abandoned all desire for "worldly distinction." Although many knew of his disillusionment with politics, this abrupt change of career—this act of martyrdom (the term is Mann's)—dazzled and amazed his friends. Here truly was a man dedicated to duty! To one friend, he wrote he had abandoned jurisprudence for "the larger sphere of mind and morals." Having found it impossible to change his peers, he wrote in his journal, he would henceforth transfer his efforts to the young: "Men are cast iron; but children are wax. Strength expended upon the latter may be effectual, which would make no impression upon the former."

＊

Back in 1820 that irresolute Whig Daniel Webster had characterized popular education in Massachusetts as a "wise and liberal system of police"—it served as a political safeguard against violence, revolution, and licentiousness. Horace Mann, also a Whig, shared this conception of popular education at the time he assumed his initial duties as secretary to the board of education.

One of the first things Mann did as secretary was to go on a lecture tour to persuade "the friends of education" to revitalize the common schools in their own districts. Traveling over five hundred miles on horseback, he visited every region of the state. At each convention his message was the same. He told the people that the state board of education wanted to universalize and make permanent the local improvements that already existed. But the board, in turn, had to rely upon the people themselves to promote popular education. The members of the board, he explained, "have no voice, they have no organ by which they can make themselves heard, in the distant villages and hamlets of this land, where those juvenile habits are now forming, where those processes of thought and feeling are, now, today, maturing, which, some twenty or thirty years hence, will find an arm, and become restless might, and will uphold, or rend asunder, our social fabric."

As he saw it, the relationship between education and social order was direct: "The mobs, the riots, the burnings, the lynchings, perpetrated by the *men* of the present day, are perpetrated, because of their vicious or defective education when children."

The following year, in his second annual lecture tour, he patiently explained why the state had to interfere with the parents' right to raise children. Quite simply: those children will soon be citizens. (Like other states during the first half of the nineteenth century, Massachusetts in 1822 had abolished the property qualifications for voting.) When a child came of age, he explained, society must accept him "be he sot, brawler, libeller, poisoner, lyncher." So society must protect itself. Public, or common schools protect us against such people: education is a preventative.

In his early annual reports to the board of education—published and widely distributed throughout the state—Mann revealed the inadequacies of popular education in Massachusetts. Yet one wonders just how inadequate education was in the Bay State, since the 1850 census reported a mere 10 percent illiteracy among white adults for the nation—compared to 50 percent illiteracy in Europe. The answer, of course, is that for Horace Mann "real" education went beyond mere literacy. Real education, he insisted, was moral training. In his first report he noted that recent observers had discovered that in France the highest incidence of crimes occurred in those provinces where most of the inhabitants could read and write. According to Mann the explanation was easy: France gave its children an inadequate education—it neglected moral training at the expense of training the mind. The cultivated intellect, he counseled, "presents to the uncultivated feelings, not only a larger circle of temptations, but better instruments for their gratification."

The notion that moral training comprised the essential ingredient of real education was not an idiosyncratic opinion in the least. It was good Whig doctrine, embodied in the Massachusetts law concerning the duties of teachers, a law passed long before Horace Mann became secretary:

> It shall be the duty of all instructors of youth to exert their best endeavors to impress on the minds of children and youth, committed to their care and instruction, the principle of piety, justice, and a sacred regard to truth, love to their country, humanity, and universal benevolence, sobriety, industry, and frugality, chastity, moderation, and temperance, and those other virtues, which are the ornament of human society, and the basis upon which a republican constitution is founded; and it shall be the duty of such instructors to endeavor to lead their pupils, as their ages and capacities will admit, into a clear understanding

of the tendency of the above-mentioned virtues to preserve and perfect a republican constitution, and secure the blessings of liberty, as well as to promote their future happiness, and also to point out to them the evil tendency of the opposite vices.

A tall order to the teachers of Massachusetts. Yet it was not that Horace Mann found teachers merely falling short of such high expectations—he discovered they were completely ignoring the fact that students have moral natures and social affections. Teachers, he complained, addressed themselves to "the culture of intellect mainly." Not from base motives; they just were not trained teachers. Few outside the city of Boston ever remained permanently in the profession, and those transient educators who staffed most schools had no understanding of their responsibilities. Obviously Massachusetts had need for a corps of professional teachers well trained in the theory and principles of teaching and dedicated to their occupation.

In addition to a lack of trained teachers the common schools suffered from an absence of supervision and control. The school committees, according to the law, were supposed to obtain "evidence of the good moral character of all instructors" along with examining them as to "their literacy qualifications and capacity for the government of the schools." In most cases, Mann discovered, the school committees never examined the teachers.

The school committees were supposed to decide what books were to be used in schools. Most did not, with the result that children came to school with a multiplicity of textbooks. This meant educational inefficiency—every recitation had to be individualized—and often introduced religious controversy into the schools when children, in direct violation of the law, brought in books "calculated to favor the tenets of particular sects of Christians."

The school committees were supposed to supervise the regulation and discipline in the schools. Few did. Consequently, teachers kept no attendance records and permitted students to come to school tardy and irregularly. These habits of idleness and truancy in the present children, Mann admonished, "are laying the foundations of vagrancy, poverty, and vice in the future men."

Finally, the school committees were supposed to visit the

schools regularly—thereby breaking the monotony of the school, spurring the slothful, and rewarding "the emulous and aspiring." Mann found that fewer than one committee in six had visited a school in 1837.

With untrained teachers staffing the common schools and functioning without supervision and control, it became clear why those who could afford it had abandoned them for the academies and private schools. At this very moment, Horace Mann reported, one-sixth of those in school are not in the common schools. Agreeing with Carter, he construed this trend among the more affluent as a threat to the stability of society. It would lead to divisiveness. The only remedy and preventative was the elevation of the common schools so that *all* would willingly attend them.

✻

In the year following his widely acclaimed first annual report, Horace Mann composed myriad bills which the legislature promptly voted into law. These included a requirement that school committees keep records and make annual reports to the secretary of the state board of education. To sweeten the burden of increased supervisory responsibilities, Mann recommended that committee members receive a salary from the state education fund. Another statute endowed the board with the power to draw up a list of "approved" books, to be included in each district school library. (The legislature, at Mann's recommendation, had appropriated funds to support the purchase of such libraries.)

Perhaps the most important legislation passed in these early years was the bill to create state-controlled teacher-training institutions. Armed with $10,000 donated by Edmund Dwight, a member of the board of education, Mann secured a matching amount from the legislature. Within a year the first of three normal schools opened. Governor Everett, speaking at the opening ceremonies as ex-officio president of the state board of education, outlined the course of studies future teachers would pursue. First, they would review all that was to be taught in the common school; second, they would learn how to teach; third, they would "practice" teaching in a school under the direction of a principal. But, most important, the governor said, were their studies in the government of the school: learning how to exercise a moral influence "most favorable to the improvement of the pupil."

In his second annual report Mann noted that the origin of reform of the common school was "the intelligence of the people, stimulated by duty." In other countries, such as Prussia, they could use the absolute power of the government to remodel their schools and educate every child in the kingdom. Their approach was faster; ours, more permanent. Considering the means employed, Horace Mann "confidently stated" that some accomplishments had occurred; moreover, he saw "sure auguries of a speed in progression hereafter."

By the time he got around to his third annual report in 1839, however, Mann sensed some new auguries: a number of people openly expressed dissatisfaction with the way things were going, not the pace of educational reform. What bothered them was how it was taking place: from the top down. More and more people grumbled about the power the state board exercised over education.

Yet, after taking note of this, Mann insensitively went ahead with typical presumption to use the annual report to dictate educational policy to the common schools. What started out as a plea to the local school committees to create libraries to supplement the instruction dispersed in the schools, soon turned into a harangue against the reading habits of the populace. The attempt to impose his personal views as educational dogma sprang, as always, from his morbid fear of social unrest and instability. He rejected books of history as appropriate fare for children since they record naught but conflict, plunder, pillage—actions that appeal to the reader's lower instincts. He dismissed all books written in Great Britain for British readers: "Such books do not contain the models according to which the growth of a Republic should be formed." Most of his hostility he reserved for novels, books that appeal to the emotions not the intellect; strengthening the feelings, they ill prepare men for their sound duties, where the emotions must be guided by intellect. In the district school libraries Mann recommended "useful" reading: works of natural history, the biographies "of great and good men," and colonial history—books on "the great subjects of art, of science, of duty."

By 1840 lots of people were fed up with the increasingly powerful state board of education and its autocratic secretary. Not that they opposed popular education. Far from it. They simply believed that the people should manage their own common schools. The new Democratic governor, Marcus Morton, put it plainly in his inaugural address of 1840: the towns and district meetings—"those little pure democracies"—should direct and govern the schools without any adventitious supervision from the state. At the suggestion of the new governor, and with the endorsement of the Democratic-controlled legislature, the House Committee on Education soon undertook an assessment of the work of the state board of education.

Within four days the committee reported out a bill. Praising the board and its secretary (an ominous beginning), the committee declared that the annual reports bore strong testimony to "beneficial influence." Then, conscious of its own temerity, it proposed to kill the board of education. This was not an attack on the common schools—they had existed prior to the board; indeed, adherence to the schools themselves had led to the judgment to abolish the board since its operations "are incompatible with those principles upon which our common schools have been founded and maintained."

The committee argued that the so-called advisory power of the board had, predictably, become a power of regulation. The board "has a tendency, and a strong tendency, to engross to itself the entire regulation of our common schools." And the legislature had, unfortunately, become "a mere instrument for carrying its plans into execution."

As to the collection and diffusion of information about education—the purported reason for the creation of the board—the committee allowed that this could better be accomplished, as it had been in the past, via the work of voluntary associations of teachers. (Parenthetically, the committee took note of the fact that such associations had appreciably declined since the coming of the board.) At bottom, the committee construed the board as no more than a governmental agency for the aggrandizement of the teaching profession. "Undoubtedly, in all . . . professions great improvements might be made, but it is better to leave them to private industry and free competition, than for the legislature to put them under the superintendence of an official Board."

Then, with political acumen, the committee delivered its harshest blow: the board was trying to mold the Massachusetts system of public instruction after the example of the French and Prussian systems. The committee found the ideal of a uniform, centrally controlled system of education—the European model— incompatible with the traditional system of local authority. Local control—and here it cites Tocqueville—encourages the zeal, interest, and activity of the people themselves in improving their own welfare, whereas centrally dictated reforms deaden such initiative. Most important, a centrally controlled education system is more "a means of political influence," more "a means of strengthening the hands of government," than merely a means for the diffusion of knowledge. The creation of the board of education is just the first step toward a system of centralization and monopoly of power in the hands of a few—opposed, in every respect, to "the true spirit of our democratical institutions." Unless we speedily check it, the committee concluded, it may "lead to unlooked for and dangerous results."

Then, one by one, the committee blasted the "reforms" Horace Mann had worked so diligently for. The rules and regulations designed to secure "minute and complicated registers of statistics" merely monopolized the teachers' time with paper work and took them away from teaching. The school districts had gone along with these bureaucratic demands only because their share of the state school fund depended upon such compliance. The project of furnishing a school library for each district "under the sanction of the Board" had led the state into the hateful arena of censorship and the promulgation of "approved" books.

Finally, the committee turned to the normal schools—another project imported from France and Prussia. Such institutions simply were unnecessary; academies and high schools did and can continue to furnish an adequate supply of teachers. Good teachers will appear, the committee predicted, not as the result of special training, but as the result of higher salaries. State normal schools represent another attempt to use the government to create a profession of educators. Abolish them; and give Mr. Dwight his $10,000 back.

❋

The report of the House Commit-
tee on Education completely shattered Horace Mann. "Political
madmen," he called them. He accused them, correctly, of an act of
partisan politics.

The Democrats—in power for the first time in Massachusetts
—were out to subvert the "abuses" of power perpetrated by the
Whigs. In the matter of popular education, the Democrats—as in
most matters—looked back to Thomas Jefferson for guidance. Like
Jefferson, the members of the House Committee on Education
construed the system of public schools as "a mere means of
diffusing elementary knowledge." They rejected as "Prussian" the
notion of a system devised "for the purpose of modifying the
sentiments and opinions of the rising generation, according to a
certain government standard." The purpose of popular education,
as Jefferson had seen it, was to help people protect themselves. And
the Massachusetts Constitution of 1780 had borne testimony to this
very notion: "Wisdom and knowledge, as well as virtue, diffused
generally among the body of the people . . . [are] necessary for the
preservation of their rights and liberties."

As the Democrats saw it in 1840, the Whigs had totally
abandoned this conception of education. They had heard Daniel
Webster voice the Whig position on popular education when he
called it a "wise and liberal system of police." Now other Whigs,
like Horace Mann and those on the Massachusetts Board of
Education, had actually institutionalized this conception of popular education. Instead of an agency to help people protect
themselves, popular education had become an engagement to
protect society *against* people!

From the angle of vision of the Democrats, the Whigs were
"British aristocrats," using the government to secure advantages
for themselves—advantages of wealth, advantages of power. The
Democrats wanted to get the government out of all projects and
activities that benefited a single class—activities such as the
regulation of the currency, internal improvements, *and* state-controlled education. Like Jefferson, they stood for weak government.

Or almost. The Democrats never opposed government participation in activities that benefited *all* men. As Andrew Jackson put it, the government should "shower its favors alike on the high and the low, the rich and the poor." And this was how many Democrats saw the system of popular education: a system to help men advance in life. Thus, many Democrats thought the government should see to it that everyone had an education. As Robert Rantoul, the first Democratic member of the state board of education, put it: "We have a right to have the career kept fairly open to talent, and to be brought equally and together up to the starting point at the public expense; after that we must shift for ourselves."

This notion—that the schools existed to promote mobility or advancement—saved the state board of education. When some Democratic legislatures asked Rantoul what he thought about the proposal to abolish the board, he told them the project was a good one "if they wished to abolish education." On March 18 the House rejected the report of the committee. The board was saved.

Until the next year. For in February 1841 the Democrat opponents to the board again launched an attack in the legislature. This time using financial retrenchment as the argument, the House Committee on Education proposed to transfer the powers and duties of the board of education to the governor and council. (Assuredly, Governor Morton would then promptly remand all power to the town and district school committees—"those little pure democracies.") The committee suggested that the secretary of state assume the work of the secretary of the board of education. To his immense relief Horace Mann saw the legislature once again turn back the committee—this time with much less debate, but by a much smaller margin of votes.

❋

The impact of the attack—two years running—was not lost on Horace Mann. Never again would he be so imperious in his annual reports. No more would he construe the function of education in such a narrow, Whiggish way as he had in his first three years as secretary.

During the early 1840s Whigs all over the nation began to discover the spring of the Democratic revolution that had taken place in American society. At last many saw what Jacksonian Democrats truly were: not Jacobins, not levelers, merely incipient capitalists who wanted the opportunity to advance themselves. The moment they saw what the Democrats were, the Whigs discovered themselves. They were Americans, too, not transplanted British aristocrats; hence, democrats (with a small "d") who really believed in the liberal spirit of equality of opportunity. The Whig "discovery" of democracy in 1840 catapulted their candidate, William Henry Harrison, the Indiana farm boy, to the White House.

And in Massachusetts the secretary of the state board of education shared with his fellow Whigs this discovery of democracy. Once he realized that he, too, was a democrat and that all Democrats (big "D" and little "d") wanted was the opportunity to advance, Horace Mann began casting the common school in a new way: as the engine of advancement.

This transformation of outlook clearly emerges from a comparison of two speeches Mann delivered on the political function of education. The first, "The Necessity of Education in a Republican Government," he gave in 1838, before the attacks of the House Committee on Education; the second, "An Oration on the Fourth of July," he gave in 1842, after the attacks on the board.

In the 1838 lecture Mann presented education as the safeguard against "a variety and extent of calamities as no nation on earth has ever suffered." Here he displayed the typical Whig phobia of the people—they had a propensity to indulge their baser human instincts, a propensity enlarged and encouraged through living and growing up in a free society. Popular education, he declared, was necessary to cultivate the higher instincts—those of piety, love, benevolence—and subdue the baser ones. Unless the people are educated, he warned, we will have a situation where "every wealthy, and every educated, and every refined individual and family stand in the same relation to society in which game stands to the sportsman!"

The oration of 1842 contained virtually the same message. Mann dragged up the traditional argument: a good society is the result of good rulers, and good rulers are men of intelligence and virtue which, in turn, are the product of education. In the United States the people are the rulers; hence, it follows that to have a good society we must educate the people so they become intelligent and virtuous.

Yet in the Fourth of July oration the tone and stress were different. "I rejoice," Mann declared, "that power has passed irrevocably into the hands of the people." Granted, this brought "imminent peril" to all public and private interests. But this was God's doing, Mann explained. Providence had transferred power from the few to the many in order to extort from the few by means of fear what should have sprung from their feelings of philanthropy: concern for the welfare of inferiors. Some recalcitrant royalists and hierarchs might want to strip the people of their power—disenfranchise them—but this was unthinkable. Indeed, he announced, he would sooner see the ignorance and venality of the people destroy the Republic.

The democratic revolution, he concludes, is that "great lesson" heaven has tried to teach us for six thousand years: nothing is more precious to God than the intellectual and moral nature of man—we must cultivate this nature in all men.

In this oration Horace Mann has transformed his battle for common schools into a religious crusade for the advancement of all mankind. He still views popular education as the means for protecting society, but the task now becomes one of pure philanthropy. The Whig construction of popular education as a liberal system of police has been transmuted into a program to equalize the conditions of men, by raising up the less fortunate.

❋

Horace Mann had always recognized that the success of his work depended upon the support of the people. After the attacks on the board in the early 1840s, he realized that people would support him only if his work actually helped them to advance. From this point on, in every annual report, he explained how the common schools he was promoting helped people improve their condition in life.

In the 1841 annual report, for example, he devoted thirty-six pages to "showing the effects of education upon the worldly fortunes and estates of men." Presenting arguments, statistics, and testimonials from successful men—and employers—he demonstrated that education led to prosperity. Education "is not only the most honest and honorable, but the surest means of amassing property."

In this report of 1841 Mann was clearly somewhat embarrassed by his blatant affirmation of the economic worth of education. Lest his readers suspect him of having become totally corrupt, he inserted a final caveat reasserting his belief in the real value of education: "However deserving of attention may be the *economical* view of the subject which I have endeavored to present, yet it is one that dwindles into insignificance when compared with those loftier and more sacred attributes of the cause which have the power of converting material wealth into spiritual well-being, and of giving to its possessor lordship and sovereignty alike over the temptations of adversity, and the still more dangerous seducements of prosperity, and which—so far as human agency is concerned—must be looked to for the establishment of peace and righteousness upon earth, and for the enjoyment of glory and happiness in heaven."

Further reflection on the "*economical* view of the subject" stilled Mann's embarrassment, however. Gradually he came to see the full political and economic significance of universal education: it destroyed the scarcity principle that had so long dominated all societies. Equality of opportunity had never really been possible before, since—sooner or later—a lucky few captured all the wealth of the community. The poor stayed poor, or became poorer; while the rich stayed rich, or became richer. The grandeur of education was that it actually increased the wealth in any society. Education was the sword to cut the Gordian knot that lashed man to a life of scarcity. Education converted consumers into producers. And more: it increased the producer's producing power.

In his monumental twelfth annual report—the last one—Mann ticked off the inventions *educated* men had drawn from "the weight of waters, the velocity of winds, the expansive force of heat and other kindred agencies." Enlisted in the service of man, these powers of nature increase the total wealth of the society. Pointing with pride to his own state he attributed the unexampled prosperity of the people of Massachusetts to—what else?—education.

In paying more heed to how the common schools helped people to advance themselves, Horace Mann redirected his attention to the curriculum. What studies were appropriate for those who sought advancement? In his report of 1842 he decried the fact that in the common schools more studied algebra than bookkeeping. (Algebra was "a branch which not one man in a thousand has occasion to use in the business of life; whereas bookkeeping every man, even the day laborer, should understand.") And why should geometry take precedence (among farmers and road-makers!) over surveying? Throughout the 1840s Mann took every opportunity to play up the vocational relevance of common-school studies. In the 1844 annual report he argued that the "pecuniary well-being" of society necessitated study of all branches of natural philosophy (science) in the common school; otherwise we "exclude those seminal ideas and principles upon which and with which inventive genius afterwards works." Here, he also argued for the inclusion of navigation, geometry, bookkeeping—all commercial studies—to prepare people to engage in foreign commerce. Chemistry, too: it is "intimately connected with agriculture, with many of the mechanical trades, and with not a few of the household arts."

Academies and colleges already offered these advanced studies. Restricting the common schools to rudimentary studies simply creates inequality. This breeds social unrest and chaos. Americans, Mann warns, must not create educational arrangements that separate people into social classes. They do this in Europe. There, those destined for manual labor receive one kind of education; those headed for skilled or mechanical work, another; while a third kind of education goes to those bound for intellectual work. Incongruous and absurd notions, he democratically asserts, for our nation, where the poorest boy in the land can grow up to become President!

In construing the common schools as agencies for advancement, one of Mann's recurring themes was the improvement of health. In his 1841 report he insisted that the most important subject beyond the elementary studies was physiology: the laws of health and life. Nothing was more fundamental or more useful; it increased "our abilities to perform the arduous duties and to bear the inevitable burdens of life." Knowledge of the laws of health prepared us to enter any field of activity; sound health was indispensable for any industrial avocation.

The diffusion of knowledge—especially useful knowledge—

and the cultivation of health helped men to advance themselves. It improved society, too. But more important than health and intelligence was virtue. Horace Mann never lost his long-held conviction that moral training stood first in the duties of the school. Now, during the 1840s, it took the guise of moral improvement. Unless men improved in virtue they would remain forever trapped in poverty, villainy, and unhappiness. Neglect moral education in the schoolrooms, he warned in 1845, and we reap the consequences: an exchange shaken by stupendous frauds, perjuries invading the tribunals of justice, hypocrisy and intolerance in the sanctuaries of religion, political profligacy in the council halls of the nation, and streams of corruption through all the channels of government.

Without moral education, social reform can never occur. There is nothing wrong with the appeals and arguments of the pacifists, the abolitionists, and the advocates of temperance, Mann explains. They fail only because those they seek to reform lack education—moral arguments cannot move them. It is not better arguments these reformers need, but listeners capable of appreciating argument.

In his famous eleventh annual report of 1847 Mann reported the results of a survey he conducted: teachers believed that, with some necessary but *minor* modifications, the common schools could morally reclaim 99 percent of their students. The teachers said the common schools could stamp out profane swearing, intemperance, censoriousness, lying, and general dishonesty—as well as graver offenses against the rights of property, reputation, and life.

Moral education is possible, Mann explains, because all men have the desire of bettering their condition. And in the United States "every man sees that the gratification of the desire is within his reach." But for moral advancement to take place, the schools must gain *more* control over the young. Two changes are necessary: first, the teachers must assume the mantle of complete authority in the classroom; second, the state must require all children between the ages of four and sixteen to attend school for ten months each year.

Earlier Mann had described the prototype for his authoritative teacher. The annual report for 1843 contained a glowing account of the Prussian schoolmasters. That year, with his new wife, Mary Peabody, in tow, Mann had spent six months in Europe. Mary later wrote that it was his habit to spend every day from seven A.M. to five P.M. visiting schools, prisons, and the men who were interested in these; "his evenings he spent reading documents which he gathered in his progress." Still smarting from the attack made on his work in 1840, Mann wanted to dispel the myth that he was modeling the Massachusetts common schools on the Prussian system. The report makes evident his awareness of the evils of the Prussian system: it teaches passive obedience to government, blind adherence to the articles of a church. But his contention is that this *spirit* of the system is separable from the *manner* of teaching itself. And here American teachers can learn much.

The Prussian schoolmaster, he discovered, combined *complete* mastery of subject matter with superb pedagogical finesse. They taught from "the head," never relying on a textbook. Beginning not with abstract theories—neither principles, rules, nor axioms—but with objects and phenomena familiar to each child, these master teachers encompassed elements of reading, spelling, writing, grammar, drawing, and general information into every lesson. Students in the Prussian schools, unhampered by the artificial formalisms of rote memorization, enjoyed learning; they liked their teachers and held them in high esteem. The teachers rarely used physical punishment; they secured discipline through the affection and respect—even awe—the students had for them. The Prussian schoolmaster was the complete authority; children unquestionably accepted and believed what he said.

Horace Mann dreamed of making American teachers as authoritative as their Prussian counterparts. He saw the fledgling normal schools in Massachusetts as a first step in staffing the classrooms with truly professional teachers.

Qualified teachers were necessary to carry out the task of moral redemption of the young. The other necessary condition was compulsory education. A controversial matter, to be sure. Employers of child labor would probably oppose it. Yet, Mann reports, he heard from a woolen mill manufacturer that children under fifteen are poor workers; he employed them only "from motives of charity." Diverting children from the factories to the schools until they are sixteen will supply better workers physically, intellectually, and morally. Compulsory education, he concludes, would neither impair the industrial resources of the state nor diminish the marketable value of its products.

Of course, parents who are poor might oppose it. But many of these simply exploit the labor of their children. And for those really destitute—Mann believed "the class not a very large one"—the public purse could pay for the children's books and supply the family's deficiencies. The only parents who would have to be coerced to send their children to school are those who have no right to be parents: "persons capable, like brutes, of bringing children into the world but impervious to those moral considerations which should impel them to train up these children in the way they should go." Such persons, Mann decided, forfeit their parental rights.

Mann looked forward confidently to the enactment of compulsory-education legislation. Nor was his confidence misplaced. Three years later—two years after Mann resigned his post as secretary to fill the congressional seat left vacant by the death of John Quincy Adams—Massachusetts passed the first compulsory-education law in the United States.

❊

Horace Mann rooted the common school deep in the liberal tradition of America. A free society holds out the promise of opportunity to all its people, but at the same time it generates fears of chaos and anarchy. As Mann saw more clearly than anyone else, the common schools—the public schools, as we now call them—could assuage the people's fears and fulfill their dreams. Once construed this way, the American schools moved center stage in the American way of life. The "father of common school" did his work well.

Perhaps too well. For by his very success in making our schools part of the liberal tradition Horace Mann helped to perpetuate a kind of authoritarianism in the education enterprise. Most American schools continue to function as agents of socialization. They teach the young to accept—and give thanks for—the existing political, economic, and social arrangements. The schools celebrate America. They are the American Dream Machine producing often not an understanding of the real world, but rather a belief in grand ideals—coupled with a conviction that our problems would vanish if only all people lived up to those ideals. Most schools discourage criticism, disagreement, and conflict as evils that spring from ignorance or lack of faith.

The role of many schoolteachers is to secure unquestioning acceptance. Professionalism is equated with authoritativeness. The teacher's job is to impart; the student's, to learn (what is imparted). The schoolteacher is, or seeks to be, the intellectual, moral, and often the psychological authority; he tells children what is true, what is good, and often tells them how they should feel.

Of course, education has always been authoritarian. Schools have always socialized; teachers have always imposed ideas, values, and attitudes. But authoritarianism is harder to perceive (or easier to ignore) when implanted in a liberal tradition. In despotic societies we can readily spot it—as Mann himself did, however incompletely, in Prussia.

In our liberal society, because they fulfill people's dreams of opportunity and still their fears of social chaos, the schools are not usually perceived as obstacles to social improvement. Yet they often are. And the more "effective" our schools become, the more fully they socialize the young to the existing political, social, and economic arrangements—making it more difficult to improve those arrangements. All this is not to say we should abandon the liberal tradition but simply that we must construct a more self-conscious and self-critical liberalism—one that constructs educational institutions that actually do help improve the society.

WORKS AND COMMENTARY

Mary Peabody Mann edited the five-volume *Life and Works of Horace Mann* (Boston, 1891) which contains her biography of her husband and all twelve annual reports he made as secretary to the board of education. Jonathan Messerli has written a masterful biography, *Horace Mann* (New York: Alfred A. Knopf, 1972). *The Republic and the School* (New York: Teachers College Bureau of Publications, 1957), edited by Lawrence Cremin, contains excerpts and summaries of the twelve annual reports and an excellent essay on "Horace

Mann's Legacy." Cremin's *The American Common School* (New York: Teachers College Bureau of Publications, 1951) describes the evolution of this institution. Rush Welter discusses the political influences on educational thinking of this period in *Popular Education and Democratic Thought in America* (New York: Columbia University Press, 1962). His *American Writings on Popular Education: The Nineteenth Century* (Indianapolis: Bobbs-Merrill, 1971) contains the 1840 "Report of the Committee on Education of the House of Representatives." Documents pertaining to the history of the struggle of 1840 are in volume 2 of *The Common School Journal* (Boston, 1841).

What follows is Mann's report for 1848, reprinted from Volume 4 of the *Life and Works of Horace Mann*, pages 245–83.

Report for 1848

Intellectual Education as a Means of Removing Poverty, and Securing Abundance

Another cardinal object which the government of Massachusetts, and all the influential men in the State, should propose to themselves, is the physical well-being of all the people,—the sufficiency, comfort, competence, of every individual in regard to food, raiment, and shelter. And these necessaries and conveniences of life should be obtained by each individual for himself, or by each family for themselves, rather than accepted from the hand of charity or extorted by poor-laws. It is not averred that this most desirable result can, in all instances, be obtained: but it is, nevertheless, the end to be aimed at. True statesmanship and true political economy, not less than true philanthropy, present this perfect theory as the goal, to be more and more closely approximated by our imperfect practice. The desire to achieve such a result cannot be regarded as an unreasonable ambition; for, though all mankind were well fed, well clothed, and well housed, they might still be but half civilized.

Poverty is a public as well as a private evil. There is no

physical law necessitating its existence. The earth contains abundant resources for ten times—doubtless for twenty times— its present inhabitants. Cold, hunger, and nakedness are not, like death, an inevitable lot. There are many single States in this Union which could supply an abundance of edible products for the inhabitants of the thirty States that compose it. There are single States capable of raising a sufficient quantity of cotton to clothe the whole nation; and there are other States having sufficient factories and machinery to manufacture it. The coal-fields of Pennsylvania are sufficiently abundant to keep every house in the land at the temperature of sixty-five degrees for centuries to come. Were there to be a competition, on the one hand, to supply wool for every conceivable fabric, and, on the other, to wear out these fabrics as fast as possible, the single State of New York would beat the whole country. There is, indeed, no assignable limit to the capacities of the earth for producing whatever is necessary for the sustenance, comfort, and improvement of the race. Indigence, therefore, and the miseries and degradations incident to indigence, seem to be no part of the eternal ordinances of Heaven. The bounty of God is not brought into question or suspicion by its existence; for man who suffers it might have avoided it. Even the wealth which the world now has on hand is more than sufficient to supply all the rational wants of every individual in it. Privations and sufferings exist, not from the smallness of its sum, but from the inequality of its distribution. Poverty is set over against profusion. In some, all healthy appetite is cloyed and sickened by repletion; while in others, the stomach seems to be a supernumerary organ in the system, or, like the human eye or human lungs before birth, is waiting to be transferred to some other region, where its functions may come into use. One gorgeous palace absorbs all the labor and expense that might have made a thousand hovels comfortable. That one man may ride in carriages of Oriental luxury, hundreds of other men are turned into beasts of burden. To supply a superfluous wardrobe for the gratification of one man's pride, a thousand women and children shiver with cold; and, for every flash of the diamonds that royalty wears, there is a tear of distress in the poor man's dwelling. Not one Lazarus, but a hundred, sit at the gate of Dives. Tantalus is no fiction.

The ancient one might have been fabulous; but the modern ones are terrible realities. Millions are perishing in the midst of superfluities.

According to the European theory, men are divided into classes,—some to toil and earn, others to seize and enjoy. According to the Massachusetts theory, all are to have an equal chance for earning, and equal security in the enjoyment of what they earn. The latter tends to equality of condition; the former, to the grossest inequalities. Tried by any Christian standard of morals, or even by any of the better sort of heathen standards, can any one hesitate, for a moment, in declaring which of the two will produce the greater amount of human welfare, and which, therefore, is the more conformable to the divine will? The European theory is blind to what constitutes the highest glory as well as the highest duty of a State. Its advocates and admirers are forgetful of that which should be their highest ambition, and proud of that which constitutes their shame. How can any one possessed of the attributes of humanity look with satisfaction upon the splendid treasures, the golden regalia, deposited in the Tower of London or in Windsor Palace, each "an India in itself," while thousands around are dying of starvation, or have been made criminals by the combined forces of temptation and neglect? The present condition of Ireland cancels all the glories of the British crown. The brilliant conception which symbolizes the nationality of Great Britain as a superb temple, whose massive and grand proportions are upheld and adorned by the four hundred and thirty Corinthian columns of the aristocracy, is turned into a loathing and a scorn when we behold the five millions of paupers that cower and shiver at its base. The galleries and fountains of Versailles, the Louvre of Paris, her Notre Dame, and her Madeleine, though multiplied by thousands in number and in brilliancy, would be no atonement for the hundred thousand Parisian *ouvriers* without bread and without work. The galleries of painting and of sculpture at Rome, at Munich, or at Dresden, which body forth the divinest ideals ever executed or ever conceived, are but an abomination in the sight of Heaven and of all good men, while actual, living beings—beings that have hearts to palpitate, and nerves to agonize, and affections to be crushed or corrupted—are experimenting all around them upon the capacities of human nature for suffering and for sin. Where standards like these exist, and are upheld by council and by court, by fashion and by law, *Christianity is yet to be discovered;* at least, it is yet to be applied in practice to the social condition of men.

Our ambition as a State should trace itself to a different origin, and propose to itself a different object. Its flame should be lighted at the skies. Its radiance and its warmth should reach the darkest and the coldest abodes of men. It should seek the solution of such problems as these: To what extent can competence displace pauperism? How nearly can we free ourselves from the low-minded and the vicious, not by their expatriation, but by their elevation? To what extent can the resources and powers of Nature be converted into human welfare, the peaceful arts of life be advanced, and the vast treasures of human talent and genius be developed? How much of suffering, in all its forms, can be relieved? or, what is better than relief, how much can be prevented? Cannot the classes of crimes be lessened, and the number of criminals in each class be diminished? Our exemplars, both for public and for private imitation, should be the parables of the lost sheep and of the lost piece of silver. When we have spread competence through all the abodes of poverty, when we have substituted knowledge for ignorance in the minds of the whole people, when we have reformed the vicious and reclaimed the criminal, then may we invite all neighboring nations to behold the spectacle, and say to them, in the conscious elation of virtue, "Rejoice with me," for I have found that which was lost. Until that day shall arrive, our duties will not be wholly fulfilled, and our ambition will have new honors to win.

But is it not true that Massachusetts, in some respects, instead of adhering more and more closely to her own theory, is becoming emulous of the baneful examples of Europe? The distance between the two extremes of society is lengthening, instead of being abridged. With every generation, fortunes increase on the one hand, and some new privation is added to poverty on the other. We are verging towards those extremes of opulence and of penury, each of which unhumanizes the human mind. A perpetual struggle for the bare necessaries of life, without the ability to obtain them, makes men wolfish. Avarice, on the other hand, sees, in all the victims of misery around it, not objects for pity and succor, but only crude materials to be worked up into more money.

I suppose it to be the universal sentiment of all those who mingle any ingredient of benevolence with their notions on political economy, that vast and overshadowing private fortunes are among the greatest dangers to which the happiness of the people in a republic can be subjected. Such fortunes would create a feudalism of a new kind, but one more oppressive and unrelenting than that of the middle ages. The feudal lords in England and on the Continent never held their retainers in a more abject condition of servitude than the great majority of foreign manufacturers and capitalists hold their operatives and laborers at the present day. The means employed are different; but the similarity in results is striking. What force did then, money does now. The villein of the middle ages had no spot of earth on which he could live, unless one were granted to him by his lord. The operative or laborer of the present day has no employment, and therefore no bread, unless the capitalist will accept his services. The vassal had no shelter but such as his master provided for him. Not one in five thousand of English operatives or farm-laborers is able to build or own even a hovel; and therefore they must accept such shelter as capital offers them. The baron prescribed his own terms to his retainers: those terms were peremptory, and the serf must submit or perish. The British manufacturer or farmer prescribes the rate of wages he will give to his work-people; he reduces these wages under whatever pretext he pleases; and they, too, have no alternative but submission or starvation. In some respects, indeed, the condition of the modern dependant is more forlorn that that of the corresponding serf class in former times. Some attributes of the patriarchal relation did spring up between the lord and his lieges to soften the harsh relations subsisting between them. Hence came some oversight of the condition of children, some relief in sickness, some protection and support in the decrepitude of age. But only in instances comparatively few have kindly offices smoothed the rugged relation between British capital and British labor. The children of the work-people are abandoned to their fate; and notwithstanding the privations they suffer, and the dangers they threaten, no power in the realm has yet been able to secure them an education; and when the adult laborer is prostrated by sickness, or eventually worn out by toil and age, the poor-house, which has all along been his destination, becomes his destiny.

Now, two or three things will doubtless be admitted to be true, beyond all controversy, in regard to Massachusetts. By its industrial condition, and its business operations, it is exposed, far beyond any other State in the Union, to the fatal extremes of overgrown wealth and desperate poverty. Its population is far more dense than that of any other State. It is four or five times more dense than the average of all the other States taken together; and density of population has always been one of the proximate causes of social inequality. According to population and territorial extent, there is far more capital in Massachusetts —capital which is movable, and instantaneously available— than in any other State in the Union; and probably both these qualifications respecting population and territory could be omitted without endangering the truth of the assertion. It has been recently stated in a very respectable public journal, on the authority of a writer conversant with the subject, that from the last of June, 1846, to the first of August, 1848, the amount of money invested by the citizens of Massachusetts "in manufacturing cities, railroads, and other improvements," is "fifty-seven millions of dollars, of which more than fifty has been paid in and expended." The dividends to be received by citizens of Massachusetts from June, 1848, to April, 1849, are estimated by the same writer at ten millions, and the annual increase of capital at "little short of twenty-two millions." If this be so, are we not in danger of naturalizing and domesticating among ourselves those hideous evils which are always engendered between capital and labor, when all the capital is in the hands of one class, and all the labor is thrown upon another?

Now, surely nothing but universal education can counterwork this tendency to the domination of capital and the servility of labor. If one class possesses all the wealth and the education, while the residue of society is ignorant and poor, it matters not by what name the relation between them may be called: the latter, in fact and in truth, will be the servile dependants and subjects of the former. But, if education be equably diffused, it will draw property after it by the strongest of all attractions; for such a thing never did happen, and never can happen, as that an intelligent and practical body of men should be permanently poor. Property and labor in different classes are essentially antagonistic; but property and labor in the same class are essentially fraternal. The people of Massachusetts have, in some degree, appreciated the truth, that the unexampled prosperity of the State—its comfort, its competence, its general intelligence and virtue—is attributable to the education, more or less perfect, which all its people have received: but are they sensible of a fact equally important; namely, that it is to this same education that two-thirds of the people are indebted for not being to-day the vassals of as severe a tyranny, in the form of capital, as the lower classes of Europe are bound to in the form of brute force?

Education, then, beyond all other devices of human origin, is the great equalizer of the conditions of men,—the balance-wheel of the social machinery. I do not here mean that it so elevates the moral nature as to make men disdain and abhor the oppression of their fellow-men. This idea pertains to another of its attributes. But I mean that it gives each man the independence and the means by which he can resist the selfishness of other men. It does better than to disarm the poor of their hostility towards the rich: it prevents being poor. Agrarianism is the revenge of poverty against wealth. The wanton destruction of the property of others—the burning of hay-ricks and corn-ricks, the demolition of machinery because it supersedes hand-labor, the sprinkling of vitriol on rich dresses—is only agrarianism run mad. Education prevents both the revenge and the madness. On the other hand, a fellow-feeling for one's class or caste is the common instinct of hearts not wholly sunk in selfish regards for person or for family. The spread of education, by enlarging the cultivated class or caste, will open a wider area over which the social feelings will expand; and, if this education should be universal and complete, it would do more than all things else to obliterate factitious distinctions in society.

The main idea set forth in the creeds of some political

reformers, or revolutionizers, is, that some people are poor *because* others are rich. This idea supposes a fixed amount of property in the community, which by fraud or force, or arbitrary law, is unequally divided among men; and the problem presented for solution is, how to transfer a portion of this property from those who are supposed to have too much to those who feel and know that they have too little. At this point, both their theory and their expectation of reform stop. But the beneficent power of education would not be exhausted, even though it should peaceably abolish all the miseries that spring from the co-existence, side by side, of enormous wealth and squalid want. It has a higher function. Beyond the power of diffusing old wealth, it has the prerogative of creating new. It is a thousand times more lucrative than fraud, and adds a thousand-fold more to a nation's resources than the most successful conquests. Knaves and robbers can obtain only what was before possessed by others. But education creates or develops new treasures,—treasures not before possessed or dreamed of by any one.

Had mankind been endowed with only the instincts and faculties of the brute creation, there are hundreds of the irrational tribes to which they would have been inferior, and of which they would have been the prey. Did they, with other animals, roam a common forest, how many of their fellow-tenants of the wood would overcome them by superior force, or outstrip them by greater fleetness, or circumvent them by a sharper cunning! There are but few of the irrational tribes whose bodies are not better provided with the means of defence or attack than is the body of a man. The claws and canine teeth of the lion and of the whole tiger family, the beak and talons of the eagle and the vulture, the speed of the deer and of other timid races, are means of assault or of escape far superior to any we possess; and all the power which we have, like so many of the reptile and insect classes, of secreting a deadly venom, either for protection or for aggression, has relation to moral venom, and not to physical.

In a few lines, nowhere surpassed in philosophic strength and beauty, Pope groups together the remarkable qualities of several different races of animals,—the strength of one class, the genial covering of another, the fleetness of a third. He brings vividly to our recollection the lynx's vision of excelling keenness, the sagacity of the hound that reads a name or a sign in the last vanishing odor of a footprint, the exquisite fineness of the spider's touch, and that chemical nicety by which the bee discriminates between honey and poison in the same flower-cup. He then closes with an interrogatory, which has human reason both for its subject and its object:—

> "The powers of all subdued by thee alone:
> *Is not thy reason all these powers in one?*"

When Pope, now a little more than a century ago, mingled these beauties with his didactic strains, he had no conception, the world at that time had no conception, of other powers and properties, infinitely more energetic and more exhaustless than all which the animal races possess, to which the reason of man is an equivalent. It was not then known that God had endued the earth and the elements with energies and activities as much superior to those which animals or men possess as the bulk and frame of the earth itself exceeds their diminutive proportions. It was not then known that the earth is a great reservoir of powers, and that any man is free to use any quantity of them if he will but possess himself of the key of knowledge,—the only key, but the infallible one, by which to unlock their gates. At that time, if a philosopher wished to operate a mechanical toy, he could lift or pump a few gallons of water for a moving-power: but it was not understood that Nature, by the processes of evaporation and condensation, is constantly lifting up into the sky, and pouring back upon the earth, all the mass of waters that flow in all the rivers of the world; and that, in order to perform the work of the world, the weight of all these waters might be used again and again in each one of their perpetual circuits.* The power-press and the power-loom, the steam-boat and the locomotive, the paper-machine and the telegraph, were

---

* The waters of the Blackstone River, which flows partly in Massachusetts, and partly in Rhode Island, are used for driving mills, twenty-five times over, in a distance of less than forty miles.

not then known. All these instruments of human comfort and aggrandizement, and others almost innumerable, similar to them, are operated by the energies and the velocities of Nature; and, had Pope grouped together all the splendid profusion and prodigality of her powers, he might still have appealed to man, and said,—

"Is not thy reason all these powers in one?"

To the weight of waters, the velocity of winds, the expansive force of heat, and other kindred agencies, any man may go, and he may draw from them as much as he pleases without money and without price: or rather, I should say, any educated man may go; for Nature flouts and scorns, and seems to abhor, an ignorant man. She drowns him, and consumes him, and tears him in pieces, if he but ventures to profane with his touch her divinely-wrought machinery.

Now, these powers of Nature, by being enlisted in the service of man, ADD to the wealth of the world,—unlike robbery or slavery or agrarianism, which aim only at the appropriation, by one man or one class, of the wealth belonging to another man or class. One man, with a Foudrinier, will make more paper in a twelvemonth than all Egypt could have made in a hundred years during the reign of the Ptolemies. One man, with a power-press, will print books faster than a million of scribes could copy them before the invention of printing. One man, with an iron-foundery, will make more utensils or machinery than Tubal-Cain could have made had he worked diligently till this time.* And so in all the departments of mechanical labor, in the whole circle of the useful arts. These powers of Nature are able to give to all the inhabitants of the earth, not merely shelter, covering, and food, but all the means of refinement, embellishment, and mental improvement. In the most strict and

* In 1740, the whole amount of iron made in England and Wales was seventeen thousand tons; in 1840, it was more than a million tons, notwithstanding all that had been manufactured and accumulated in the intervening century. What would a Jewish or a Roman artificer have said to an annual product of a million tons of iron?

literal sense, they are bounties which God gives for proficiency in knowledge.

The above ideas are beginning to be pretty well understood by all men of respectable intelligence. I have adverted to them, not so much on their own account, as by way of introduction or preface to two or three considerations, which certainly are not understood, or not appreciated, as they deserve to be.

It is a remarkable fact, that human progress, even in regard to the worldly interests of the race, did not begin with those improvements which are most closely allied to material prosperity. One would have supposed, beforehand, that improvements would commence with the near rather than with the remote. Yet mankind had made great advances in astronomy, in geometry, and other mathematical sciences; in the writing of history, in oratory, and in poetry: it is supposed by many to have reached the highest point of yet attained perfection in painting and in sculpture, and in those kinds of architecture which may be called regal or religious, centuries before the great mechanical discoveries and inventions which now bless the world were brought to light. And the question has often forced itself upon reflecting minds, why there was this preposterousness, this inversion of what would appear to be the natural order of progress. Why was it, for instance, that men should have learned the courses of the stars, and the revolutions of the planets, before they found out how to make a good wagon-wheel? Why was it that they built the Parthenon and the Colosseum before they knew how to construct a comfortable, healthful dwelling-house? Why did they construct the Roman aqueducts before they constructed a saw-mill? Or why did they achieve the noblest models in eloquence, in poetry, and in the drama, before they invented movable types? I think we have now arrived at a point where we can unriddle this enigma. *The labor of the world has been performed by ignorant men,* by classes doomed to ignorance from sire to son, by the bondmen and bond-women of the Jews, by the helots of Sparta, by the captives who passed under the Roman yoke, and by the villeins and serfs and slaves of more modern times. The masters—the aristocratic or patrician orders—not only disdained labor for themselves and their children, which was one fatal mistake, but they supposed that knowledge was of no use to a laborer, which was a mistake still more fatal. Hence, ignorance, for almost six thousand years, has gone on plying its animal muscles, and dropping its bloody sweat, and never discovered any way, nor dreamed that there was any way, by which it might accomplish many times more work with many times less labor. And yet nothing is more true than that an ignorant man will toil all his life long, moving to and fro within an inch of some great discovery, and will never see it. All the elements of a great discovery may fall into his hands, or be thrust into his face; but his eyes will be too blind to behold it. If he is a slave, what motive has he to behold it? Its greater profitableness will not redound to his benefit; for another stands ready to seize all the gain. Its abridgment of labor will not conduce to his ease; for other toils await him. But the moment an intelligent man applies himself to labor, and labors for his own benefit or for that of his family, he begins to inquire whether the same task cannot be performed with a less expenditure of strength, or a greater task with an equal expenditure. He makes his wits save his bones. He finds it to be easier to think than to work; nay, that it is easier both to think and work than to work without thinking. He foresees a prize as the reward of successful effort; and this stimulates his brain to deep contrivance, as well as his arms to rapid motion. Taking, for illustration, the result of an experiment which has been actually made, let us suppose this intelligent laborer to be employed in moving blocks of squared granite, each weighing 1080 pounds. To move such a block along the floor of a roughly-chiselled quarry requires a force equal to 758 pounds. An ignorant man, therefore, must employ and pay several assistants, or he can never move such a block an inch. But to draw the same block over a floor of planks will require a force of only 652 pounds. The expense of one assistant, therefore, might be dispensed with. Placed on a platform of wood, and drawn over the same floor, a draught of 606 pounds would be sufficient. By soaping the two surfaces of the wood, the requisite force would be reduced to 182 pounds. Placed on rollers three inches in diameter, a force equal to 34 pounds would be sufficient. Substituting a wooden for a stone floor, and the requisite force is 28 pounds. With the same rollers on a wooden platform, 22 pounds only would be required. And now, by the invention and use of locomotives and railroads, a traction or draught of between *three* and *four* pounds is found to be sufficient to move a body weighing 1080 pounds. Thus the amount of force necessary to remove the body is reduced about two hundred times. Now, take away from these steps the single element of intelligence, and each improvement would have been impossible. The ignorant man would never have discovered how nearly synonymous are freight and friction.

If a savage will learn how to swim, he can fasten a dozen pounds' weight to his back, and transport it across a narrow river or other body of water of moderate width. If he will invent an axe, or other instrument, by which to cut down a tree, he can use the tree for a float, and one of its limbs for a paddle, and can thus transport many times the former weight many times the former distance. Hollowing out his log, he will increase what may be called its tonnage, or rather its *poundage;* and, by sharpening its ends, it will cleave the water both more easily and more swiftly. Fastening several trees together, he makes a raft, and thus increases the buoyant power of his embryo water-craft. Turning up the ends of small poles, or using knees of timber instead of straight pieces, and grooving them together, or filling up the interstices between them in some other way, so as to make them water-tight, he brings his rude raft literally into *ship-shape.* Improving upon hull below and rigging above, he makes a proud merchant-man, to be wafted by the winds from continent to continent. But even this does not content the adventurous naval architect. He frames iron arms for his ship; and, for oars, affixes iron wheels, capable of swift revolution, and stronger than the strong sea. Into iron-walled cavities in her bosom he puts iron organs of massive structure and strength, and of cohesion insoluble by fire. Within these he kindles a small volcano; and then, like a sentient and rational existence, this wonderful creation of his hands cleaves oceans, breasts tides, defies tempests, and bears its living and jubilant freight around the globe. Now, take away intelligence from the ship-builder, and the steamship—that miracle of human art—falls back into a floating log; the log itself is lost; and the savage swimmer, bearing his dozen pounds on his back, alone remains.

And so it is, not in one department only, but in the whole circle of human labors. The annihilation of the sun would no more certainly be followed by darkness than the extinction of human intelligence would plunge the race at once into the weakness and helplessness of barbarism. To have created such beings as we are, and to have placed them in this world without the light of the sun, would be no more cruel than for a government to suffer its laboring classes to grow up without knowledge.

In this fact, then, we find a solution of the problem that so long embarrassed inquirers. The reason why the mechanical and useful arts,—those arts which have done so much to civilize mankind, and which have given comforts and luxuries to the common laborer of the present day, such as kings and queens could not command three centuries ago,—the reason why these arts made no progress, and until recently, indeed, can hardly be said to have had any thing more than a beginning, is, that the labor of the world was performed by ignorant men. As soon as some degree of intelligence dawned upon the work-man, then a corresponding degree of improvement in his work followed. At first, this intelligence was confined to a very small number, and therefore improvements were few; and they followed each other only after long intervals. They uniformly began in the nations and among the classes where there was most intelligence. The middle classes of England, and the people of Holland and Scotland, have done a hundred times more than all the Eastern hemisphere besides. What single improvement in art, or discovery in science, has ever originated in Spain, or throughout the vast empire of the Russias? But just in proportion as intelligence—that is, education—has quickened and stimulated a greater and a greater number of minds, just in the same proportion have inventions and discoveries increased in their wonderfulness, and in the rapidity of their succession. The progression has been rather geometrical than arithmetical. By the laws of Nature, it must be so. If, among ten well-educated children, the chance is that at least one of them will originate some new and useful process in the arts, or will discover some new scientific principle, or some new application of one, then, among a hundred such well-educated children, there is a moral certainty that there will be more than ten such originators or discoverers of new utilities; for the action of the mind is like the action of fire. One billet of wood will hardly burn alone, though dry as suns and north-west winds can make it, and though placed in the range of a current of air; ten such billets will burn well together; but a hundred will create a heat fifty times as intense as ten, will make a current of air to fan their own flame, and consume even greenness itself.

For the creation of wealth, then,—for the existence of a wealthy people and a wealthy nation,—intelligence is the grand condition. The number of improvers will increase as the intellectual constituency, if I may so call it, increases. In former times, and in most parts of the world even at the present day, not one man in a million has ever had such a development of mind as made it possible for him to become a contributor to art or science. Let this development precede, and contributions, numberless, and of inestimable value, will be sure to follow. That political economy, therefore, which busies itself about capital and labor, supply and demand, interest and rents, favorable and unfavorable balances of trade, but leaves out of account the element of a widespread mental development, is nought but stupendous folly. The greatest of all the arts in political economy is to change a consumer into a producer; and the next greatest is to increase the producer's producing power,—an end to be directly attained by increasing his intelligence. For mere delving, an ignorant man is but little better than a swine, whom he so much resembles in his appetites, and surpasses in his powers of mischief.

But there is a class of persons who are not unwilling to concede the advantages which education has over ignorance, both in the more rapid and perfect performance of all kinds of labor, and in the creation of all those mechanical instruments through which Nature stands ready to do the work of the world: but, while they acknowledge all this, they seem to think that the argument in favor of knowledge has lost much of its force, because mechanical ingenuity and scientific discovery must have nearly reached the outermost limit of possible advancement; that either the powers of Nature are exhausted, or human genius is in its decrepitude. The past achievements of the mind excite their admiration, but not their hope. They are regarded as the measure of what man can perform, but not as the promise of what he is yet to perform. They are accepted, not as a little earnest-money, but as full payment.

Now, the view which I am constrained to take of the history and destiny of man is exactly the contrary of this one. I hold all past achievements of the human mind to be rather in the nature of prophecy than of fulfilment,—the first-fruits of the beneficence of God in endowing us with the faculties of perception, comparison, calculation, and causality, rather than the full harvest of their eventual development. For look at the magnificent creation into which we have been brought, and at the adaptation of our faculties to understand, admire, and use it. All around us are works worthy of an infinite God; and we are led, by irresistible evidence, to believe, that, just so far as we acquire his knowledge, we shall be endued with his power. From history and from consciousness, we find ourselves capable of ever-onward improvement: and therefore it seems to be a denial of first principles—it seems no better than impiety—to suppose that we shall ever become such finished scholars, that the works of the All-wise will have no new problem for our solution, and will, therefore, be able to teach us no longer. Nor is it any less than impiety to suppose that we shall ever so completely enlist the powers of Nature in our service, that exhausted Omnipotence can reward our industry with no further bounties. This would be to suppose that we shall arrive at a period when our active and progressive natures will become passive and stationary; when we shall have nothing to do but to sit in indolent and inglorious contemplation of past achievements; and when, all aspirations having been lost in fruition, we shall have outlived the joys of hope and the rewards of effort, and no new glories will beckon us onward to new felicities.

Neither our faculties, nor their spheres of action, seem to have been projected on any such narrow plan. Ever-expanding powers are within us; eternity lies before us; and an Infinite Being, amidst his works, is the adorable object of these faculties throughout this eternity. These, no height of attainment which our powers will ever reach, and no length of duration to which the cycles of eternity shall ever have run, will enable us to exhaust or fully to comprehend. To affirm the contrary would be to affirm that our finite minds can embrace and encircle their infinite Author, as his mind embraces and encircles ours. Our relation to our Maker, then, is a moral phase of the problem of the asymptote,—a line forever approaching a point which it can never reach.

And, if we believe in our individual capacity for indefinite improvement, why should we doubt the capacity of the race for continued progress as long as it dwells upon the earth? Can man, "by searching, find out God" in a physical sense any more than in a moral one? or can all the generations of the race, by the longest and the profoundest investigations, ever fathom the depths of eternal wisdom and power as they are incorporated into this earthly frame? However far, then, science and art may push their explorations, there will always be a frontier bounding their advances; there will always be a *terra incognita* beyond the regions they have surveyed,—beyond the utmost verge of the horizon which the eye can see from the topmast pinnacle of existing discoveries. Each new adventurer can gain new trophies by penetrating still deeper into the illimitable solitudes where alone Omnipotence dwells and works. The most perfect instrument which the brightest genius of any age may ever construct will be excelled by another instrument, made after a higher ideal of perfection by the brighter genius of a succeeding age. The most rapid processes of art known to any generation will be accelerated in the generation that shall follow it, and science will be found not only a plant of perennial growth, but, in each succeeding age, it will bear blossoms of a more celestial splendor, and fruits of beneficence unknown before.

Astronomers now tell us, that the sun is not a stationary orb, fixed and immovable at one place in the heavens, as, since the days of Copernicus, it had been supposed to be, but that, in some far-off region of immensity, at a distance wholly inconceivable by us, there is a central point of attraction, around which our sun, with its attendant train of planets, is performing a magnificent revolution; just as, within their narrow orbits, the planets of our local system are revolving about the sun. They tell us, further, that the circumference of this solar orbit is so vast, that, during the six thousand years which are supposed to have elapsed since the creation of Adam, the sun has not yet travelled through so much as one of the three hundred and sixty degrees that make up its mighty circle; not through so much as one of those hundreds of astronomical spaces through which it must move before it will complete a single revolution. What number of these immense circuits the earth is destined to perform, or what part even of a single revolution it will accomplish, before it will meet with some such catastrophe as will unfit it to be the abode of a race like ours, we know not; but we have no reason to believe, even if the mighty years of the solar revolutions should equal the number of our terrestrial years since the creation of Adam, that the race will ever have exhausted the earth of all the latent capacities for ministering to the improvement and happiness of man with which God has endued it. No invention or discovery will ever be made, upon which the author can stand, and lift up his proud voice, and exclaim, *"I have found the last miracle of the miracle-working God!"*

Now, so far as these natural and yet undeveloped resources of the earth are hereafter to be brought to light, and made the ministering servants of human welfare, we suppose they are to be brought to light by the exercise of the human faculties, in the same way that all the scientific and mechanical improvements of past times have been brought to light,—that is, by education. And the greater the proportion of minds in any community which are educated, and the more thorough and complete the education which is given them, the more rapidly, through these sublime stages of progress, will that community advance in all the means of enjoyment and elevation, and the more will it outstrip and outshine its less educated neighbors. The advance-guard of education and intelligence will gather the virgin wealth of whatever region they explore, as the reward of their knowledge, just as the Portuguese reaped the great harvest of the riches of India as their reward for discovering the new route to India.

I know that it may be said, and said, too, not without a

certain measure of truth, that when a more intelligent community has made a discovery in science, or devised or perfected the processes of any art, a less intelligent community by its side may adopt and copy them, and thus make the improvements their own by possession, though the invention belonged to another. After a bold navigator has opened a new channel of commerce, and while he is gathering the first-fruits of his sagacity, the stupid or the predatory may follow in his wake, and share the gains of his enterprise. Dr. Franklin may discover the uses of the lightning-rod; but when once discovered, and the manner of its use exhibited, any half-taught son of Vulcan can make and erect one by copying the given model. When a school-boy of New England has invented the cotton-gin, or perfected cotton machinery, the slaves of the South, stupid and ignorant as cattle, "according to the form of the statute in such cases made and provided," can operate them with a greater or less degree of success and profit. But there are two considerations which show how inferior the condition of the aping community must always be to that of the originating one.

In the first place, all copying is in the nature of empiricism. The copyist operates blindly, and not on principle; and therefore he is constantly exposed to failure. In untried emergencies, he never knows what to do, for the light of example shines only in one direction; while it is the very nature of principle, like its divine Author, to circumfuse its beams, and so to leave no darkness in any direction.

And, in the second place, even supposing the aping community to be able, after long delays and toils, to equal the originating one, still, before the period shall have elapsed which the pupil will require for studying out or copying the old lesson, his master will have studied out some new one; will have discovered some new improvement, diffusive of new utility, and radiant with new beauty: so that the distance will be kept as great as ever between him and the learner.

The slave States of this Union may buy cotton machinery made by the intelligent mechanics of the free States, and they may train their slaves to work it with more or less skill; but should they succeed ever so well, should they eventually become able to meet their entire home demand, it will nevertheless be true, that, in the mean time, the new wants and refinements generated by the progress of the age will demand some new fabric, requiring for its manufacture either more ingeniously-wrought machinery, or greater skill in the operator: and thus will the more educated community forever keep ahead of the less educated one. The progress of mankind may be compared to an ascending spiral. In moving upward along this spiral, the less intelligent community will see the more intelligent one at a point above its head. It will labor on to overtake it, and, making another toilsome circuit, will at length reach the place where the victor had been seen; but, lo! the victor is not there: he, too, has made a circuit along the ascending curve, and is still far aloft, above the head of his pursuer.

Another common idea is this: it is supposed that intelligence in workmen is relatively less important in agricultural labors than in the mechanic and manufacturing arts. The great agricultural staples of the country—corn, cotton, sugar, rice, and so forth—have been stigmatized, or at least characterized, as "coarser" products, and, therefore, requiring less skill and science for their culture and improvement than the fabrics of the loom and the workshop. This may be true; but I am by no means convinced of its truth. It seems to me that there is, as yet, no adequate proof that skill and science, if applied to agriculture, will not yield practical benefits as copious and as wonderful as any that have rewarded the mechanician or the artisan in any department of their labors. Why vegetable growths, so exquisite in their organization, animated by the mysterious principle of life, and so susceptive of all the influences of climate, whether good or ill,—why these should be called "coarser" than iron-ore or other unorganized metals, or any kind of wealth that is found in mines; or why cotton or flax, wool or leather, wood or grain, should be denominated "coarser" before they have been deprived of the principle of life than after it, and before they have lost the marvellous power of assimilating inorganic matter to their own peculiar substance,—it is not easy to perceive. May it not yet be found that a better knowledge of the laws that govern vegetable growth; a better knowledge of the properties and adaptations of different soils; a better knowledge of the conditions of fructification and germination, and of the mysterious chemistry that determines the quality of texture, color, flavor, and perfume; a better knowledge of the uncombined gases, and of the effect of light, heat, electricity, and other imponderable agents, upon the size, rapidity, and variegation of vegetable growths,—in fine, a better knowledge of vegetable physiology, and of that, too, which may be called vegetable pathology,—will redeem the whole circle of agricultural occupations from the stigma of requiring less intelligent cultivators than are required for other pursuits, and thus supply a new and irresistible argument in favor of diffusing a vastly-increased amount of knowledge among our free field-laborers and our rural population generally? The marvellous improvements which have been made under the auspices of the Massachusetts Horticultural Society, in horticulture, flori-culture, and pomology, already betoken such a result.*

Now, it is in these various ways that all the means of human subsistence, comfort, improvement, or what, in one word, we call wealth, are created,—additional wealth, new wealth, not another man's earnings, not another nation's treasures or lands, tricked away by fraud or wrested by force, but substantially, and for all practical purposes, knowledge-created, mind-created wealth; as much so as though we had been endued with a miraculous power of turning a granite quarry into a city at a word, or a wilderness into cultivated fields, or of commanding harvests to ripen in a day. To see a community acquiring and redoubling its wealth in this way; enriching itself without impoverishing others, without despoiling others,—is it not a noble spectacle? And will not the community that gains its wealth in this way, ten times faster than any robber-nation ever did by plunder,—will not such a community be a model and a pattern for the nations, a type of excellence to be admired and

---

* As an illustration of the value of knowledge in agricultural pursuits, it may be mentioned, that the researches and discoveries by M. Meneville, in regard to the fly which was lately so destructive to the olive in the south of France, have increased the annual product of this fruit almost a million of dollars' worth. When would an ignorant man, or a slave, have made such a discovery?

followed by the world? Has Massachusetts no ambition to win the palm in so glorious a rivalry?

But suppose that Massachusetts, notwithstanding her deplorable inferiority in all natural resources as compared with other States, should be content to be their equal only in the means of education, and in the development of the intelligence of her present children and her future citizens, down, down to what a despicable depth of inferiority would she suddenly plunge! Her ancient glory would become dim. No historian, no orator, no poet, would rise up among her children. Her sons would cease, as now, to fill chairs in the halls of learning in more than half the States of the Union. Her jurists would no longer expound the laws of Nature, of nations, and of States, to guide the judicial tribunals of the country. Her skilled artisans and master-mechanics would not be sought for, wherever, throughout the land, educated labor is wanted. Her ship-captains would be driven home from every ocean by more successful competitors. At home, a narrowing in the range of thought and action, a lowering of the tone of life and enterprise, a straitening in the means of living and of culture, a sinking in spirit and in all laudable and generous ambitions, the rearing of sons to obscurity and of daughters to vulgarity, would mark the incoming of a degenerate age,—an age too ignorant to know its own ignorance, too shameless to mourn its degradation, and too spiritless even to rise with recuperative energy from its guilty fall. But little less disastrous would it be to stop where we now are, instead of pressing onward with invigorated strength to a further goal. What has been done is not the fulfilment or consummation of our work. It only affords better vantage-ground from which our successors can start anew in a nobler career of improvement. And if there is any one thing for which the friends of humanity have reason to join in a universal song of thanksgiving to Heaven, it is that there is a large and an increasing body of people in Massachusetts who cannot be beguiled or persuaded into the belief that our common schools are what they may and should be; and who, with the sincerest good-will and warmest affections towards the higher institutions of learning, are yet resolved that the education of the people at large—of the sons and daughters of farmers, mechanics, tradesmen, operatives, and laborers of all kinds—shall be carried to a point of perfection indefinitely higher than it has yet reached.*

---

* In the letter of the Hon. Abbott Lawrence, making a donation of fifty thousand dollars for the purpose of founding a scientific school at Cambridge (to which he has since added fifty thousand dollars more), the following expression occurs: "Elementary education appears to be well provided for in Massachusetts." And in the Memorial in behalf of the three colleges,—Harvard, Amherst, and Williams,—presented to the legislature in January, 1848, and signed by each of the three presidents of those institutions, it is said, "The provision [in Massachusetts] for elementary education . . . seems to be all that can be desired, or that can be advantageously done by the legislature." The average salaries of female teachers throughout the State, at the time when these declarations were made, was only $8.55 a month (exclusive of board), which, as the average length of the schools was only eight months, would give to this most faithful and meritorious class of persons but $68.40 a year. The whole value of the apparatus in all the schools of the State was but $23,826; and the whole number of volumes in their libraries was only 91,539, or an average of but twenty-five volumes for each school. In accordance with the prayer of the Memorial, the Committee on Education reported a bill, making a grant of half a million of dollars to the colleges. The House of Representatives, after maturely considering the bill, changed the destination of the money from the colleges to the common schools, and then passed it. The donation of Mr. Lawrence will be beneficial to the few hundreds of students who will have the direct enjoyment of his munificence; and, through them, it will also benefit the State. So, too, would the contemplated grant to the colleges. Thus far, it is believed, all liberal minds will agree. But what is needed is the universal prevalence of the further idea, that there are two hundred thousand children in the State, each one of whom would be far more than proportionally benefited by the expenditure for their improved education of one-tenth part of sums so liberal.

4
Ralph
Waldo
Emerson

$\mathbf{F}$ive years before Horace Mann gave up his position as president of the Senate to become secretary of the Massachusetts Board of Education, a young clergyman resigned his pastorate at the ancient and respectable Second Church in Boston. Like Horace Mann, who had abandoned law and politics for "the larger sphere of mind and morals," Ralph Waldo Emerson forsook the ministry in order to ascend to a higher world. "A sect or party," he wrote in his journal, "is an elegant incognito devised to save a man from the vexation of thinking." Having come to believe that religion was the relation of the soul to God, he concluded that "the progress of sectarianism marks the decline of religion."

The decision to leave the ministry did not come easy to Emerson. He was descended from a long line of ministers. They had initially borne witness to the austere Calvinism of colonial New England. That religion of his fathers had evolved into Unitarianism, replacing the grim doctrine of predestination with the belief that all men are good. But even Unitarianism, the freest of all Christian religions, the young Emerson found restrictive. The difficulty, he wrote, "is that we do not make a world of our own, but fall into institutions already made, and have to accommodate ourselves to them to be useful at all, and this accommodation is, I say, a loss of so much integrity and, of course, of so much power." The age had altered, but men still worshiped in "the lead forms of their forefathers." In order to be a good minister, he found it necessary to leave the ministry.

✻

Emerson sought no less than to create a new religion. The first statement of the principles of that religion appeared in 1838 in an essay he published anonymously, simply titled *Nature.* This essay charts Emerson's passage from the position of philosophical idealism to the spiritual idealism for which he is famous.

Starting with the notion of the primacy of ideas over nature, Emerson shows that under whatever guise we contemplate it, nature leads us to the world of ideas. When man considers nature as a commodity—the beasts, fire, water, stones, and corn that serve him—he perceives that each benefit is instrumental to some higher good: commodities point to a final cause, the Good. When man contemplates nature as beauty, he does behold an intrinsic worth of nature, it is true, but such beauty is only a mirage—something higher, a spiritual element, is essential to its perfection. Beauty in nature is not ultimate; it is the herald of inward and eternal beauty, and is not alone a solid and satisfactory good. A third way man can contemplate nature is as a language. Here, it is the symbol of spirit; spirit manifests itself in material forms, "day and night, river and storm, beast and bird, acid and alkali, preexist in necessary Ideas in the mind of God."

Finally, man can contemplate nature as a discipline. It educates both our Understanding and our Reason. For Emerson, Reason was primarily a power of the mind to feel moral and religious truths, while Understanding deals with the expedient and the customary—what we call empirical truth. As a discipline nature conveys to man "the unspeakable but intelligible and practical meaning of the world."

In Emerson's hands idealism became a radical force, useful for attacking the deadening influence of the past. Instead of seeing through someone else's eyes, men should behold nature face to face, have an original perception of the universe. In the famous opening lines of *Nature,* he wrote: "Our age is retrospective. It builds the sepulchres of the fathers. It writes biographies, histories, and criticism. The foregoing generations beheld God and nature face to face; we through their eyes. Why should not we also enjoy an original relation to the universe?"

Philosophical idealism, however, could not be the basis for a *continuous* original relation to the universe. From Plato onward— after initially bringing about a revolution in thought—philosophi- cal idealism had always become the philosophy of conservatism; once the true ideas were revealed the task became one of preserving and perpetuating them. But in the last chapters of *Nature* Emerson sets forth a novel philosophical construction that will permit continuous engagement in an original relation to the universe.

Idealism tells us that nature is not real, that spirit alone is real. But spirit is within, and for Emerson this means that God is within man's soul. Thus man is the creator of nature. "Spirit, that is the Supreme Being, does not build up nature around us, but puts it forth through us, as the life of the tree puts forth branches and leaves through the pores of the old. . . . Once inhale the upper air, being admitted to behold the absolute nature of justice and truth, and we learn that man has access to the entire mind of the Creator, is himself the creator of the finite."

This is mystical. If God is within the soul, then man can have a continuous original relationship with nature, since man then becomes the creator of nature. But at this point Emerson is merely proclaiming. The ideas are unclear, the significance unexplored. What is clear is that man must right himself, must rely upon reason, not understanding, to pursue wisdom. But beyond this gnosiological dictum of philosophic idealism, Emerson promises man mastery of nature—a mastery, Emerson tells us, now glimpsed only in acts of heroism, in art, in poetry.

Through this self-recovery of man's soul, Emerson foresaw the coming of a new era—an age of freedom and mastery. "As fast as you conform your life to the pure idea in your mind, that will unfold its great proportions. A correspondent revolution in things will attend the influx of the spirit. So fast will disagreeable appearances, swine, spiders, snakes, pests, mad-houses, prisons, enemies, vanish; they are temporary and shall be no more seen. The sordor and filths of nature, the sun shall dry up and the wind exhale. As when the summer comes from the south the snowy banks melt and the face of the earth becomes green before it, so shall the advancing spirit create its ornaments along its path, and carry with it the beauty it visits and the song which enchants it; it shall draw beautiful faces, warm hearts, wise discourse, and heroic acts, around its way, until evil is no more seen. The kingdom of man over nature, which cometh not with observation,—a dominion such as now is beyond his dream of God,—he shall enter without more wonder than the blind man feels who is gradually restored to sight."

❋

After leaving the ministry, Emerson supported himself through public lecturing; the lecture became his sermon, the lyceum his church. His fame grew as each year he made the rounds with a new series of lectures: on Natural History (1833–34) on Biography (1835) on English Literature (1835–36) and the Philosophy of History (1836–37). In August 1837 the Phi Beta Kappa Society of Harvard invited him to deliver an address. Here he presented his most famous oration, *The American Scholar*, called by many the second American declaration of independence: a declaration of literary and artistic independence.

Repeating the same spiritualist themes set forth in *Nature*, Emerson now applies them directly to the scholar. Analyzing how nature, books, and action influence him, Emerson reveals that the scholar actually creates nature, books, and actions: the scholar is the cause, not the effect. This happens when the scholar trusts himself, when he accepts the fact that he is not simply an observer, a reader, a participant: the scholar is Man; he is Man thinking. For the scholar, self-trust is everything. He must be free, and he must be brave. The deafness, the stone-blind custom, the overgrown error—all exist only through the sufferance of the scholar. He—if he is free, if he is brave, if he has self-trust—can shatter and destroy all ignorance. It is wrong to think that the world was finished a long time ago: "As the world was plastic and fluid in the hands of God, so it is ever to so much of his attributes as we bring to it." Only the ignorant adapts to the world; for the scholar, for Man thinking, "the firmament flows before him and takes its signet and form."

The office of the scholar is to cheer, to raise, to guide men by showing them facts amid appearances. Yet this task is really revolutionary. For Emerson would have the scholar domesticate the ideas of culture—have him illuminate the minds of all men by making them part of Man thinking. "For a man, rightly viewed, comprehendeth the particular natures of all men. Each philosopher, each bard, each actor has only done for me, as by a delegate, what one day I can do for myself. The books which once we valued more than the apple of the eye, we have quite exhausted. What is that but saying that we have come up with the point of view which the universal mind took through the eyes of one scribe; we have been that man, and have passed on."

The times, Emerson says, are ripe for such a revolution. One of the signs is the emergence of a new literature embracing the near, the low, the common: "The literature of the poor, the feelings of the child, the philosophy of the street, the meaning of household life, are the topics of the times. It is a great stride." This new literature—the work of Goldsmith, Burns, Cowper, and that of Goethe, Wordsworth, and Carlyle—gives form and order to the everyday world: "There is no trifle, there is no puzzle, but one design unites and animates the farthest pinnacle and the lowest trench."

Emerson sees the same movement toward unity in another sign of the times: individualism, the new political importance given to the single person. Insulated and alone, each man comes to feel the world is his and learns to treat others with natural respect. Individualism thus leads to union—each man treating another as a sovereign state treats a sovereign state. Individualism brings union as well as greatness.

The signs of the times—romanticism in literature, individualism in politics—beckon the scholar. The moment is right for him, right for the revolution; the domestication of culture awaits his awakening. "The scholar is that man who must take up into himself all the ability of the time, all the contributions of the past, all the hopes of the future. He must be a university of knowledges. If there be one lesson more than another which should pierce his ear, it is, The world is nothing, the man is all; in yourself is the law of all nature, and you know not yet how a globule of sap ascends; in yourself slumbers the whole of Reason; it is for you to know all; it is for you to dare all."

In the last paragraph of the oration Emerson heralds the emergence of the new age, an American age of arts and letters. The American scholar must forsake the "courtly muses of Europe." Americans must walk on their own feet, work with their own hands, speak their own mind. If the American scholar plants himself "indomitably on his instincts and there abide, the huge world will come round to him." Then, Emerson promises, "a nation of men will for the first time exist, because each believes himself inspired by the Divine Soul which also inspires all men."

❋

Following the spectacularly successful *American Scholar* oration, the seniors of the Harvard Divinity School invited Emerson to deliver an address. This Divinity School address, delivered in the summer of 1839, did not bring Emerson the accolades of the previous speech. For when he applied his spiritualism directly to Christianity, the result, to many, was heresy. Even the most liberal Unitarians could not accept the command to become self-reliant and recognize that God is within man.

Emerson began his address with a hauntingly beautiful paean to nature. "In this refulgent summer, it has been a luxury to draw the breath of life. The grass grows, the buds burst, the meadow is spotted with fire and gold in the tint of flowers. The air is full of birds, and sweet with the breath of the pine, the balm of Gilead, and the new hay." But, however beautiful nature is, there is a more overpowering beauty that appears to man when his heart and mind open to the sentiment of virtue.

The delight and reverence man takes from virtue springs from divine laws, laws that cannot be stated adequately, yet we read them hourly. These laws execute themselves: "He who does a good deed is instantly ennobled. He who does a mean deed is by the action itself contradicted. He who puts off impurity, thereby puts on purity." Nor can these laws be contravened: "Thefts never enrich, alms never impoverish; murder will speak out of stone walls." All this suggests that the world is the product of one will, one mind, everywhere active: "in each ray of the star, in each wavelet of the pool; and whatever opposes that will is everywhere balked and baffled, because things are made so, and not otherwise."

Man can unite himself with this will and mind; and while he seeks good ends, he is strong. But when he roves from those ends, "he bereaves himself of power, or auxiliaries; his being shrinks out of all remote channels, he becomes less and less, a mote, a point, until absolute badness is absolute death." The principles of this Divine Law awakens the religious sentiment, which divines and deifies man, revealing "the fountain of all good to be in himself."

Yet this sentiment, this wisdom, is had only through an intuition. "I cannot receive it second-hand from another. I can accept nothing on the word of another; what he announces I must find true in me, or reject." This self-reliance is possible, and veracious, Emerson explains once again, because the Divine dwells in each one of us.

But today, Emerson laments, this divine nature of man, this indwelling of the Supreme Spirit, is denied with fury. Instead Christians attribute the divine nature to but one or two persons. Christ, Emerson admits, saw the mystery of the soul; with his heart and life he declared God was within him: "Thus is he the only soul in history who has appreciated the worth of man."

Having perverted Christ's message of man's divinity, the Christian church no longer teaches. Only the man through whom the soul speaks can teach: "Courage, piety, love, wisdom, can teach; and every man can open his door to these angels, and they shall bring him the gift of tongues. But the man who aims to speak as books enable, as synods use, as the fashion guides, and as interest commands, babbles. Let him hush."

*

In his *American Scholar* oration
and in his Divinity School address, Emerson had characterized
both the scholar and the clergyman as educators. Educators who
abandoned the traditional approaches, educators who deserted the
customary arrangements. He had depicted both the scholar and the
clergyman as educators who helped others to become more fully
human, which meant, paradoxically, to recognize the divine spirit
dwelling within. As he elaborates his construction of the educational process, Emerson clarifies and expands the spiritualism of his
earlier works.

In 1840 Emerson delivered a series of lectures on the theme
The Present Age. One of the topics he treated was "Education." Our
education, he begins, like the other institutions and formularies of
the present age, is poor. It has no breadth. It speaks in a dialect. As
we construe it, education refers to a narrow circle of experiences,
powers, and a literature of its own. Education should be as broad
as man, fostering and demonstrating whatever elements are in him.
If he is dexterous, analytical, or a synthesizer; if he is jovial,
mercurial or greathearted; if he is a strong commander; if he is a
good ally; if he is ingenious or useful or elegant or witty, a prophet
or a diviner—education should make it appear, respect his talents,
and help improve them.

Today's education does none of this. We confront the
narrowness and vanity of our education when we look at its result:
society. "What gloomy wrecks we daily meet drifting along this sea
of life. What parrots of routine. What men of pasteboard, what
triflers, what madmen whose culture is only a paint or enamel that
never ennobles the lump. Now and then the mask is lifted and we
see the clown still. Where is the wisdom that ought to look out on
us from every eye; the religion that should hallow us perforce as we
approached its atmosphere; the cheerfulness that should make us
glad; the salient vivacity that should take possession of society?
Should not every man we meet affect us as a magazine of
unexhausted resources? Should not everyone new paint the landscape and exalt our interest in the world because he had shown us

of it a new side? But we do not care for those whose opinions we can predict."

Everyone recognizes the numbing boredom of all that falls under the rubric "education": a treatise on education, a convention for it, a lecture about it, a system of education—each affects us with "slight paralysis and a certain yawning of the jaws." We are not encouraged, Emerson adds, "when the law touches it with its fingers."

If the vast and the spiritual are untouched by education, so are the practical and the needful. After being shut up in school for ten or fifteen years, we come out not knowing a thing. "We cannot use our hands or our legs or our eyes or our arms. We do not know an edible root in the woods. We cannot tell our course by the stars nor the hour of day by the sun. It is well if we can swim and skate." If at least a man learned to plant, to fish, or to hunt, he could secure his subsistence and not be painful to his friends and fellow men. Schools teach us words—concealing truth and reality. Men transformed by books become simple praters; they have no power, inspire no awe.

If the results of education dismay us, so also should the mode: it is profane. Educators aim to expedite, to save labor. Thus they use emulation and display. This saves time, works with good as well as slow students, and is easy to apply—any schoolmaster in his first term can employ it. But this mode of instruction profanes education. True education (Emerson had taught school from 1818 to 1826) employs simple discipline and follows nature. True education is time-consuming and difficult, and it makes great demands on the teacher—only to think of using it implies "piety and profoundness."

If the results are poor and the mode is profane, what about the philosophy of our present education? It is, he says, a philosophy of despair: "We do not believe in the power of Education. We do not think we can call out God in man and we do not try. We renounce all high aims. We sacrifice the genius of the pupil, the unknown possibilities of his nature to a neat and safe uniformity."

Whence this corruption of the philosophy of education, the perversion of its mode, the despondency of its results? "Well," Emerson replies, "language of this spirit is heard in the street, in the

senate, in the household, and in the college. It has infected and
paralyzed the enterprise of education."

Here, assuredly, was an attack on Horace Mann—delivered,
like the other blows Mann received, in the fateful year of 1840. But,
unlike the attacks leveled by the politicians, Horace Mann worried
little about Emerson's abstract, philosophical criticism. In a testy
letter to Elizabeth Peabody, who had repeated some of Emerson's
theoretical questions about the common-school reform movement,
Mann wrote:

> Oh my dear lady! If a tough question were before a District
> School Meeting about doing something for the school;—or
> before a Town Meeting about helping any side or limb of
> humanity forward, how think you, your oracle [Emerson] would
> lead or manage the minds of people, which we call great by
> country! Oh these Reformers and Spiritualizers who can do
> everything well on paper! They can tell exactly how a road
> ought to be laid between here and New Orleans, but can they
> lay it?"
>
>   Quoted in Jonathan Messerli, *Horace Mann: A Biography*
>   (New York: Alfred A. Knopf, 1972), p. 336.

To counter the despair embodied in the educational arrangements of the present age, we need, Emerson claims, a revolution in
hope. And this can come about through recognizing the infinitude
of every man. This infinitude is amply demonstrated by the fact of
our perpetual youth; however old we become, we remain subject
always to circumstances, we do not control them: "We come
greenhorns to every conversation." This gives us temporary unhappiness, but in it we can see a deeper good: continual growth, we
can always improve. "As long as things change and invite our
energies, we grow and advance. We learn evermore."

To become true educators, teachers must admit their ignorance; confess they do not know the good or understand how
learning takes place: "He who sees moral nature out and out and
thoroughly knows how knowledge is acquired and character
formed, is a pedant." Teachers must replace pedantry with hope:
"We judge of a man's wisdom by his hope."

Hope, the leitmotiv of all real education, is born from

skepticism. For once we recognize that what passes among us for erudition is still ignorance, once we realize that there are no permanent wise men, then it is difficult to avoid skepticism. The young and aspiring feel this and are tortured by it. But when we perceive that our despair of ever knowing absolute truth, of ever doing pure good, is itself rooted in a sense of the perfect that "accompanies, overhangs us always," skepticism disappears. Hope is born when we realize that we can continually improve, advance closer and closer to—but never attain—absolute truth and pure good. For Emerson, as for the Italian philosopher Giambattista Vico, "man is a finite being who tends toward the infinite."

After insisting that hope must inform any worthy theory of education, Emerson turns to the arrangements necessary for it. He credits little to schooling: a few arts, a few rules, reading and writing, "undeniable conveniences though very low ones in a scale where into all humanity enters." Our real education takes place outside schools: "My life, my work and play, my pleasure and pain, my loves and quarrels, my own reading, my business, my friends, the stranger, the observation of people pursuing their own affairs, their coldness from which I suffered; their cordiality which warmed me, the winter's frost, the summer's fruit—it is these which have taught me that lore which I cannot spare." Educational institutions are nugatory. Education, he concludes, is not there.

Although true education needs no institutions to promote it, teachers are indispensable. To effect education the teacher must be a man—more so than other men. And what method shall he use? The secret, Emerson explains, lies in respecting the child. The teacher cannot choose what the child shall know, what he shall do. That, Emerson says, is foreordained. The student, alone, holds the key. The teacher's tampering, thwarting, and too much governing may hinder the student from his end. Each child is unique: "Nature never rhymes her children; never makes two men precisely alike." The teacher who works on the assumption that one child resembles some other, defeats "his proper promise and produce[s] the ordinary and mediocre."

To respect the child demands great patience from the teacher —tolerance of his want of taste, his lack of perception, his sensualism. And here Emerson calls upon his famous law of compensation: "If he has his own vice, he has its correlative virtue." If every mind is allowed to make its own statement in action, he insists, "its balance will appear." This is not to say that teachers should indulge their students, or pander to them; the teacher must respect himself. He can love his students' virtues but hate their vices.

Yet education is not up to the teacher. Scholars must work. Learning does not come ready-made to fit like a coat. *To be taught,* Emerson says, is the great design hung out in the sky and earth. The student must accept this. "He that has no ambition to be taught let him creep into his grave. What is he doing among good people? The play is not worth the candle—the laborer is not worthy of his meat—the sun grudges him light and the air his breath—who stands with his hands folded in this great school of God and does not perceive that all are students, all are learning the art of life, the discipline of virtue, how to act, how to suffer, how to be useful, and what their Maker designed them for. It is this persuasion only that can invest existence with any dignity or hope, and make the life of a man better than a brute's. And this will do it. If you believe that every step not only enables you to make another, but also brings you within reach of influences before inert acts—like Day, which not only brings more objects in view every moment but brings out new properties in every particular object—you will then accept instruction as the greatest gift of God and anxiously put yourself in the attitude of preparation."

Still we are faithless. True education needs only hope to inform it, teachers who are men, and students who will work—but we do not believe it can occur. Too many people, we say, are ineducable: society is but a hospital of incurables. Because we lack faith we give our students opiates, diversions, and alleviations instead of education.

But, Emerson insists, we should take less account of the kinds of talents and the quality of the skills our student has, and pay heed instead to the great inner force, a force that distinguishes him from the animals. Teachers must bring each student to perceive that he has access to the universal. Each student can recognize that he tends toward infinity: he can always advance, always improve. When each sees his self in relation to the perfect he recognizes that comparisions with others is meaningless. In relation to the perfect there is no difference between a profound mind and one not so profound: the ignorance of all men is infinite (thus we say, "in the eyes of God all men are equal"). Man's calling is not to excel others, but to "suffice to himself"—a task without end. Inferiority to others becomes null when man measures himself by the perfect, toward which he tends.

And this leads Emerson to touch briefly on the content of education, what is to be studied. Man's proper study is men—representative men, men of genius. Students will study their lives and their works. This is to say no more than that they will study philosophy (e.g., Plato), religion (e.g., Swedenborg), belle lettres (e.g., Montaigne), history (e.g., Napoleon), poetry (e.g., Shakespeare), and science (e.g., Goethe). These were the representative men Emerson selected to lecture on in 1845.

Great men teach us the self-subsistency of man. The child who understands Plato is already Plato so far: "The best picture makes us say, I am a painter also; the poem, I also am a poet." These men of genius—their works, their lives—awaken us to something new, and yet old: the recognition that the infinite, the Divine, God, flows "through every willing heart of man."

Still we lack faith. Not seeing education as the pursuit of perfection, the movement of the finite being toward the infinite, we purvey a trivial commodity as education. We teach feats and games; we do not improve or advance man. Our education conceals, saves appearances, solaces our students. "Worst of all, it tends to insanity by amusing the man with this show of accomplishments instead of exposing to him his fatal want."

True education will take place only when we incorporate into it the realization that "a man is not a man who does not draw on the eternal and universal Soul." It lies within—it lies behind us all. Everyone—the dullest drone, the shallowest fop, the least profound—is capable of that sentiment. Each can know his relation to the All; each can be ennobled. And the finite mind that discovers it is related to the Supreme Mind, the finite will that perceives it is related to the Supreme Will; thus, man finds himself related to all the works men have created and so travels "a royal road to particular knowledges and powers."

As to practical proposals to reform education (*pace,* Mr. Mann), Emerson finds himself at a loss (*carpe diem,* Mr. Mann). "A vicious society cannot have virtuous schools. A society which wishes its youth bred to certain dexterities cannot have schools which condemn that end." So we must, Emerson concludes, simply abandon all hope of educational reform within institutions.

In place of institutions we must depend upon men. Emerson's last words are an appeal for all men to become educators: "To whatsoever upright mind,—to whatsoever beating heart I speak,— to you it is committed to educate men. By simple living,—by true speech,—by just action,—by an illimitable soul, you inspire, you correct, you instruct, you raise, you embellish. . . . Consent yourself to be an organ of your highest thought, and lo! suddenly you put all men in your debt and are the fountain of an energy that goes pulsing on with waves of benefit to the borders of society, to the circumferences of things."

*

In the lecture "Education," Emerson introduced a new dimension to his spiritualism, an element absent in his earlier works. Here we find an evolutionary spiritualism. God is within man as an evolutionary force, enabling finite man to tend toward the infinite, toward the Perfect. Because God exists within, man is creative, indeed because of this divine inner force man can create without end.

Emerson later elaborated this evolutionary spiritualism in his *Essays, First Series,* published in 1841. In the essay called "Love," he explains that man's ability to love can always expand, always deepen. There are moments when we are absorbed in the love of some one person or persons, but, in time, we transcend this: "That which is so beautiful and attractive as these relations must be succeeded and supplanted only by what is more beautiful, and so on, forever."

The essay "Circles" contains his fullest exposition of the evolutionary spiritualism. Man evolves, or can advance in knowledge and virtue; he can improve every idea, better every act. "Beware when the great God lets loose a thinker on this planet. Then all things are at risk. . . . There is not a piece of science, but its flank may be turned tomorrow; there is not any literary reputation, not the so-called eternal names of fame, that may not be revised and condemned." As to virtue: "There is no virtue which is final; all are initial. The virtues of society are vices of the saint. The terror of reform is the discovery that we must cast away our virtues, or what we have always esteemed such, into the same pit that has consumed our grosser vices."

Because man can evolve or improve—in love, in knowledge, in virtue—he is perpetually a learner. Hence all men are equally educable; all can continually improve. Such a magnificent conception of the enterprise of education could not but view the current practices of schools and teachers as Emerson did: poor, expedient, trivial, and despairing. Yet this noble construction of the process of education had little influence on the course of educational thought in America. True, many of Emerson's criticisms of education reappear in the work of the romantic educational theorists of the 1960s. But most of them knew nothing of their affinity to Emerson, and none of them offered so penetrating or so complete a theory as he.

Darwinism eclipsed Emerson's evolutionary spiritualism. Emerson claimed that man evolved in knowledge, virtue, and love—but he failed to explain how this evolution took place. As a result Emerson winds up sounding like a rather naive, even simpleminded believer in inevitable human progress. Lacking any explanatory theory of how it takes place, he ignored the fact that often improvement does *not* occur: people sometimes become dogmatic about their ideas; and instead of expanding their love for others, some people constrict it and become selfish; nor do people inevitably become more virtuous, as some stay rooted to habitual vicious behavior.

Actually, although he himself never sought such a reconciliation, Darwinism is not incompatible with Emerson's theory of spiritual evolution—indeed it helps make it more acceptable. According to Darwin, evolution takes place through the critical encounter of organisms with their environment. Newborn organisms are always, in some way, different from their parents; the environment rejects (kills) those organisms that are unfit. The same critical encounter accounts for the advancement of knowledge and the improvement of behavior. That is, criticism reveals and rejects ideas that are contradictory and behavior that harms others. This leads man to create new and *better* ideas and behavior. Thus man's knowledge and behavior evolves if and when it is subjected to critical analysis.

In an analogous way, love can expand and grow. For the lover often dominates and seeks to possess the beloved. This stymies growth. Love grows through a critical engagement between the lover and the beloved. The beloved must be free to be herself, or himself, to react, to respond to the love tendered. The lover then refines and modifies his or her expressions of love in light of the response of the beloved.

Because Emerson thought that the evolution of knowledge, virtue, and love occurred naturally and inevitably, he failed to see the importance of institutions. Institutions are necessary for human evolution. In the first place, institutions such as the state provide the freedom necessary for improvement or advancement to take place. As Jefferson saw, unless people are protected against harm from those who are stronger and smarter, they will not develop or evolve. But Emerson thought that men could do without government—perhaps not just yet, but soon men would be good enough, wise enough, and loving enough. In "Politics" he wrote: "The appearance of character makes the state unnecessary. The wise man is the State. He needs no army, fort, or navy—he loves men too well." He admitted that men had never tried to use "the power of love" as the basis for the state, but he believed that this was the tendency of the times.

Emerson did not see that institutions, such as schools, can not only protect the young so that they have the freedom to evolve and develop, but they can also promote and foster evolution and development. The schools can do this, in a Darwinian way, by becoming critical agencies, the critical environment in which and through which children test their ideas and behaviors, continually improving their skills, ideas, and dispositions.

Emerson's incisive criticism of the education of his day still holds: education is still narrow, still impractical; its mode remains that of expedience, and its philosophy one of despair. We still need a revolution of hope. That revolution, as Emerson preached, can spring from the realization of the infinitude within every child. We must respect the child, admit our ignorance and fallibility as educators, forswear the task of imposing wisdom on them, and take up the more human enterprise of helping them to improve the knowledge they already possess—recognizing that improvement is endless. For, as Emerson saw, man tends toward the infinite.

WORKS AND COMMENTARY

There are numerous editions of Emerson's works. Harvard University Press is issuing the most definitive edition, *The Collected Works of Ralph Waldo Emerson* (Cambridge, Mass.: 1971 et seq.). Harvard is also issuing a new edition of Emerson's *Journals*. This will replace an earlier edition edited by his son, *Journals of Ralph Waldo Emerson*, 6 vols. (Boston, 1909). The best biography remains that of Ralph Leslie Rusk, *The Life of Ralph Waldo Emerson* (New York: Columbia University Press, 1949). A good brief biography is that by Robert E. Spiller in his *Literary History of the United States* (New York: Collier-Macmillan, 1964). Howard Mumford Jones has edited a collection of Emerson's writings on education, *Emerson on Education* (New York: Teachers College Bureau of Publications, 1966). Unfortunately this collection contains the synthetic essay "Education" pieced together from a number of Emerson's writings by his friend and literary executor, James Elliot Cabot, and published in *Lectures and Biographical Sketches* in 1883. While it contains large parts of the original 1840 lecture, it lacks the coherence, force, and beauty of the original. The 1840 lecture, reprinted below, is in volume 3 of the *Early Lectures of Ralph Waldo Emerson*, edited by Robert E. Spiller and Wallace E. Williams (Cambridge, Mass.: Harvard University Press, 1972).

Milton Konvitz and Stephen E. Whicher edited an excellent collection of critical essays, *Emerson* (Englewood Cliffs: Prentice-Hall, 1962). Stephen Whicher wrote an incisive study of Emerson's inner life, *Freedom and Fate* (Philadelphia: University of Pennsylvania Press, 1953). Morton White has a highly critical analysis of Emerson's philosophy in *Science and Sentiment in America* (New York: Oxford University Press, 1972).

Education

We have considered in the foregoing discourses the literature, the politics, the domestic life, the philanthropic projects of the present day, and lastly at some length the aspect of the religious institutions and the relation which the institution holds to the eternal Conscience. In the last lecture I endeavored to give a sketch of that natural theology which conversation, fiction, proverbs, and the very thoughts of men at the present day, seem to strive to embody. I pass by natural connexion of topics this evening to the subject of Education.

But I have still one more remark to make upon the Church which will sum up all I have had to say upon the institutions and formularies which represent to the nations at the present epoch the deepest Idea in Man. Namely, it is poor. The instructions of the Church have no adequate breadth. It speaks in a dialect. It refers to a narrow circle of experiences, persons, and a literature of its own. What I hear of there, I never meet elsewhere. I cannot make it sufficient to me but by contracting myself,—and lovers of rest do this. It does not explain to me my fortune, nor my form, my affections, my talent, my disease, my trade; I see it not in the sunset; I hear it not in music; if I glance from the catechism to natural history the connexion of the two things is not quite obvious. The thermometer and microscope have a very unbelieving look. The very vane on the church steeple is little better.

Now it is plain to me that the very mark of a truth is, that it is rich, all related, all explaining. How impoverished is our popular statement of belief will appear by seeing the attraction that the doctrine of Swedenborg has for men. It classifies the world for the receiver. It explains his marriage, his fever, his dreams, his vocation, life and death, his presentiments, his insanity. See the attraction which phrenology has for the people. That instantly offers to give them an insight of the true order of temperament of taste, of talent, of fortune, of success. And thus, although nothing can be more rude or premature than the present state of this so-called *science,* yet the eagerness with which it is embraced by thousands and the contentment this shadowy classification gives them, shows plainly enough what they demand of a religion—what they are looking for.

The Church is not broad enough for man. What difference do we make in our view if we alter the word and say Education? The same remark is still to be made. Education should be as broad as man. Whatever elements are in him, *that* should foster and demonstrate. Is not the Vast an element of his being? Yet what teaching or book of today appeals to the Vast? If he be dexterous his tuition should make it appear. If he be capable of dividing men by the trenchant sword of his Thought, Education should unsheath it. If he is one to cement society by his all-reconciling affinities, o hasten their action. If he is jovial, if he is mercurial, if he is greathearted, if he is a cunning artificer, if he is a strong commander, if he is a good ally, if he be ingenious or useful or elegant or witty, a prophet or a diviner, society has need of all. The vanity of Education is felt in our surveys of its result. Society is its result. Yet what a variety of misfortune, disaster, incapacity, ruin it offers us. What gloomy wrecks we daily meet drifting along this sea of life. What parrots of routine, what men of pasteboard, what triflers, what madmen whose culture is only a paint or enamel that never ennobles the lump. Now and then the mask is lifted and we see the clown still. Where is the wisdom that ought to look out on us from every eye; the religion that should hallow us perforce as we approached its atmosphere; the cheerfulness that should make us glad; the salient vivacity that should take possession of society? Should not every man we meet affect us as a magazine of unexhausted resources? Should not every one new paint the landscape and exalt our interest in the world because he had shown us of it a new side? But we do not care for those whose opinions we can predict.

But do those on whom society has concentrated its choicest means and lights, whom it has installed in its seminaries and there recited to it all its learning, repay its care by their expanding and productive genius? Or have we not seen many times the sad spectacle when a youth after ten years of public education comes out ready for his voyage of life—that the entire ship is made of rotten timber, of rotten, honeycombed, traditional timber without so much as an inch of new plank in the hull.

It is wonderful and ominous—a presumption of crime—that this word Education has so cold, so hopeless a sound. A treatise on Education, a convention for Education, a lecture, a system, affects us with slight paralysis and a certain yawning of the jaws. We are not encouraged when the Law touches it with its fingers. It is not broad enough for man. If the vast and the spiritual are beyond it and omitted, so are the practical and the needful. An education in things is not. We are all involved in the condemnation of words, an age of words. We are shut up in schools and college recitation rooms for ten or fifteen years and come out at last with a bag of wind, a memory of words, and do not know a thing. We cannot use our hands or our legs or our eyes or our arms. We do not know an edible root in the woods. We cannot tell our course by the stars nor the hour of the day by the sun. It is well if we can swim and skate. We are afraid of a horse, of a cow, of a dog, of a cat, of a spider. The Roman rule was to teach a boy nothing that he could not learn standing. It seems as if a man should learn to plant, to fish, or to hunt that he might secure his subsistence at all events and not be painful to his friends and fellowmen. It seems at least that pains should be taken to make the lessons of science as experimental as they can be. The sight of the star through a telescope is worth all the course on astronomy. The shock of the electric fluid in the elbow out-values all the theories; the taste of the nitrous oxide, the making of an artificial volcano better than volumes of chemistry.

One man seems often as much enervated by words as another by luxury. It makes little difference in what manner a man loses truth and reality. How many men can measure themselves with a ton of coals and not lose by the comparison? Over a thing power and awe hang inseparably. In every moment and change it represents Nature, a fresh, genuine, aboriginal force, but men transformed by books become impotent praters.

Our modes of Education are avowedly profane. That is they aim to expedite; to save labor; to do for masses what can never be done for masses; what must be done reverently,—one by one;—say rather, the whole world is needed for the tuition of each pupil. What else is this system of emulation and display? The advantages of it are so prompt and obvious; it is such a time-saver; it is so energetic on slow and on bad natures; and is of so easy application,—needing no sage or poet, but any tutor or schoolmaster in his first term can apply it,—that it is not strange that this *calomel* of culture should be a popular medicine. On the other hand, total abstinence from this drug, and the adoption of simple discipline and the following of Nature involves at once immense claims on the time, the thoughts, on the life of the teacher. It requires principles instead of expedients; character instead of rules. It requires time, use, insight, event,—all the great lessons and assistances of God, and only to think of using it implies piety and profoundness; and to enter on this course of discipline, is to be good and great. It is precisely analogous to the difference between the use of corporal punishment and the methods of love. It is so easy to bestow on a bad boy a blow, overpower him, and get obedience without words, that, in this world of hurry and distraction,—who can wait for the returns of reason and the conquest of self in the uncertainty, too, whether that will ever come? And yet the familiar observation of the universal compensations might suggest the fear that so summary a stop of a bad humour was more jeopardous than its continuance, it is driven into the constitution, and has infected the brain and the heart.

Our system is a system of despair. We do not believe in a power of Education. We do not think we can call out God in man and we do not try. We renounce all high aims. We sacrifice the genius of the pupil, the unknown possibilities of his nature to a neat and safe uniformity, as the Turks whitewash the costly mosaics of ancient art which the Greeks left on their temple-walls.

Well, language of this spirit is heard in the street, in the senate, in the household, and in the College. It has infected and paralysed the theory of Education.

Certainly this despondency is not in the plan of things. Not for this, not to be thus deserted and betrayed was he created and endowed the heir of Nature.

I call then our system a system of despair and I find all the correction, all the revolution that is needed and that the best spirits of this age promise, in one word,—in Hope.

Let me say before all other considerations that I think it the main guard to a correct judgment, I may say the bulwark of all that is sacred in man—not to accept degrading views. It is a primal instinct and duty of the human mind to look with a sovereign eye of hope on all things. Let us apply to this subject the same torch under whose light we have looked at all the phenomena of the Time; the infinitude, namely, of every man. Everything teaches that. One fact constitutes all my satisfaction, inspires all my trust, viz. this perpetual youth, which as long as there is any good in us we cannot get rid of. Is it not strange how long our noviciate lasts; that the period of our mastership still loiters, that, as long as we continue growing, and do not inveterate we are always subject to circumstances and do not control them? Many and many a time, we have said, how long will this false shame, how long this excess of sympathy, how long this malign sorcery of ungenial and antagonistic natures endure? Shall we not presently learn to surmount the irritations, the apathy, the gloom with which events and politics and company still torment us? But we do not mend or rise. All the circumstances, like chemical agents, act with energy on us, and we come greenhorns to every conversation. The young, the knowing, the fashionable, the practical, the political, the belle, the Pharisee, the Sadducee put us out; all overact on us and make us dumb.

Who does not see in this temporary unhappiness a deeper good? As long as we are working up to things, we are young, we are safe. As long as things change and invite our energies, we grow and advance. We learn evermore. In smooth water we discover the motion of our boat by the motion of trees and houses on shore; so the progress of the mind is proved by the perpetual change in the persons and things we daily behold. A wonderful perception of the simplicity and identity of all things is united in us with a profound ignorance and inexpectancy of all particular facts. In saying that man is always a youth, what say we but that the Universe will never let him exhaust it and know it to the end.

The simplicity of the Universe is very different from the simplicity of a machine. He who sees moral nature out and out and thoroughly knows how knowledge is acquired and charac-ter formed is a pedant. The simplicity of nature is not that which may easily be read, but is inexhaustible. The last analysis can in no wise be made. We judge of a man's wisdom by his hope, knowing that the perception of the inexhaustibleness of nature is an immortal youth. The wild fertility of nature is felt in comparing our rigid names and reputations with our fluid consciousness. We pass in the world for sects and schools, for erudition and piety, and we are all the time jejune babes. One sees very well how Pyrrhonism grew up. Every man sees that he is the middle point, that everything may be affirmed and denied of him with equal reason. He is old, he is young, he is very wise, he is altogether ignorant. He hears and feels what you say of the seraphim and of the tin pedlar. There is no permanent wise man except in the figment of the stoics. We side with the hero as we read or paint against the coward and the robber. But we have been ourselves that coward and robber, and shall be again, not in the low circumstance but in comparison with the grandeurs possible to the soul.

This fact that always we are astonished by the events of the new day, that all the accumulations of our past experience will never bring us quite even with the new fact,—what is it but a mode in which the immense wealth of nature is made known to us? Why is it that we are always green? why that we are always abashed by new emergences? Only that a sense of the Perfect accompanies, overhangs us alway.

For this reason I greet the complaints of the young and aspiring. I congratulate them on their despondency and skepticism when they ask, What shall I do? How shall I live? They are not to be pacified by pointing them to the uncultivated and pious. No: they ask, Could these bear the ordeal of cultivation and leisure? If not we do not wish to be whipped by toil all day and whipped to bed at night. These mourners shall have their reward. Let them learn this fact that their sorrows are the ebbs of a happiness as delicate and spiritual and if they are proportionate to the preceding flux so are they also the preparation of a new tide.

Let us be unhappy, let us be unquiet, ashamed, and always tormented by riddles we cannot expound, if this is all the price we pay for docility and intimacy with an Excellence which abashes us by its splendors.

I speak with diffidence on this subject because it really seems to me more embarrassing than others and I would rather offer my thoughts as conjectures than as opinions.

It seems to me that our experience does not justify the separation of education into distinct institutions, the separating education as an act or system of acts. In a wise society the education of the youth would be accomplished by the ordinary activity of the seniors. All men delight to teach what they know and to do what they can do well. The curiosity of youth meets the communicativeness of the mature and both find their account.

If we rigorously render account to ourselves of what we have owed to instruction,—deliberate, premeditated, organized instruction,—I think it is a very evanescent quantity. Like the poor man in the Arabian nights, day by day we received a bright new sequin and going at last to the drawer where we laid them, there is nothing but a bunch of dry leaves. We owe a few arts, a few rules, reading and writing the Latin grammar and the rule of three, which to me seem undeniable conveniences though very low ones in a scale where into all humanity enters. A few of our attainments, these few I speak of, we keep alive by use and affection but far the greater part of our acquisitions, bought by so much time and labor, and labor too of those at home who pinched themselves that we might want for nothing, have died in the waste of the memory. My academical hours have yielded thus much.

But my life, my work and play, my pleasure and pain, my loves and quarrels, my own reading, my business, my friend, the stranger, the observation of people pursuing their own affairs, their coldness from which I suffered, their cordiality which warmed me, the winter's frost, the summer's fruit—it is these which have taught me that lore which I cannot spare. Or rather it is these daily showers of facts under the light of that omnipresence which makes all these—illustrations of itself;—and what share has a college, a school, or an apprenticeship in this? One sees these organizations recede very fast in a true scale. Indeed always they seem to be nugatory. The college does not have more fine wits than the same population without a college, and it does not have less. It neither helps nor hinders. It is attended by this harm, that it causes those to be sent to study who ought not to go to study and those to be employed to teach who have no vocation to teach. The real advantage of the college is often the simple, mechanical one, I may call it, of a chamber and a fire which the parents will allow the boy without hesitation at Cambridge or at Andover, but do not think needful at home. Undoubtedly they give us leisure and books and the separation from secular pursuits. This is of the highest importance as preparation but it is only that. But this good is to a degree neutralized by rigorous and inflexible courses of instruction not adapted to individuals but to large numbers.

The sum of my criticism on the institutions and systems of education is that education is not there, that it quite transcends all the methods on which they most rely, that it may be procured equally well near them or far from them, but must descend from higher sources than any routine of classbooks or academical exercises can ever supply.

I believe that our own experience instructs us that the secret of education lies in respecting the pupil. It is not for you to choose what he shall know, what he shall do. It is chosen and foreordained and he only holds the key to his own secret. By your tampering and thwarting and too much governing, he may be hindered from his end and kept out of his own. But being born for himself alone, he can never be coaxed or chided or drilled into your place, form, and faculty. You have deprived him of himself and the world of a man to add another to the army of drones and blunderers and artisans which fill the towns and postpone the hope and faith of all beholders.

Respect the child. Be not too much his parent. Trespass not on his solitude. Fathers would be the fathers of the mind as well as the body of their children. Wait and see the new product of nature. Nature never rhymes her children; never makes two men precisely alike. She loves analogies but not repetitions. But a low self-love in the parent desires that his child should repeat his character and fortune; an expectation which the child, if justice is done him, will nobly disappoint. By working on the theory that this resemblance exists, we shall do what in us lies to defeat his proper promise and produce the ordinary and mediocre.

Let us wait and see what is this new creation, of what new organ the great Spirit had need when it incarnated this new Will. A new Adam in the garden, he is to name all the beasts in the field, all the gods in the sky. And jealous provision seems to have been made in his constitution that you shall not invade and contaminate him with the worn weeds of your language and opinions. It is very certain that the coming age and the departing age seldom understand each other. The old man thinks the young man has no distinct purpose for he could never get anything intelligible and earnest out of him. Perhaps the young man does not think it worth his while to explain himself to so hard and inapprehensive a confessor. Do not think that the youth has no force because he cannot speak to you seniors. For months perhaps you have got from him no reasonable word. Hark in the next room who spoke so clear and emphatic? It was he. It seems he knows how to speak to his contemporaries. Bashful or bold then, he will know how to make us seniors very unnecessary.

Let us respect the child and the youth. Let him be led up with a longsighted forbearance, and let not the sallies of his petulance or folly be checked with too much disgust or indignation or despair.

So to regard the young child, the young man, requires, no doubt, rare patience:—a patience that nothing but faith in the remedial forces of the soul can give. You see his sensualism; you see his want of those tastes and perceptions which make the power and safety of your character. Very likely. But he has something else. If he has his own vice, he has its correlative virtue. Every mind should be allowed to make its own statement in action, and its balance will appear. In these judgments, one needs that foresight which was attributed to an eminent reformer, of whom it was said, "his patience could see in the bud of the aloe the blossom at the end of a hundred years."

But I hear the outcry which replies to this suggestion— Would you verily throw up the reins of private and public discipline; would you leave the young child to the mad career of his own passions and whimsies, and call this anarchy a respect of the child's nature? I answer, Respect the child, respect him unto the end, *but also respect yourself.* Be the companion of his thought, the friend of his friendship, the lover of his virtue,—but no kinsman of his sin. Let him find you so true to yourself that you are the irreconcileable hater of his vice, and the imperturbable slighter of his trifling.

It is plain that the right education of youth requires a wise society as well as wise individuals. If all men were self-respecting, the miscreant would find his vice bruised and repelled everywhere by the walls of character. That man has not read his own biography who underestimates the tacit energy of the true and self-relying in us. The costliest influence is that of character, that plant of slowest growth, the mutual veneration which grows up between men who have seen each other in every variety of event and never knew a tie of civility or of sanctity but the faith of boyhood still sacred and fragrant.

So perfect is my confidence in that uplifting energy that I think the reason why Education is false and poor, is because there are few men,—there are no men. Let us be men, and the youth will learn of us to measure

> the ideal track of right
> More fair than heaven's broad pathway paved with stars
> Which Dion learned to measure with delight.

We are faithless. We believe the defects of all these limitary people who make up society are organic; and so society is but a hospital of incurables. We do not believe that any education, any system of philosophy, any influence of genius, will lead a mind not profound to become profound. Having settled ourselves into this infidelity our utmost skill is expended to procure alleviations, diversion, opiates. We adorn the doomed victim with manual skill, his tongue with languages, his eye with agreeable forms, his body with inoffensive and comely manners. So have we cunningly hid the tragedy of limitation and inner death which we cannot cure. Is it wonderful that society should be devoured by a secret melancholy which breaks through all the smiles, and all the gaiety and games?

But if we made less account of special skills and talents, and more of that great inner force by which a man is distinguished from the more cunning animals it is possible that we might even come to think that a mind not profound could become profound. That which is best in nature, the highest prize of life, is the perception in the private heart of access to the Universal. How is a man a man? How can he weave relations of joy and good with his brother, but because he is inviolable, alone, perfect? I stand here glad at heart of all the sympathies I can awaken and share, clothing myself with them as with a garment of shelter and beauty and yet knowing that it is not in the power of all who surround me to take from me the smallest threat I call mine. If all things are taken away I have still all things in my relation to the Eternal. But the very worth and essence of this faith consists in its impersonality. It is not mine; it is not thine. It knows not names or person or sex or accident. If I have any vantage of my brother I can lead him to feel that I do not wish to excel him but to suffice to myself. If I have any inferiority to him it becomes null, I know it not, it pains me not when I adore this Perfect which solicits me.

Is not the whole mission of genius always to reveal this gospel to men? What else do they teach—those great bards that in all ages have raised the hope and history of man and whose memory we associate with flowers and stars, with laurel and palm—what teach they but the insulation and selfsubsistency of a man; by the heart, by the soul and not by what roof he lives under, what stem he sprung from, man is great; and that what is of the heart and mind eludes all laws of property; and the child who understands Plato is already Plato so far. The costliest benefit of books is that they set us free of themselves also. The best picture makes us say, I am a painter also; the poem, I also am a poet. And is not that the charm, the highest charm of all works of art, that we feel this marble or canvas to be no prison of beauty but that it gleams with something essentially radiant and unconfinable, apprising us that the artist had risen into a region from which lustre played on all forms and objects and that whatever thing he did he had adorned? And conveying too by implication his own deep sense that no walls less broad than nature, no privilege, no preference could set limit or bound to this overflowing of God through every willing heart of man.

All social influences do daily labor to teach me the same thing. The office of conversation is to give me selfpossession. I lie torpid as a clod. Virtue, wisdom sound to me fabulous, all cant. I am an unbeliever. Then comes by a sage and gentle spirit who spreads out in order before me his own life and aims not as experience but as the good and desireable. Straightway I feel the presence of a new and yet old, a genial, a native element. I am like a southerner who having spent the winter in a polar climate feels at last the south wind blow, the rigid fibres relax, and his whole frame expand to the welcome heats. In this bland, flowing atmosphere I regain one by one my faculties, my organs: life returns to a finger, a hand, a foot. A new nimbleness, almost wings unfold at my side, and I see my right to the heaven as well as the farthest fields of the earth. The effect of the conversation resembles the effect of a beautiful voice in a church choir which insinuates itself as water into all chinks and cracks and presently floats the whole discordant choir and holds it in solution in its melody. Well, I am a ship aground; and the bard directs a river to my shoals, relieves me of these perilous rubs and strains, and at last fairly uplifts me on the waters and I put forth my sails and turn my head to the sea.

There is an upper influence in external nature too which always addresses man with the like admonition, an influence which detaches him, which does not speak to masses nor to select companies nor to a pair of friends but which speaks alone to the alone. It cannot be interpreted in human language. Nature will not have us fret and fume. She does not like our benevolence or our learning much better than she likes our frauds and wars. When we come out of the Caucus or the Bank or the Abolition Convention or the Temperance Meeting or the Literary Club into the fields and woods she says to us, "So hot? my little Sir." There is an intimation breathed by the sea and land more intelligible when our ear is open: that our life is not obedient and concordant with theirs and that when it shall be we shall understand their speech.

I say that what is called Education in the world fails because of its low aim. It aims to make amends for the Fall of Man by teaching him feats and games. It aims not to retrieve but to conceal; to save appearances; at best to solace him. It offers a jest to the sick. It rouges the cheek which is pale with death. Worst of all, it tends to insanity by amusing the man with this show of accomplishments instead of exposing to him his fatal want. Now to what end have good and great men walked in the world,—sane souls from time to time,—Moses, and Jesus, Zoroaster, and Zeno, to what end philosophy, poetry, Christianity; to what end these affecting experiences, never omitted in any private life, the influence of conversation, the relation of absolute truth which love, which terror, which need, do not fail to establish between each of us, and some of his mates, to what end this instruction of genius, of society, of external nature, if the truth is not [in] some manner to be incorporated into our schools,—that a man is not a man who does not yet draw on the eternal and universal Soul? It lies within,—it lies behind us all,—the dullest drone, the shallowest fop. Those unhappy who come into every one's thought when the question is proposed —Can a mind not profound,—by education become profound? —those unhappy persons are capable of this sentiment. They can be ennobled and made to know their relation to the All. They are capable of humility, of justice, of love, of aspiration. The clay can be tempered with this fire. If of these, then are they already on a platform that commands the sciences and arts, speech and poetry, action and grace. For whoso dwells in this perception does already anticipate those special powers which you prize so highly, just as love does justice to all the gifts of the object beloved. The lover has no talent, no skill which passes for quite nothing with his enamoured maiden, however little she may possess of related faculty. And the heart which abandons itself to the Supreme Mind finds itself related to all his works and will find a royal road to particular knowledges and powers.

I confess myself utterly at a loss in suggesting particular reforms proposed in our modes of teaching. No discretion that can be lodged with a school committee,—with the Overseers or Visiters of an Academy, a College, can at all avail to reach a wrong as deepseated and intrinsic as this. A vicious society cannot have virtuous schools. A society which wishes its youth bred to certain dexterities cannot have schools which condemn that aim. But all difficulties and perplexities solve themselves when we leave institutions and address individuals. To whatsoever upright mind,—to whatsoever beating heart I speak,—to you it is committed to educate men. By simple living,—by true speech,—by just action,—by an illimitable soul, you inspire, you correct, you instruct, you raise, you embellish all.

By your own act you teach the beholder how to do the practicable. According to the depth from which you draw your life such is the depth not only of your strenuous effort, but of your last act, of your manners, and presence. The beautiful nature of the world has here blended your happiness with your power. Work straight on in absolute duty, and you lend an arm and an encouragement to all the youth of the Universe. Consent yourself to be an organ of your highest thought, and lo! suddenly you put all men in your debt and are the fountain of an energy that goes pulsing on with waves of benefit to the borders of society, to the circumference of things.

5
Charles W. Eliot

In the halcyon days of transcendentalism Emerson had complained that America was not up to the best and brightest of her young, at least not up to those he knew in New England. America was too commercial, too materialistic for those of an idealist or spiritual persuasion. Hence, he noted, many intelligent and religious persons "withdraw themselves from the common labors and competitions of the market and the caucus, and betake themselves to a certain solitary and critical way of living." Feeling a disproportion between their faculties and the work offered them, they hold themselves aloft: "They are striking work, and crying out for something worthy to do."

Because they withdraw from the labors of the world, they are not, he admits, good citizens: they take no part in public charities or reform movements, participate neither in religious rites nor the enterprise of education. They do not even like to vote. Yet Emerson requests patience and charity for them—tolerance of these "children," who skulk and play "a mean, shiftless and subaltern part in the world." They are, he insists in his essay "Transcendentalism," really rare and gifted men; "possibly some benefit may yet accrue from them to the state."

Possibly. But the nation had no time to wait for these "rare and gifted men." America was on the make. And as the nation expanded, the political, social, and economic arrangements underwent dramatic changes. If the best and brightest of New England refused to take up the task of tending to these arrangements, then others would gladly take over.

Although we are unsure just how much to credit the influence of transcendentalism, the national influence of the New Englanders clearly waned in the years before the Civil War. True, we find New Englanders in the front ranks of every moral crusade: abolition, temperance, education, the care of the sick and infirm. But few rose to national prominence in the arena of politics, and none embodied the common will of the populace. Moreover, the obsessions of the patrician class of New England with moral purity and righteousness (e.g., Horace Mann) and with intellectual elegance (e.g., Emerson) kept them out of the front ranks of economic leadership. Content to remain largely in the reputed fields of commerce and banking, most of the "better people" had no truck with the rampant industrial development taking place beneath their noses.

Increasingly these Brahmins and their epigones in other parts of the nation became more and more isolated from what was happening in America. Throughout the country these men of superior intellect and culture, "the educated classes," formed an ineffectual, maybe even an effete class. Nothing symbolized this more clearly than the way people had come to regard Harvard College.

❋

In the 1850s Harvard experienced one of its most intense periods of public criticism. During this decade the Massachusetts House of Representatives created a special committee "to consider and report what legislation, if any, is necessary to render Harvard University more beneficial to all the people of the commonwealth."

In its final report the committee concluded that Harvard fell short of "the just expectations of the people." The chief charges: Harvard failed to provide practical instruction, and it admitted too few students. (In the eyes of astute observers, the first failure gave rise to the second.) Enrollment figures corroborated the indictment: between 1855 and 1864, population in New England increased over 16 percent; but college enrollment rose by less than 4 percent. Obviously the colleges were not supplying what the community wanted.

What were the colleges supplying? Well, they continued to turn out men of culture with supposedly disciplined intellects. But this no longer seemed adequate. The course of studies pursued had changed little over the last hundred years. (Some critics said "two hundred years.") All studied the same courses in Greek, Latin, and mathematics; and in the senior year took a course in moral philosophy. This uniform, prescribed course of studies—elementary from beginning to end—developed grammatical and mathematical discipline. But it did little to prepare young men to assume roles of leadership in the society.

By the 1860s some "modern" subjects had begun to appear at Harvard. But these were quite limited. Considered by the faculty as less educationally worthy than the classical subjects, the "modern" ones were never prescribed, but students could elect them. By 1868 the Harvard catalog announced one elective study in English in each of the sophomore, junior, and senior years. Here, students were introduced to the study of Anglo-Saxon and Chaucer. This was the only instruction offered in English literature.

The strong prejudice against modern subjects prevented expansion of course offerings, thereby forcing instruction in them to remain at an elementary level. Under these conditions, no teacher of modern subjects could become a specialist. The professor of belle lettres, for example, had responsibility for instruction in Italian, Spanish, French, and German.

Science was not even permitted to be taught in the college proper. Back in 1847, Abbott Lawrence had donated $500,000 for scientific studies at Harvard. Hoping that the college would emphasize engineering, the philanthropist saw his money used to establish a new undergraduate school, the Lawrence Scientific School. There, its director, Louis Agassiz—a comparative zoologist—fostered natural science. The students in this school were marked as second-rate scholars: admission requirements were lower than for admission to the college, the program lasted three years instead of four, and graduates received a different kind of degree, a Bachelor of Science.

Until after the Civil War, all attempts to break the hold of the classical curriculum at Harvard made as little headway as they did at other colleges. The ending of the war signaled the opening of a new period in American history. Would the college continue to take its cues from an increasingly irrelevant past, ignoring the demands of an expanding industrial nation? Might not the college simply disappear, to be replaced by one of the technical schools now being set up in all of the larger cities across the nation? These technical schools *were* supplying what the society wanted. One of the most heralded of these new institutions, the Massachusetts Institute of Technology, had recently opened its doors within shouting distance of Harvard itself.

In response to the threat of extinction, the Board of Overseers of Harvard College established a committee to study the needs of the college. In its report—issued in 1869, after two years of deliberation—the committee recognized "the vigorous technological schools everywhere springing up." Harvard, the committee insisted, must awaken from its lethargy and adopt "all the best practical methods of education, whether they have been customary or not."

The board of overseers concurred with the committee report. The stage was now set for a dramatic transformation of Harvard. The overseers sought more than simply keeping up with MIT; they wanted to surpass it, maybe even embrace it. They wanted no less than to transform Harvard College into a true university. In a college, as the committee report explained, all students are taken through the same prescribed curriculum; in a university, students have many and various departments of knowledge offered to them. "A college is a place to which a young man is *sent* to go through an appointed list of studies; a university, one to which he *goes* to get instruction and help in his pursuit of science." A university, the report continues, provides faculties in language, science, law, theology, medicine, engineering, architecture, and all the arts— adding that it also should have museums, libraries, botanic gardens, and an observatory.

The final paragraph of the report left little doubt about the direction it wished Harvard to go.

> We should all labor together to make Harvard a noble University,—a seat of learning which shall attract the best teachers and most ardent students,—a University which shall retain all the good of the past, and go forward to welcome the advancing light of the future. So may the priceless gift of our fathers be transmitted to our children, not only unimpaired, but constantly renewed and bettered. Let each generation do its part to make it more worthy of this great country, this advancing civilization.

The report came at an opportune time. It served as a guideline in the search for a new president for Harvard, someone to succeed Thomas Hill, who had resigned in September 1868. Searching for someone who could convert Harvard into a "noble university," the board of overseers finally decided upon Charles W. Eliot, a professor of chemistry at Massachusetts Institute of Technology.

❋

Charles W. Eliot was no stranger to Harvard. He had graduated from the college in 1853, following which he served on the faculty of the Lawrence Scientific School. (As an undergraduate he had studied chemistry with Josiah Cooke, a professor in the Lawrence Scientific School.)

As a faculty member, Eliot's obvious administrative skills had led President Hill to make him a part-time administrative assistant. Eliot left Harvard in 1863 after another, older man received the appointment to a professorship he had coveted. After spending two years in Europe observing the educational systems of England, France, and Germany, Eliot returned to New England. As professor of chemistry at MIT he devoted most of his attention to the methods of teaching science—organizing the laboratory method of instruction and writing the first textbook in English on inorganic chemistry.

A bona fide member of the patrician class, Eliot traced his roots in New England back to the seventeenth century. For generations the family name had been familiar to Harvard students. Charles's grandfather, a prosperous merchant, had founded the Eliot Professorship in Greek. His father had served as treasurer of the university. One cousin, Charles Eliot Norton, was an established Harvard professor; another cousin was a member of the board of overseers. Charles himself was elected an overseer in 1868.

But he was a scientist—in a school of technology! Many of the faculty and some of the overseers had serious reservations about his suitability for the presidency of Harvard. Would he attempt to transform Harvard into a technical school?

For a while it looked as if he might. In an article written while he was still a professor at MIT, and published before his final confirmation as Harvard's president, Eliot announced that the nation needed engineers, architects, chemists, superintendents of mines and works, and constructors of machinery; it needed a steady supply of men well trained in recognized principles of science and art, and well informed about established practices.

But when he came to deliver his inaugural address, the thirty-five-year-old president of Harvard began by allaying some of the fears of his critics:

> The endless controversies whether language, philosophy, mathematics, or science supplies the best mental training, whether general education should be chiefly literary or chiefly scientific, have no practical lesson for us today. This University recognizes no real antagonism between literature and science, and consents to no such narrow alternatives as mathematics or classics, science or metaphysics. We would have them all, and at their best.

Harvard was not to become a technical school. Here *all* subjects would be taught at their best: Harvard was to become a true, a noble university.

But what did this mean? For Eliot it simply meant that Harvard had to become more like the European universities. In Europe the universities were professional schools, institutions for the training of experts, who then took up the leadership roles in the society.

Yet Eliot did not want to "Europeanize" Harvard. He sought, he wrote to a friend before his inauguration, to bring the American college and the European professional school to understand and respect each other. Harvard and "the educated classes" had to realize that America no longer needed men equipped with a broad general education. America needed professionals, each equipped with the expertise appropriate to his speciality. "As a people," Eliot warned in his inaugural address, "we do not apply to mental activities the principle of division of labor; and we have but a halting faith in special training for high professional employments. The vulgar conceit that a Yankee can turn his hand to anything we insensibly carry into high places when it is preposterous and criminal. . . . This lack of faith in the . . . value of a discipline concentrated upon a single object, amounts to a national danger."

Eliot realized that the university must take its cues from the manpower demands within the existing society. This was even more necessary in America than in Europe, for here the universities had no support from an established church or an aristocracy. Here generations could, if repelled, "pass the university by." Reform of the university was a matter of survival.

Yet Eliot was after more than mere survival. He wanted to make Harvard into a great American university. And he astutely realized that by serving the various professions—improving the expertise of the practitioners, thus raising their status and power— the university could secure the support and allegiance of the professional classes. In every other civilized country, he wrote, the higher educational institutions receive support from the professions simply because of the fact that "only through them can the professions be reached." Once universities controlled entry into the professions, the thousands of ignorant and undisciplined practitioners that now abounded would be driven out. As a result, the grateful "professionals" would honor and revere the universities.

Eliot's plan to transform Harvard into a school for the training of professionals boded no subservient role for the university, simply because the university was going to determine the criteria for each profession. The university now became the agency to professionalize the various occupations. In constructing this new function, Eliot moved the university—and, ultimately, the total school system—into a central position in American society. Henceforth universities would actually recruit, train, and certify the leaders and guardians of society's progress. America's leaders were to acquire their expertise, their knowledge, their licenses, and their power from schools.

*

"We mean to build here, securely and slowly, a university in the largest sense" prophesied Eliot at the first commencement over which he presided, in 1870. Within three years he had reformed the law school and the divinity school, reconstructed the medical school, and created a new graduate school of arts and sciences.

In 1869 the three professors of the law school—*the* law school—signed a report that began: "The condition of the school at the present time is eminently satisfactory." The new president thought otherwise. The school admitted students without any evidence of academic requirements; the classes were not graded; students entered at any time and attended the lectures then in progress; the school never examined the students, who left after eighteen months of lectures—with a degree.

Eliot insisted that a school for training professionals adhere to three inviolable principles: high admission standards, a graded course of study, and rigorous standards of examination for the awarding of degrees. By adhering to these principles a school gained credibility. People respected and had faith in its graduates. Initially, enrollments might drop, and they did. But, in time, the quality of the school would attract more students than it could handle. It did.

By installing his own appointee, Christopher Langdell, as the first dean of the law school, Eliot got his written examinations, a progressive three-year course of studies, and—as an added bonus— a new method of instruction. Langdell introduced the widely acclaimed case-study method, which other law schools throughout the country soon copied. Finally, in response to Eliot's prodding, the law school in 1893 required a college degree for admission, making it the first graduate school of law in the nation.

Enrollment figures justified Eliot's reforms. By the 1880s the number of students studying law at Harvard had risen again to

120—equaling the enrollment of 1869. By 1909, the year Eliot retired, the school had 684 students and a faculty of 17.

Eliot found it more difficult to reform the medical school. When he asked the medical faculty in 1870 if it would be possible to substitute an hour's written examination for graduation in place of the five-minute oral exam then administered, the answer came promptly from the head of the faculty: "Written examinations are impossible in the Medical School. A majority of the students cannot write well enough."

This was understandable. The school had no requirements for admission; a young man did nothing more than register his name and pay a fee. The program consisted of lectures and clinical demonstrations which a student attended for sixteen weeks, although he had to wait three years for his degree. In the final oral examination—the only exam he took—a student who successfully answered four questions out of five got his medical degree.

Through tenacity and patience, President Eliot imposed upon a long-time, independent medical faculty, all of whom were part-time professors, his principles for a professional training program: stiff entrance examinations; a progressive three-year course for all; written examinations, all of which must be passed, at the end of each year.

The divinity school—which when Eliot arrived consisted of "three mystics, three sceptics, and three dyspeptics"—underwent similar reforms under the firm, determined guidance of the president. Although originally the school had required a Bachelor's degree for admission, it had gradually begun to admit people on the basis of examinations—which grew weaker and weaker. In 1869 the divinity school announced that a knowledge of Latin and Greek were no longer requirements for admission. "There is reason to hope," Eliot commented sarcastically, "that the school has now touched bottom." Not unexpectedly, then, the school restored the admission requirements of Latin and Greek the next year; and it set up periodic examinations of all students, as well as final examinations for the awarding of degrees.

Eliot's construction of education for the professions included more than a concern for rigorous standards and a graded course of studies. Perhaps even more significant for the history of American education was his conception of the content of professional education. He abhorred the shallow pragmatism that stressed ability to perform. He denied that practitioners make the best professors of law, or medicine, or theology—or any profession. All his reforms at Harvard moved the faculties of the professional schools away from practical preparation for a craft toward the study of the scientific principles and theories that underlay practice.

The divinity school, for example, Eliot construed as "an institution for the scientific collation of the vast body of various learning which is grouped around theology." Likewise with the medical school. In opposition to Henry Bigelow, head of the medical faculty, who warned that pure science might distract medical students from the practical and the useful, Eliot construed the medical school as "an institution for the teaching of medical science instead of one which an association of practitioners conduct." Eliot's views triumphed, of course, as witnessed by his appointment of a new dean of the medical school in 1883: Henry P. Bowditch, a physiologist.

When Eliot became convinced, late in his presidency, that the field of business had become a highly intellectual operation, with scientific principles underlying its practice, he fought for, and got, a graduate school of business administration—converting the "oldest of the arts" into the youngest of the professions.

One of the most dramatic educational consequences of this scientific ideal of professional education was the revolution it precipitated in instructional practices and procedures. In his inaugural address Eliot had bluntly declared that "the actual problem to be solved is not what to teach, but how to teach." Few then understood what he had in mind. But thirty years later, the meaning was clearly embodied in the instructional process at Harvard —and in most institutions of learning in America.

When Eliot came on the scene in 1869, almost all instruction was expository: through lectures and recitations teachers imparted information to students. The scientific idea of professional training replaced this goal with the notion of developing skills—skills of observation, of recording, of reasoning; and skills for expressing ideas of significance in a given field or profession. Lectures and recitations could never develop such skills. New modes of instruction were called for. They soon appeared: laboratories, clinics, seminars, conferences, field observations, written reports, and elaborate demonstrations. This new approach to teaching, with its emphasis on the development of skills, meant that students had to engage in activities; they could not passively absorb information imparted to them. With the development of these new methods, the material needs of a school sharply increased. The new modes of instruction required more laboratory equipment and supplies; enormous collections of books in numerous libraries, plus great collections in every branch of natural history—stuffed animals, dried plants, fossils, rocks and minerals; museums to house archeological artifacts and museums for the fine arts; botanical gardens full of trees, shrubs, and flowers.

The purpose of all this—the collections, the equipment, the arrangements—was to improve instruction. Through them the university teachers could shape the future professionals, disciplining their powers to observe, reason, and express, thus preparing them for leadership positions in their chosen fields of endeavor.

A second educational consequence of Eliot's scientific ideal of professional education was the inexorable stimulus it gave to research. Research now became one of the essential roles of a university. In Eliot's construction of the function of a university, research and teaching became welded together inextricably. The university's primary task was to teach; research simply made advanced teaching possible—it broadened and deepened the material to be taught. Nowhere did Eliot more clearly express this than in his defense of the graduate school of arts and sciences he created in 1872.

Eliot construed the graduate school—he called it the "true university"—as a professional school, "for teachers, men of letters, journalists, naturalists, physicists, chemists, and mathematicians." Initially some of the faculty expressed the fear that a graduate school might weaken the college. Not so, Eliot replied firmly: "It will strengthen the college. As long as our teachers regard their work as simply giving so many courses for undergraduates, we shall never have first class teaching here. If they have to teach graduate students as well as undergraduates, they will regard their subjects as infinite, and keep up that constant investigation which is necessary for first-class teaching."

The graduate school, as Eliot knew it would, functioned as the research arm of the university. And as research deepened and broadened the knowledge in all fields, the subject-matter departments within the university became larger and more complex. New fields of study came into being: comparative literature, international law, social ethics, meteorology, paleontology, genetics. In time whole new departments emerged: a department of government sprang from history; philosophy begat economics, psychology, and sociology. Instruction in the fine arts, first offered in 1874, grew into the Department of Fine Arts replete with its own Fogg Museum. The Department of Architecture, created in 1906, had its beginning in a single course first offered in 1893. The physics department revived the study of astronomy in 1891. Twelve years later the astronomers had their own observatory.

Eliot gloried in this expansion. Frequently he invoked Ezra Cornell's famous remark: "I would found an institution in which one may study anything." Nothing short of this, Eliot would add, is the true aim of a university: "It should cover the whole field of human knowledge, and be able to bring its students to the very frontiers of original scholarship." But since the graduate school was a professional school, scholarship and research remained subservient to teaching. The primary task of the graduate school was to discipline and train the future leaders who could use these skills in their chosen occupations. Through teaching, the university converted knowledge into power—and the great desideratum of education today, Eliot wrote, is "the development of power in action."

The rise in enrollment at Harvard during Eliot's forty-year tenure as president would seem to corroborate the claim that Harvard was now supplying the community with what it wanted. In 1869 Eliot had taken over an institution that enrolled 383 students; by 1909 Harvard had 3,500 students. Yet Eliot had done more than transform Harvard College into a great university. He had created a model, an exemplar, imitated—with varying degrees of success—by most of the other American institutions of higher learning.

But what about Harvard College? What was the program for undergraduates? What changes had Eliot wrought here? Quite simply, Eliot had professionalized it, too.

*

In a retrospective evaluation in 1894 Eliot declared that the development of the elective system "has proved to be the most generally useful piece of work which this university has ever executed." Through the elective system Eliot revolutionized undergraduate education at Harvard—indeed, throughout the land, since other institutions followed his lead in the academic procession of educational change.

When Eliot became president in 1869, Harvard College prescribed most of the studies for all students. He moved slowly but deliberately to abolish the prescription of studies, finishing the task in the 1890s. Since electives had existed before, Eliot's promotion of them did not in itself constitute a revolution. What did, was his insistence that modern subjects introduced via the elective system were of equal educational worth to the traditional studies. Eliot simply denied that there were any *essential* studies. He was, he admitted, "fundamentally a sceptic as to the necessity of any subject whatever as an element in the education of a gentleman and a scholar."

This doctrine of the equivalence of studies emerged from Eliot's recognition that the college could no longer "force subjects of study, or particular kinds of mental discipline, upon unwilling generations." He felt that Harvard had inflicted "gratuitous injury" on itself, and on the nation, by refusing to grant the educational worth and the disciplinary value of the modern languages, literatures, and sciences.

To secure acceptance of his radical ideas about the equivalence of all studies, Eliot concocted a new, persuasive definition of liberal studies: "all studies which are pursued in the scientific spirit for truth's sake and as a means of intellectual discipline." The definition itself was not original; educators had long construed the liberal arts as those that "enlarged the mind and disciplined the intellect." What was original was Eliot's contention that according to this definition the modern subjects were liberal studies.

Each age, Eliot argued, takes the best intellectual and moral materials existing in its day and makes them the substance of a liberal education. Inevitably, then, the content of a liberal education changes over time. The original seven liberal arts, consisting of the trivium—grammar, rhetoric, and logic—and the quadrivium—arithmetic, geometry, music, and astronomy—changed in the eleventh century when metaphysics and theology replaced most of the quadrivium. Then, in the sixteenth century, Greek became one of the liberal arts. Today, he concluded, our best intellectual and moral materials are the modern subjects: English, German, French, history, political economy, and natural science. They therefore merit inclusion as liberal studies.

Moreover, Eliot insisted, the program of studies offered by the college must contain more than surveys or elementary introductions to each subject—otherwise these studies would lose their disciplinary value. He believed that each subject matter had disciplinary value. Through each one students could learn how to observe, record, reason, and make significant claims *within* a specific field of inquiry. To secure such intellectual discipline each subject matter had to have an orderly and consecutive schedule of courses "rising from the elementary comprehensive course through courses of greater and greater difficulty."

Eliot thus revolutionized the college curriculum by turning the established notion of electives on its head. In place of a course of study prescribed *by the faculty,* with a minimal degree of student freedom to elect certain less worthwhile subjects, a liberal education under Eliot's regime became something constructed completely *by the student,* out of the myriad of "liberal studies" the college offered.

The very act of "freeing" higher education from faculty control transformed, as Eliot knew it would, liberal education into a program of professional training. In the inaugural address of 1869 Eliot had lauded the elective system because it gave the student the freedom to discover his own natural talents, the talents he must develop for his life's work: "When the revelation of his own peculiar taste and capacity comes to a young man, let him reverently give it welcome, thank God, and take courage. Thereafter he knows his way to happy, enthusiastic work, and, God willing, to usefulness and success." Through the elective system each student could now select those studies that best prepared him for his future profession. The college student who knows what his profession is to be will, Eliot explained, find that some of his college studies are practically prescribed for him: the young man destined for engineering will "inevitably" choose a large amount of mathematics and physics during his college years; the one destined for medicine will study chemistry, physics, biology, French, and German on the way to his first degree.

Yet, most college students do not know from the start what calling they are to follow. For the student who has no clue to the profession he will take up, the elective system allows him, "wisely," to be guided in his selection of college studies by "his individual tastes, inclinations, and capacities." If a student follows this guidance, Eliot comments, "it will probably turn out, when he chooses his profession, that he has already taken in college subjects related to his future professional work, for the wise choice of the profession will be based upon the same consideration of his tastes and powers, which determined his choice of college studies." Then, hammering home this identification of a liberal education with professional training, he concludes: "In both kinds of choice, the wise choices will rely on the same sort of guidance."

Eliot admitted to qualms about the dangers of overspecialization, confessed fears about capricious and irresponsible selection of courses, and even acknowledged that the elective system might lead to social alienation since it intermixed students in all courses. Yet he found that even these unwanted consequences vindicated the wisdom of the elective system. For even these choices, taken freely, helped a student to discover what kind of life's work best suited him. Discovering and preparing for one's future occupation was what education was all about.

Eliot used the career of his own son, Charles, to justify the elective system. As a college student Charles had no idea what his profession would be, and his choice of electives appeared incoherent. Yet, his father noted, he chose courses remarkably appropriate to his later needs as a professional landscape artist. Continually Eliot pointed out how a liberal education could and did terminate in a profession; at the same time he used the job descriptions of existing professions to demonstrate that the preparatory education Harvard College offered was appropriate—and liberal.

One consequence of the elective system Eliot frequently pointed to was the professionalization of scholarship. As long as the college curricula had been prescribed, professors had had little to stimulate them to broad and deep intellectual attainments. The elective system changed all that. Now each professor had advanced students with whom he could pursue and share investigations. Each could now become a specialist, a scholar and researcher advancing and disseminating knowledge in his own area of specialization.

The elective system also furthered the professionalization of scholarship by enabling universities to provide complete graduate-training programs for future professors. This permitted universities to raise the standards of selection in hiring professors; colleges now looked for professors who had already demonstrated in graduate school their capacity for persistent, productive, scholarly work. This growth of professionalism among professors in turn led to the creation of scholarly associations and societies which brought together all the scholars in their specialities from the universities and scientific establishments across the country.

The American scholar had arrived. He was a professional—systematically produced in and for the higher institutions of education.

＊

During his tenure in office Eliot often confronted critics who accused him of being an enemy to the liberal arts college. To one such critic he replied: "The task before me during the first twenty years of my presidency was to develop a university out of a college without doing the college anything but good, and just that is what I believe to have done."

From Eliot's angle of vision he had done the college good. Through the elective system he had "professionalized" liberal education—making the college a central institution in preparing leaders for American society. Moreover, through his efforts the college had become a crucial link in the hierarchical system of American education. At Harvard he had insisted upon requiring the A.B. degree for admission to graduate schools, and by 1901 the three main professional schools—divinity, law, and medicine—also required a Bachelor's degree. Other universities followed Harvard's example. Forever after, undergraduate education in Harvard—in America—remained subservient to the graduate schools.

President Eliot's dream of a complete hierarchical system of

American education extended beyond the walls of Harvard University. As early as his 1869 inaugural address he had declared that the whole structure of education needed rebuilding from the foundations. At that time he lamented the fact that the American college had to supplement the work of the American school, supplying whatever elementary instruction the secondary schools failed to give. The preparatory schools, he maintained, should enrich and enlarge their course of studies. Intuitively he realized that the pressure for reform had to come from the colleges: "Schools follow universities, and will be what universities make of them." Just as he had enthralled the curriculum of the college to the graduate schools, Eliot now sought to annex that of the secondary schools to the colleges.

Eliot's interest in the entire educational system sprang directly from his overriding concern to secure power and influence for the educated classes. To do this he would educate them as experts—professionals with a grounding in the scientific bases of their fields of specialization. For such an education to take hold, the students had to be adequately prepared. The preparation must begin in the secondary schools, or even, Eliot sometimes argued, in the elementary schools. In order to force the secondary schools to enlarge and enrich their curricula, Harvard began to broaden its entrance requirements to the college; within a decade of Eliot's inauguration the college had added entrance requirements in physical geography, English composition, French or German, and physical science.

In this battle to raise college-entrance requirements the chief obstacle Eliot encountered was the requirement of Greek. For, as long as the college insisted upon its incoming freshmen knowing Greek, the secondary schools could spend little time bringing students to a level of proficiency in any other subject-matter field. Eliot continually fought for options to the Greek requirement, declaring that it was "the greatest question of university policy which has arisen is likely to arise, in this generation." Most of the opposition came from the faculty, who viewed any change in the Greek requirement as a lowering of standards, or at least a diminution of "tone." But Eliot had the force of public opinion outside the university on his side, and through persistence he finally, in 1886, secured options to the Greek requirement. In 1894 the faculty further liberalized entrance requirements.

At the same time he battled the resistance of his faculty to changes at Harvard, Eliot sought to restrain the "reckless" changes taking place in other universities. While he was trying to raise admission standards, they were actually lowering them. Eliot particularly opposed the "certificate" system. With this a university admitted, without examination, graduates possessing a certificate from a high school approved by an inspector (usually a university faculty member). Begun at the University of Michigan in 1870, this system spread throughout the state universities of the Midwest. Eliot castigated this "dangerous experiment" as a blatant lowering of standards. He denounced the inspection system as totally inadequate; one faculty member spent one day in the high school every three years.

Other than issue scathing denunciations, what could Eliot do about the admission requirements of other institutions? A new strategy was called for.

In the late 1880s, after obtaining the new admission requirements at his own institution, Eliot set about to influence directly the program of studies in American secondary schools. In his bid to become a national educational leader of secondary education Eliot chose as his forum the recently established National Education Association (NEA), the professional organization of American schoolteachers and administrators.

At the 1888 convention of the NEA Eliot spoke to the division composed of school administrators on the topic "Can School Programs Be Shortened and Enriched?" His answer was "yes, they can"—if the elementary schools took up some of the instruction presently given in the secondary schools—English grammar and literature, for example, and arithmetic and history. The students in the elementary schools did not have enough "meat" in their diet, the president of Harvard told his audience. He ended with some practical recommendations to make the lower schools more efficient: teachers should abandon the goal of complete mastery of subject matter; they should stop making children repeat grades; and the schools should have longer hours and shorter vacations.

Later, in another speech to the NEA on the same topic, Eliot

issued specific curriculum recommendations to the elementary or
grammar schools. They could shorten their programs by eliminating the esoteric parts of arithmetic, grammar, and geography; as
well as by abandoning completely the subject of bookkeeping
which, as taught, had no relation whatsoever to the real world of
business. With the time thus saved, Eliot claimed, the grammar
schools could *enrich* their programs by adding algebra, geometry, a
foreign language, and science.

If the elementary schools shortened and enriched their program of studies, then what about the secondary school program?
Eliot returned to the NEA convention in 1890 to tell the members
of that professional association that the secondary schools were the
weakest part of the educational system in the nation. "No state in
the American union possesses anything which can be properly
called a system of secondary education," he announced. The
existing collection of public high schools, endowed academies,
college preparatory departments, and private schools conformed to
no common standards and were under no common control. The
rural areas completely lacked public high schools, while the urban
high schools languished under control of local committees that
rarely looked beyond the immediate community interests. In
Massachusetts, Eliot noted, where supposedly the best public
secondary schools existed, fewer than one in ten maintained a
course of study that prepared students to enter Harvard College or
any other college in the state.

To overcome this nationwide gap between the colleges and the
"tolerably organized" common or elementary school system, Eliot
insisted upon two changes: more schools; and higher, common
standards in the existing schools.

Eliot had little to say about how new schools were to be
created, except to recommend the strategy of consolidation of
school districts to create sufficient support for one secondary
school. Here, he sagely noted, some form of public transportation
was a necessary ingredient. But with regard to the matter of
uniform high standards, he was quite explicit, strongly recommend-
ing more state supervision and control over the secondary school
curriculum. He cited two examples: Minnesota, where a state high
school board inspected all high schools; and the examination
system set up by the New York Board of Regents.

Eliot, of course, dreamed of something more grandiose than state-by-state supervision and control of the secondary school curriculum. Couldn't the National Education Association itself secure *national* high uniform standards?

The opportunity came at the 1892 convention. After four years of studying the matters of uniform standards and college-admission requirements, the Committee on Secondary Education of the NEA recommended the creation of a new committee! Made up of ten representatives from both colleges and secondary schools, this "blue ribbon" committee was to formulate "a plan for complete adjustment between secondary schools and colleges." As its chairman, this committee of ten had the national educational leader, Charles W. Eliot.

❉

Under the forceful direction of Eliot, the Committee of Ten completed its work and submitted its report within the space of one year. The U.S. commissioner of education, William T. Harris, who was a member of the committee, called it "the most important educational document ever published in this country." He had it quickly and widely, and freely, distributed by the U.S. Bureau of Education to schoolmen, school-board members, and other interested parties. In 1904 the commissioner corroborated his own original estimate of the significance of the report: "The scheme of studies recommended by the Committee of Ten as Secondary School studies to the National Education Association has become the model for all secondary or high schools, public and private."

The bulk of the report was made up of individual reports from nine different conferences. The Committee of Ten had chosen ten representatives from various colleges and schools for each one of these conferences. In December 1892 these representatives met at various locations around the country and for three days deliberated on the question of the appropriate secondary school program in a specific subject-matter area. The conference on Latin and Greek took place at the University of Michigan, that on English at Vassar College, the University of Wisconsin hosted the conference on history (and government and political economy).

Eliot received all the conference reports and, as chairman, compiled a final report for the council of the NEA. There was, he noted, remarkable unity in the conference reports. But the uniformity was really not so remarkable at all, since every conference had focused on a list of specific questions drawn up by the Committee of Ten under the guidance of its chairman. These questions about the organization and arrangement of studies were, not surprisingly, the very ones Eliot had been raising in his various appearances before the NEA for the past five years: What subjects should the secondary schools teach? When should they teach them? How should they teach them? And how long should they teach them? These questions set up a framework within which each conference inevitably came up with the uniform program of secondary school studies that Eliot had ordained.

In 1892, just three days after his appointment as chairman of the Committee of Ten, and *before* the committee had held any meetings, Eliot delivered an address to the NEA entitled "Undesirable and Desirable Uniformity in the Schools." This speech clearly presaged the message that would come later in the report from the Committee of Ten. Desirable uniformity, Eliot explained, was uniform subjects with predetermined topics, all beginning at the same grade level, with a uniform time allocation for each subject and with predetermined, uniform methods of instruction. He believed, he told his audience, that the best way to bring about such desirable uniformity was through the pronouncement of "judicious experts" acting under the sanction of a national association such as the NEA. This, he felt, would lead to adoption by leading cities and institutions, followed by many others in all parts of the country.

The Committee of Ten supplied the judicious experts, the nine conferences prescribed the desirable uniformity. All the conferences, as requested, stipulated the topics to be covered in each subject, how much time to allot to each subject, and how it should be taught. Significantly, all the conferences followed Eliot in conflating liberal and professional education. One of the questions put to each conference was: "Should the subject be treated differently for pupils who are going to college, for those who are going to a scientific school, and for those who, presumably, are going to neither?" This question, as Eliot announced in his final report, "is answered unanimously in the negative by the conferences." The Committee of Ten agreed that "every subject which is taught at all in a secondary school should be taught in the same way and to the same extent to every pupil so long as he pursues it, no matter what the probable destination of the pupil may be, or at what point his education is to cease."

Just as Eliot had converted undergraduate liberal education into professional training, so now he—with the support of nine judicious experts—declared that there was no difference between college preparatory studies and those studies that prepared for life. All studies prepared for life, for one's probable future destiny.

The report of the Committee of Ten provided a detailed plan for "closing the gap" between the colleges and the elementary schools. By following such a plan the secondary schools could ensure that every youth who entered college would have spent four years studying a few subjects thoroughly. It would make no difference which of the nine subject areas he studied—all were considered equivalent in educational rank for admission to college. Any combination of these studies would yield "four years of strong and effective mental training," provided the student pursued them for the prescribed length of time and provided they were taught according to the prescribed methods.

In spite of this blueprint for a national system of secondary education, Eliot recognized that the gap was not yet completely closed. The original problem had been twofold. On the one side were the state universities that admitted students simply on the basis of graduation from a "certified" high school. Here the proposals of the Committee of Ten, when adopted, would raise the academic standards of the "certified" schools and so supply better-educated students to the state universities. The other side of the problem was the admission policies of the private colleges and universities. Located in the East, primarily, these institutions admitted students on the basis of examinations. Here, Eliot reasoned, the only way to secure uniform high standards of admission was to initiate some system of cooperation in entrance examinations among the various colleges and universities.

Thus, the year after submitting his report to the NEA, Eliot shifted his attention to the eastern regional associations of colleges and secondary schools. In 1894 he made a proposal for a cooperative "board of examiners" to the Association of Colleges of New England, but nothing came of it. He continued promoting the idea, however, and finally succeeded in influencing the regional association of the Middle Atlantic states. At its 1899 meeting, the Association of Colleges and Secondary Schools of the Middle Atlantic States and Maryland, with Eliot prominently in attendance, adopted a plan for a College Entrance Examination Board (CEEB). The board was formally organized the following year, and five years later Eliot dragged a hesitant Harvard University into its membership. "The Harvard faculty moves slowly," Eliot wrote, "but it moves."

Eliot seized another opportunity to secure uniform high standards in the nation's secondary schools when he became, in 1905, the first chairman of the board of trustees of the newly established Carnegie Foundation for the Advancement of Teaching. One of the ways the foundation sought to "advance teaching" was to pension off the older, and more recalcitrant, college professors—making room for new, young professors, more open to innovation and change. The board of trustees decided to pay the pensions directly to the colleges, who would then dispense them to the retiring professors. But before they could allocate the funds, the trustees had to decide what, exactly, qualified as a college. They decided that a college must have at least six full-time professors, a four-year liberal arts course, and must require a high school education for admission.

What counted as a high school education? The trustees decided that it should consist of 16 units of 120 classroom clock hours in one subject each. As to the subjects making up these sixteen units, they indicated their general agreement with the subjects identified by the College Entrance Examination Board—a list of subjects not noticeably different from the list set out by Eliot's Committee of Ten.

Since most colleges eagerly sought Carnegie pensions, they set about, as Eliot knew they would, to pressure the high schools to adopt the "Carnegie Unit" as the basis for curriculum construction. Most high schools complied, and within a short time practically all high schools measured their work in terms of the unit defined by the Carnegie Foundation.

✳

Although Eliot continually talked about closing the "gap" between the elementary schools and the colleges, it would be incorrect to view his calculated actions to secure uniform high standards in secondary schools solely as the effort of a self-interested college president endeavoring to obtain a ready supply of qualified students for his institution. He was concerned with recruitment, but more important was his genuine desire to enhance equality of opportunity in American education. "The essence of freedom," he said, "is in equality of opportunities, and the opportunity of education should be counted the most precious of all." Many students—and their parents—never realized that they might go to college when they began high school. Better then to keep the doors open by providing all with a course of studies that would prepare for college.

And yet it is even more incorrect to cast Eliot as one who saw the high school solely as an agency for college preparation. In the report of the Committee of Ten he wrote: "The secondary schools of the United States, taken as a whole, do not exist for the purpose of preparing boys and girls for colleges. Only an insignificant percentage of the graduates of these schools go to colleges or scientific schools." Then he went on to say: "Their main function is to prepare for the duties of life that small proportion of all the children in the country—a proportion small in number, but very important to the welfare of the nation—who show themselves able to profit by an education prolonged to the eighteenth year, and whose parents are able to support them while they remain so long at school."

Ultimately, for Eliot, the importance of the secondary schools was political—their graduates had a vital role to play in the working of the American democracy. Their function, so important to the welfare of the nation, was to pave and smooth the way for the professionals, the experts who were to assume the burden of decision making in the emerging American civilization.

Eliot elaborates this notion fully in his speech "The Democratic Function of Education." In the conduct of private corporations and business, Eliot notes, people recognize that the employment of experts is "the only rational and successful method": no one would think of building a bridge, constructing a dam, setting up a power station, or establishing a cotton mill without relying absolutely on the advice of intelligent experts. So it must be in our governmental affairs, declares Eliot. Municipal, state, and national governments must employ experts and abide by their decisions. "Such complicated subjects as taxation, finance, and public works cannot be wisely managed by popular assemblies or their committees, or by executive offices who have no special acquaintance with these most difficult subjects." Then, referring to the experiences of the last twenty years, Eliot concludes that it demonstrates that "popular assemblies have become absolutely incapable of dealing wisely with any of these great subjects."

If we are to have a truly expert society, one in which the decision-making authority rests in the hands of the professional specialists, then, Eliot insists, people must learn to acquiesce to the authority of experts. This is the function of popular education, especially secondary education. In schools, especially high schools, where the student learns exact observation and how to reason, he "will naturally acquire a respect for these powers when exhibited by others in fields unknown to him." And then, too, he will learn how hard it is to determine a fact, to state it accurately, and to draw from it the justly limited inference—coming thereby to recognize that "he himself cannot do these things, except in a very limited field." Thus popular education, Eliot assures us, will dispel the "mischievous delusion" that a Yankee can turn his hand to anything. Once his education reveals the great range of knowledge and capacity needed in the business of the world, the student will come to respect capacities he sees developed in great diversity in other people. Through his education, Eliot concludes, the student "will come to respect and confide in the expert in every field of human activity."

*

The spell of Charles W. Eliot is broad and deep in American education. He was the pioneer educational statesman, the principal architect of our present educational system. Moreover, through his leadership in creating graduate professional schools, in conflating liberal studies with professional training at the college level, and in equating high school preparation for college with preparation for life, Eliot "professionalized" American education, creating thereby its dominant ideology: the proper function of the school system is to determine the "probable destinies" of the young.

Eliot always thought that the actual decision about a student's probable destiny should be postponed as long as possible, thus ensuring the maximum equality of opportunity for all. At first he fought to prevent the high schools from making such a decision, as is clear from his report for the Committee of Ten. But, later, when more and more of the young began to attend high schools, Eliot went along with the demand to introduce vocational studies into the high school curriculum—thus tacitly conceding that the course of study a student took in high school would determine his probable destiny. The *elementary schools,* he argued, had to take on the job of sorting people out for their probable destinies. The elementary schools had "no function more important," Eliot proclaimed at a 1908 meeting of the Society for the Promotion of Industrial Education.

Now the task of sorting people out for their probable destinies is not an educational activity—it is an administrative one. Inevitably, then, Americans have come to construe their educational enterprise in the language and concepts of administration. They talk about the content and the process of education in terms of *points, credits, units,* and *grades,* as well as *class periods, clock hours, courses* and *semesters taken, spent,* or *endured.* Because education is now construed this way, the administrative structure has come to determine American educational policies and dictate the American educational process. Anyone who seeks to bring about educational change finds himself locked into a hierarchical educational system. The would-be innovator must always accommodate—sometimes compromise—to the administrative "realities" of requirements, standards, and expectations imposed from above: the expectations of the secondary school dominate the elementary school, those of the college dominate the secondary school, the graduate school dominates the college, and the world of work dominates the entire system by insisting upon diplomas, degrees certificates, transcripts, and records for entry into the marketplace.

The administrative educational system he did so much to create has gone far toward creating that expert society Eliot envisioned throughout his entire career. Through the administration of bureaucratized standards it controls entry into occupations and provides guarantees to the public that the holders of its diplomas and certificates have "fulfilled all requirements" and so are bona fide experts. The system has sorted out, trained, and helped the best and the brightest to gain positions of influence and power in our society.

But in recent decades we witness a growing disillusionment with the distribution of power in our expert society. The arrogance of those in power, their refusal to admit to human fallibility, has annoyed, dismayed, and angered many. The experts in government lead the nation into tragic and senseless wars. The experts in industry have polluted our environment and depleted our natural resources. The experts in business have screwed the consumers.

By professionalizing it and creating administrative arrangements that sort and prepare people for their probable destinies, Charles Eliot cast the educational system into the center of American civilization. Which is one of the reasons why, when people become critical of that civilization, they turn on the schools.

WORKS AND COMMENTARY

Many of Eliot's speeches and addresses on education are contained in two collections: *American Contributions to Civilization and Other Essays* (New York, 1897) and *Educational Reform: Essays and Addresses* (New York, 1898). Some of these essays are also in *Charles W. Eliot: The Man and His Beliefs*, 2 vols. (New York, 1926), edited by William A. Neilson; and in *Charles W. Eliot and Popular Education* (New York: Teachers College Bureau of Publications, 1961), edited by Edward A. Krug.

There are a number of biographies of Eliot; the one by Henry James is excellent: *Charles W. Eliot: President of Harvard University, 1869–1909*, 2 vols. (Boston: 1930). The most recent and best biography is Hugh Hawkins, *Between Harvard and America* (New York: Oxford University Press, 1972).

The standard history of Harvard is Samuel Eliot Morison's

Three Centuries of Harvard (Cambridge: Harvard University Press, 1936). Lawrence Veysey's *The Emergence of the American University* (Chicago: University of Chicago Press, 1965) is a superb history of the American university during its formative period.

The selection that follows is from Eliot's *Educational Reform: Essays and Addresses*, pages 401–18.

The Function of Education in Democratic Society

What the function of education shall be in a democracy will depend on what is meant by democratic education.

Too many of us think of education for the people as if it meant only learning to read, write, and cipher. Now, reading, writing, and simple ciphering are merely the tools by the diligent use of which a rational education is to be obtained through years of well-directed labor. They are not ends in themselves, but means to the great end of enjoying a rational existence. Under any civilized form of government, these arts ought to be acquired by every child by the time it is nine years of age. Competent teachers, or properly conducted schools, now teach reading, writing, and spelling simultaneously, so that the child writes every word it reads, and, of course, in writing spells the word. Ear, eye, and hand thus work together from the beginning in the acquisition of the arts of reading and writing. As to ciphering, most educational experts have become convinced that the amount of arithmetic which an educated person who is not some sort of computer needs to make use of is but small, and that real education should not be delayed or impaired for the sake of acquiring a skill in ciphering which will be of little use either to the child or to the adult. Reading, writing, and arithmetic, then, are not the goal of popular education.

The goal in all education, democratic or other, is always receding before the advancing contestant, as the top of a mountain seems to retreat before the climber, remoter and higher summits appearing successively as each apparent summit is reached. Nevertheless, the goal of the moment in education is always the acquisition of knowledge, the training of some permanent capacity for productiveness or enjoyment, and the development of character. Democratic education being a very new thing in the world, its attainable objects are not yet fully perceived. Plato taught that the laborious classes in a model commonwealth needed no education whatever. That seems an extraordinary opinion for a great philosopher to hold; but, while we wonder at it, let us recall that only one generation ago in some of our Southern States it was a crime to teach a member of the laborious class to read. In feudal society education was the privilege of some of the nobility and clergy, and was one source of the power of these two small classes. Universal education in Germany dates only from the Napoleonic wars; and its object has been to make intelligent soldiers and subjects, rather than happy freemen. (In England the system of public instruction is but twenty-seven years old.) Moreover, the fundamental object of democratic education—to lift the whole population to a higher plane of intelligence, conduct, and happiness—has not yet been perfectly apprehended even in the United States. Too many of our own people think of popular education as if it were only a protection against dangerous superstitions, or a measure of police, or a means of increasing the national productiveness in the arts and trades. Our generation may, therefore, be excused if it has but an incomplete vision of the goal of education in a democracy.

I proceed to describe briefly the main elements of instruction and discipline in a democratic school. As soon as the easy use of what I have called the tools of education is acquired, and even while this familiarity is being gained, the capacities for productiveness and enjoyment should begin to be trained through the progressive acquisition of an elementary knowledge of the external world. The democratic school should begin early—in the very first grades—the study of nature; and all its teachers should, therefore, be capable of teaching the elements of physical geography, meteorology, botany, and zoölogy, the whole forming in the child's mind one harmonious sketch of its complex environment. This is a function of the primary-school teacher which our fathers never thought of, but which every passing year brings out more and more clearly as a prime function of every instructor of little children. Somewhat later in the child's progress toward maturity the great sciences of chemistry and physics will find place in its course of systematic training. From the seventh or eighth year, according to the quality and capacity of the child, plane and solid geometry, the science of form, should find a place among the school studies, and some share of the child's attention that great subject should claim for six or seven successive years. The process of making acquaintance with external nature through the elements of these various sciences should be interesting and enjoyable for every child. It should not be painful, but delightful; and throughout the process the child's skill in the arts of reading, writing, and ciphering should be steadily developed.

There is another part of every child's environment with which he should early begin to make acquaintance, namely, the human part. The story of the human race should be gradually conveyed to the child's mind from the time he begins to read with pleasure. This story should be conveyed quite as much through biography as through history; and with the descriptions of facts and real events should be entwined charming and uplifting products of the imagination. I cannot but think, however, that the wholly desirable imaginative literature for children remains, in large measure, to be written. The mythologies, Old Testament stories, fairy tales, and historical romances on which we are accustomed to feed the childish mind contain a great deal that is perverse, barbarous, or trivial; and to this infiltration into children's minds, generation after generation, of immoral, cruel, or foolish ideas, is probably to be attributed, in part, the slow ethical progress of the race. The common justification of our practice is that children do not apprehend the evil in the mental pictures with which we so rashly supply them. But what should we think of a mother who gave her child dirty milk or porridge, on the theory that the child would not assimilate the dirt? Should we be less careful of mental and moral food-materials? It is, however, as undesirable as it is impossible to try to feed the minds of children only upon facts of observation or record. The immense product of the imagination in art and literature is a concrete fact with which every educated human being should be made somewhat familiar, such products being a very real part of every individual's actual environment.

Into the education of the great majority of children there enters as an important part their contribution to the daily labor of the household and the farm, or, at least, of the household. It is one of the serious consequences of the rapid concentration of population into cities and large towns, and of the minute division of labor which characterizes modern industries, that this wholesome part of education is less easily secured than it used to be when the greater part of the population was engaged in agriculture. Organized education must, therefore, supply in urban communities a good part of the manual and moral training which the coöperation of children in the work of father and mother affords in agricultural communities. Hence the great importance in any urban population of facilities for training children to accurate hand-work, and for teaching them patience, forethought, and good judgment in productive labor.

Lastly, the school should teach every child, by precept, by example, and by every illustration its reading can supply, that the supreme attainment for any individual is vigor and loveliness of character. Industry, persistence, veracity in word and act, gentleness, and disinterestedness should be made to thrive and blossom during school life in the hearts of the children who bring these virtues from their homes well started, and should be planted and tended in the less fortunate children. Furthermore, the pupils should be taught that what is virtue in one human being is virtue in any group of human beings, large or small—a village, a city, or a nation; that the ethical principles which should govern an empire are precisely the same as those which should govern an individual; and that selfishness, greed, falseness, brutality, and ferocity are as hateful and degrading in a multitude as they are in a single savage.

The education thus outlined is what I think should be meant by democratic education. It exists today only among the most intelligent people, or in places singularly fortunate in regard to the organization of their schools; but though it be the somewhat distant ideal of democratic education, it is by no means an unattainable ideal. It is the reasonable aim of the public school in a thoughtful and ambitious democracy. It, of course, demands a kind of teacher much above the elementary-school teacher of the present day, and it also requires a larger expenditure upon the public school than is at all customary as yet in this country. But that better kind of teacher and that larger expenditure are imperatively called for, if democratic institutions are to prosper, and to promote continuously the real welfare of the mass of the people. The standard of education should not be set at the now attained or the now attainable. It is the privilege of public education to press toward a mark remote.

From the total training during childhood there should result in the child a taste for interesting and improving reading, which should direct and inspire its subsequent intellectual life. That schooling which results in this taste for good reading, however unsystematic or eccentric the schooling may have been, has achieved a main end of elementary education; and that schooling which does not result in implanting this permanent taste has failed. Guided and animated by this impulse to acquire knowledge and exercise his imagination through reading, the individual will continue to educate himself all through life. Without that deep-rooted impulsion he will soon cease to draw on the accumulated wisdom of the past and the new resources of the present, and, as he grows older, he will live in a mental atmosphere which is always growing thinner and emptier. Do we not all know many people who seem to live in a mental vacuum—to whom, indeed, we have great difficulty in attributing immortality, because they apparently have so little life except that of the body? Fifteen minutes a day of good reading would have given any one of this multitude a really human life. The uplifting of the democratic masses depends on this implanting at school of the taste for good reading.

Another important function of the public school in a democracy is the discovery and development of the gift or capacity of each individual child. This discovery should be made at the earliest practicable age, and, once made, should always influence, and sometimes determine, the education of the individual. It is for the interest of society to make the most of every useful gift or faculty which any member may fortu-

nately possess; and it is one of the main advantages of fluent
and mobile democratic society that it is more likely than any
other society to secure the fruition of individual capacities. To
make the most of any individual's peculiar power, it is important to discover it early, and then train it continuously and
assiduously. It is wonderful what apparently small personal gifts
may become the means of conspicuous service or achievement,
if only they get discovered, trained, and applied. A quick eye for
shades of color enables a blacksmith to earn double wages in
sharpening drills for quarrymen. A delicate sense of touch
makes the fortune of a wool-buyer. An extraordinarily perceptive forefinger gives a surgeon the advantage over all his
competitors. A fine voice, with good elocution and a strong
memory for faces and parliamentary rules, may give striking
political success to a man otherwise not remarkable. In the ideal
democratic school no two children would follow the same
course of study or have the same tasks, except that they would
all need to learn the use of the elementary tools of education—
reading, writing, and ciphering. The different children would
hardly have any identical needs. There might be a minimum
standard of attainment in every branch of study, but no
maximum. The perception or discovery of the individual gift or
capacity would often be effected in the elementary school, but
more generally in the secondary; and the making of these
discoveries should be held one of the most important parts of
the teacher's work. The vague desire for equality in a democracy has worked great mischief in democratic schools. There is
no such thing as equality of gifts, or powers, or faculties, among
either children or adults. On the contrary, there is the utmost
diversity; and education and all the experience of life increase
these diversities, because school, and the earning of a liveli-
hood, and the reaction of the individual upon his surroundings,
all tend strongly to magnify innate diversities. The pretended
democratic school with an inflexible programme is fighting not
only against nature, but against the interests of democratic
society. Flexibility of programme should begin in the elementary school, years before the period of secondary education is
reached. There should be some choice of subjects of study by
ten years of age, and much variety by fifteen years of age. On

the other hand, the programmes of elementary as well as of secondary schools should represent fairly the chief divisions of knowledge, namely, language and literature, mathematics, natural science, and history, besides drawing, manual work, and music. If school programmes fail to represent the main varieties of intellectual activity, they will not afford the means of discovering the individual gifts and tendencies of the pupils.

As an outcome of successful democratic education, certain habits of thought should be well established in the minds of all the children before any of them are obliged to leave school in order to help in the support of the family. In some small field each child should acquire a capacity for exact observation, and as a natural result of this acquirement it should come to admire and respect exact observation in all fields. Again, in some small field it should acquire the capacity for exact description, and a respect for exact description in all fields. And, lastly, it should attain, within the limited range of its experience and observation, the power to draw a justly limited inference from observed facts. I need not say that this power of just inference is an admirable one, which many adults never attain as the combined result of their education in childhood and their experience in after life. Yet democratic institutions will not be safe until a great majority of the population can be trusted not only to observe accurately and state precisely the results of observation, but also to draw just inferences from those results. The masses of the people will always be liable to dangerous delusions so long as their schools fail to teach the difference between a true cause and an event preceding or accompanying a supposed effect. Thus, a year ago our nation came to the very brink of a terrible disaster because millions of our people thought the fall in the price of silver during the past twenty years was the cause of the fall in price of many other American products; whereas the prime cause of the general fall of prices, including the price of silver, was the immense improvement which has taken place since the Civil War in the manufacture and distribution of mechanical power—an operating cause which, in the near future, is going to produce much more striking effects than it has yet produced.

Any one who has attained to the capacity for exact

observation and exact description, and knows what it is to draw a correct inference from well-determined premises, will naturally acquire a respect for these powers when exhibited by others in fields unknown to him. Moreover, any one who has learned how hard it is to determine a fact, to state it accurately, and to draw from it the justly limited inference, will be sure that he himself cannot do these things, except in a very limited field. He will know that his own personal activity must be limited to a few subjects, if his capacity is to be really excellent in any. He will be sure that the too common belief that a Yankee can turn his hand to anything is a mischievous delusion. Having, as the result of his education, some vision of the great range of knowledge and capacity needed in the business of the world, he will respect the trained capacities which he sees developed in great diversity in other people. In short, he will come to respect and confide in the expert in every field of human activity. Confidence in experts, and willingness to employ them and abide by their decisions, are among the best signs of intelligence in an educated individual or an educated community; and in any democracy which is to thrive, this respect and confidence must be felt strongly by the majority of the population. In the conduct of private and corporation business in the United States the employment of experts is well recognized as the only rational and successful method. No one would think of building a bridge or a dam, or setting up a power station or a cotton mill, without relying absolutely upon the advice of intelligent experts. The democracy must learn, in governmental affairs, whether municipal, State, or national, to employ experts and abide by their decisions. Such complicated subjects as taxation, finance, and public works cannot be wisely managed by popular assemblies or their committees, or by executive officers who have no special acquaintance with these most difficult subjects. American experience during the last twenty years demonstrates that popular assemblies have become absolutely incapable of dealing wisely with any of these great subjects. A legislature or a Congress can indicate by legislation the object it wishes to attain; but to devise the means of attaining that object in taxation, currency, finance, or public works, and to expend the money appropriated by the constituted authorities for the object, must be functions of experts. Legislators and executives are changed so frequently, under the American system of local representation, that few gain anything that deserves to be called experience in legislation or administration; while the few who serve long terms are apt to be so absorbed in the routine work of carrying on the government and managing the party interests, that they have no time either for thorough research or for invention. Under present conditions, neither expert knowledge nor intellectual leadership can reasonably be expected of them. Democracies will not be safe until the population has learned that governmental affairs must be conducted on the same principles on which successful private and corporate business is conducted; and therefore it should be one of the principal objects of democratic education so to train the minds of the children, that when they become adult they shall have within their own experience the grounds of respect for the attainments of experts in every branch of governmental, industrial, and social activity, and of confidence in their advice.

The next function of education in a democracy should be the firm planting in every child's mind of certain great truths which lie at the foundation of the democratic social theory. The first of these truths is the intimate dependence of each human individual on a multitude of other individuals, not in infancy alone, but at every moment of life—a dependence which increases with civilization and with the development of urban life. This sense of mutual dependence among multitudes of human beings can be brought home to children during school life so clearly and strongly that they will never lose it. By merely teaching children whence come their food, drink, clothing, and means of getting light and heat, and how these materials are supplied through the labors of many individuals of many races scattered all over the world, the school may illustrate and enforce this doctrine of intricate interdependence, which really underlies modern democracy—a doctrine never more clearly expressed than in these two Christian sentences: "No man liveth to himself," and "We are every one members one of another." The dependence of every family, and indeed every person, on the habitual fidelity of mechanics, purveyors, railroad servants, cooks, and nurses can easily be brought home to children. Another mode of implanting this sentiment is to trace in history the obligations of the present generation to many former generations. These obligations can be easily pointed out in things material, such as highways, waterworks, fences, houses, and barns, and, in New England at least, the stone walls and piles of stone gathered from the arable fields by the patient labor of predecessors on the family farm. But it may also be exhibited to the pupils of secondary schools, and, in some measure, to the pupils of elementary schools, in the burdens and sufferings which former generations have borne for the establishment of freedom of conscience and of speech, and of toleration in religion, and for the development of the institutions of public justice. Of course history is full of examples of the violation of this fundamental democratic doctrine of mutual help. Indeed, history, as commonly written, consists chiefly in the story of hideous violations of this principle, such as wars and oppressions, and the selfish struggles of class against class, church against church, and nation against nation. But these violations, with the awful sufferings that follow from them, may be made to point and emphasize the truth of the fundamental doctrine; and unless the teaching of history in our public schools does this, it were better that the subject should not be taught at all.

Democratic education should also inculcate in every child the essential unity of a democratic community, in spite of the endless diversities of function, capacity, and achievement among the individuals who compose the community. This is a doctrine kindred with that just mentioned, but not identical. It is a doctrine essential to diffused democratic contentment and self-respect, but materially different from the ordinary conception of equality of condition as a result of democracy; for unity is attainable, while equality of condition is unnatural and unattainable. The freedom and social mobility which characterize the democratic state permit, and indeed bring about, striking inequalities of condition; and if the surface of democratic society should be leveled off any day, inequalities would reappear on the morrow, unless individual freedom and social mobility should be destroyed. The children of a democratic society should, therefore, be taught at school, with the utmost explicitness, and with vivid illustrations, that inequalities of condition are a necessary result of freedom; but that through all inequalities should flow the constant sense of essential unity in aim and spirit. This unity in freedom is the social goal of democracy, the supreme good of all ranks of society, of the highest no less than of the lowest.

Another ethical principle which a democracy should teach to all its children is the familiar Christian doctrine that service rendered to others is the surest source of one's own satisfaction and happiness. This doctrine is a tap-root of private happiness among all classes and conditions of men; but in a democracy it is important to public happiness and well-being. In a democracy the public functionary is not a master, but a trusted servant. By excellence of service he earns not only a pecuniary consideration, but also respect and gratitude. This statement applies just as well to a letter-carrier, a fireman, or a village selectman, as it does to a high-school teacher, a judge, or a governor. Democracy applies literally the precept, "If any man would be great among you, let him be your servant." The quality of this faithful service and its rewards should be carefully taught in school to all children of a democracy. The children should learn that the desire to be of great public service is the highest of all ambitions; and they should be shown in biography and in history how the men and women who, as martyrs, teachers, inventors, legislators, and judges, have rendered great service, have thereby won enduring gratitude and honor.

Since it is a fundamental object of a democracy to promote the happiness and well-being of the masses of the population, the democratic school should explicitly teach children to see and utilize the means of happiness which lie about them in the beauties and splendors of nature. The school should be a vehicle of daily enjoyment, and the teacher should be to the child a minister of joy. Democratic society has already learned how to provide itself—at least, in the more intelligent communities—with open grounds in cities, and parks in suburbs, and has in these ways begun to provide directly for the wholesome pleasures of the population. It should be a recognized function of the democratic school to teach the children and their parents how to utilize all accessible means of innocent enjoyment.

Finally, the democratic school must teach its children what the democratic nobility is. The well-trained child will read in history and poetry about patricians, nobles, aristocrats, princes, kings, and emperors, some of them truly noble, but many vile; and he will also read with admiring sympathy of the loyalty and devotion which through all the centuries have been felt by generous men and women of humbler condition toward those of higher. He will see what immense virtues these personal loyalties have developed, even when the objects of loyalty have been unworthy; and he will ask himself, "What are to be the corresponding virtues in a democracy?" The answer is, Fidelity to all forms of duty which demand courage, self-denial, and zeal, and loyal devotion to the democratic ideals of freedom, serviceableness, unity, toleration, public justice, and public joyfulness. The children should learn that the democratic nobility exists, and must exist if democracy is to produce the highest types of character; but that it will consist only of men and women of noble character, produced under democratic conditions by the combined influences of fine inherited qualities, careful education, and rich experience. They should learn to admire and respect persons of this quality, and to support them, on occasion, in preference to the ignoble. They should learn that mere wealth has no passport to the democratic nobility, and that membership in it can be transmitted to children only through the transmission of the sound mental and moral qualities which are its sole warrant. This membership should be the rightful ambition of parents for their children, and of children for their future selves. Every person of the true quality, no matter what his station or vocation, is admitted of right to this simple democratic nobility, which home, church, and school unite in recruiting; and there are, consequently, more real nobles under the democratic form of government than under any other.

6
Booker
T.
Washington

In 1903 Booker T. Washington attended the alumni dinner at Harvard University where he was introduced as "one of the whitest souls in our country." Nothing better depicts the legacy Washington bequeathed to the United States. He, a black man, had made it. Through merit alone he had succeeded—on the white man's terms.

❋

Booker Taliaferro Washington was born a slave in Virginia—as he was fond of recounting—where his bed was nothing but a pile of rags. Barely nine years old at the Civil War's end, Booker vividly recalled the day the slaves received the news that they were free; he remembered "great rejoicing, and thanksgiving, and wild scenes of ecstacy." He had few memories of his times as a slave, but one was unforgettable: his uncle Monroe—stripped naked, tied to a tree—being whipped by a cowhide. At each blow his uncle cried out, "Pray master! Pray master!" The absolute power of the white man was indelibly stamped into the mind of the frightened young black boy.

When his mother took him and his brother to live with his stepfather in Malden, West Virginia, young Booker discovered that although they were no longer slaves, the white man still had all the power. In Malden he worked in a salt mine, working harder than he ever had as a slave. It is not clear just how long he worked beside his father, pounding salt into barrels. But by the age of twelve he had a new job as houseboy for the wife of one of the richest men in Malden. His mistress, Viola Ruffner, became the single most important influence in his future development.

A Vermont-bred Yankee woman, Viola Ruffner firmly implanted the puritan ethic deep into the very being of her young servant. According to the puritan ethic, only those who were good merited salvation. When they applied this to economic life Christians secularized the spiritual doctrine into the notion that in this world—ruled as it is by Divine Providence—material success came only to those who merited it. In this life God rewards industry, perseverance, and thrift with material wealth. Only the shiftless and the lazy remain poor and unsuccessful.

Initially, Booker resisted Mrs. Ruffner's exacting demands and badgering tone. He ran away several times, once going as far as Cincinnati. But where could he go? Always he came back, and every time he persuaded her to let him take up his old position.

Although he had at first feared her—even trembled in her presence—in time he came to understand Mrs. Ruffner, later to agree with her, and finally—as the years passed—to love and know her as one of his great benefactors.

As Washington applied it to himself, the puritan ethic of success through merit underwent a further transmutation. More than the salvation of his soul, or even the acquisition of material wealth, the young black came to believe that industry, hard work, and perseverance would win him acceptance as a human being equal to white people. Just as the Christian willingly placed his future in the hands of God, and the economic entrepreneur accepted the outcome of the free competition of the marketplace, so Washington believed that the future of the black man depended on white people. The acquiescence to white supremacy did not engender feelings of fatalism about the future—not his own, or that of his race—no more than the beliefs of the Christian and the capitalist made them fatalistic. Like them, Washington regarded the universe as a just order: the good Christian merited salvation, the good capitalist merited wealth, so the good Negro merited the status of a full-fledged human being. A number of consequences follow from Washington's transmutation of the puritan ethic into a social philosophy—consequences that unfolded and became reality as Washington, in time, emerged as the leader and accepted spokesman for his people.

First, since he applied it to an entire race, not simply to individuals, this social philosophy entails acceptance of a racist society where one race is not only socially superior but is the authority for determining how worthy, if at all, the inferior race is. This confers a kind of legitimacy on the opinion *any* white person might have of the black race, or of any individual member of that race.

Second, with this construction of social reality blacks could never "succeed" simply because according to it blacks could succeed only if whites judged them; *but* as long as whites *did* act as judges, blacks could *never* succeed—they would remain inferior in the society. The only way for blacks to succeed was to stop being black, a course open to but a small percentage of those who could "pass" as white. The rest had to suffice with attempts to conceal their Negritude: by trying to lighten their skin, straighten their hair, and looking to have children lighter than themselves. Black was a stigma of inferiority.

Not only did the doctrine of merit make it impossible for blacks to "succeed," it enthralled them to lives of complete surveillance and control. This ceding of absolute power to the white race meant that any white was the legitimate judge of each and every act a black person made. By accepting this doctrine, the black person could never ascertain his own worth; some white person had to disclose it. "Am I getting on?" That, Mrs. Ruffner was to recall, was Booker Washington's principal—and continual —question.

In spite of the impossibility of success, in spite of the complete surveillance and control, the doctrine of merit generated optimism and hope. This emerged from the fact that, according to the doctrine, one's place in society depended upon oneself. Through the development and exercise of the appropriate virtues—thrift, industry, perseverance—one (and one's race) could "move up." Progress was up to the black man.

The final consequence of accepting the notion of success through merit as a sound doctrine was the creation of a *peaceful* racist society. Only when blacks ceased to believe in this doctrine did American racism precipitate discord and violence. But it was a long time before this happened. Not until the second half of the twentieth century did black Americans break the spell of Booker T. Washington. Many white Americans still remain under that spell.

❋

When at the age of sixteen Booker left the service of Viola Ruffner, it was to place himself under the tutelage of another apostle of the puritan ethic, General Samuel Chapman Armstrong, "the noblest, rarest, human being that it has been my privilege to meet," Washington later testified.

In 1869 General Armstrong had established Hampton Institute, a normal school for the education of black teachers. The son of a clergyman, Armstrong grew up in Hawaii, where his father served as minister of education in addition to maintaining a Presbyterian mission. When after the war the young general decided "to minister rather than become a minister," it was the Hawaiian school system for Polynesians that suggested the plan of the Hampton School. It was to be a place to educate a people "in the early stages of civilization," a school to teach the black people "to crawl before they could walk."

When Booker Washington arrived at Hampton Normal and Agricultural Institute in October, 1872, the first person he met was Miss Mary Mackie, the lady principal—another Yankee lady cast from the same mold as Viola Ruffner. He had made the 500-mile trip from Malden on foot, so it was a dirty, disheveled, young man with but fifty cents in his pocket who presented himself for admission. After some hesitation Miss Mackie gave him his entrance examination: "The adjoining recitation-room needs sweeping. Take the broom and sweep it."

Washington recounts what happened in his autobiography, *Up from Slavery*:

> Never did I receive an order with more delight. I knew I could sweep, for Mrs. Ruffner had thoroughly taught me how to do that when I lived with her.
>
> I swept the recitation-room three times. Then I got a dusting cloth and I dusted it four times. All the woodwork around the wall, every bench, table and desk, I went over four times with my dusting cloth. Besides every piece of furniture had been moved and every closet and corner in the room had been thoroughly cleaned. I had the feeling that in a large measure my future depended upon the impression I made upon the teacher in the cleaning of that room. When I was through I reported to the head teacher. She was a "Yankee" woman who knew just where to look for dirt. She went into the room and inspected the floor and closets; then she took her handkerchief and rubbed it on the woodwork about the walls, and over the table and benches. When she was unable to find one bit of dirt on the floor, or a particle of dust on any of the furniture, she quietly remarked "I guess you will do to enter this institution."

Miss Mackie had made him "the happiest student ever to enter Hampton Institute." She approved of him!

Once admitted to Hampton Institute, Booker T. Washington became janitor of the Academic Building. This helped to pay part of his tuition and board; it also provided him with close contact with the teachers and General Armstrong himself.

Although the purported purpose of Hampton was to prepare Negro teachers for elementary schools of the South, industrial education was the heart of its educational program. As Armstrong construed it, industrial education at Hampton was not designed to teach marketable skills to the blacks, it was simply a means of inculcating virtues: industry, perseverance, and thrift. He saw industrial education as the salvation for the Negro race: it would root out their "natural" tendencies to laziness, improvidence, and sensuality.

Thus at the very moment industrial education was becoming specialized and professionalized in white colleges and institutes, Armstrong was laying the foundation for undifferentiated, simple, industrial education for blacks—an education to teach a work ethic with little heed to teaching specialized work skills.

Years of working for Mrs. Ruffner had well prepared Washington for his Hampton education. The doctrine of success through merit now became an integral part of his life and thought. "At Hampton," he later wrote, "I found an opportunity for class-room education and for practical training in industrial life, opportunity to learn thrift, economy and push. Amid Christian influences I was surrounded by an atmosphere of business, and a spirit of self-help that seemed to awaken every faculty in me and caused me for the first time to realize what it means to be a man instead of a piece of property." During this period Washington accepted, and made his own, the attitudes Armstrong prescribed for Negroes:

> Be thrifty and industrious. Command the respect of your neighbors by a good record and a good character. Own your own houses. Educate your children. Make the best of your difficulties. Live down prejudice. Cultivate peaceful relations with all. As a voter act as you think and not as you are told. Remember that you have seen marvellous changes in sixteen years. In view of that be patient—thank God and take courage.

General Samuel Chapman Armstrong had developed the doctrine of success through merit into a fullblown ideology for American Negroes. As his most faithful disciple, Booker Washington would demonstrate, in his life and in his work, that such an ideology inevitably led to a life of accommodation—accommodation to whatever conditions the white man would decree.

❊

After graduating from Hampton, Washington spent two years teaching school in his home town of Malden, West Virginia. Education had helped him to move up. Now he wanted to help others of his race "improve themselves." In a letter to the Charlestown *West Virginia Journal* in August 1877 on the matter of improvement of the colored people, Washington declared that education was the key. Unfortunately, too few of his race took advantage of the existing opportunities: "I think there are many who, if they would count up the time spent by them in vain and idle street talk, would find it to amount to hours and days enough in which they might have obtained for themselves a valuable and respectable education."

The notion of using education to improve the race is ambiguous. It can mean using education to help the race to improve the conditions under which it presently lives. Or it can mean using education to improve the quality—the intellectual and the moral quality—of the people themselves. His fantastic commitment to the doctrine of success through merit led Washington to this second construction of education. As Washington viewed it, improvement of the conditions under which black people lived *follows*—"is merited by"—improvement in the quality of the people themselves. "If the colored man will only improve his opportunities and persevere," he wrote, "I believe the time is not far distant when a great portion of them will be equal in education, in wealth, equal in civilization, and equal in everything that tends toward human advancement, to any nation or people on earth."

Washington's construction converts education into an authoritarian enterprise, in this case, a racist enterprise; education becomes the imposition of "correct" ideals, values, beliefs, attitudes, and habits, on an inferior race of people. And in spite of its philanthropic and meliorist rhetoric, this authoritarian, racist education actually perpetuates what it is supposed to eliminate. A racist education cannot bring about improved conditions for blacks simply because such an education teaches blacks to accommodate themselves to what exists, to accept white superiority. So, ironically—no, tragically—this construction of education transformed schools into traps that locked young blacks into the existing social, political, and economic arrangements in the South.

Booker Washington never perceived the fateful consequences of his construction of education. So throughly had he internalized the dogma of white superiority that he could not conceive of success in any way except through acceptance by whites. So, for him, his own experiences were a testimonial to the validity of his ideas about education. For him it worked. He was getting on, wasn't he?

*

Yes indeed! Booker T. Washington was getting on. He made another important step upward when he accepted General Armstrong's invitation to return to Hampton as a teacher—the first black teacher in the school. He taught a "night class" made up of students who worked in the sawmill or the laundry from seven in the morning until six in the evening and then attended school from seven to nine thirty at night. After his success with this "plucky class" (the sobriquet is Washington's), General Armstrong put him to work teaching some Indians the government had sent to Hampton from western reservations.

Washington enthusiastically tackled the educational experiment, determined to show "that the Indian is a man." At the end of the year he reported how well education had worked. Bear's Heart, for example, had been an army prisoner when he had left the Indian Territory. Look at him after a few years at Hampton: he wore the school's gray uniform decorated with sergeant's stripes and color bearer's insignia; instead of a tomahawk, he carried a box of carpenter's tools, knapsack, and Bible. "His long hair and moccasins he has long since forgotten, and instead of the weak, dirty, ignorant piece of humanity that he was, with no correct idea of this life or the next—his only ambition being to fight the white man—he goes back a strong, decent, Christian *man*."

In the spring of 1881 Washington abruptly left Hampton to "move up" even higher. The opportunity came in the form of a letter to General Armstrong from the commissioners of a Negro normal school in Tuskegee, Alabama. They asked Armstrong to recommend a principal, hoping for one of his teachers or some other white man imbued with "his ideas" about educating black people. Within a week the general tersely replied: "The only man I can suggest is one Booker T. Washington, a graduate of this institution, a very competent mulatto, clear headed, modest, sensible, polite, and a thorough teacher and superior man. The best man we ever had here."

Washington got the job and immediately left for Alabama. Expecting to find the school already in operation, a surprised and disappointed young man discovered that the hesitant state legislature would not grant any money for the nonexisting school until the following October. Undaunted, the resolute new principal set out to establish and open a school by July 4. He rented a building, secured some secondhand books and equipment from Hampton, recruited students through speeches delivered in the local churches, and laid plans for initiating a manual labor system so students could pay their own way.

The new school did open on July 4. As the news spread that Tuskegee had a school for training teachers, enrollments rose— reaching 60 by September and 88 in November. The school moved to new quarters: a farm bought with money borrowed from one of the teachers at Hampton. And Washington hired three new teachers.

By attempting to model Tuskegee on Hampton Institute, Washington created serious financial problems for the fledgling school. His determination that the school must own its own property and must be a boarding school—like Hampton—forced him to spend a great deal of time "up north," begging and borrowing funds to keep the school going. (During Washington's tenure at Tuskegee the appropriation from the state of Alabama never exceeded $3,000 a year.) Moreover, his determination to make the school independent forced the students literally to build the school: they made the bricks, laid the foundations, and erected all the school buildings. In addition, they planted, grew, harvested, and sold food crops. Washington viewed these arduous tasks as educational opportunities. Through them students learned the dignity of labor, self-help, and perseverance (especially educative in this last regard were the initial attempts of faculty and students to make bricks: they made and ruined three kilns before producing any bricks at all). And most important, these challenges supplied the opportunity to demonstrate that Negroes could create and run a school by themselves.

Washington was correct. Undoubtedly the onerous labors of the teachers and students did create a community, did inculcate a work ethic, and did evince the respect of some whites. In 1893 Washington had occasion to recount the achievements of Tuskegee Institute when he delivered a memorial address at Hampton Institute in honor of the late General Armstrong. Tuskegee, Washington explained, was a living memorial to the ideas and ideals of the general:

Eleven years ago there were 30 students and one teacher; now
there are 600 students and 38 teachers; then scarcely a dollar
and not a foot of land; now 1400 acres of land, 20 buildings and
rent and personal property worth $180,000; then one blind
horse; now 260 head of livestock. Then the plantation where the
Tuskegee Institute stood had known naught but the labor forced
by the lash; today there are nineteen industries kept in motion
by 600 as happy hearts as can be found in America; then some
feared that the Negro youth would be ashamed to work for his
education, but these students have made and laid into the
buildings with their own hands 2,000,000 bricks, and of 20
buildings, 17 have been built and furnished by the students
themselves.

The record is truly impressive. And yet Washington's work at
Tuskegee exacerbated the plight of the blacks in the South. For one
thing, the school, with its permeating ethos of success through
merit, "cooled out" bright young blacks, training them to accommodate themselves to the status quo. At Tuskegee everyone learned
to construe the status quo as a testing ground where one could
demonstrate one's merit to white people.

Moreover, through his efforts to make his school independent
—like Hampton Institute—Washington identified it with the
northern white aristocracy, thus eliminating any possible alliances
with southern whites, especially the lower classes. This made the
school, the faculty, and the students susceptible and vulnerable to
reprisals from its white neighbors. So long as the Negroes did not
become "uppity," however, the white citizens tolerated them. But
whenever a student or a faculty member tried to move beyond his
"place," the whites of the city of Tuskegee came down on
him—very hard.

When one graduate tried to start a newspaper in the town, he
was requested to suspend publication. Another student was forced
to leave school after writing to a Negro newspaper in Mississippi
about a recent effort by a mob to lynch a Negro prisoner.
Washington acquiesced to, even cooperated with, these curtail-
ments of free speech. In an apology that painfully revealed his own
powerlessness and the vulnerability of the school, he said, "It has
always been and is now the policy of the Normal School to remain
free from politics and the discussion of race questions that tend to

stir up strife between the races, and whenever this policy is violated it is done without the approbation of those in charge of the school." He then went on to claim that he took pride in the fact that in the seven-year period of the school's existence there were not "a half dozen acts performed or utterances made at which any one took offense."

In his efforts to minimize the threats his school posed to the white community, Washington fought all attempts to convert it into a college. He even forbade the teaching of Latin and Greek—too uppity. Academic subjects were taught, but they "dovetailed" into the industrial work that comprised the heart of the curriculum.

※

In advocating industrial education for the students of Tuskegee, Washington followed the lead of his mentor, General Armstrong. But he placed a different emphasis on the function of industrial education. Armstrong had stressed the pedagogical value of combining manual with mental training and, most of all, the social value of industrial education in teaching Negroes the dignity of work. Washington accepted these claims, but more and more he came to point to its economic value to blacks. Industrial education, he argued, "kills two birds with one stone." It ensured the survival of the blacks, and it secured the cooperation of the whites.

Industrial education was the principal strategy in Washington's campaign to help his race succeed through merit. Unlike Armstrong and many other paternalistic whites who spoke of it in pseudo-ethical terms, Washington had come to a hard-headed construction of the doctrine of success through merit as it applied to black people. Rather than appeal to the conscience of white people, or to abstract principles of social justice, Washington based all his arguments for the merit of black people on simple economic grounds: he appealed to the self-interest of the southern whites.

In a speech before the NEA in Wisconsin in 1884, Washington explained his interpretation of the doctrines of merit: "Harmony will come in proportion as the black man gets something that the white man wants, whether it be of brains or material." If a Negro, he argued, because of his knowledge about agriculture, can raise fifty bushels of corn to the acre, while his white neighbor can raise only thirty, then "the white man will come to the black man to learn. . . . They will sit down on the same train, in the same couch and on the same seat to talk about it."

Washington's argument is clear: industrial education of the southern Negro is in the interest of the southern white. In the same speech he repeated what a former slaveowner had recently said to him: "I can see every day the change that is coming about. I have on one of my plantations a colored man who can read and write and he is the most valuable man on the farm. In the first place I can trust him to keep the time of the others or with anything else. If a new style of plow or cotton planter is taken on the place, he can understand its construction in half the time that any of the others can."

As Washington saw it, neither political action nor legislation could help the Negro. When, in 1883, the Supreme Court struck down the Civil Rights Act of 1875, Washington took it complacently. In a speech in Saratoga, he declared, "The best thing to do in regard to civil rights bills, and bills of like interest, in the South, is to let them alone, and throw our force to making a business-man of the negro. I find that our Southern people are much like people elsewhere. Harmony between the two races will come in proportion as the black man gets something that the white man wants."

Washington continually used the appeal to the economic self-interest of whites to combat concrete cases of racial discrimination. His argument in all cases was the same: the Negro did not merit such discrimination because it brought undesirable consequences for the white man. When a wedding party made up of teachers from Tuskegee suffered continuous harassment and threats on a train trip through Alabama, Washington wrote a letter of complaint to a Montgomery newspaper. His initial sentences were: "I wish to say a few words from a purely business standpoint. It is not a subject with which to mix racist equality or anything bordering on it. To the Negro it is a matter of dollars and cents." He did not complain against separation itself, but against the crowded old uncarpeted cars, where drunken white men were free to sprawl when they were ostracized from the white people's railroad cars. If the railroad did not want blacks in first-class cars with whites, then "let them give us a separate one just as good in every particular and just as exclusive, and *there will be no complaint.*" If the railroads did not want to give blacks first-class accommodations, he concluded, "then let them sell us tickets at reduced rates."

Washington's argument against racial discrimination had limited force and restricted applicability. It applied only in those cases where Negroes actually had something that whites wanted: money, skills, knowledge. For this reason, education, industrial education, played such a crucial role in Washington's grand strategy. From Tuskegee he dispatched teachers throughout the entire rural South. Good schoolteachers, he said, would be more potent in settling the race question than civil rights bills.

By basing his grand strategy on universal education, Washington was forced to counsel gradualism: white acceptance of the entire race would take many, many years. Negroes must begin at the bottom, learn the elemental skills of economic survival, and, gradually, move up the occupational ladder. Washington's school supplied an industrial education in manual and semiskilled crafts: blacksmithing, brickmaking, carpentry, sewing, printing, farming, and laundry work. This is where the Negro must begin. In defending his strategy Washington often cited the example of the founders of New England. Those colonists, he noted, "first made themselves masters of the soil, their sons were schooled and taught trades, then came the small factories and trading houses, then they began to multiply their colleges and professional schools, then followed those learned in the professions and fine arts. Thus following the great law of the condition and the conditioned they have built up a civilization which is a beacon light to the world."

Such an approach demanded an almost superhuman patience and magnanimity on the part of blacks, a willingness to endure injustice and affronts that few besides Booker T. Washington possessed. His certainty about the correctness of his grand strategy conferred on Washington an imperturbable omniscience—an omniscience that helped him to endure, to understand, to excuse, and sometimes even to control the course of events.

As part of the commencement ceremonies at Tuskegee in 1896, the governor of Alabama, John C. Oates, was scheduled to deliver an address. The speaker immediately preceding him, a black politician from North Carolina, said some things that the governor interpreted as a call for black militancy. When he rose to speak Governor Oates refused to deliver his prepared address. Waving it admonishingly at his audience, he shouted: "I want to give you niggers a few words of plain talk and advice. No such address as I have just listened to is going to do you any good; it's going to spoil you. You had better not listen to such speeches. You might as well understand that this is a white man's country, as far as the South is concerned, and we are going to make you keep your place. Understand that. I have nothing more to say to you."

As the audience muttered in indignation, an unruffled Washington stepped up and announced: "Ladies and gentlemen: I am sure you will agree with me that we have had enough eloquence for one occasion. We shall listen to the next speaker on another occasion, when we are not so fagged out. We will now rise, sing the doxology, and be dismissed."

Earlier that year, the governor had written to the Alabama delegation in Congress in support of Washington's bid for a federal land grant to the school. ("Anything that Congress may do by way of helping this school will be the very best disposition that can be made of that amount of public land.") Washington's imperturbable demeanor at the commencement exercises retained a valuable ally. The governor did not withdraw his support for the school. And within a short time he was telling people that Booker T. Washington was "the smartest Negro in the world."

Yet, however adamant Washington was about his grand strategy, and however adroitly and resolutely he pursued it, the logical unfolding of that grand strategy inexorably exacerbated America's racial problem.

❋

By the mid-1890s the tragic consequences of the doctrine of success through merit were evident to all. Adherence to the doctrine had led Washington to accept disfranchisement of the Negroes in the South and to acquiesce in the creation of a racially segregated, caste society.

Acceptance of the disfranchisement of blacks—by means of literacy tests and property requirements—followed logically from

Washington's doctrine: illiterate, propertyless blacks did not *merit* the franchise. True, he did object to gimmicks like the "grandfather clause," which allowed illiterate and propertyless whites to vote because *their* grandfathers had been voters. Washington secretly financed court cases to test the constitutionality of such laws. But literacy and property tests—applied equally to both races—were, he thought, just. Throughout the 1890s state after state in the South encountered little opposition as they passed laws that effectively disenfranchised most Negroes.

Acquiescence to the separation of the races into two castes also followed from the doctrine of merit. For as long as blacks did not "merit" white acceptance, they had to remain segregated. And as long as blacks aspired to integration into white society they tacitly acquiesced to membership in an inferior caste. Moreover, although the blacks became a separate caste, the doctrine of merit destroyed any basis of a black solidarity simply because all blacks were in competition for the scarce prize of white acceptance. As a result, among those who cared, blacks became highly censorious of one another, each trying to become more acceptable than the other—each trying to be a "good nigger."

Explicit recognition of these consequences of the doctrine of success through merit came in Washington's famous speech at the Atlanta Exposition of 1895—the speech many blacks later referred to as the "Atlanta Compromise."

In this widely publicized address, Washington once again based his argument for the merit of Negroes on the economic self-interest of whites. Speaking directly to the southern whites, Washington pointed out that "sixteen million hands will aid you in pulling the load upward, or they will pull against you the load downward. We shall constitute one-third of the ignorance and crime of the South, or one-third of its intelligence and progress; we shall contribute one-third to the business and industrial prosperity of the South, or we shall prove a veritable body of death, stagnating, depressing, retarding every effort to advance the body politic."

He admits that Negroes must begin at the bottom of the occupational ladder: "No race can prosper till it learns that there is as much dignity in tilling a field as in writing a poem."

Then, making citizenship conditional upon economic wealth,

he explicitly accepts disfranchisement for blacks—until they merited it.

> The wisest among my race understand that the agitation of questions of social equality is the extremist folly, and that progress in the enjoyment of all the privileges that will come to us must be the result of severe and constant struggle rather than of artificial forcing. No race that has anything to contribute to the markets of the world is long in any degree ostracized. It is important and right that all privileges of the law be ours, but it is vastly more important that we be prepared for the exercises of these privileges.

Finally, and most dramatically, Washington announces that a racially separated, caste society is compatible with the economic self-interest of both races. Raising his hand, with fingers spread wide apart, he declares: "In all things that are purely social we can be as separate as the fingers, yet one as the hand in all things essential to mutual progress."

The response of the white southerners was electric. When he finished speaking Governor R. F. Bullock rushed across the stage to shake his hand. The handshaking, backthumping, and hearty congratulations were such that Washington had difficulty getting out of the building. Papers in all parts of the United States published the address in full, and for months afterward there were complimentary editorial references to it. The editor of the *Atlanta Constitution* wrote, in part: "I do not exaggerate when I say that Professor Booker T. Washington's address yesterday was one of the most notable speeches, both as to character and as to warmth of its reception, ever delivered to a southern audience. The address was a revelation. The whole speech is a platform upon which blacks and whites can stand with full justice to each other." A few days after the Atlanta address Washington received a congratulatory message from Grover Cleveland, the President of the United States.

Perhaps the most poignant comment of all came from a reporter for the *New York World*, who noticed that at the end of the speech "most of the Negroes in the audience were crying, perhaps without knowing just why."

In 1896, the year after the Atlanta speech, the Supreme Court of the United States legalized segregation of the races, when in *Plessy* v. *Ferguson*, they declared that states could create and maintain separate, but equal, arrangements for Negroes.

Booker T. Washington now emerged as *the* spokesman for his race. Groups everywhere invited him to speak. Gladly and willingly he accepted, charming and mollifying whites throughout the country with his message of success through merit. Invited to write the story of his life, he wrote two autobiographies (with the assistance of some ghostwriters). One was for blacks: *The Story of My Life and Work*, and one was for white readers: *Up from Slavery*. Both books carried the message of success through merit. *He* had succeeded. *He* had risen higher than any other black in the history of the nation. He was the black Horatio Alger.

Increasingly, white politicians and men of influence consulted Washington on the appointment of blacks to various political offices—from post office clerk to undersecretaries of the President's cabinet. And finally, just as it always comes to Alger heroes, Washington gained his ultimate triumph—the hightest accolade. On October 16, 1901, President Theodore Roosevelt invited him to dinner at the White House. That night marked the symbolic confirmation of Booker T. Washington as "king of a captive people." Later, Harvard University bestowed on him a fitting crown: an honorary Master's degree, and introduced him at the alumni dinner as "one of the whitest souls in our country."

❋

Booker T. Washington died in 1915. Although his personal power and influence had waned even before his death, his ideas long dominated American thought. Not until the 1950s did most Americans begin to challenge his central doctrine of success through merit.

Since then, most have begun to see that the doctrine of racial merit has no place in the political, social, economic, and educational arrangements of the nation. Blacks are citizens; they do not have to "merit" the franchise. Nor do they have to "merit" a "white man's job," or admittance to a "white neighborhood" or a "white school."

During the second half of the twentieth century, Americans

witnessed the dismantling of the doctrine of racial merit from American life: first the consequences, then the underlying assumptions, finally, the principle itself.

In the 1950s the battle was against the racially segregated, caste society that Washington had condoned. Sparked by the *Brown* case, Americans began to eliminate racial segregation in schools, in public places, in restaurants, on public conveyances, and in public housing. Later the focus broadened to combat directly the disfranchisement of blacks—which Washington had also condoned. Here, the Civil Rights Acts of 1957 (the first since Reconstruction), 1960, and 1964 paved the way for the legal dismemberment of racially imposed restrictions. These changes did not come easily. Strikes, boycotts, protest marches, demonstrations, and riots augmented the legal processes of legislation and adjudication. But once begun, the irrevocable logic of reversal moved inexorably to expunge the doctrine of racial merit from American society.

In the 1960s many became conscious of the racist prejudices rooted deep in the souls of white Americans—prejudices institutionalized in the existing social, economic, and political arrangements. This came about as blacks massively rejected the assumption underlying the doctrine of success through merit—the assumption of white superiority. As blacks became more conscious of their own worth and dignity, there emerged a new widespread appreciation of black culture past and present. Henceforth no self-respecting black person aspired to being a "good nigger" (in street talk "bad" became good); many forswore the label "Negro" in favor of "black." Most now took pride in their negritude (Black is beautiful) and ceased trying to look like white people.

Once they had rejected the racist assumption of white superiority underlying the doctrine of success through merit, it was a short step (although an impossible one for many Americans) to the total repudiation of that doctrine itself. In place of winning jobs and positions or securing admission to schools and colleges on the basis of "merit," many Americans now insisted that jobs and admission to educational institutions must be based on a quota system—ensuring a place for a certain percentage of blacks. (Other oppressed groups soon used the same argument: Spanish-speaking Americans and women, for example.)

In repudiating the merit system, these Americans rejected the social accommodationist philosophy of Booker Washington insofar as selection for a job or selection for admission to a school on the basis of "merit" presumes that those selected will accommodate to the status quo, not improve it, not change it in any way. Those who repudiate selection by merit envision more dynamic and open-ended occupational and educational arrangements where jobs and schools will change *because* new kinds of people enter them. And this, ultimately, will mean a new, open society, one where we will change and refine the existing social and economic arrangements in order to accommodate *them* to all members of the society.

But before this can take place, Booker T. Washington's conception of the function of formal education must be put aside. As we saw, he construed schools as the means to mobility, status, and position. This was an essential part of his social philosophy. Through the process of schooling blacks were to become meritorious; the schools were to ascertain just who were meritorious and so certify them.

Most of the educational thought of comtemporary blacks continues to perpetuate this notion of schooling as the process of economic socialization to the world of work, together with the corollary notion that schools are credential agencies. This conflation of the social function of education into economic socialization is but a continuation of Booker T. Washington's theory of economic determinism—a theory shattered by the course of events: material wealth did not win equality for those blacks who attained it. This conception of education does not accept people as they are; it invites educators to change, modify, process young blacks to fit into predetermined economic and social arrangements. Like everything else connected with his doctrine of racial merit, this Washingtonian conception of education is authoritarian.

If education is to help secure improvement for blacks, then educators must set aside the legacy of Booker T. Washington and set up a direct *educational* engagement with existing social conditions. Rather than trying to change the young, educators would try to help them learn how to protect themselves, so that each may live as *he* sees fit—so long as he does not harm others. This would mean a new social function for the schools: teaching people how to accommodate the arrangements in society to all the members of that society—in other words, improving the society rather than adjusting to it. Today there is some cause to expect the emergence of this kind of education in America: the consciousness, tolerance, patience and pluralism it requires is already manifest among many of the young of our society.

WORKS AND COMMENTARY

So far, four volumes of *The Booker T. Washington Papers* (Urbana: University of Illinois Press, 1973 et seq.), edited by Louis R. Harlan, have appeared. Volume 1 contains the autobiographical writings, including *Up from Slavery* and *The Story of My Life and Work.* Washington's *Selected Speeches* (New York: 1932) contains some important addresses not yet published in the *Papers.*

Louis R. Harlan has recently published a superb study of Washington, *Booker T. Washington: The Making of a Black Leader, 1856–1901* (New York: Oxford University Press, 1972). Useful, critical studies of Washington appear in Rayford W. Logan, *The Negro in American Life and Thought: The Nadir, 1877–1890* (New York: Dial Press, 1954); August Meier, *Negro Thought in America, 1880–1915* (Ann Arbor: University of Michigan Press, 1963); and in the collection of articles edited by Hugh Hawkins, *Booker T. Washington and His Critics* (Boston: D. C. Heath, 1962).

The selection that follows is from *Selected Speeches,* pages 1–11.

The Educational Outlook in the South

An Address Delivered Before the National Educational Association Madison, Wisconsin, July 16, 1884

Mr. President, Ladies and Gentlemen:

Fourteen years ago it is said that Northern teachers, in the South for the purpose of teaching in colored schools, were frightened away by the whites from the town of Tuskegee, Alabama. Four years ago the Democratic members of the

Alabama legislature from Tuskegee voluntarily offered and had passed by the General Assembly a bill, appropriating $2,000 annually to pay the salaries of teachers in a colored normal school to be located at Tuskegee. At the end of the first session of the school the legislature almost unanimously passed a second bill appropriating an additional $1,000 annually, for the same purpose. About one month ago one of the white citizens of Tuskegee who had at first looked on the school in a cold, distant kind of a way said to me, "I have just been telling the white people that the Negroes are more interested in education than we, and are making more sacrifices to educate themselves." At the end of our first year's work, some of the whites said, "We are glad that the Normal School is here because it draws people and makes labor plentiful." At the close of the second year, several said that the Normal School was beneficial because it increased trade, and at the close of the last session more than one said that the Normal School is a good institution, it is making the colored people in this state better citizens. From the opening of the school to the present, the white citizens of Tuskegee have been among its warmest friends. They have not only given of their money but they are ever ready to suggest and devise plans to build up the institution. When the school was making an effort to start a brick yard, but was without means, one of the merchants donated an outfit of tools. Every white minister in town has visited the school and given encouraging remarks. When the school was raising money to build our present hall, it occurred to one of the teachers that it would be a good idea to call on the white ladies for contributions in the way of cakes, etc., toward a fair. The result was that almost every lady, called on, gave something and the fair was made up almost entirely of articles given by these friends. A former slaveholder working on a Negro normal school building under a Negro master carpenter is a picture that the last few years have made possible.

Any movement for the elevation of the Southern Negro, in order to be successful, must have to a certain extent the coöperation of the Southern whites. They control government and own the property—whatever benefits the black man benefits the white man. The proper education of all the whites will benefit the Negro as much as the education of the Negro will benefit the whites. The Governor of Alabama would probably count it no disgrace to ride in the same railroad coach with a colored man, but the ignorant white man who curries the Governor's horse would turn up his nose in disgust. The president of a white college in Tuskegee makes a special effort to furnish our young men work that they may be able to remain in school, while the miserable unlettered "brother in white" would say, "You can't learn a nigger anything." Brains, property, and character for the Negro will settle the question of civil rights. The best course to pursue in regard to the civil rights bill in the South is to let it alone; let it alone and it will settle itself. Good school teachers and plenty of money to pay them will be more potent in settling the race question than many civil rights bills and investigating committees. A young colored physician went into the city of Montgomery, Alabama, a few months ago to practise his profession—he was the first to professionally enter the ex-Confederate capital. When his white brother physicians found out by a six days' examination that he had brains enough to pass a better examination, as one of them said, than many of the whites had passed, they gave him a hearty welcome and offered their services to aid him in consultation or in any other way possible—and they are standing manfully up to their promise. Let there be in a community a Negro who by virtue of his superior knowledge of the chemistry of the soil, his acquaintance with the most improved tools and best breeds of stock, can raise fifty bushels of corn to the acre while his white neighbor only raises thirty, and the white man will come to the black man to learn. Further, they will sit down on the same train, in the same coach and on the same seat, to talk about it. Harmony will come in proportion as the black man gets something that the white man wants, whether it be of brains or of material. Some of the county whites looked at first with disfavor on the establishing of a normal school in Tuskegee. It turned out that there was no brick yard in the county; merchants and farmers wanted to build, but bricks must be brought from a distance or they must wait for one house to burn down before building another. The Normal School with student labor started a brick yard. Several kilns of bricks were burned; the whites came from miles around for bricks. From examining bricks they were led to examine the workings of the school. From the discussion of the brick yard came the discussion of Negro education—and thus many of the "old masters" have been led to see and become interested in Negro education. In Tuskegee a Negro mechanic manufactures the best tinware, the best harness, the best boots and shoes, and it is common to see his store crowded with white customers from all over the county. His word or note goes as far as that of the whitest man.

I repeat for emphasis that any work looking towards the permanent improvement of the Negro South must have for one of its aims the fitting of him to live friendly and peaceably with his white neighbors both socially and politically. In spite of all talks of exodus, the Negro's home is permanently in the South: for coming to the bread-and-meat side of the question, the white man needs the Negro, and the Negro needs the white man. His home being permanently in the South, it is our duty to help him prepare himself to live there an independent, educated citizen.

In order that there may be the broadest development of the colored man and that he may have an unbounded field in which to labor, the two races must be brought to have faith in each other. The teachings of the Negro in various ways for the last twenty years have been rather too much to array him against his white brother than to put the two races in coöperation with each other. Thus Massachusetts supports the Republican party, because the Republican party supports Massachusetts with a protective tariff, but the Negro supports the Republican party simply because Massachusetts does. When the colored man is educated up to the point of reasoning that Massachusetts and Alabama are a long way apart and the conditions of life are very different, and if free trade enables my white neighbor across the street to buy his plows at a cheaper rate it will enable me to do the same thing, then will he be consulted in governmental questions. More than once have I noticed that when the whites were in favor of prohibition the blacks, led even by sober upright ministers, voted against it simply because the whites were in favor of it, and for that reason the blacks said that they knew it was a "Democratic trick." If the whites vote to levy a tax to build a schoolhouse, it is a signal for the blacks to oppose the measure, simply because the whites favor it. I venture the assertion that the sooner the colored man South learns that one political party is not composed of all angels and the other of all devils, and that all his enemies do not live in his own town or neighborhood, and all his friends in some distant section of the country, the sooner will his educational advantages be enhanced many fold. But matters are gradually changing in this respect. The black man is beginning to find out that there are those even among the Southern whites who desire his elevation. The Negro's new faith in the white man is being reciprocated in proportion as the Negro is rightly educated. The white brother is beginning to learn by degrees that all Negroes are not liars and chicken thieves. A former owner of seventy-five or one hundred slaves and now a large planter and merchant said to me a few days ago, "I can see every day the change that is coming about. I have on one of my plantations a colored man who can read and write and he is the most valuable man on the farm. In the first place I can trust him to keep the time of the others or with anything else. If a new style of plow or cotton planter is taken on the place, he can understand its construction in half the time that any of the others can."

My faith is that reforms in the South are to come from within. Southern people have a good deal of human nature. They like to receive the praise of doing good deeds, and they don't like to obey orders that come from Washington telling them that they must lay aside at once customs that they have followed for centuries, and henceforth there must be but one railroad coach, one hotel, and one schoolhouse for ex-master and ex-slave. In proof of my first assertion, the railroads in Alabama required colored passengers to pay the same fare as the whites, and then compelled the colored to ride in the smoking car. A committee of leading colored people laid the injustice of the matter before the railroad commissioners of Alabama, who at once ordered that within thirty days every railroad in the State should provide equal but separate accommodations for both races. Every prominent newspaper in the

State pronounced it a just decision. Alabama gives $9,000 annually towards the support of colored normal schools. The last legislature increased the annual appropriation for free schools by $100,000, making the total annual appropriation over $500,000, and nearly half of this amount goes to colored schools, and I have for the first time to hear of any distinction being made between the races by any state officer in the distribution of this fund. Why, my friends, more pippins are growing in the South than crab apples, more roses than thorns.

Now, in regard to what I have said about the relations of the two races, there should be no unmanly cowering or stooping to satisfy unreasonable whims of Southern white men, but it is charity and wisdom to keep in mind the two hundred years' schooling in prejudice against the Negro which the ex-slaveholders are called upon to conquer. A certain class of whites South object to the general education of the colored man on the ground that when he is educated he ceases to do manual labor, and there is no evading the fact that much aid is withheld from Negro education in the South by the states on these grounds. Just here the great mission of

Industrial Education

coupled with the mental comes in. It "kills two birds with one stone," viz.: secures the coöperation of the whites, and does the best possible thing for the black man. An old colored man in a cotton field in the middle of July lifted his eyes toward heaven and said, "De cotton is so grassy, de work is so hard, and de sun am so hot, I believe this darkey am called to preach." This old man, no doubt, stated the true reason why not a few enter school. Educate the black man, mentally and industrially, and there will be no doubt of his prosperity; for a race who has lived at all, and paid, for the last twenty years, twenty-five and thirty per cent interest on the dollar advanced for food, with almost no education, can certainly take care of itself when educated mentally and industrially.

The Tuskegee Normal School, located in the black belt of

Alabama, with an ignorant, degraded Negro population of twenty-five thousand within a radius of twenty miles, has a good chance to see the direct needs of the people; and to get a correct idea of their condition one must leave the towns and go far out into the country, miles from any railroad, where the majority of the people live. They need teachers with not only trained heads and hearts, but with trained hands. Schoolhouses are needed in every township and county. The present wrecks of log cabins and bush harbors, where many of the schools are now taught, must be replaced by comfortable, decent houses. In many schoolhouses rails are used for seats, and often the fire is on the outside of the house, while teacher and scholars are on the inside. Add to this a teacher who can scarcely write his name, and who is as weak mentally as morally, and you then have but a faint idea of the educational condition of many parts of the South. It is the work of Tuskegee, not to send into these places teachers who will stand off and tell the people what to do, or what ought to be done, but to send those who can take hold and show the people *how* to do. The blacksmiths, carpenters, brickmasons, and tinners, who learned their trades in slavery, are dying out, and slavery having taught the colored boy that labor is a disgrace, few of their places are being filled. The Negro now has a monopoly of the trades in the South, but he can't hold it unless the young men are taught trades while in school. The large number of educated loafers to be seen around the streets of our large cities furnishes another reason in favor of industrial education. Then the proud fop with his beaver hat, kid gloves, and walking cane, who has done no little to injure the cause of education South, by industrial training, would be brought down to something practical and useful. The Tuskegee Normal School, with a farm of five hundred acres, carpenter's shop, printing office, blacksmith's shop, and brick yard for boys, and a sewing department, laundry, flower gardening, and practical housekeeping for girls, is trying to do its part towards furnishing industrial training. We ask help for nothing that we can do for ourselves; nothing is bought that the students can produce. The boys raise the vegetables, have done the painting, made the brick, the chairs, the tables, the desks; have built a stable, a carpenter's shop, and a blacksmith's shop. The girls do the entire housekeeping, including the mending, ironing, and washing of the boys' clothes; besides they make many garments to sell.

The majority of the students are poor and able to pay but little cash for board; consequently the school keeps three points before it: first, to give the student the best mental training; secondly, to furnish him with labor that will be valuable to the school, and that will enable the student to learn something from the labor *per se;* thirdly, to teach the dignity of labor. A *chance* to help himself is what we want to give to every student; this is the chance that was given me ten years ago when I entered the Hampton Institute with but fifty cents in my pocket, and it is my only ambition in life to do my part in giving it to every other poor but worthy young man and woman.

As to morals, the Negro is slowly but surely improving. In this he has had no standard by which to shape his character. The masses in too many cases have been judged by their so-called leaders, who are as a rule ignorant, immoral preachers or selfish politicians. The number of these preachers is legion. One church near Tuskegee has a total membership of two hundred, and nineteen of these are preachers.

Poverty and ignorance have affected the black man just as they affect the white man. They have made him untruthful, intemperate, selfish, caused him to steal, to be cheated, and made the outcast of society, and he has aspired to positions which he was not mentally and morally capable of filling. But the day is breaking, and education will bring the complete light. The scales of prejudice are beginning to drop from the eyes of the dominant classes South, and through their clearer and more intelligent vision they are beginning to see and recognize the mighty truth that wealth, happiness, and permanent prosperity will only come in proportion as the hand, head, and heart of both races are educated and Christianized.

7
John
Dewey

During his college days at the University of Vermont, John Dewey tells us that he recognized "the disorganized character of western modern culture." From the beginnings, he said, he traced that "disorganization" to "a disintegrative individualism." The search for a solution to this problem of cultural disorganization became the overriding quest in Dewey's intellectual career. In graduate school at Johns Hopkins (1882–84) he discovered that the German philosopher Georg Hegel had made similar criticisms of Western civilization. Hegel went beyond criticism to offer a solution—a mode of synthesizing or regulating social life. Yet, although Hegel impressed him deeply, Dewey reports that he "drifted away from Hegelianism in the next fifteen years."

Dewey came to realize that Hegelianism, like all absolutist philosophies, was authoritarian. Born in the aftermath of Germany's war for independence, it reflected the social struggle of the period: a struggle "to subordinate the individual to the established state in order to check the disintegrating tendencies of liberalism." Hegel had concocted the notion of the state as "god on earth," the absolute reality—maintaining that individuals have objective existence, truth, and morality only in their capacity as members of the state. Gradually, Dewey came to see that this solution to the problem of cultural disorganization was inappropriate for America.

First and foremost a nineteenth-century American dedicated to American democracy and confident of America's social progress, John Dewey held out for a nonauthoritarian solution to the problem of social disorganization—a solution in accord with Democracy and progress. His quest for this progressive, democratic solution began in his first monograph, *The Ethics of Democracy*, published in 1888.

✳

In *The Ethics of Democracy* Dewey sought to rebut Sir Henry Maine's devastating attack on democracy. In a book of essays titled *Popular Government* (1886), Maine had declared that the cultural disorganization that so troubled all thinking men of the nineteenth century was the result of the growth of popular government, or democracy.

In his initial essay Maine had raised two devastating criticisms against democracy. First, as an empirical criticism—based on the actual events of the preceding century—he argued that democracy was a most unstable form of government. As history reveals, it produces what he called "irreconcilable bodies" within the mass of population, who insist on the immediate redemption of the pledge "of a new and good time at hand" and "utterly refuse to wait until a popular majority gives effect to their opinions."

Maine's second criticism of democracy emerges from what he calls its "inherent nature." Democracy, he says, prevents progress; it obstructs new ideas, rejects new discoveries and inventions, impedes new arts of life. "Universal suffrage," he declares, "which today excludes free trade in the United States, would certainly have prohibited the spinning jenny and the power loom. It would certainly have forbidden the threshing machine. It would have prevented the adoption of the Gregorian calendar and it would have restored the Stuarts." Democracy, he concludes, is opposed to science.

In his second essay Maine raised a third criticism of democracy—he calls it "the greatest, most permanent, and most fundamental of all the difficulties of democracy": the absence of a common will. "On the complex questions of politics," he says, "the common determination of the multitude is a chimerical assumption."

In his rebuttal to Maine, the young Dewey focuses on a philosophical question: "What is democracy?" First, democracy is not, as Maine thought, merely a form of government: it is a way of life. Government, therefore, is not to be construed, as Maine construed it, in terms of sovereignty—the governors and the governed—but as a way of expressing the *will* of the society. Thus Dewey rejects the notion propounded by many, including Maine, that the distinguishing characteristic of democracy is "rule by many." Democracy, for Dewey, is form of association. This is an ethical conception. Democracy differs from all other forms of association because it is more ethical: it allows for the greatest amount of participation in determining the common good. In a democracy no elite imposes its version of the "common good" on the rest of the people. For Dewey, a democracy offers "an individualism of freedom, of responsibility, of initiatives to and for the ethical ideal."

This conviction that democracy is the most ethical form of human association because it allows all to participate in the creation of the common good became the single most important notion in John Dewey's social and political philosophy. But at this stage of his intellectual career, this notion precipitated more problems than it solved. For, even if one accepts the construction of democracy as an ethical form of association—i.e., a form of association that permits all to participate in decision making—the objections Sir Henry Maine raised come back with renewed force: the participation of all people simply leads to social instability, the obstruction of progress, and the disappearance of a societal common will. Ethical though democracy may be, can any society afford it?

In this early monograph Dewey tried to use Hegelian notions to rebut Maine's dire predictions. He argued that society and the individual are "organic" to each other, which led him to conclude that a democratic society *does* have a common will, is the *most* stable of all forms of society, and offers the *most* opportunity for the individual to progress, to realize himself most fully as a person. So, in direct opposition to Sir Henry Maine, Dewey now argues that democracy was the cure for—not the cause of—the problem of cultural disintegration.

But he didn't prove it. Nowhere does he really reply to Maine's criticisms of democracy. His argument from philosophical idealism did not speak to the empirical claims that democracies are unstable forms of government (or society). They either are unstable, or they are not. More important, can Dewey tell us how to prevent instability? Nor could philosophical idealism guarantee the actual existence of a common will. A common will exists, or it does not. Moreover, if a democracy could possess a common will, then can Dewey tell us how it comes into existence? And how it functions? Nor, finally, does the notion of individual self-realization inherent in philosophical idealism, actually confront the question of social progress. Can Dewey tell us how individual self-realization leads to social progress for all?

If he was to continue to maintain that democracy is the solution to the problem of cultural disorganization, then, Dewey realized, he must confront these empirical and practical questions. Moreover, he saw that the solution to them lay in a reconstruction of social philosophy based on the notion of the common good. He had to come up with a construction that allowed for common participation in determining the common good, but which, at the same time, would ensure—or at least not endanger—social progress and social stability. In preparation for such a reconstruction Dewey tells us he now undertook "a systematic study of ethics." A study that culminated in the publication of *Ethics* in 1908.

❊

Before publishing his *Ethics*, Dewey wrote two textbooks for use in his college courses at the University of Michigan. These, together with the later *Ethics*, reveal his long struggle to reconstruct moral philosophy.

In the first book—*Outlines of a Critical Theory of Ethics*, published in 1891—Dewey remained very much the Hegelian. Here he repeats his conviction that the chief end of man is "self-realization." In his next book—*The Study of Ethics: A Syllabus*, published in 1894—Dewey began to move away from absolute idealism toward what he called "Experimental Idealism." At this point, as

Morton White has carefully demonstrated, Dewey abandoned the
a priori notion of self-realization for an experimental one. "Some
acts tend to narrow the self, to introduce friction into it, to weaken
its power, and in various ways to *disintegrate* it, while other acts
tend to expand, invigorate, and harmonize, and in general organize
the self." According to this new organicism those acts that
disintegrate the self are "bad," those that integrate it, "good." We
learn which are bad and which are good only through experiment
or experience.

Dewey always conceived individuals as existing within a social
context, so when he abandoned the a priori notion of the good for
an experimental one, that good ever remained a social, or common
good. That is, those acts that integrate the self are—must be—acts
that integrate the society; those that disintegrate the self, disintegrate the society.

In his *Ethics* of 1908 Dewey makes clear how individual
self-realization maintains social stability. "The essential factor in
morality," he declares, is "the constant discovery, formation, and
reformation of the self in the ends which an individual is called
upon to sustain and develop in virtue of his membership in a social
whole." There is hardly a whiff of philosophical idealism here.
Self-realization takes place *only* within a social context—it takes
place *only* after an individual recognizes and accepts the ends
inherent in the society.

This sounds like the individual is subordinate to, indeed the
captive of, the social group. But here Dewey makes an important
distinction between a static society and a progressive one. In a
static society the emphasis is on those ends, or values, already
shared. But a progressive society is one in which there is an
opportunity to initiate, to create new values that will be socially
shareable. In short, a progressive society is one where all individuals can contribute to the common good.

Dewey deliberately eschews what he calls a "monastic"
morality, one that retreats "from social affairs for the sake of
cultivating personal goodness." For him, the moral quality resides
"in the habitual dispositions of an agent . . . it *consists* of the
tendency of those dispositions to secure (or hinder) values which
are socially shared, or shareable." He concludes that the moral and
the social are one: morality "is simply the means of social

reconstruction." Yet this new "social morality" can emerge only in a progressive, or (*pace*, Sir Henry Maine) democratic society—one that has customs, institutions, laws, and organizations that set free individual capacities "in such a way to make them available for the development of the general happiness or the common good."

Here we must note that Dewey's conception of a progressive society is quite different from that used by Sir Henry Maine. Dewey's conception emerges from his notion of social morality: a progressive society is one that allows all or most people to initiate change, to create new, socially shareable values. Maine, however, speaks of progress and progressive societies solely in terms of results; i.e., some changes are demonstrably progressive, e.g., the spinning jenny, the Gregorian calendar, etc. Societies that permit or allow such changes are progressive. His contention is that allowing all people to participate in initiating social change will, in fact, obstruct actual progress. For Dewey a democracy is a progressive society by definition; for Maine, a democracy is empirically not a progressive society.

So if he is to meet Maine's arguments Dewey will have to show that the participation of all does lead to progress in Maine's sense of that term, i.e., he must demonstrate progressive results. Dewey begins to work toward an answer to this when he points out that the freedom accorded to individuals in a progressive (democratic) society carries with it responsibility—the responsibility for all to be intelligent or reflective. Indeed, by 1908 Dewey had adopted the term "reflective morality" for his experimental ethics. Reflective morality supplied no final ends or final rules or precepts for men to follow. All human acts are potentially moral, since all acts have consequences that affect others. Reflection will help men determine the right course of action in each concrete situation. Those acts or actions are right that contribute to the general or social well-being.

Yet, although he sought to replace traditional "customary morality" with "reflective morality," Dewey nowhere in the *Ethics* explains how reflection takes place, what it consists of. Nor does he really explain how reflective morality will maintain stability within the society and, at the same time, insure progress. In his next book, *How We Think*, he takes care of all these loose ends by explaining that reflection is simply thinking—and thinking, real thinking, follows the method of science.

❋

In the first chapter of *How We Think*, published in 1910, Dewey defines reflective thought as "active, persistent, and careful consideration of any belief or supposed form of knowledge in the light of the grounds that support it, and the further conclusions to which it tends." The central factor in reflective thinking, he notes, is "that operation in which present facts suggest other facts (or truths) in such a way as to induce belief in the latter upon the ground or warrant of the former."

This search for justifications or warrants for our beliefs begins with a problem, or a "felt difficulty." Four logically distinct steps follow: "(1) location and definition of the difficulty or problem; (2) suggestion of possible solution; (3) development by reasoning of the bearings of the suggestion; (4) further observation and experiment leading to its acceptance or rejection; that is the conclusion of belief or disbelief." Thinking—reflective thinking—Dewey says, is problem solving.

Next, Dewey explains, or proposes, an appropriate model for problem solving. He reformulates problem solving into two phases of systematic inference: inductive discovery and deductive proof. Through induction we come up with an idea, a conjecture, an hypothesis—to solve the problem, overcome the difficulty. Then, through deduction, we develop the idea, or hypothesis, by reasoning out consequences or certain additional particulars—not yet experienced—that ought to be forthcoming, if the hypothesis is acted upon. Finally, we check, or test, or experiment—to see if these particulars are the case. Confirmation corroborates the original hypothesis. For example:

> I discover my room in a state of disorder. (Problem) I infer (induce) that a burglary has taken place. Next I infer (deduce) that *if* a burglary has taken place, *then* the doors or windows will show signs of tampering. I check; find they have been tampered with, and thereby confirm that a burglary has taken place.

The essence of reflective thinking, Dewey says, is suspended judgment: the reflective thinker must be cautious in deciding, what the problem actually is, cautious in coming to an hypothesis or possible solution, cautious in tracing consequences, and cautious in testing for them. The model or exemplar for *cautious, careful* inquiry or reflection is science. Science, or the scientific method, is *the* method for problem solving or reflective thought. Through the scientific method we "observe" and "amass" data that facilitate the formation of significant hypothesis (induction). And through that method we draw conclusions from the hypothesis (deduction) and then experiment to test for them. For example:

> The scientist who is a physician by careful observation induces from the amassed data that the patient has typhoid fever. Then, he deduces that if this hypothesis is correct that the patient will have (the yet undiscovered) condition p. Condition p will be observable through symptom o, which can be measured by instrument q. The physician next performs a test or experiment to confirm (or disconfirm) his hypothesis.

Now that he has explained what he means by reflective thought, Dewey is well on the way to solving the problem that has so long troubled him: cultural disorganization. He had traced cultural disorganization to "a disintegrative individualism" which could be combated, he argued, by democracy—a form of association where all participated in making decisions. But Sir Henry Maine had warned that such popular participation simply led to social instability and hindered progress as well. Dewey's answer to this was the construction of a new "social morality," a reflective morality. According to this, people would make decisions about what is good by using the scientific method. Certainly no one—not even Sir Henry Maine—could deny that employment of the method of science would ensure both progress and stability!

But Sir Henry Maine had raised a third criticism of democracy—"the greatest, most permanent, and most fundamental of all the difficulties of democracy": the absence of a common will. And precisely at this point this difficulty looms up to confront Dewey's proposal to have people in a democracy follow the method of science. For unless there already exists a common will, unless people already share common ends, they cannot use the scientific method to create the common good. The scientific method begins, Dewey says, with a problem. But problems are perceived, or experienced, as obstacles, difficulties, hindrances, to an end-in-view. So if people have different ends—lack a common end—then they will perceive, or experience, different problems. Thus each individual or each group will employ the scientific method to solve his own, or its own, problem. Each will use the scientific method to secure or create an individual or private good, not the common good.

At this point Dewey must come up with a common end that all men do *and should* share. One is already at hand, inherent in the naturalism Dewey now professes, a naturalism far removed from the absolute idealism of his early career. The common end all men share is growth. Later, in *Reconstruction in Philosophy* (1920) Dewey will declare: "Growth itself is the only moral 'end.' "

To help people see that growth is the common end of all is the task of education. In addition, education must help people understand how to promote growth. Thus a democracy—a form of association where all are able to pursue their shared or common interests—demands a special kind of education. This is the message of *Democracy and Education*, which appeared in 1916.

❋

Dewey begins *Democracy and Education* with a discussion of education as a "necessity of life." Continuous, intergenerational self-renewal of social life demands education. All societies rely on education to maintain their continuous existence. This process is one of controlling and directing the growth of both the immature individual and the group in which he lives. What is crucial, Dewey points out, is how one construes "growth."

In a static society education aims at the preservation of established customs, traditions, behaviors: the young *grow into* predetermined roles and habits. The educators in a static society know what the common good is—they know what is best for the general welfare of the society—and they impose it on the young under the label "education."

But in a progressive society, a democratic society, the common good is not known beforehand. Here growth has no predetermined end, no final stopping place. In a democracy educators promote growth—for more growth. Thus education in a democracy faces a paradox: the end of education is growth, but growth is not an end, a state, or condition—it is a process. Thus education has no end, save further education. As Dewey puts it in *Reconstruction in Philosophy*: "The best thing that can be said about any special process of education, like that of the formal school period, is that it renders its subject capable of further education: more sensitive to conditions of growth and more able to take advantage of them."

How, then, does growth take place? What is Dewey's theory of growth? We must, he insists, reject both the theory that takes growth as the "unfolding of latent powers from within," *and* the theory that views growth as "formation from without." Both conceptions are widely held by many educators, he notes in *Democracy and Education*, but both are a priori hence authoritarian, antidemocratic. His own notion, or theory, is that growth is a constant reorganizing or reconstruction of experience. Here is his "technical" definition of education: "It is that reconstruction, or reorganization of experience which adds to the meaning of experience, and which increases ability to direct the course of subsequent experience."

To understand this "technical" definition of education one must understand how Dewey uses the term "experience." He construes experience as the interaction of the self with its environment. The self is active: it has impulses and instincts and purposes, or ends. The environment supports, permits, or promotes that activity, whether it be walking, breathing, eating, or whatever. But the environment also, at times, hinders, frustrates, or stops that activity. The environment can present us with a problem.

These experiences—problems—present us with opportunities for growth. So long as the environment supports the activity of the self, there is no need to change, to alter behavior. But once it encounters an obstacle, a problem—once, that is, its habitual patterns of behavior are no longer adequate—then it must, if it can, develop new and different ways of behaving, ways that will overcome the obstacle or problem. And the method for overcoming obstacles, the method to solve problems, of course, is the scientific method. Growth, in short, consists of problem solving, or reflective thinking—the employment of the scientific method. It is through the scientific method that we reorganize or reconstruct experience, thereby adding to the meaning of experience; and at the same time we increase our ability to direct the course of subsequent experience.

※

Education was not a new topic for Dewey. Very early in his career he had publicly lamented what he called the "chaos" in moral training in the schools. Then, in 1897 he published *Ethical Principles Underlying Education* (which in 1909 he republished under the title *Moral Principles in Education*). Here he criticized the schools for continuing educational practices that encouraged the "disintegrative individualism" that lay at the root of the present cultural disorganization.

The practice of having children in any given class all do the same work—study, recite, and regurgitate—for a grade leads to competition and rivalry: "The weaker gradually lose their sense of capacity, and accept a position of continuous and persistent inferiority. . . . The stronger grow to glory, not in their strength, but in the fact that they are stronger." The upshot of such educational practices is that the child is launched into "individualistic competition" in areas where competition is least applicable, in intellectual and spiritual matters. There, Dewey insists, the rule is (or ought to be) cooperation and participation.

The individualistic, competitive practices common in the schools engender selfish dispositions in the young. Educators must replace these practices, Dewey counsels, with ones that engender dispositions to social service and social usefulness. More is involved than simply the introduction of new pedagogical practices. For if the school is actually to perform a moral function—which for Dewey is ever a social function—then, he claims, we must reconstruct the school itself as a *social* institution, we must develop *social* methods of learning and we must cast the school studies in such a way that students perceive their social significance.

In 1894 Dewey left the University of Michigan to go to Chicago as chairman of the combined Departments of Philosophy,

Psychology, and Pedagogy. There he proposed that the scholarly research facilities be brought to bear on the problems of education. To "test and exhibit in actual working order the results of the theoretical work," Dewey founded what came to be called "the laboratory school." In the late 1890s he delivered a series of lectures to explain what the "new education" was all about. These came out as a book in 1899, under the title *The School and Society*.

The "new education," Dewey explained, can be understood only in the context of the cultural disorganization brought about by social changes—changes "writ so large that he who runs may read." Industrialization had removed children from those agencies of informal education they had encountered in their normal process of growing up on the farm or in the small village. Then, by merely observing and helping his parents and other adults in their daily rounds of work and labor, the child had learned how men solved their shared problems of daily living. Then, too, the normal process of growing up had included experiences that developed moral character. For as part of the community, every child had such chores to perform as milking the cow or gathering firewood— duties, the neglect of which could lead to dire consequences. These responsibilities developed character.

The society now emerging in America had eclipsed that educative community. Living in the ever more industrialized city, segregated and cut off from the world of work, children were losing contact with the real world; they no longer understood how men solved their existential problems; they lacked the elemental knowledge of how men secured food, clothing, shelter. The "new education," Dewey explained, was a response to these social changes.

Now, according to Dewey, the schools had to perform the functions previously performed by the community itself. What in earlier times they had learned informally, children now had to learn in formal institutions. But to carry out these new responsibilities we must transform the school into a community, an embryonic community. A community is "a number of people held together because they are working along common lines, in a common spirit, and with reference to common aims." So for a school to become a true community the methods of learning and doing must change. Students must engage in "common and productive activity." In the

University of Chicago Laboratory School the spirit of cooperation replaced the traditional school spirit of competition. There, mutual assistance was no longer a "crime"; pupils freely communicated and exchanged ideas—silence wasn't "golden"; pupils were making and doing—not passively receiving instruction or timorously reciting. In brief, students were learning by doing.

And to create social methods of learning meant the transformation of the school studies themselves. In the Laboratory School, children studied the occupations of cooking, sewing, carpentry, gardening. They investigated how people have solved the problems of securing food, clothing, and shelter at different times and in different places. Thus, they learned history and geography as well as science and mathematics, and the communication arts of reading and writing; but they learned them in ways that made such "subject matter" socially meaningful. Through these "real life" activities the school became "a genuine form of active community life, instead of a place set apart in which to learn lessons."

The function of the school was decidedly social: to train "each child of society into membership within such a little community, saturating him with the spirit of service, and providing him with the instruments of effective self direction." This, Dewey claimed, "was the deepest and best guarantee of a larger society which is worthy, lovely, and harmonious."

The "new education" was not confined to the Laboratory School at the University of Chicago. In a book he wrote in collaboration with his daughter, Evelyn, called *Schools of Tomorrow* (1915), Dewey presented vignettes of numerous schools that had independently sprung up across the nation. In Fairhope, Alabama, an experimental school had been recently founded by Marrietta Johnson . . . at the University of Missouri, Professor J. L. Meriam was directing an elementary school . . . the Francis Parker School in Chicago, the Cottage School at Riverside, Ill., and the "play" school in New York City all practiced the "new education" . . . as did the school at Interlaken, Indiana, and the Little School in the Woods at Greenwich, Connecticut . . . while the public schools in Chicago, Cincinnati, Indianapolis, and, above all, Gary, Indiana, all manifested signs of the "new education." What is common to all these schools, Dewey tells us, is that they have abandoned the traditional school program designed for a small and specialized social class, in favor of a program "truly representative of the needs and conditions of a democratic society."

The conventional type of education, Dewey says, is suited to an autocratic society: "it trains children to docility and obedience, to the careful performance of imposed tasks because they are imposed, regardless of where they lead." A democracy, Dewey insists, must have schools that allow children freedom, and help them develop active qualities of initiative, independence, and resourcefulness; only, then, Dewey claims, will "the abuses and failures" of democracy disappear.

*

In *Democracy and Education* (1916), Dewey presents the philosophic underpinnings for the "new education." In his earlier books on education he had stressed the social function of education in a democracy, stressing occupational studies as a way to confront the young with the "real problems" men faced in securing food, clothing, shelter, and other necessities for survival and progress. Now he demonstrates that reflective thought—scientific method—is the method whereby men actually solve their problems. In this book, Dewey proposes that in a democracy scientific problem solving should be the aim, the method, and the subject matter of education.

Here Dewey equates democracy and science. Science is an activity through which men solve their problems. So with democracy. It is that form of association in which all engage in joint activity to solve common, or shared problems. The result of this joint activity is the creation of the common good—that good created by and shared by all.

There are obstacles to an education that takes scientific problem solving as its aim, method, and content. These obstacles, Dewey reveals, are rooted in a vestigal prescientific (hence predemocratic) philosophy—a philosophy that separates mind and body, spirit and matter, and, most importantly, a philosophy that holds mind superior to matter. Dewey finds these philosophical dualisms manifest in the traditional distinctions people have made between labor and leisure, between vocation and culture, between

practical and intellectual culture. Moreover, societies have histori-
cally embodied these distinctions in rigidly marked-off, hierarchi-
cally stratified social classes and groups, prohibiting those in the
lower classes from participating in leisure, cultural, or intellectual
activities. In these prescientific, predemocratic societies, an elite—
the upper classes—alone determined the common good, imposing
it upon the rest.

If we are ever to have a truly democratic society, we must,
Dewey insists, root out all vestiges of this prescientific philosophy.
This philosophy originated, he claims, in "the conflicts and duties
of social life." Every philosophical system records the main
lineaments and difficulties of the society and culture in which it is
born. So the way to liquidate prescientific philosophy is to
eradicate all predemocratic social and class distinctions. And we
can do this by developing new social and cultural dispositions in
the young—democratic dispositions. We can use the schools to
reconstruct the society by making them schools for *all* and
converting them into democratic communities where the young
learn how to work together to solve the problems shared by all
people.

Thus the schools are the key to creating a true democracy, a
society where all participate in creating the common good.

✽

Dewey left the University of Chi-
cago in 1904 to become a member of the philosophy department of
Columbia University and never again engaged in the kind of
professional educational activities he had conducted at the Laboratory School in Chicago. After the publication of *Democracy and
Education* in 1916, he confined his writing on education to minor
articles and to lectures that merely defended, explained, and
corrected misinterpretations of the educational philosophy he had
already developed.

Dewey now became *the* sage, *the* wise man of educational
thought. He acquired legions of self-styled disciples in teacher-
training institutions who expounded, interpreted, and defended his
social texts. Most American educators accepted the notion that a
democratic society required some kind of "new education." Many

found what they were looking for in the works of John Dewey. The overwhelming influence of Dewey's thought on American educators continued, largely unchallenged until his death in the 1950s; in some quarters it continues to this day. At first blush this is surprising, if only because his educational philosophy comes predicated on a picture of a democracy that never existed, and probably never could exist; there is an empirical emptiness about it.

Throughout our history, even during the so-called progressive period, a (somewhat open) ruling class has made our public decisions. (In Dewey's terminology: a ruling class determined the common good.) And this ruling class has rarely made its decisions on purely scientific or even "rational" grounds. The actual decisions made usually result from compromises with the diverse pushes and pulls exerted by other groups within the society. In our "democracy" elitism, pluralism, and irrational emotions have continually played central roles. Dewey sought—vainly, I think—to replace this functioning democracy with an ideal construct where *all* people, following the quintessentially *rational* scientific method, would participate in the making of public decisions in light of their shared, or *common* end of growth.

Similarly, Dewey's educational philosophy depicts a school or school enterprise that never existed and probably never could exist. To carry it out would require superteachers and superstudents. Dewey expects teachers to have a thorough understanding of his philosophy plus a knowledge of the subject matter, including its history, its logical structure, and its connection with other subject matters, plus a social-psychological understanding of the child and his development. Now, perhaps we could find some teachers who could pull this off, but hardly enough to staff a complete school, and surely not enough to run a nationwide educational enterprise. Likewise we can find *some* pupils who are, or who can become, dedicated scientists, indefatigable in the pursuit of inquiry into the problems of men—but we probably cannot find enough to fill a school.

Yet once we realize that Dewey's ideal school became, like all ideals, a club to smash and destroy what actually existed, then the mystery of his long-standing appeal to American educators begins to clear up. Educators seized upon Dewey's philosophy not because they wanted to reconstruct American society (although some did) but because they wanted to reconstruct the schools. They wanted to democratize them (although perhaps in a way quite different from what Dewey intended).

Demographic changes after the American Civil War set afoot a series of events that inexorably led to the transformation of American schools. The dramatic increase in population—as a result of immigration as well as natural growth—together with the industrialization and urbanization of the society all combined to render children, especially children of the lower classes, a social problem. In the underpopulated agrarian society of antebellum days, children had been an asset; they had had useful work to do. Not after the war. Thus we find adult workers, in self-protection, fighting against child employment in the factories and mills, while the philanthropic-minded of the middle class opposed child labor on moral grounds.

Without work the children simply "got into trouble" in the streets and alleys of the cities. The only solution was to force them to go to school. Compulsory schooling laws, passed in every state and enforced by truant officers, brought the kids into the schools. It was up to the teachers to keep them there. To do this the teachers realized they had to destroy the traditional school; they had to create a new atmosphere in the schools, adopt new methods, introduce new subjects, concoct new aims. John Dewey supplied the strategies, the rhetoric, and the theoretic rationale for transforming the American school.

Throughout the first half of the twentieth century, generation after generation of teachers streamed from the schools of education armed with some (usually inchoate) understanding of, and powerful belief in, Dewey's philosophy of education. Their primary article of faith was that education—by which they meant "schooling"—was a good thing . . . for all people. Resolutely they set about to democratize American schools from the elementary level to the college, making them institutions that all children would attend and stay in for as long as possible.

Thus teachers permitted pupils to be more active in school: Pupils "learned by doing." Teachers subsumed a concern with subject matter to a concern for children themselves—their problems, their needs, their interests: Schools became "child-centered." They tried to relate what went on in the school with the outside world: providing students with "real life educative experiences." They replaced the pedagogical aim of mastery with the more human, although less rigorous, aim of growth: "education is growth; growth is education." Although few schools ever became "embryonic democratic communities," most did become more informal, more relaxed, more friendly than they had been before.

Of course, the logic of institutional change prevented most schools from immediate, radical reconstruction. Tending to the business of keeping the schools going took up most of the educators' time and energy. And the zeal for reconstruction found in most new teachers tended to wane in a few years. Frequently the most zealous departed in disillusionment. Yet most of the teachers continued to believe in what they thought Dewey stood for—even if they had to compromise in practice.

When critics scoffed and scolded them for the changes they had made in the schools, the educators rolled out John Dewey's ideal democracy. And few critics had the temerity to reject that ideal simply because that ideal—of an equal, unified, rational society—was embedded deep in the consciousness of Western man. It was the ideal used during the Enlightenment to shatter the inequality, the pluralism, and the irrationalism of feudalism. Hence educators could successfully defend the new education not as an effort to make schooling fun, but as a sincere effort to create a "truly democratic society."

And all the while, John Dewey, proud of the unified, holistic character of his complete philosophy, continually complained in hurt tones: "that is not what I meant . . . that is not what I meant at all!" Dewey was like the man in the crazy-house-of-mirrors who discovers a distorted, truncated, misshapen reality everywhere he looks, yet knows full well that what he perceives is his own reflection.

As the new education percolated up through grade after grade and level after level of the educational system, more and more children remained longer and longer in the schools. The enrollment figures dramatically tell the story of the democratization of American education.

Enrollment rates increased twice as much in the sixty years

after 1900 as in the sixty years before. The actual number of children aged five to seventeen enrolled in school more than doubled between 1900 and 1960, going from 16.7 million to 38.8 million. The number of high school graduates rose from 62,000 in 1900 to 1,627,000 in 1960. By 1960 98 percent of youths aged seven to thirteen were enrolled in school; for those fourteen to seventeen the figure was 88 percent. Perhaps just as revealing is the fact that the percentage of enrolled pupils attending schools rose from 68.6 percent in 1900 to 90 percent in 1960.

By 1960 it was clear that the schools had become democratized—they just about served *all* American youth. Now Dewey's philosophy was no longer needed as a club to smash the traditional school; the traditional school had disappeared. Now educators could take Dewey's educational philosophy seriously as a model, a blueprint, for education. Those who followed this course—the romantic school of educators of the 1960s and '70s—relentlessly carried out the logic of that philosophy.

To other Americans, especially those who approached education from the perspective of the international "cold war" with communism, the democratization of education raised haunting fears. Did the new education endanger America's chance for survival?

WORKS AND COMMENTARY

John Dewey wrote some forty books and over seven hundred articles. Southern Illinois University Press has published five volumes of his early works and expects to publish forty more. Dewey's three most important books on educational theory are still in print: *The School and Society* (Chicago: University of Chicago Press, 1956), *Democracy and Education* (New York: Macmillan Co., 1961), and *Experience and Education* (New York: Collier-Macmillan 1963). Dewey's plans for the Laboratory School at Chicago appear in a book written by two former teachers in that school; see Katherine Camp Mayhew and Anna Camp Edwards, *The Dewey School* (New York: D. Appleton-Century Co., 1936). Reginald D. Archambault has collected Dewey's most important articles on education in *John*

Dewey on Education: Selected Writings (New York: Random House, 1964). Martin Dworkin has edited a similar, smaller collection called *Dewey on Education* (New York: Teachers College Bureau of Publication, 1959).

John Dewey wrote a brief intellectual biography, "From Absolutism to Experimentalism" published in *Contemporary American Philosophy*, edited by George P. Adams and William P. Montague (New York: 1930). His daughter, Jane, also wrote a "Biography of John Dewey" for the first volume in the Library of Living Philosophers, *The Philosophy of John Dewey*, edited by Paul A. Schlipp (Evanston: Northwestern University Press, 1939). One of Dewey's most famous pupils, Sidney Hook, wrote *John Dewey: An Intellectual Portrait* (New York: John Day 1939). George Dykhuizen has recently published an authoritative biography: *The Life and Mind of John Dewey* (Carbondale, Ill.: Southern Illinois University Press, 1973).

Comprehensive analyses of Dewey's educational thought appear in Melvin C. Baker's, *Foundations of John Dewey's Educational Theory* (New York: King's Crown Press, 1955), and Arthur G. Wirth's *John Dewey as Educator* (New York: John Wiley & Sons, 1966). Lawrence Cremin's *The Transformation of the School* (New York: Alfred A. Knopf, 1961) is the best historical analysis of John Dewey's place in the history of American education. Other historical studies are in Oscar Handlin's *John Dewey's Challenge to Education* (Westport, Conn.: Greenwood Press, 1959) and Richard Hofstadter's *Anti-Intellectualism in American Life* (New York: Alfred A. Knopf, 1963).

The best collection of critical analyses of Dewey's philosophy is the Schlipp volume mentioned above. Reginald D. Archambault has edited a collection of critical analyses of Dewey's educational thought: *Dewey on Education: Appraisals* (New York: Random House, 1966).

The selection that follows is taken from John and Evelyn Dewey's *Schools of Tomorrow* (New York: Dutton, 1962), pages 207–26.

Democracy and Education

The schools that have been described were selected not because of any conviction that they represent all of the best work that is being done in this country, but simply because they illustrate the general trend of education at the present time, and because they seem fairly representative of different types of schools. Of necessity a great deal of material that would undoubtedly prove just as suggestive as what has been given, has been omitted. No attempt has been made to touch upon the important movement for the vitalization of rural education: a movement that is just as far-reaching in its scope and wholesome in its aims as anything that is being done, since it purposes to overcome the disadvantages of isolation that have handicapped the country schoolteacher, and to make use of the natural environment of the child to give him a vocational education, in the same way that the city schools use their artificial environment. And except as their work illustrates a larger educational principle, very little attention has been given to the work of individual teachers or schools in their attempt to teach the conventional curriculum in the most efficient way. While devices and ingenious methods for getting results from pupils often seem most suggestive and even inspiring to the teacher, they do not fit into the plan of this book when they have to do simply with the better use of the usual material of the traditional education.

We have been concerned with the more fundamental changes in education, with the awakening of the schools to a realization of the fact that their work ought to prepare children for the life they are to lead in the world. The pupils who will pass this life in intellectual pursuits, and who get the necessary training for the practical side of their lives from their home environment, are such a small factor numerically that the schools are not acting wisely to shape all the work for them. The schools we have been discussing are all working away from a curriculum adapted to a small and specialized class toward one which shall be truly representative of the needs and conditions of a democratic society.

While these schools are all alike in that they reflect the new spirit in education, they differ greatly in the methods that have been developed to bring about the desired results; their surroundings and the class of pupils dealt with are varied enough to suggest the influence that local conditions must exercise over methods even when the aim is identical. To the educator for whom the problems of democracy are at all real, the vital necessity appears to be that of making the connection between the child and his environment as complete and intelligent as possible, both for the welfare of the child and for the sake of the community. The way this is to be accomplished will, of course, vary according to the conditions of the community and to a certain extent according to the temperament and beliefs of the educator. But great as the differences are between the different schools, between such a plan as that worked out by Mr. Meriam in Columbia, Mo., and the curriculum of the Chicago public schools, an analysis of the ideas back of the apparent extreme divergence of views, reveals certain resemblances that seem more fundamental than the differences. The resemblances are more fundamental because they illustrate the direction that educational reform is taking, and because many of them are the direct result of the changes that modern science and psychology have brought about in our way of looking at the world.

Curiously enough, most of these points of similarity are found in the views advocated by Rousseau, though it is only very recently that they have begun to enjoy anything more than a theoretical respect. The first point of similarity is the importance that is accorded to the physical welfare of the pupils. The necessity of ensuring the health of all young people as the foundation on which to build other qualities and abilities, and the hopelessness of trying to build where the body is weak, ill-nourished, or uncontrolled, is now so well recognized that it has become a commonplace and needs only a passing mention here. Health is as important from the social point of view as from the individual, so that attention to it is doubly necessary to a successful community.

While all schools realize the importance of healthy pupils, the possibilities of using the activities of the child that are employed in giving him a strong healthy body, for general educational purposes, are not so well understood. As yet it is the pioneer in education who realizes the extent to which young children learn through the use of their bodies, and the impossibility of ensuring general intelligence through a system which does not use the body to teach the mind and the mind to teach the body. This is simply a restatement of Rousseau's proposition that the education of the young child rests largely on whether he is allowed to "develop naturally" or not. It has already been pointed out to what an extent Mrs. Johnson depends on the physical growth of her pupils as a tool for developing their intellectual ability, as well as the important part that muscular skill plays in the educational system of Madame Montessori. This seems not only reasonable but necessary when we think of the mere amount of movement, handling, and feeling of things that a baby must indulge in to understand the most familiar objects in its environment, and remember that the child and the adult learn with the same mental machinery as the very small child. There is no difference in the way the organism works after it is able to talk and walk; the difference lies in the greater complexity of activities which is made possible by the preliminary exercises. Modern psychology has pointed out the fact that the native instincts of a human being are his tools for learning. Instincts all express themselves through the body; therefore education which stifles bodily activities, stifles instincts, and so prevents the natural method of learning. To the extent of making an educational application of this fact, all the schools described are using the physical activities of their pupils, and so the means of their physical development, as instruments for training powers of judgment and right thinking. That is to say, the pupils are learning by doing. Aside from the psychological reasons for teaching by this method, it is the logical consequence of a realization of the importance of the physical welfare of the child, and necessarily brings changes in the material of the schoolroom.

What are the pupils to do in order to learn? Mere activity, if not directed toward some end, may result in developing muscular strength, but it can have very little effect on the mental development of the pupils. These schools have all answered the question in the same general way, though the definite problems on which they work differ. The children must have activities which have some educative content, that is, which reproduce the conditions of real life. This is true whether they are studying about things that happened hundreds of years ago or whether they are doing problems in arithmetic or learning to plane a board. The historical facts which are presented must be true, and whether the pupils are writing a play based on them or are building a Viking boat, the details of the work as well as the main idea must conform to the known facts. When a pupil learns by doing he is reliving both mentally and physically some experience which has proved important to the human race; he goes through the same mental processes as those who originally did these things. Because he has done them he knows the value of the result, that is, the fact. A statement, even of facts, does not reveal the value of the fact, or the sense of its truth—of the fact that it is a fact. Where children are fed only on book knowledge, one "fact" is as good as another; they have no standards of judgment or belief. Take the child studying weights and measures; he reads in his textbook that eight quarts make a peck, but when he does examples he is apt, as every schoolteacher knows, to substitute four for eight. Evidently the statement as he read it in the book did not stand for anything that goes on outside the book, so it is a matter of accident what figure lodges in his brain, or whether any does. But the grocer's boy who has measured out pecks with a quart measure *knows*. He has made pecks; he would laugh at anybody who suggested that four quarts made a peck. What is the difference in these two cases? The schoolboy has a result without the activity of which it is the result. To the grocer's boy the statement has value and truth, for it is the obvious result of an experience—it is a *fact*.

Thus we see that it is a mistake to suppose that practical activities have only or even mainly a utilitarian value in the schoolroom. They are necessary if the pupil is to understand the facts which the teacher wishes him to learn; if his knowledge is to be real, not verbal; if his education is to furnish standards of judgment and comparison. With the adult it is undoubtedly true that most of the activities of practical life have become simply means of satisfying more or less imperative wants. He has performed them so often that their meaning as types of human knowledge has disappeared. But with the schoolchild this is not true. Take a child in the school kitchen; he is not merely preparing that day's midday meal because he must eat; he is learning a multitude of new things. In following the directions of the *recipe* he is learning accuracy, and the success or failure of the dish serves as an excellent measure of the pupil's success. In measuring quantities he is learning arithmetic and tables of measures; in mixing materials, he is finding out how substances act when they are manipulated; in baking or boiling he is discovering some of the elementary facts of physics and chemistry. Repetition of these acts by adults, after the muscular and intellectual mastery of the adjustments they call for has been established, gives the casual thinker the impression that pupils also are doing no more than wasting their time on insignificant things. The grocer's boy knows what a peck is because he has used it to measure things with, but since his stock of knowledge is not increased as he goes on measuring out peck after peck, the point is soon reached where intellectual discovery ends and mere performance of a task takes its place. This is the point where the school can see that the pupil's intellectual growth continues; while the activity of the mere worker who is doing the thing for its immediate practical use becomes mechanical. The school says the pupil has had enough of this particular experience; he knows how to do this thing when he needs to and he has understood the principles or facts which it illustrates; it is time he moved on to other experiences which will teach him other values and facts. When the pupil has learned how to follow a recipe, how to handle foodstuffs and use the stove, he does not go on repeating the same elementary steps; he begins to extend his work to take in the larger aspects of cooking. The educative value of the cooking lessons continues because he is now studying questions of food values, menus, the cost of food, and the chemistry of foodstuffs, and cooking. The kitchen becomes a laboratory for the study of a fundamental factor in human life.

The moral advantages of an active form of education reenforce its intellectual benefits. We have seen how this method of teaching necessitates greater freedom for the pupil, and that this freedom is a positive factor in the intellectual and moral development of the pupils. In the same way the substitution of practical activities for the usual isolated textbook study achieves positive moral results which are marked to any teacher who has used both methods. Where the accumulation of facts presented in books is the standard, memory must be relied upon as the principal tool for acquiring knowledge. The pupil must be stimulated to remember facts; it makes comparatively little difference whether he has to remember them in the exact words of the book, or in his own words, for in either case the problem is to see that he does store up information. The inevitable result is that the child is rewarded when his memory is successful, and punished by failure and low marks when it is not successful. The emphasis shifts from the importance of the work that is done to the pupil's degree of external success in doing it. Since no one's performance is perfect, the failures become the obvious and emphasized thing. The pupil has to fight constantly against the discouragement of never reaching the standard he is told he is expected to reach. His mistakes are constantly corrected and pointed out. Such successes as he achieves are not especially inspiring because he does no more than reproduce the lesson as it already exists in the book. The virtues that the good scholar will cultivate are the colorless, negative virtues of obedience, docility, and submission. By putting himself in an attitude of complete passivity he is more nearly able to give back just what he heard from the teacher or read in the book.

Rewards and high marks are at best artificial aims to strive for; they accustom children to expect to get something besides the value of the product for work they do. The extent to which schools are compelled to rely upon these motives shows how dependent they are upon motives which are foreign to truly moral activity. But in the schools where the children are getting their knowledge by doing things, it is presented to them through all their senses and carried over into acts; it needs no feat of memory to retain what they find out; the muscles, sight, hearing, touch, and their own reasoning processes all combine to make the result part of the working equipment of the child. Success gives a glow of positive achievement; artificial inducements to work are no longer necessary, and the child learns to work from love of the work itself, not for a reward or because he is afraid of a punishment. Activity calls for the positive virtues—energy, initiative, and originality—qualities that are worth more to the world than even the most perfect faithfulness in carrying out orders. The pupil sees the value of his work and so sees his own progress, which spurs him on to further results. In consequence, his mistakes do not assume undue importance or discourage him. He can actively use them as helps in doing better next time. Since the children are no longer working for rewards, the temptation to cheat is reduced to the minimum. There is no motive for doing dishonest acts, since the result shows whether the child has done the work, the only end recognized. The moral value of working for the sake of what is being done is certainly higher than that of working for rewards; and while it is possible that a really bad character will not be reformed by being placed in a situation where there is nothing to be gained excepting through an independent and energetic habit of work, the weak character will be strengthened and the strong one will not form any of those small bad habits that seem so unimportant at first and that are so serious in their cumulative effect.

Another point that most of the present-day reformers have in common, in distinction from the traditional way of looking at schoolwork, is the attempt to find work of interest to the pupils. This used to be looked at as a matter of very little importance; in fact, a certain amount of work that did not interest was supposed to be a very good thing for the moral character of the pupil. This work was supposed to have even greater disciplinary qualities than the rest of the work. Forcing the child to carry through a task which did not appeal to him was supposed to develop perseverance and strength of character. There is no doubt that the ability to perform an irksome duty is a very useful accomplishment, but the usefulness does not lie in the irksomeness of the task. Things are not useful or necessary because they are unpleasant or tiresome, but in spite of these characteristics. The habit of giving work to pupils solely for the sake of its "disciplinary" value would seem to indicate a blindness to moral values rather than an excess of moral zeal, for, after all, the habit is little more than holding up a thing's defects as its virtues.

But if lack of interest is not to be admitted as a motive in selection of classwork, it is fair enough to object that interest cannot serve as a criterion, either. If we take interest in its narrowest sense, as meaning something which amuses and appeals to the child because of its power of entertainment, the objection has truth. The critic of the new spirit in education is apt to assume that this narrow sense is what is meant when he hears that the pupils ought to be interested in what they are doing. Then, logically enough, he goes on to point out that such a system lacks moral fiber, that it caters to the whims of children, and is in reality an example of the general softening of the social fiber, of everyone's desire for the easy way. But the work is not made easy for the pupils; nor yet is there any attempt to give the traditional curriculum a sugar coating. The change is of a more fundamental character and is based on sound psychological theory. The work given to the children has changed; the attempt is not to make all the child's tasks interesting to him, but to select work on the basis of the natural appeal it makes to the child. Interest ought to be the basis for selection because children are interested in the things they need to learn.

Everyone is familiar with the way a baby will spend a long time making over and over again the same motions or feeling of some object, and of the intense interest children two and three years old take in building a tower of blocks, or filling a pail with sand. They do it not once but scores of times, and always with the same deep absorption, for it is real work to them. Their growing, unformed muscles have not yet learned to act automatically; every motion that is aimed at something must be repeated under the conscious direction of the child's mind until he can make it without being aware of effort toward an adjustment. Since the little child must adjust the things about him, his interests and his needs are identical; if they were not he could not live. As a child grows older his control over his immediate needs so rapidly becomes automatic, that we are apt to forget that he still learns as the baby does. The necessary thing is still, as it will be all his life, the power of adjustment.

Good adjustment means a successful human being, so that instinctively we are more interested in learning these adjustments than in anything else. Now the child is interested in adjusting himself through physical activity to the things he comes up against, because he must master his physical environment to live. The things that are of interest to him are the things that he needs to work on. It is then the part of wisdom in selecting the work for any group of children, to take it from that group of things in the child's environment which is arousing their curiosity and interest at that time. Obviously as the child grows older and his control of his body and physical environment increases he will reach out to the more complicated and theoretical aspects of the life he sees about him.

But in just this same way the work in the classroom reaches out to include facts and events which do not belong in any obvious way to the child's immediate environment. Thus the range of the material is not in any way limited by making interest a standard for selection. Work that appeals to pupils as worthwhile, that holds out the promise of resulting in something to their own interests, involves just as much persistence and concentration as the work which is given by the sternest advocate of disciplinary drill. The latter requires the pupil to strive for ends which he cannot see, so that he has to be kept at the task by means of offering artificial ends, marks, and promotions, and by isolating him in an atmosphere where his mind and senses are not being constantly besieged by the call of life which appeals so strongly to him. But the pupil presented with a problem, the solution of which will give him an immediate sense of accomplishment and satisfied curiosity, will bend all his powers to the work; the end itself will furnish the stimulus necessary to carry him through the drudgery.

The conventional type of education which trains children to docility and obedience, to the careful performance of imposed tasks because they are imposed, regardless of where they lead, is suited to an autocratic society. These are the traits needed in a state where there is one head to plan and care for the lives and institutions of the people. But in a democracy they interfere with the successful conduct of society and government. Our famous, brief definition of a democracy, as "government of the people, for the people and by the people," gives perhaps the best clew to what is involved in a democratic society. Responsibility for the conduct of society and government rests on every member of society. Therefore, everyone must receive a training that will enable him to meet this responsibility, giving him just ideas of the condition and needs of the people collectively, and developing those qualities which will ensure his doing a fair share of the work of government. If we train our children to take orders, to do things simply because they are told to, and fail to give them confidence to act and think for themselves, we are putting an almost insurmountable obstacle in the way of overcoming the present defects of our system and of establishing the truth of democratic ideals. Our State is founded on freedom, but when we train the State of tomorrow, we allow it just as little freedom as possible. Children in school must be allowed freedom so that they will know what its use means when they become the controlling body, and they must be allowed to develop active qualities of initiative, independence, and resourcefulness, before the abuses and failures of democracy will disappear.

The spread of the realization of this connection between democracy and education is perhaps the most interesting and significant phase of present educational tendencies. It accounts for the growing interest in popular education, and constitutes a strong reenforcement to the arguments of science and psychology for the changes which have been outlined. There is no doubt that the textbook method of education is well suited to that small group of children who by environment are placed above the necessity of engaging in practical life and who are at the same time interested in abstract ideas. But even for this type of person the system leaves great gaps in his grasp of knowledge; it gives no place to the part that action plays in the development of intelligence, and it trains along the lines of the natural inclinations of the student and does not develop the practical qualities which are usually weak in the abstract person. For the great majority whose interests are not abstract, and who have to pass their lives in some practical occupation, usually in actually working with their hands, a method of education is necessary which bridges the gap between the purely intellectual and theoretical sides of life and their own occupations. With the spread of the ideas of democracy, and the accompanying awakening to social problems, people are beginning to realize that everyone, regardless of the class to which he happens to belong, has a right to demand an education which shall meet his own needs, and that for its own sake the State must supply this demand.

Until recently school education has met the needs of only one class of people, those who are interested in knowledge for its own sake—teachers, scholars, and research workers. The idea that training is necessary for the man who works with his hands is still so new that the schools are only just beginning to admit that control of the material things of life is knowledge at all. Until very recently schools have neglected the class of people who are numerically the largest and upon whom the whole world depends for its supply of necessities. One reason for this is the fact that democracy is a comparatively new thing in itself; and until its advent, the right of the majority, the very people who work with their hands, to supply any of their larger spiritual needs was never admitted. Their function, almost their reason for existence, was to take care of the material wants of the ruling classes.

Two great changes have occurred in the last century and a half which have altered men's habits of living and of thinking. We have just seen how one of these, the growth of democratic ideals, demands a change in education. The other, the change that has come about through scientific discoveries, must also be reflected in the classroom. To piece together all one's historical information into a rough picture of society before the discovery of the steam engine and of electricity, will hardly serve to delineate sufficiently the changes in the very fundamentals of society that these and similar discoveries have brought about. The one possibly most significant from the point of view of education is the incredible increase in the number of facts that must be part of the mental furniture of anyone who meets even the ordinary situations of life successfully. They are so many that any attempt to teach them all from textbooks in school hours would be simply ridiculous. But the schools, instead of facing this frankly and then changing their curriculum so that they could teach pupils how to learn from the world itself, have gone on bravely teaching as many facts as possible. The changes made have been in the way of inventing schemes that would increase the consumption of facts. But the change that is demanded by science is a more radical one; and as far as it has been worked out at present, it follows the general lines that have been suggested in this book. This includes, as the curricula of these different schools have shown, not alone teaching of the scientific laws that have brought about the changes in society since their discovery, but the substitution of real work which itself teaches the facts of life for the study and memorization of facts after they have been classified in books.

If schools are to recognize the needs of all classes of pupils, and give pupils a training that will ensure their becoming successful and valuable citizens, they must give work that will not only make the pupils strong physically and morally and give them the right attitude toward the state and their neighbors, but that will as well give them enough control over their material environment to enable them to be economically independent. Preparation for the professions has always been taken care of; it is, as we have seen, the future of the worker in industry which has been neglected. The complications of modern industry due to scientific discoveries make it necessary for the worker who aspires to real success to have a good foundation of general education on which to build his technical skill, and the complications of human nature make it equally necessary that the beginner shall find his way into work that is suited to his tastes and abilities. A discussion of general educational principles is concerned only with industrial or vocational education which supplies these two needs. The questions of specific trade and professional training fall wholly outside the scope of this book. However, certain facts connected with the movement to push industrial training in its narrower sense have a direct bearing on the larger question. For there is great danger just at present, that, as the work spreads, the really educative type of work that is being done in Gary and Chicago may be overlooked in favor of trade training.

The attention of influential citizens is more easily focused on the need of skilled workers than on that of a general educational readjustment. The former is brought home to them by their own experience, perhaps by their self-interest. They are readily impressed with the extent to which Germany has made technical trade training a national asset in pushing the commercial rivalries of that empire. Nothing seems so direct and practical as to establish a system of continuation schools to improve workers between the ages of fourteen and eighteen who have left school at the earliest age, and to set up separate schools which shall prepare directly for various lines of shop work, leaving the existing schools practically unchanged to prepare pupils for higher schools and for the walks of life where there is less manual work.

Continuation schools are valuable and important, but only as palliatives and makeshifts; they deal with conditions which ought not to exist. Children should not leave school at fourteen, but should stay in school until they are sixteen or eighteen, and be helped to an intelligent use of their energies and to the proper choice of work. It is a commonplace among teachers and workers who come in contact with any number of pupils who leave school at fourteen to go to work, that the reason is not so much financial pressure as it is lack of conviction that school is doing them any good. Of course there are cases where the child enjoys school but is forced to leave at the first opportunity in order to earn money. But even in these rare instances it would usually be wiser to continue the family arrangements that were in vogue up to the child's fourteenth birthday, even if they include charity. The wages of the child of fourteen and fifteen are so low that they make a material difference only to the family who is already living on an inadequate scale.

The hopelessness of the situation is increased by the fact that these children increase their earning capacity much more slowly and reach as their maximum a much lower level than the child who is kept in school, so that in the long run the loss both to the child and his family more than offsets the precarious temporary gain. But the commonest reason advanced by pupils for leaving school is that they did not like it, and were anxious to get some real work to do. Not that they were prepared to go to work, or had finished any course of training, but simply that school seemed so futile and satisfied so few of their interests that they seized the first opportunity to make a change to something that seemed more real, something where there was a visible result.

What is needed then is a reorganization of the ordinary schoolwork to meet the needs of this class of pupils, so that they will wish to stay in school for the value of what they are learning. The present system is bungling and shortsighted; continuation schools patch up some of its defects; they do not overcome them, nor do they enable the pupils to achieve a belated intellectual growth, where the maladjustment of the elementary school has served to check it. The ideal is not to use the schools as tools of existing industrial systems, but to use industry for the reorganization of the schools.

There is danger that the concentrated interests of businessmen and their influential activity in public matters will segregate training for industry to the damage of both democracy and education. Educators must insist upon the primacy of educational values, not in their own behalf, but because these represent the more fundamental interests of society, especially of a society organized on a democratic basis. The place of industry in education is not to hurry the preparation of the individual pupil for his individual trade. It should be used (as in the Gary, Indianapolis, and other schools) to give practical value to the theoretical knowledge that every pupil should have, and to give him an understanding of the conditions and institutions of his environment. When this is done the pupil will have the necessary knowledge and intelligence to make the right choice of work and to direct his own efforts toward getting the necessary technical skill. His choice will not be limited by the fact that he already knows how to do one thing and only one; it will be dictated only by his ability and natural aptitude.

The trade and continuation schools take their pupils before they are old enough or have knowledge enough of their own power to be able to make a wise choice, and then they drill them in one narrow groove, both in their theoretical work and in their manual skill, so that the pupil finds himself marked for one occupation only. If it proves not to be the right one for him it is still the only one he is trained for. Such a system does not give an opportunity for the best development of the individual's abilities, and it tends to keep people fixed in classes.

The very industries that seem to benefit most by receiving skilled workers for the first steps of the trade will lose by it in the more difficult processes, for the workers will not have the background of general knowledge and wider experience that the graduate of a technical high school or vocational school should have acquired. But the introduction of the material of occupations into the schools for the sake of the control of the environment brought by their use will do much to give us the proportion of independent, intelligent citizens that are needed in a democracy.

It is fatal for a democracy to permit the formation of fixed classes. Differences of wealth, the existence of large masses of unskilled laborers, contempt for work with the hands, inability to secure the training which enables one to forge ahead in life, all operate to produce classes, and to widen the gulf between them. Statesmen and legislation can do something to combat these evil forces. Wise philanthropy can do something. But the only fundamental agency for good is the public school system. Every American is proud of what has been accomplished in the past in fostering among very diverse elements of population a spirit of unity and of brotherhood so that the sense of common interests and aims has prevailed over the strong forces working to divide our people into classes. The increasing complexity of our life, with the great accumulation of wealth at one social extreme and the condition of almost dire necessity at the other, makes the task of democracy constantly more difficult. The days are rapidly passing when the simple provision of a system in which all individuals mingle is enough to meet the need. The subject matter and the methods of teaching must be positively and aggressively adapted to the end.

There must not be one system for the children of parents who have more leisure and another for the children of those who are wage-earners. The physical separation forced by such a scheme, while unfavorable to the development of a proper mutual sympathy, is the least of its evils. Worse is the fact that the overbookish education for some and the over-"practical" education for others brings about a division of mental and moral habits, ideals, and outlook.

The academic education turns out future citizens with no sympathy for work done with the hands, and with absolutely no training for understanding the most serious of present-day social and political difficulties. The trade training will turn out future workers who may have greater immediate skill than they would have had without their training, but who have no enlargement of mind, no insight into the scientific and social significance of the work they do, no education which assists them in finding their way on or in making their own adjustments. A division of the public school system into one part which pursues traditional methods, with incidental improvements, and another which deals with those who are to go into manual labor means a plan of social predestination totally foreign to the spirit of a democracy.

The democracy which proclaims equality of opportunity as its ideal requires an education in which learning and social application, ideas and practice, work and recognition of the meaning of what is done, are united from the beginning and for all. Schools such as we have discussed in this book—and they are rapidly coming into being in large numbers all over the country—are showing how the ideal of equal opportunity for all is to be transmuted into reality.

8
James B. Conant

James Bryant Conant entered "Mr. Eliot's university" as a freshman in 1910. Eliot had turned over the presidency to Abbott Lawrence Lowell the previous year, but Harvard, Conant assures us, was still "Mr. Eliot's university." Yet by the time the precocious young Conant received his bachelor's degree, the university had, as President Lowell was wont to put it, "gone off on a new tack."

Whereas Eliot had taken the German universities as his model, Lowell's ideas about education were greatly influenced by his intimate knowledge of Oxford and Cambridge. For Eliot, undergraduate education was but preparation for a professional degree in law or medicine, or a Ph.D. from the faculty of arts and sciences. Not so with President Lowell. During his twenty-four years in office, his primary concern was for the college; this is revealed in the methodical way he set about reforming the educational program for undergraduates.

The most significant change Lowell effected was the replacement of the "free elective system" with a plan for "concentration and distribution." This created a common framework for the education of all undergraduates. No longer could a student study only a single field, nor could one any longer elect only elementary courses in many different fields. Now every student had to take courses in a variety of fields—this was distribution—*and* the same number of courses in a single field—concentration.

In addition to modifying the elective system, Lowell repudiated Eliot's plans to reduce the undergraduate years to three. And to ensure that Harvard undergraduates would get four years of broad as well as deep education, Lowell inaugurated comprehensive final examinations that all seniors had to take before graduating. To assist undergraduates in preparing for them he appointed in all fields tutors who lived with the students in dormitories, or houses, especially built for the undergraduate student body. Inexorably, Harvard College came to resemble Oxford and Cambridge.

As an undergraduate, James Conant reacted negatively to the reforms of President Lowell, especially when a dean tried (unsuccessfully) to dissuade him from completing his studies for his Bachelor's degree in three years. (Within three more years Conant, at the age of twenty-three, had completed work for a Ph.D. in chemistry.) As for his general education, Conant recounts that he got this not from lectures in courses taken to fulfill the distribution requirement, but from his membership in a highly selective literary club, the Signet. Many years later, in his autobiography, *My Several Lives*, Conant voiced his approval of the advanced placement program introduced into higher education in the 1950s, which, "once again" allowed students to complete their requirements for an A.B. degree in three years.

After becoming an assistant professor in the chemistry department, Conant took a trip to Germany that served to strengthen his opposition to "the new tack" Harvard was taking under President Lowell. In Europe he discovered that it was the German university that made German science so fruitful. By institutionalizing a highly competitive and elaborate screening process of all students in all the sciences, a screening process that continued long after the award of the Ph.D., the German universities had fostered a ruthless demand for excellence. "Success" came to a German scientist only with his appointment to a first-class university as *the* professor in a given field. There he directed, and took credit for, the research conducted by his associates, while delegating the training of Ph.D. candidates to associate professors. Captivated by the German model, Conant returned to the United States where he successfully used an "offer" from the newly created California Institute of Technology to exhort a "research budget" from Harvard, thus becoming the first American organic chemist to establish and direct a research laboratory staffed with faculty research associates.

Yet, in spite of the support he received from Harvard, Professor Conant remained unhappy with his alma mater: there was a lack of commitment to the pursuit of excellence. This was typified, he thought, in President Lowell's decision to grant permanent appointments to tutors. Tutors merely provided instruction to undergraduates—they did nothing to contribute to the advancement of knowledge. (The chemistry department had refused to hire tutors, a policy Conant continued when he became chairman of that department.) Lowell's action, Conant believed, led to the permanent appointment of mediocre men. The quality of those appointed to life positions was fundamental: to be the *best* university the permanent professors had to be the best scholars in the country. Harvard, he lamented, was going downhill.

Chairman Conant voiced all this to a member of the Harvard Corporation (board of trustees) in the winter of 1933. Shortly thereafter he found himself the leading contender to replace Lawrence Abbott Lowell, who had announced his plans to retire. In May 1933, James Bryant Conant became president of Harvard University.

✽

While an undergraduate, James Conant had learned what he called the "strategy" and the "tactics" of scientific research. From Theodore Richards, the chairman of the department (who became his father-in-law when Conant was a graduate student), he had learned "the grand strategy of scientific advancement": the need to identify and work on those crucial problems related to the fundamental theories of science. From Elmer Kohler, professor of organic chemistry, he had learned the tactics of research: the art of dealing effectively with the concrete puzzles one confronts in the science laboratory.

Throughout his "several lives" James Bryant Conant was to reveal himself as an astute strategist and a brilliant tactician. When he became president of Harvard University he adopted a simple yet far-reaching strategy: the fundamental problem for Harvard University was the pursuit of excellence. Only through the active pursuit of excellence could it advance as an educational institution.

At his first meeting with the Harvard Corporation in 1933 the new president boldly announced that what Harvard needed now were men, not buildings. Whereas his predecessor had spent money for new buildings, now it must be spent for scholarships and professorships. Harvard had to secure excellent students and excellent professors. Nothing short of excellence would do. The surest way to ruin a university faculty, President Conant was fond of saying, is to fill it with good men.

But this was 1933, the height of the depression. To carry out his grand strategy in the face of restricted funds and declining enrollments, James Conant had to summon all his skill and ingenuity as a tactician.

One way to make room for the appointment of outstanding scholars was to get rid of those who were no longer productive, especially those who were elderly. During his first year in office the thirty-nine-year-old president introduced a retirement plan. Prior to this, Harvard had had no retirement age. Henceforth, a faculty member would be requested to retire at sixty-six or, if he was in good health, allowed to continue on a year-to-year basis until the age of seventy-six. In dealing with the delicate matter of the already overage, "eminent scholars" in their seventies, President Conant's tactic was to "explore" with each one individually the possibility of the matter becoming a subject of public altercation. As a result, every one of them agreed to announce his voluntary retirement without reference to the conversation with the president.

A second tactic for thinning out the ranks of the existing faculty and making room for the appointment of outstanding scholars was to get rid of some of the less promising younger men still on temporary appointments. During his first year in office the new president worked out a plan to link promotion with permanent appointment. According to this "up or out" policy, a faculty member had to be promoted within the first six years of being hired, or else he was let go.

As in the past, all recommendations for promotion originated in the department, and such recommendations were subject to review by the president. In spite of the fact that this placed the president in the untenable position of assessing the professional judgments of each department about its own faculty, this arrangement had caused no problems until now. For, in the past, a department had frequently refused to promote one of its members, allowing him to remain on a temporary annual appointment. By 1933 more than two-thirds of the faculty were on temporary appointments. Under the new "up or out" policy, a department had to promote a man or turn him out on the streets. Few departments would refuse to promote one of its members, especially during a depression. What heretofore had been a workable sharing of power between the faculty and the president now broke down completely. When President Conant refused to promote two members of the economics department the faculty rebelled.

Confronted with a formal motion that threatened to wrest the traditional power of appointment from the president and confer it on the faculty, Conant averted a crisis by making a public apology to the faculty, pleading with them not to take "a hasty step which might affect Harvard adversely for years to come." Next, he devised the ingenious tactic of creating ad hoc committees to review all recommendations for permanent appointment. Each ad hoc committee, appointed by the president, usually had one member from the department concerned, with other members drawn from related departments and from other institutions. The committee considered the merits of the department's choice as well as the qualifications of possible candidates outside the university; its job was to report who was the best-qualified candidate *in the nation* for permanent appointment to Harvard University.

Because he never lost sight of his grand strategy, James Conant was quite willing to give up his own awesome power to make all permanent appointments in exchange for a regularized procedure that better guaranteed that Harvard would grant permanent appointments only to the best scholars in every field.

One of Conant's most ingenious schemes to set Harvard in

pursuit of excellence was his plan to cast the tercentary year (1936) of Harvard's founding as a 300th Anniversary Fund drive for new money for national scholarships and university professorships. Conant invented the position of university professor to ward off competition among departments for new faculty appointments. The university professor was to be an outstanding scholar appointed by the president "with a roving commission, whose teaching and creative work shall not be hampered by departmental considerations." Primarily research scholars, university professors could teach if, and when, and where they wanted.

Through his scheme for national scholarships the new president sought to bolster Harvard's declining enrollments. Originally construed solely for a group of midwestern states, he presented this invention to the Corporation as a way to secure new students who would not otherwise come to Harvard. Prior to the creation of the national scholarships Harvard had purely honorary scholarships that contained no stipend. The new national scholarship was, like the old, awarded solely on merit, but it provided a stipend according to the need of the student, one large enough to cover all essential expenses for four years. The first year Harvard awarded ten scholarships. By 1936 the number of awards had risen to thirty-one. Harvard, more than one critic complained, was robbing the Midwest.

❋

In his continuing search for excellent students for his university, James Conant became deeper and deeper involved in the educational problems of the nation. Inevitably, his actions had a profound impact on the course of American educational history in the area of educational testing, in the training of teachers, and in educational theory.

Conant's influence on the area of educational testing emerged directly from his plan for national scholarships. When he first presented the plan to the Corporation, everyone lauded the notion of recruiting new students from outside New England. But some wondered what criteria would be used in awarding the scholarships. For, as President Conant soon discovered, rigorous, sustained instruction in the traditional college preparatory subjects—math, science, Latin, Greek, French, and German—had disappeared in most secondary schools, both private and public. Indeed, only in the large eastern cities did public schools offer a course of studies that prepared students to enter Harvard. (Which was why the present student body consisted almost totally of youth from private preparatory schools, and those from public schools in eastern cities.)

The only reasonable criteria for selecting outstanding high school graduates, Conant informed the Corporation, was "the potential for success in collegiate work." But how does one measure this? Conant turned this problem over to two assistant deans, who discovered that the College Boards had developed a Scholastic Aptitude Test (SAT) *not* predicated on the mastery of any particular subject matter. The test simply ascertained how much potential a candidate had for scholastic work by testing his verbal and mathematical aptitudes. Harvard not only adopted the test for awarding scholarships, but also began to use it as a general admissions test as well.

In the late 1930s Conant reports that he became a zealous convert to aptitude tests—going so far as to believe that, armed with the SAT, colleges need no longer trouble themselves with subject-matter admission tests or pay heed to the secondary school records of their applicants. He later restrained his intemperate faith in the power of the SAT, although he continued to regard aptitude tests as one of the significant measures for discovering "worthwhile young men" for entrance to college.

Conant never abandoned his conception of psychological testing as the basis for predicting success or failure. In 1937 he addressed a convention of education test-makers, urging them to merge their efforts—instead of competing with one another—in order to develop predictive tests for all sorts of vocations and avocations. Conant's ardent support helped to channel the educational testing movement into the business of selecting and sorting people for, in Eliot's famous phrase, "their probable destiny."

The proposed merger of the various testing agencies did not come off until 1947, with Conant continually playing a significant role. The College Entrance Examination Board merged with both the Carnegie Foundation for the Advancement of Teaching and the American Council on Education to become one cooperative testing agency: the Educational Testing Service (ETS). The first president of ETS was Henry Chauncey, one of the two then unknown assistant deans President Conant had asked in 1933 to solve the problem of measuring "potential for success in collegiate work."

The creation of ETS marked the institutionalization of selecting and sorting as the primary function of educational testing in America. ETS continues to supply a vast battery of tests that determine the future destinies of many Americans. These include the Preliminary Scholastic Aptitude Test as well as the Scholastic Aptitude Test, the Advanced Placement Examination and the College Placement Tests, the College Board Admission Test, and the Graduate Record Examination. In addition, ETS supplies tests for entry into a number of professions: teaching, obstetrics and gynecology, speech pathology and audiology, insurance underwriting, and the U.S. Foreign Service.

※

The department of teacher-training established during the reign of Charles Eliot had, by Conant's time, become the Harvard Graduate School of Education. Conant had no special enthusiasm for the school, but instead of abolishing it forthwith, he suggested to an admittedly worried Dean Henry Holmes that, together, they "explore" the question of "the basis for the existence of the school."

Conant's search for bright students "on the other side of the Allegheny Mountains" had brought him to deplore the existing low quality of secondary school instruction. Could it be improved? He thought so: by improving the academic education of future teachers. Thus it came to pass that his "explorations" with the dean of the Graduate School of Education resulted, in 1935, in the creation of a new degree for school teachers, the Master of Arts in Teaching (MAT). For this degree the departments of the faculty of arts and sciences set the standards and examined the candidates' knowledge of the subject matter; the Graduate School of Education had charge of the study of professional material and practice teaching.

Following World War II, a number of colleges and universities—in some cases with financial support from the Ford Foundation—adopted MAT programs: Yale, Wesleyan, Oberlin, Chicago, for example. These programs usually had substantial scholarship aid, thus attracting many bright young people into the teaching profession. And in some institutions the program helped to overcome some of the opposition of faculties of arts and sciences to schools and departments of education. But probably the most significant result of the MAT program was the fostering and spreading of the belief—Conant's belief—that the improvement of teacher training was simply a matter of deepening and enriching the academic preparation—the subject-matter studies—of educators. Such a notion undermined serious efforts to develop teacher-training programs that focus on the actual and diverse educational problems that teachers encounter in the actual practice of their profession.

Yet just such a belief guided and directed Conant in the study he made years later, in 1961, of the education of American teachers. The initial chapter of his book lays bare this long-standing belief. Here he portrays the problem of teacher education as essentially a political battle between professors of education and professors of arts and sciences. With typical magnanimity Conant declares that he has "found much to criticize strongly on both sides of the fence that separates faculties of education from those of arts and sciences." But this declaration presages a determination to diminish the power of the educationists.

The entire process of teacher certification, Conant reveals, is in the hands of the educational establishment, an interlocking directorate made up of state departments of education, professors of education, and teachers' associations. In order to destroy the educational establishments across the land, Conant calls for each state to inaugurate a policy whereby the certification of teachers will be placed completely in the hands of the universities within each state with the explicit understanding that each university will have a *university-wide* committee to direct and control the program for teacher preparation.

With one masterful scheme Conant would preempt the power of all departments and schools of education in America. Yet, his proposal is supposed to be a compromise, so he does not ban professors of education from the university. He keeps them on—at least three or four in each college or school, as "clinical professors" —to teach the methods of teaching and to supervise practice teachers. They never attain permanent appointment in the university since they are to "go back to the schools" every five years or so to reestablish their ties with the real work of schoolteachers. The traditional "foundations" courses, if they be taught at all, are to be taught by professors in the college of arts and sciences, i.e., historians will teach history of education, psychologists teach educational psychology, sociologists, educational sociology. The subject-matter courses—what the future teacher will teach—will, of course, be taught by the professors of arts and sciences.

In *The Education of American Teachers* Conant rivets his attention to the courses and subjects that future teachers should study. With amazing presumption he pays no heed at all to the tasks and functions teachers actually perform in schools. He ignores completely all questions about the professional relevance of existing programs of teacher preparation. Nor does he say anything about the professional relevance of *his* proposed program for teacher preparation. For Conant, good teacher preparation is the study of academic subjects under the guidance of professors of arts and sciences. This, he believes, is so self-evident as to need no argument or proof. Significantly, the longest chapter in the book is "The Academic Preparation of Teachers." There, with the help of tables, he lays out a program of studies to give future teachers the "breadth" and "depth" they need to carry out their appointed tasks.

Not unexpectedly, Conant's book infuriated professional educators (Conant's "establishment"). What upset them most was the framework Conant had used. By casting the problem of teacher preparation as a political issue, he had put the educators into a position whereby whatever criticisms they made of his proposals would brand them as antiintellectuals. Here, then, Conant's superb tactical skills backfired. *The Education of American Teachers* so alienated American educators that he could no longer count on them as allies to bring to fruition his grand strategy for American society.

＊

     During the 1930s, as he continued to pursue his grand strategy to improve Harvard, Conant came more and more to see it as a grand strategy for the nation itself. By the early 1940s he began to work out a tactic for joining the needs of Harvard to the welfare of the nation. Once again, it was his doings with the National Scholarship Plan that pointed the direction he was to take.

The National Scholarship Plan, he explained in his annual report for 1936–37, had very important social implications. Harvard University, he maintained, was rendering a worthwhile service to the nation by widening opportunities for higher education. And to those who complained that Harvard was stealing able students from institutions in their own sections of the country, he replied that "the number of high-ranking, all-around students is large enough to give each institution its share." Moreover, he added, there are a large number of promising boys who are financially unable to attend college even in their own sections. By 1940 he was talking about how national scholarships equalized educational opportunity by helping to overcome the geographical and financial barriers that prevented many from pursuing higher education.

Conant now began to concoct an "educational philosophy" for American education according to which the schools would function as the agencies to restore what he persisted in calling a "classless society." The first public pronouncement of this "philosophy" came in an address he delivered at the University of California in 1940, "Education for a Classless Society."

Until fairly recently, he told his audience, Americans took for granted that theirs was a classless society, one that had no *hereditary* classes or castes. Social mobility is the essence of a classless society. But today, Conant warns, we see less mobility than existed earlier; throughout the country we find the development of a hereditary aristocracy of wealth.

We can recapture the classless society of the past, Conant promises, *if* we develop a "continuous process" by which power and privilege may be automatically redistributed at the end of each generation. This simply means a more equitable distribution of opportunity. And the "continuous process" through which we can so redistribute opportunity is, he declares, our educational system. Picturing our secondary school system as "a new type of social instrument" that we do not yet fully understand, Conant announced that we are only now learning how to operate it for the public good. It can aid us in recapturing social flexibility, help us regain opportunity.

To restore equality of opportunity, Conant insists, the secondary schools must assess abilities, develop talents, and guide ambitions. They must equip the young "to step onto the first rung of whatever ladder of opportunity seems appropriate."

Here, then, is Conant's ingenious tactic for binding the needs of Harvard to the welfare of the nation. His grand strategy for Harvard—and now for the nation—is the relentless pursuit of excellence. Harvard—and now the nation's secondary schools—must seek out and promote the talented and the gifted. Conant's tactic to get the secondary schools to accept this function of selecting and promoting the talented is to present it as a means of securing equality of opportunity for all. Rigorous selection and promotion of the talented will ensure social mobility for this group. It will guarantee that positions of power and leadership will be filled on the basis of merit alone. Thus, the wealth of one's parents, one's religion, or one's race will no longer be relevant to social mobility.

Conant, with typical modesty, denied any originality for this conception of the social function of the schools. He claims to have found it in Thomas Jefferson (thus conferring an aura of historical legitimacy on the conception). He roots his proposal for the secondary school in Thomas Jefferson's plan for "culling the natural aristocrats from among the common people."

❋

But what about those who are not gifted, those who are not "college material"? What could the schools do for them? During the 1940s Conant became more and more aware of this large group of students in the secondary schools, especially after he joined the Educational Policies Commission (EPC) of the National Educational Association and the

American Association of School Administrators. As a member of
this commission he learned about the realities of the public schools.

In 1944 the EPC published a manifesto called *Education For
ALL American Youth*, dedicated to the proposition that "every youth
in these United States—regardless of sex, economic status, geo-
graphic location, or race—should experience a broad and balanced
education." James Conant agreed with this proposition, and in his
own writings about education now began to use the label "general
education" to characterize that education all American youths
should receive. He distinguished general education from education
for a career, insisting all youths should have both.

"General education" was the focus of the series of lectures he
delivered at Teachers College, Columbia University, in 1945,
published three years later under the title *Education in a Divided
World.* As the book makes clear, the cold war between the United
States and the Soviet Union (the "divided world") gave a new
urgency to his concern with general education. Since he saw the
cold war as an ideological battle, Conant insisted that if they were
to win it, Americans had to be united ideologically. General
education could bring this about.

General education, he explains, is the common, or core
learnings that "will unite in one cultural pattern the future
carpenter, factory worker, bishop, lawyer, doctor, sales manager,
professor and garage mechanic." Under the rubric general education, Conant lumped the humanities, social studies, and the
sciences. Yet, since some of these subjects were part of "career
education"—for those going to college—Conant adds that it was
not the subjects themselves but the way they were taught that made
them a part of general education. General education raised the
students' level of understanding of the world he lived in—its
political, social, and economic arrangements, as well as the
physical environment and modern technology. Such understanding
conferred stability and coherence on the society by making it easier
for the young to accommodate to the existing arrangements. In
short, general education is socialization to what exists, and to the
ideology that underlies it.

Now what underlies the existing arrangements in our society is
the ideology of meritocracy: power and leadership in social,
political and economic spheres is, or ought to be, in the hands of

the most talented. Therefore, in addition to providing general education—in order to secure cohesion and stability in the society—the schools must provide opportunity for the talented to rise. This, Conant admits, creates an educational dilemma. For the more fully we aim to give a general education on a democratic basis for *all* American youth, the more we fail to give the best specialized professional training for a selected few. Yet, he says, he is confident we can create arrangements in our secondary schools that do not overlook gifted youth. But in this book he doesn't really explain how we can do this. He merely recommends differentiated programs in English, math, foreign languages, and science for "those students headed in different directions."

Nor does he come to grips with this "dilemma" in his next book, *Education and Liberty*, published in 1953. Here, once again, he presents his educational proposals for selecting and promoting the gifted as a means of enhancing equality of opportunity: "If we so desire, we can, through our schools, annually restore a great degree of fluidity to our social and economic life and in so doing make available for the national welfare reservoirs of potential professional talent now untapped." And once again he insists that at the same time, through general education, we can use the schools to "promote the social and political ideals necessary for the harmonious operation of our economic system." Finally, he once more construes the schools as instruments of national policy in the cold war with the Russians, thus dramatizing how crucial it is to move in the direction he suggests: "The nearer we approach, through the management of our schools to our goal of equality of opportunity . . . and the better we teach the basic tenets of American democracy, the more chance there is for personal liberty to continue in the United States."

Until the time he retired from Harvard University in 1953 to become U.S. high commissioner of Western Germany and, later, ambassador, Conant continued to insist that the so-called opposition between education for *all* American youth and education for the gifted is a "false antithesis"—a notion we must expunge from our minds. True, he admitted, there were very few schools where those of "high intellectual ability" receive "adequate stimulus and sound instruction." Nevertheless, he continued to insist that comprehensive secondary schools could pull it off. And when he retired his ambassadorship in 1957 and returned to education, James Bryant Conant was ready to tell us how we could do it.

✳

Conant's timing was perfect. His book *The American High School Today*, more frequently referred to as "the Conant Report," appeared just months after the Russians had launched *Sputnik I*. Many Americans had converted this blow to their technological supremacy into an educational defeat: the Russians were ahead of us because they had better schools. Into the storm of criticism that had erupted stepped the calm, assured James Conant, to deliver his "First Report to Interested Citizens."

Conant had laid plans for this report while he was still ambassador to Germany, and had actually begun his "investigation" ten months before the launching of the Soviet satellite. With a grant from the Carnegie Corporation—administered by ETS—Conant declared that he had set out to see whether the American comprehensive high school could satisfactorily fulfill three functions: "Can a school at one and the same time provide a good general education for *all* the pupils as future citizens of a democracy, provide education programs for the majority to develop useful skills, and educate adequately those with a talent for handling advanced academic subjects—particularly foreign languages, and advanced mathematics." (His real concern, as he wrote in his original proposal to John Gardner of the Carnegie Foundation, was to study "the education of the talented youth" in American comprehensive high schools.)

Conant claimed to have based his report on visits to fifty-nine high schools in some sixteen states. In each school he asked if all the able students (the top 15 percent) took twelfth-grade science, math, and foreign-language courses. Because the responses were largely impressionistic, Conant devised an "academic inventory" to get some reliable data on the courses of study the talented students took. The "academic inventory" consisted of a record of each student's actual program for four years together with a measure of his or her potential academic ability as measured by scholastic aptitude tests.

In his report Conant announced that he found eight schools

that "were satisfactorially fulfilling the three main objectives of a comprehensive high school." In addition to adequate general education and significant nonacademic programs, the academic inventory showed that over half of the academically talented in these eight schools had studied at least seven years of math and sciences, as well as seven years of English and social studies.

If these eight could do it, all comprehensive schools could do it. In the second half of his book Conant presented twenty-one recommendations for improving American secondary education.

He directed his first recommendation at beefing up the counseling systems in all schools: "Counseling should start in the elementary school. . . . There should be one full-time counsellor for every two-hundred and fifty to three-hundred pupils in the high school. . . . The counsellor should be on the lookout for the bright boy or girl whose high ability has been demonstrated by the results of aptitude tests . . . but in his achievement . . . has been low."

To check on both the counseling system and the school policies, Conant recommends that school boards ask for academic inventories (Appendix H of his book contains "instructions" for preparing one). In the report he blithely suggests that the academic inventories "of the graduating class might well be published each year."

Conant develops his primary tactic for educating the highly talented in his recommendations for individualized programs and ability grouping. Through individualized programs the school eliminates classifying students according to clearly defined and labeled programs or tracks ("college preparatory," "vocational," "commercial"). When combined with ability grouping, his scheme of individualized programs would allow a student, for example, to be "in the top section in English but the middle section in history or ninth grade algebra." These combined tactics thus enable a school to maintain high standards in the all-important areas of science, math, and foreign languages—for a few, the gifted. Perhaps because he was carried away by the ingenuity of his scheme for combining in a single school the general education of *all* with the specialized education of the gifted, Conant actually proposes ability grouping of the *highly* gifted (the top 3 percent) in special classes.

The largest and most fully developed recommendation deals

specifically with the programs for the academically talented. Here is the minimum: four years of mathematics, four years of one foreign language, three years of science, in addition to four years of English and three years of social studies. Getting to the nitty-gritty, Conant adds: "This program will require at least fifteen hours of homework each week." To maintain standards in the upper-level science, math, and foreign-language courses, he insists upon a prerequisite: at least a grade of C in the previous course.

To heighten the pressures on the academically talented, he makes a couple of administrative recommendations. For example, to prevent bright students from electing easy courses in order to obtain high grades, he recommends that the graduating class not be ranked on the basis of grades obtained in *all* subjects; he also suggests an academic honors list exclusively for students taking courses recommended for the academically talented. In addition, he blatantly recommends that schools issue a supplement to the diploma—a durable transcript of the courses taken and the grades obtained. He advocates publicizing the existence of such records so that employers might ask for it rather than merely relying on a diploma when questioning an applicant for a job about his education. "The record might be a card that could be carried in a wallet," Conant suggests.

Conant ends his list of twenty-one recommendations with two intended to promote "mutual respect and understanding between students of different levels of academic ability": first, each home-room should be composed of students of all levels of ability and vocational interests; second, all students should take a common twelfth-grade course on American problems.

＊

Totally committed to his general strategy for America, Conant next undertook a nationwide speaking tour arranged by the National Citizens Council for Better Schools, to take his message to all interested citizens. Within a year he published some of these lectures in a second book, *The Child, the Parent, and the State.* Addressing himself to interested citizens, Conant urged them to assume responsibility for reforming the schools.

In this new world, this "divided world," Conant insists "we can no longer tolerate the kind of education which might have been considered adequate a generation earlier," an education, he adds, still "found in many schools today." But American education, he explains, unlike that in most countries of the world, is highly decentralized and locally controlled. Therefore the present inadequacies in our schools stem from public ignorance and inaction. Citizens must become vitally involved with improving education through effective action at both national and state levels. But the most important, and the most immediately effective approach is action at the local community level. Here is Conant's agenda for action. First, citizens must acquaint themselves with the tasks the public schools should perform (they should read his report); next, they must get the facts about their local schools (an academic inventory will reveal how well the talented are being educated). Then, armed with facts and a program, they can become a "constructive force"—perhaps through organizing a citizens group. This heady vision of a grass-roots transformation of American education stretched Conant's bland prose to new heights: "The road to better schools will be paved by the collective action of the local citizenry in thousands of communities. The responsibility for the sorely needed upgrading of our schools cannot be passed to the state legislatures or to Congress. The responsibility rests on every citizen in the land."

But then the majestic days of James Bryant Conant's position as premier educational statesman of the United States began to wane. In the early 1960s he committed two serious tactical errors that lost him important political allies in his crusade to create a secondary school system that would identify and promote the talented.

❉

In September 1961 Conant published *Slums and Suburbs: A Commentary on Schools in Metropolitan Areas.* In his original report on the comprehensive high school he had dealt with those schools outside the metropolitan areas; therefore, his recommendations, he now explained, did not apply to high schools in the suburbs or those in the slums. These schools had special problems.

As he saw it, the principal educational problem in the suburban school was to get students into colleges of the parents' choice. In the slums the problem was to prepare a student for getting and keeping a job. The reason for these two entirely different functions, Conant explains, is that the schools serve different families. "To a considerable degree," he declares, "what a school should do and can do is determined by the status and ambitions of the families being served."

Now this statement may not be new (or even true), but it is a remarkable declaration for James Bryant Conant to make. It is tantamount to admitting that the schools are not really the instruments of democracy he had long claimed them to be. He is simply saying that in the slums—where, he infers, parental ambitions are always low—the school *cannot* provide the young with equality of opportunity.

Conant makes this quite clear in the text of his book. He explains that the slum child's background, his family's status, affects his aptitudes as measured by aptitude tests. Since the tests predict the probability of academic success, and since Negro slum students score low on these tests, then, Conant concludes, "most of the pupils in the Negro Slum School will have a very difficult time with their future schooling."

After tacitly admitting that slum schools do not provide black students with equality of opportunity, Conant goes on to propose that the schools in the slums should confirm and perpetuate the inferior status of black kids. He advocates the creation of school programs that will train the students in immediately "marketable skills."

Conant closed the lid on the slum school student—and further infuriated most blacks—when he went on to declare his opposition to any attempts to transport them to other schools. Busing, or transporting students over "residential boundaries," he denounced as misguided attempts to use the schools to overcome de facto residential segregation.

Although they sparked much surprise and heated controversy, Conant's pronouncements on the education of blacks in slum schools follow logically from his grand strategy of identifying and promoting talented youth. For one of the necessary consequences of this strategy is that some—at least 85 percent of the population, according to his own estimates—will not be identified as talented and therefore not promoted to the top rungs of the educational ladder. Conant discovered that, according to both SAT scores and grades in school, few Negroes in slum schools were in the category he labeled "the academically talented." Magnanimously he insisted that there is no reason to believe that these students as a group are inherently or genetically less capable than white students.

But what can the schools do? Because his whole strategy is to "cull the talented," Conant cannot advocate a lowering of standards or accept the employment of different educational standards for Negro students. He cannot reject or repudiate the SAT because it is culturally biased, since it is the dominant white culture that defines what talent *is*. The *only* solution open to Conant was the one he took—to advocate the creation of a completely separate system of education for slum schools, one with a function different from that of the standard American comprehensive high school.

But if Conant's primary concern was with the education of the talented, which by (his) definition were white and mostly middle class, then why did he ever get into issuing pronouncements on the educational arrangements for Negro slum schools? He did it, he tells us, because of the "social dynamite" he saw building up in the inner cities. The root cause, as he saw it, was the absence of job opportunities. This led to undesirable social attitudes which, in turn, made people susceptible to the lure of communism, which "feeds upon discontented, frustrated, unemployed people." So for the welfare of our society, Conant the cold war warrior concluded, the slum schools had to develop meaningful courses and programs in vocational education.

It never occurred to James Conant to suspect that the school itself—that institution that had become society's sorting and selecting agency—contributed to the "social dynamite" in the slums. In the schools Negro children learned that they had less scholastic aptitude than whites, and therefore could not expect to be so mobile as whites. This easily leads to self-hatred. Then, when sympathetic educators explained that their inferiority was due to their bad environments, black students naturally began to hate their environment—as an obstacle, a trap, something to be destroyed, not enjoyed. Finally, the black students ended up hating the school itself; for in the name of "equality of opportunity" the school actually confirmed them as inferior and perpetuated that inferiority. Instead of enhancing and fulfilling his expectations of determining his own destiny, this educational "equality of opportunity" simply corroborated the black child's feelings of powerlessness.

In the same book where he proposed using the slum schools to keep the blacks down, Conant praised the suburban schools as "lighthouse schools"; they identified and promoted the talented white middle-class students who attended them. The parents in the suburban schools—all of whom, Conant inferred, had ambitions for their children—believe that the American high schools provide equality of opportunity. After all, the schools prepare *their* children to go to an acceptable college, or university, don't they?

As his principal recommendation for the suburban high school, Conant stressed that guidance counselors must make clear to parents that only the very best students should go to prestige universities.

＊

Conant's "Commentary on Schools in the Metropolitan Areas" was more than controversial; it raised serious questions about the whole meritocratic construction of the American educational system. And Conant's next book helped clarify these questions.

After long insisting that his strategy for America was nothing more than an expanded Jeffersonianism, Conant in 1962 published *Thomas Jefferson and the Development of American Public Education*, based on three lectures he delivered at the University of California in 1960. Here he actually reveals how different his meritocratic educational ideas are from those originally put forth by Jefferson.

Thomas Jefferson had limited his consideration of formal educational institutions to their political function: the elementary education of all future citizens and the higher education of all future political leaders. The higher education of future leaders was to help develop moral character, thus making them less likely to be tyrannical and arbitrary; the elementary education of all free white children was to help them to protect their liberties against rulers who might abuse their powers. "Every government degenerates when trusted to the rulers of the people alone. The people themselves, therefore, are its only safe depositories. And to render even them safe, their minds must be improved to a certain degree."

For Jefferson, educational institutions were supplemental— they merely helped citizens to man and utilize the political and governmental arrangements designed to protect their liberty. For James Conant, educational institutions had much broader functions. He construed universal education as "general education," the preparation of all youth for a "useful life." He saw the public elementary and secondary schools as a vast social instrument to socialize the young to adapt to the existing economic, social, and political arrangements.

Conant had expanded Jefferson's notion of the talented in order to transform the secondary schools into what he was fond of calling "instruments of democracy": the schools could and should restore fluidity to American society by identifying and promoting the academic careers of the talented; mobility would then occur on merit alone. To bring this about Conant had long labored to increase the opportunities for the talented poor to go to college— through scholarships, for example. At the same time he had worked to broaden the functions of higher education beyond even the dreams of Charles Eliot, casting the university as the agency to prepare *all* experts ("those who understand and lead") in all fields and professions. During his reign as president of Harvard he had created the Littauer School of Public Administration for the training of leaders in government; saved the Graduate School of Education from extinction (twice), so that it might turn out leaders in the field of education; established the prestigious Nieman Fellowships for the in-service training of professional journalists.

Whereas James Conant saw his grand strategy as simply an enlargement of the ideas of Thomas Jefferson, it was actually a subversion of them. Jefferson had cast education as a negative force to prevent the abuse of power. Conant cast it as a positive force to legitimize the exercise of power. In Conant's world, the schools issued credentials (based on a student's merit) that determined an individual's future position and status in the society. In the lost world of Thomas Jefferson the schools had had but a minimal influence on a person's future economic and social position and status. For Jefferson the schools functioned solely to help people to protect their liberty.

Of course Conant fretted about liberty too, but with him it was more a ("scare") tactic he used to garner support for his grand strategy of using the schools to cull the talented: the talented would protect our liberty against the threat of communism. In Conant's world—in our world—the schools have acquired tremendous power over the lives of all the young. A person now can become useful—as a citizen, as a worker, as a member of society—*only* through attending school.

✳

James Conant's pursuit of his grand strategy had led him to formulate a vision of an educational system so powerful and authoritative that he could not safely permit it to remain in the hands of the educators. As a result he proceeded to invite others to take over American education—people with broader and deeper insights, possessing no vested interests in the established enterprise.

Thus, as we have seen, in 1963 Conant released his report *The Education of American Teachers*, where he suggested taking the responsibility for the education of teachers away from the educators and giving it over to more responsible, university-wide committees in each institution. The following year he issued another report, this time directed at freeing education from the control of the "educators." *Shaping Educational Policy* was, like its predecessor, a study financed by the Carnegie Corporation. Here, after a rather ill-tempered bombasting of the educational establishment for its unfettered control of educational policy in almost every state of the union, Conant recommends the creation of an "Interstate Commission for Planning a Nationwide Education Policy." The members of the commission were to be distinguished citizens of each state "who are *not* educators" (his italics). In his autobiography Conant labels this his "major social invention."

The proposal led—with the help of John Gardner, then president of the Carnegie Corporation—to the establishment in 1966 of the Education Commission of the States. Through its annual meetings and its various publications, this commission disseminates news and reports about successful programs in the various states. It seeks to influence federal legislation favorable to the fifty-two member states and territories. Its most significant work thus far has been its assumption of the direction of the national assessment of education. Whether this or any of the work of the Educational Commission of the States will actually shape American educational policy has yet to be seen.

In 1967 James Conant published his last book on education, his "second report to interested citizens," *The Comprehensive High School.* In it he repeats his plea for the elimination of all the small high schools in the land. The opportunity for a student to study a wide variety of subjects, he points out, increases as the size of the high school increases. The larger high schools, he explains, offer four years of a foreign language, they have accepted the new science curricula, they employ ability grouping, and they have courses in automotive mechanics.

The Comprehensive High School attracted little attention when published, or since. By 1967 Conant had no constituency. He had alienated those who had a professional interest in reforming the schools—the educators; as well as those who had a personal interest in reforming them—urban blacks. True, his book had appeared at a time of widespread educational criticism, but it was now a criticism that emanated from educational values entirely different from those he professed. By 1967 Americans were in the midst of a searching reappraisal of the functions of their schools; and James Bryant Conant, for many, stood for all that was wrong with American education.

❋

James Conant had geared his entire educational career to getting educational institutions to pursue excellence. Together with the help of the Carnegie Corporation (whose one-time president, John Gardner, wrote a book called *Excellence*), he did much to institutionalize the pursuit of excellence throughout the entire American educational system.

The pursuit of excellence is praiseworthy, but attempts to institutionalize it convert what ought to be an educational enterprise into an administrative one. Thus our schools have become the nationwide agency for sorting and selecting all American youth into winners and losers. In this way James Conant's general strategy did not a little to foster social instability in America. First, those who the school system identified as lacking academic talent could not but conclude they were less worthy than others. This generated social divisiveness, resentment, and animosity. Second, as we saw, the grand strategy rendered impossible any feasible educational response to the problem of residential racial segregation. This increased the despair and disillusionment of urban blacks and heightened the privatism and racial prejudice of urban whites. Finally, this grand strategy gave birth to a generation of highly schooled young people who grew increasingly critical and ofttimes cynical of the meritocratic system that spawned them.

In the last pages of his autobiography, published in 1970, James Conant begins to question the grand strategy he had relentlessly pursued. In a plaintive, yet endearing passage he asks: "Can it be that the fetish of upholding academic standards has misled us? The educational process should continue throughout life. The knowledge and the skills required in a vocation are something quite apart. Have we in the United States unnecessarily entangled the two? Has this come about by giving to our academic institutions control over entry to the learned professions and other vocations as well? I raise these questions humbly as possible working hypotheses?"

WORKS AND COMMENTARY

James B. Conant's major educational writings are *Education in a Divided World* (Cambridge: Harvard University Press, 1949), *Education and Liberty* (Cambridge: Harvard University Press, 1958), *The American High School Today* (New York: McGraw-Hill, 1959), *The Child, the Parent, and the State* (Cambridge: Harvard University Press, 1960), *Slums and Suburbs* (New York: McGraw-Hill, 1961), *Thomas Jefferson and the Development of American Public Education* (Berkeley: University of California Press, 1962), *The Education of American Teachers* (New York: McGraw-Hill, 1963), *Shaping Educational Policy* (New York: McGraw-Hill, 1964), and *The Comprehensive High School* (New York: McGraw-Hill, 1967). His speech "Education for a Classless Society" was published as an occasional pamphlet by the

Harvard Graduate School of Education (Cambridge: 1940). He published his autobiography under the title *My Several Lives* (New York: Harper & Row, 1970).

The selection that follows is chapter 3 of *The Child, the Parent, and the State,* pages 58–83.

The Citizen's Responsibility

In the first chapter of this volume, I have sketched the governmental framework within which we operate a vast number of tax-supported schools. In the succeeding chapter, I suggested that since we are living in a world quite different from that which existed in the 1920's or 1930's, there is a new national interest in the adequacy of our schools. Because of the nature of our struggle with Soviet imperialism, many Americans feel we can no longer tolerate the kind of education which might have been considered adequate a generation earlier and which is to be found in many schools today. Thousands of high schools do not even offer the kind of instruction which challenges the academically talented students and which is essential for our future professional leaders. To a large extent, this particular inadequacy reflects the attempts of communities to operate high schools that are too small. To cure this situation, as I have pointed out, action by state legislatures is required. The entire citizenry of some states must be awakened to the necessity for radical reform in order that the states in question may not be delinquent in their duty to the nation. In almost all states, further constructive action by the state legislature is required in order to provide an adequate state contribution to the finances of many relatively impoverished districts. Here, as in the case of the reduction of the number of small high schools through consolidation, the voters in the state must be keenly conscious of the national necessity for better schools. Indeed, as I indicated in the concluding pages of the last chapter, the entire body of American citizens must face up to the necessity of either some drastic changes in the federal and state taxing systems or the federal government's becoming involved in public education on a new and very large scale. In short, an American citizen vitally concerned with improving education (as I believe all should be) has opportunities for effective action at both the national and state levels. But perhaps his most immediately effective approach to the problem of providing better schools is as a member of a local community. This chapter, therefore, is addressed to the increasing number of men and women who are anxious to improve their local schools.

The first requisite for such an undertaking is an insight into the problems faced by those who administer a school system. And to obtain an insight one must understand something of the complexities of the American pattern.

To some degree the attention devoted to the shortcomings of our public schools by the media of mass communication in the last few years has tended to confuse the layman. So, too, have the writings of certain critics. The basis of the complaints was hardly new; indeed, to those of us who had been directly involved in education for many years, the stories were quite familiar. What Sputnik accomplished was to provide an attentive audience. Criticism of public education, particularly of the high schools, was good copy. In fact, in the closing months of 1957 and the beginning months of 1958, the more violently a speaker attacked the high school, the more certain he was to have his remarks appear with large headlines on page one.

An historian with a sociological bias or a sociologist with historical training could write an interesting article about the sudden burst of highly critical interest in public education which occurred in the fall of 1957. The alarm caused by the military implications of Sputnik was combined with chagrin that the Soviets appeared to have won a scientific race. To the alarm and chagrin was added the impact of reports on Soviet education. By a strange coincidence, highly favorable reports about Soviet education were published almost at the same time as the Russian triumphs in rocketing began to disturb the public mind. To be sure, the news about Soviet education, unlike the reports about Sputnik, did not represent a sudden dramatic turn of affairs. People had been writing for several years about the extraordinarily rapid development of Soviet education; reports on the number of scientists and engineers being educated on the other side of the Iron Curtain had been publicized in the

United States in connection with a campaign to encourage more young Americans to study science and engineering. But the publication of an official U.S. Office of Education report on the ten-year schools of the Soviet Union served to dramatize the way the Russians had organized their system of education. Comparisons with American secondary education were quickly made, and the contrast appeared to put the United States schools in a most unfavorable light. All of which provided good ammunition for those who for years had been shooting at the professors of education and the administrators of the public schools.

The future historian of American education will surely ask one question about the episode I have just described. He will wonder why those who were responsible for the tax-supported schools appeared to be so vulnerable to the violent attacks; why the public seemed so ready to believe the worst about their schools. For years we had been praising our wonderful system of free schools providing education for all through the high school and, for many, through the college years. And then suddenly, as in a fit of anger, the American public seemed to be repudiating the whole adventure. I have overdrawn the picture, admittedly, yet at least one distinguished foreign visitor with whom I spoke saw the situation much as I have just described it. "What is the matter with your country?" he inquired. "Have a couple of Russian rockets set off a panic? You appear to be ready to condemn and throw overboard what you have bragged about for years—namely, your tax-supported schools. Such talk shakes the confidence of Europeans in the stability of the American people."

My European friend failed to realize that articulate American opinion, like the wind, comes in violent gusts and may quickly shift direction. I remember the case of a man named Dewey, not the philosopher but an admiral, the commander-in-chief of the U.S. naval forces in the Spanish War. He was crowned a hero by the American press and a few years later violently uncrowned. Today, the reputation of a philosopher with the same last name appears to be suffering from a similar turn of the wheel of fortune. However, the willingness of citizens to listen to those who have proposed radical reforms of

education cannot be explained solely in terms of the fickleness
of public opinion. There are several deeper causes. Perhaps the
underlying cause is widespread misunderstanding about the
nature of the problems facing school boards and school
administrators. To a considerable degree, I believe this misunderstanding can be dissipated. At all events, it is one of the
purposes of this chapter to make an effort in that direction.

The lack of understanding is by no means confined to those
who stand outside the teaching profession. Indeed, if the ranks
of the educators had presented a solid front, I think the violent
critics of public education would have hardly received a
hearing. The truth of the matter is that some of the most
virulent attacks on the American high schools have come from
within the profession itself—from professors in universities. If a
citizen hears the public high schools condemned by a professor, he is strongly inclined to believe the professor must be
right. The layman may regard professors with suspicion when
they talk about politics or economics, but surely a teacher in a
university ought to know whether the high schools are good or
bad. As a consequence of this attitude, one may encounter a
parent who is satisfied with the local high school yet is quite
willing to believe the worst about the national situation
because he has read an article by Professor X.

University teachers who are highly critical of public secondary education are to be found in the faculties of arts and
sciences and in the professional schools, but *not in the schools
of education.* In fact, for two generations, in almost every
university, there has been little except hostility between the
faculty of education and the other faculties. Nearly twenty years
ago, I ventured to speak frankly about this matter at the fiftieth
anniversary of the founding of Teachers College, Columbia
University, and entered a plea for a "Truce Among Educators."
At that time, one frequently heard the joke that 120th Street—
the east-west street separating Teachers College from the rest of
Columbia University—was the widest street in the world. I was
told not long ago by one of the younger professors at Teachers
College that the street had narrowed perceptibly in the last ten
years. I have heard reports from other campuses which point in
the same direction. But there is always a time lag in public

affairs. If a truce has been finally declared among the educators in some universities, many alumni will probably not yet have heard the news. They may recall only the college years and the way that the English, or history, or chemistry professor used to rail against his colleagues in the school of education.

Nearly five years ago a committee of the American Academy of Arts and Sciences issued a report entitled "On the Conflict Between the 'Liberal Arts' and the 'Schools of Education'." It opens with the sentence, "During the recent past the criticism of our public schools and our institutions for the training of teachers has assumed a degree of vehemence which, whether justified or not, reveals dangerous schisms in the cultural life of the nation." And towards the end of the report, which is largely an excellent historical account of the development of the tensions, the authors state:

"There exists among a considerable number of the defenders of the liberal arts a shocking ignorance of the social problems with which the modern school is confronted. Consequently, these professors attack many of the most well-meant endeavors of our public schools on the basis of inadequate and fallacious criteria. Certainly the capacity of thinking is one of the supreme criteria of man; it can never be sufficiently cultivated. Yet, our modern schools were in no position to apply this criterion as their exclusive measure of achievement. If they had tried to carry through the program of one of the foremost critics of our high schools and colleges (that every modern citizen 'should understand the great philosophers, historians, scientists and artists'), our whole national life would be in danger of collapse. It would banish into the limbo of ignorance and futility the great majority of this nation, including a considerable number of university instructors. . . .

"To repeat: though criticism is needed, there is no salvation in the present fashionable tendency to attack the public school system by the use of incommensurate criteria, forgetting completely that this school system—whatever its obvious defects—has been for about a hundred years the most important instrument in the amalgamation of millions of poor immigrants and native citizens. As a matter of fact, this great achievement has been made possible largely by the use of methods severely criticized by outsiders. Without an attempt at understanding the complexity of a school system which at the same time should fulfill the demands of equality and of quality, of justice and differentiation, of democracy and of an elite within this democracy—and without undergoing the difficult task of relating developments in education to broad changes in our social cultural pattern—without such endeavors on all sides, there can be no productive discussion."

"Without an attempt at understanding the complexity of a school system . . . there can be no productive discussion." I should amend this statement slightly to read as follows: "Without an understanding of the complexities of public education resulting from the diversities of American communities, there can be no productive discussion of the shortcomings of our tax-supported schools." What are the complexities; what are the diversities I have in mind? They are related primarily to those factors influencing American public education which are a consequence of the total social, political, and economic structure of our society—a structure which varies in some significant details from state to state and town to town.

College professors of the liberal arts and many of their friends often discuss school problems as though schools operated in the stratosphere—that is, in a social vacuum. To be sure, it is a convenient fiction to assume all children enter school with the same interests, abilities, preconceived ideas, and return to homes that are culturally identical. It is even more convenient to assume that a community has no interest in a school except as an institution for developing intellectual powers. If one needed an example to illustrate the insufficiency of such premises about education, what is happening south of the Mason-Dixon Line would provide a dramatic case.

It would be easy to multiply examples illustrating what should be the starting point of any discussion about public education—namely, the proposition that the schools in any society operate within the framework determined by that society. Talk about school problems which ignores the framework of society or, by wishful thinking, replaces the real framework with an illusory one at the best is frivolous, at the worst is dangerous. The framework is in part legal, governmental, formal; in part, it is extra-legal, determined by local traditions, customs, by economic and social considerations, and, above all, by family attitudes.

Let me be concrete and ask the reader to go with me in imagination to a high school which I visited not long ago. It is located in a district of a medium-sized city where the rents are low and where, in periods of recession, the unemployment is high. The school is attended primarily by those who live in the district but also by a few who come some distance to enroll in certain of the vocational programs, which have a good reputation. Less than ten percent of those enrolled desire to enter a college on graduation, though more than one four-year institution is located in the city and offers free tuition. Not many more than this small fraction of the student body have the ability to handle satisfactorily the usual twelfth-grade course in physics, trigonometry, or a foreign language. And the more able students (about ten percent) are, for the most part, enrolled in these courses.

The vocational courses are well staffed and well supported and cover a wide range. A girl can go a long way towards becoming an expert in stenography, in office practice work, in running a beauty parlor, in catering and professional cooking; boys on graduation will have completed the equivalent of one year of apprentice work in auto mechanics, airplane mechanics, tool and die work, metal work, and similar trades. All the students, irrespective of their elective programs, are devoting half their time to the improvement of their skill in reading and writing, to the study of some mathematics and science, history, political science, the elements of economics, and to a discussion of current problems. Many, if not all, are benefiting from the courses in art and music and are learning something about the ways of a democracy by the operation of clubs and other extra-curricular activities. The vocational courses for a vast majority represent the vital core of the school program. They represent something related directly to the ambitions of the boys and girls and their parents.

I often wonder if those who inveigh against vocational courses in our high schools have ever visited the kind of school I have just been describing. I wonder if they have ever talked to conscientious teachers in such a school and canvassed the possibility of substituting a sequence of courses in mathematics, chemistry, physics, and foreign languages for the vocational elective programs. If they have and still persist in saying that a school should be concerned only with "mental discipline" or developing intellectual powers, their conclusions have been quite different from my own.

A second illustration of the effect of outside influences on a school and I am through with my examples of community diversity. Again, let me take the reader on an imaginary journey to visit a school I know which is by no means unique, either in its setting or its organization. It is located in an area of the type which is usually referred to as a high-income residential district. The families who send their children to this school have very different ambitions for their offspring from those of the families living in the city school district I first described. There are no skilled workmen who wish their sons to follow in their footsteps. Most of the parents are professional people; almost without exception they assume their children must go to college. Some are very specific about the college the boy or girl must enter. And, if the college in question is highly selective in its admission policy, grief and frustration in the senior year may be in store for all concerned unless a wise counselor recognizes in the lower grades the limitations in academic ability which no amount of study can overcome, or recognizes that, even if perfectly acceptable, the boy or girl in question may not be accepted because of the limited size of the college freshman class.

In part as a result of the cultural habits of the parents, the number of slow readers in this school is smaller than in the other school I just portrayed; the fraction of the student body who can effectively handle mathematics and a foreign language is much larger. Nevertheless, a considerable number of the boys and girls have the greatest difficulty with eleventh- and twelfth-grade mathematics and science and can progress only very slowly in the study of a foreign language. In these cases, parental ambition often outruns student ability. As a result, in this school there is an experienced counselor whose full-time job it is to locate colleges with sufficiently low standards to admit even those who, in terms of national norms of scholastic aptitude, are in the third quarter of the high school population. Over the years, this counselor has been most successful.

I might note parenthetically that one of the factors leading to the present highly vocal discontent with public education has been the increasing demands of parents in certain suburbs for a purely academic curriculum for all their children. A generation ago the equivalent of many of these families would have sent their children to private schools. The income tax and a greater number of children have forced more than one family to rely on public education as the means of getting a son or daughter into a particular college. Thirty years ago a similar family would have turned to a private boarding school or day school which had the reputation of being a good college-preparatory school. In those days colleges were not overburdened with applicants; the admission policies were such that a boy or girl with less than average academic ability, by hard work and skillful coaching, could pass the necessary subject-matter examinations and eventually accumulate the necessary credits for admission. I need not stress how different the highly selective admission policies of many colleges are today. The trouble in some suburban communities is that the parents are still thinking in terms of the colleges of their youth. They may demand that the school accomplish the impossible—namely, transform a boy or girl with little academic talent into a brilliant pupil; and, if frustrated by the actual situation, they are only too ready to blame the superintendent, or the principal, or the school board, or probably all three.

To be intelligent about his local situation, a citizen must assess to some degree the needs of the community in regard to vocational education. He has to make an effort to see the schools as serving the children of all the families, not just his own and his friends' children. An important clue to vocational needs is the percentage of high school graduates who, year after year, enter an institution of higher learning. Clearly, there is not much demand for vocational courses in the suburban school I just described because of the large fraction of students going on to college. In regard to specific vocational offerings, one must know the kinds of jobs available to those who wish to go to work full time immediately on graduation, for vocational work in high school must be related to employment possibilities. Whether or not local opportunities for part- or full-time education in a two-year college are available is another matter of great importance, because the relation of the community college (if one exists) to the high school may affect to some degree the organization of the high school work, especially in vocational areas. In short, a variety of questions must be answered before a citizen is in a position to discuss the highly controversial subject of the extent and kinds of practical and vocational courses (if any) which should be included in the curriculum of the high school.

Whatever may be a citizen's considered opinion, after careful study, as to the need for more or fewer vocational offerings in the local high school, he is almost certain to have strong opinions about the nonvocational work. He will have read so much about the failure of the American high schools to challenge the able student that he is on the alert to discover whether or not the criticism is valid in his own hometown.

First, one must ascertain the course offerings in the high school. For example, is it possible for a student to pursue the study of a foreign language for four years? Are twelfth-grade courses in mathematics, physics, and chemistry available every year? (There are many small high schools in which this is not the case.) Second, a constructive critic of the school system ought to know the minimum requirements for a high school diploma. To my mind, they should include the study of English each of four years, the study of social studies for at least three of the four years, and at least one year each of mathematics and natural science. Third, one should try to find out whether the students who have the ability to carry courses in advanced mathematics, science, and a foreign language as well as in English and social studies are, in fact, electing such a full academic program. Not until a person is in possession of at least this much information is he in a position to pass even a first judgment on a school system.

The third item I have just listed presents difficulties, for, unlike the first two, such information is usually not available. This fact I discovered in connection with my study of the comprehensive high school to which I have already referred so often. Without some knowledge of what kinds of students are electing what sorts of courses, one cannot make meaningful statements about a school. Every school board, I believe, should ask the superintendent to request the high school principal to prepare an academic inventory of each graduating class. Each student's actual program for four years, together with a measure of his or her potential academic ability as measured by a scholastic aptitude test, should be recorded on a card. The individual cards with the students' names should be kept highly confidential, of course. But a summary of the results should be published each year. Since tests of mathematical and verbal aptitude given in the lower grades are a rough measure of each student's potentialities, the published summary should show what percentage of the potentially abler students had elected various sequences of courses. For example, in one high school from which I obtained an academic inventory, at least half the boys whose test scores placed them in the top fifteen percent of the high school population on a national basis (the academically talented) had elected four years of mathematics, three years of science, and four years of foreign language, on top of the required four years of English and three years of social studies. By way of contrast, in another school far fewer than half the boys in the same category had elected as much as four years of mathematics, just over a half had elected as much as three years of science, and only a small percentage had studied a foreign language more than two years. I have referred to the programs of boys only because under our present social mores engineering, science, and medicine are almost exclusively male preserves. It is a pity that more able girls are not electing science and mathematics in school and college, for careers are open in teaching and research, at least, for capable women well trained in these subjects.

The making of an academic inventory does not commit a school board to a policy concerning what the potentially able boys and girls ought to study. Yet I think the school board might well adopt a policy in this regard to serve as a guide to the counselors. And I think as a minimum program for the academically talented (the top fifteen percent on a national basis) the board should have in mind the following: four years of English, three years of social studies (including two of history), three years of science, four years of mathematics, and four years of one foreign language. For the academically talented boys, at least, I feel this is a minimum program. With a seven- or eight-period day, there is room for art and music too. For girls, perhaps, a second foreign language might be substituted for twelfth-grade mathematics or science, but for the boys *in this group,* a second foreign language, I believe, should be in addition to what I have just listed.

To my mind, in every school the guidance officers, who play such a vital role in a nonselective comprehensive school, should urge every pupil whose scholastic aptitude test scores and work in the lower grades indicate academic talent to start a four-year mathematical sequence and a four-year foreign language sequence. If the boy or girl in question really cannot handle the one subject or the other by the time the eleventh grade is reached, then a more restricted elective program may be in order. However, I believe the presumption should be that a student whose test scores in the eighth grade place him in the upper fifteen percent of the high school population on a national basis is capable of studying a wide academic program effectively and rewardingly. In other words, if he is academically talented, he should develop his talents as fully as possible while he is young.

The real issue will not often be an issue to be settled by the school board or the administrative officials—it will be a community issue. How hard do the parents of the able children want their children to work? To what degree will the community support the efforts of a school board to urge the academically talented to take a wide program? In many a school I have been in, the more able boys and girls complained they could not devote as much time to study as they wished because their evenings were taken up by activities arranged by organizations in the community. If the leading citizens in such cities really sense the realities of the kind of world in which we live, they will be the first to say to the bright boy or girl, "For your own sake and for the sake of the nation, do your homework."

Anyone familiar with the facts about the high school

population will recognize that it is impossible to have one standard academic curriculum for all pupils. That is, it is impossible if high standards in mathematics, science, and foreign languages are to be maintained. Of course, one can require that even pupils with very little academic ability be *exposed* to such subjects, but for a high school student to profit from the exposure he or she must have a certain minimum of ability and be prepared to work. The accumulated experience of countless teachers demonstrates that the profitable study of mathematics beyond elementary algebra or the study of a foreign language with the objective of mastery is just too difficult for certain pupils. For others, such study is relatively easy, and these are the pupils who should be urged to study these subjects. For an intermediate group—and the line between this group and the academically talented is hazy—much will depend on the attitudes of the boy or girl and the parent. What the educators call "motivation" is for this group all important. No one should attempt to be dogmatic about the size of this intermediate group or the elective programs they should study. Given sufficient ambition, many a pupil whose academic talent is not very great may, by hard work, be able to keep up with his more brilliant classmates in both mathematics and foreign languages. But there are limits to what even hard work can accomplish, as every teacher knows. Any realistic appraisal of the problems of secondary education results in the conclusion that there must be a wide variety of courses in the high school.

All right, the reader may ask, if not all pupils can handle a tough academic program, why not require just the bright students to take the tough courses? To this I would reply: How? There is no way in a free country by which organized society can *require* bright children to study hard. One can imagine a school assigning all the pupils with an I.Q. above a certain score to a prescribed, stiff program of academic studies, yet what if the students refuse the challenge and do not do the work? Drop them from the program? This would keep up standards, but the over-all objective would not have been accomplished. The chances are that the arbitrary assignment of pupils to such a program would cause resentment from some of those who were included as well as considerable pressure from parents whose children were excluded. As a matter of fact, I can hardly conceive of a community agreeing to any such arbitrary and deterministic scheme. Some high schools do attempt to solve the problem by setting up a special academic track with a prescribed course of study that a student may *elect*. However, there is no way of insuring that all the able students will choose the program and do the work; the decision of the student largely depends on the attitudes of the parents and counselors and the spirit of the school. Even if, in place of a special academic program within a high school, one established a series of special selective academic high schools (a radical innovation which would take much time), there would be no guarantee that any large fraction of those who ought to attend would, in fact, enroll. The more one studies the problem of how to develop academic talent through education in a free society, the more one concludes that attempts at compulsion are not the answer. A climate of opinion must be created which brings forth in each young person a strong desire to do his or her best in school. Then the schools must, in turn, provide the challenging courses and provide a variety so that not only the academically talented student but every student will feel his studies are worthwhile.

I have been discussing the necessity for advanced mathematics, science, and foreign languages on an *elective* basis. English and social studies, on the other hand, are *required* and are presented to all or almost all high school students irrespective of their talents. It would require a long discussion to go into the basic reasons why the study of English or history is different from the study of mathematics beyond elementary algebra, or physics, or the study of foreign language. One illustration may suffice. Almost all pupils can achieve a certain degree of competence in English composition, though the quality of the themes written, even with the best instruction, will vary enormously. Everyone agrees that one of the objectives of a high school is to improve the writing ability of every child. The poorest writer should be able to write a simple letter, while the best may be trying his or her hand at poetry. Contrast this with the study of trigonometry. Unless the student can reach a certain level of understanding and skill in handling the concepts and symbols, nothing has been accomplished by the course of study. A certain absolute level of competence must be soon reached or the rest of the course is meaningless. So, too, with other mathematical courses usually given in grades ten, eleven, and twelve; so, too, with the study of foreign languages or physics as given in grades eleven or twelve. On the other hand, the social studies courses at the high school level are like English.

I have devoted considerable attention to the kind of student who has certain talents which, when properly developed, lead to academic skills. It is interesting that we have been quite ready to recognize other kinds of talents—not only to recognize them but to stress the value of the skills that can be developed from them. I refrain from over-elaborating on our interest in athletic talent! One reason for public recognition of this particular talent is the fact that it is easily observable. Artistic and musical talents likewise are readily discernible. For this reason, and because of the long-term benefits to the individual that come from the development of musical and artistic skills, much time and money have been devoted to instruction in these fields in our public schools. As a people, we have been increasingly concerned with raising the cultural level of the country.

Until very recently the American public has shown little interest in academic ability or the manipulative talents of skilled workmen. Yet, recalling the Biblical parable, we should not bury these talents but rather develop them. If a basketball coach sees a boy over six feet tall with good coordination, he will urge the boy to try out for the basketball team. The same principle should hold true for students with academic or manipulative talents; they have certain potential skills that should be developed. Further, just as the American public has the good sense to realize that success in basketball means a combination of special talent and good coaching, so we should recognize that success in these other areas means talent combined with good teaching. Both are needed.

I pointed out in the preceding chapter that the assumption that all leaders and good citizens in society will come from the academically talented group is utterly false. It is true that most of the professional people—doctors, lawyers, engineers, scientists, and scholars—are recruited from this group. But just as one cannot possibly say that good citizens are people with basketball skills, so one cannot say that good citizenship is tied directly to skills resulting from the study of foreign languages or advanced mathematics and science.

How, then, do our schools promote what we might call the skills of good citizenship? It is my belief, as I stated earlier, that the general education required of all students, regardless of special talents, academic or otherwise, serves this purpose. The ability of students to participate in our free society as active and effective citizens will be developed by a required program in English (four years), social studies (at least three years), and some mathematics and science, together with the various out-of-class activities that mark a comprehensive high school. These courses and activities are designed to develop in every student his or her power of reasoning, as well as an understanding of our cultural heritage, the traditions of our society, and the give-and-take of democracy in action. It should go without saying that we must do all we can to protect this vitally important function of our schools.

One question which troubles many parents and many citizens who are not parents of children now in school is the following: How do we know, even if all the pupils are required to study certain subjects (such as English) for a period of years, that they will benefit from the instruction? How can we be sure, even if all the academically talented boys elect twelfth-grade mathematics and four years of a foreign language, that these students will have their talents in these fields developed to the full? In other words, what guarantees can we have that the quality of the teaching in a school is adequate?

This is an important question, and it highlights the obvious fact that good teachers are essential at every stage of our educational system. Yet, with the salary schedule what it is in most states, it is difficult to see how we are going to recruit each year a sufficient number of able young people to provide the teachers that we need. Therefore, every citizen concerned with the quality of the teaching in his schools might well be concerned with the level of the teachers' salaries.

When it comes to assessing the performance of any individual teacher, a layman should proceed with the utmost caution. Excellent teachers are usually well known and recognized in a community after a period of years. But the crucial question of determining the potentialities of a teacher on trial is not a question for outsiders to take a hand in. Only professionals with experience (particularly the superintendent and principals of the schools) are in a position to weigh all the evidence which must be considered in determining whether a teacher should be made a permanent member of the staff. The judicious use of standard achievement tests and examinations enables the administration of a school system to follow the work of various teachers, and I know of a number of schools in which such devices are constantly and wisely used. In the final analysis, the quality of the teaching depends on the skill of the administrators in recruiting the staff and providing inspiring leadership.

The last point needs underlining, for good teachers will not teach well in a system where the morale of the staff has been destroyed by unwise actions of the school board or its agents. The community should have confidence in the school board, the superintendent, and the other administrative officers. In other words, they should have confidence in the management's ability to obtain good teachers and stimulate them to do their best. And I should like to conclude this brief discussion of the key role of the teachers by stating that I have visited many high schools with a good reputation and found this reputation justified by the quality of the teachers I have met.

The title of this chapter indicates my conviction that a heavy responsibility rests on each citizen for the improvement of our schools. Let me sum up what can be done at the local level. The citizen who wishes to do his part should, first of all, orient himself to the complexities of the task we have assigned our public schools. Second, he should get the facts about the current local situation. Then, armed with this knowledge, he is in a position to be part of a constructive force. Depending on the circumstances of the time and place, he may wish to help organize a local citizens committee in support of the public schools. He certainly will do all in his power to see to it that responsible, intelligent, public-spirited citizens are candidates for election to the local school board, and in the recurring public discussion of the financing of the schools he will be ready to support energetically the school board's recommendations, provided, of course, that he has become convinced of their soundness. And in order to become convinced he will, together with other citizens, be supplied by the school board with answers to a great variety of pertinent questions. In addition to knowing the requirements for a diploma, the course offerings, and the results of an academic inventory of each graduating class, he may wish to inquire as to the instruction in English composition. Are the teachers over-loaded and, therefore, not in a position to give adequate attention to theme writing? (They are in many schools that I have visited.) Are the standards for passing an elective academic course kept sufficiently high, or has community pressure caused the superintendent to let it be known that the teachers must be careful not to fail too many? (I could name schools where this situation exists and where, as a consequence, the less able students are being deceived by thinking they have learned something about a foreign language, for example, when in fact their accomplishment is almost nil.) What, if anything, is being done for the highly gifted student (a small percentage of the population)? Such students are apt to be bored even by academic courses suitable for an academically talented boy or girl. A number of high schools are providing opportunities for these extremely able students to anticipate one or more freshman college courses in their senior high school year.

As I pointed out in the preceding chapter, there are something like four thousand high schools in the United States that are large enough to be able to provide adequately for the whole spectrum of abilities and interests to be found in the usual American community. Many of these, as I know from visits to them, are unsatisfactory in one or more respects. Some, as I judge from hearsay, are extremely inadequate in regard to the education of the more able students. Yet the faults could be remedied in almost all the instances with which I am familiar by relatively minor changes, assuming, of course, that money for the improvements is available. The conclusion of my study of the American comprehensive high school has been, therefore, that we need no radical change in the basic pattern, except as regards the schools that are too small.

Now I know that there are critics of our public schools who disagree with any such statement. These "radical reformers," as I call them, are apt to base their arguments on the alleged superiority of European schools. I happen to know something about the schools in Germany and also about those in Switzerland by first-hand observation. I also know something about the schools in France, though only indirectly. The references to European education I read in the papers lead me to believe that there is a widespread misunderstanding in the United States about this subject. Therefore, I venture to conclude this chapter by answering a question I sometimes hear—namely: Would it not be a good idea to import the European system of education into the United States?

People who incline to answer this question offhand in the affirmative have usually had experience with one type of European school—the German *Gymnasium* (or *Oberrealschulen*) or the French *lycée*. These schools, which one may conveniently designate as pre-university schools, enroll not more than a fifth of an age group; the selection of those enrolled is made at ten to eleven years of age. The other four fifths of the youth, with a few exceptions, complete their full-time education at age fourteen and go to work. The course of study in the pre-university schools is far from easy. The homework is heavy; standards are high; often as many as two thirds fail during the eight- or nine-year course. Those who succeed then take a national examination and receive a certificate that admits to any university. (I am speaking here of Germany and Switzerland.) There is no equivalent of the four-year liberal arts college in all of Europe. The pre-university school provides all the general or liberal education that the future university student will receive. A European university is the equivalent of our graduate professional schools—law, medicine, arts and science.

One may find the education obtained in the European

pre-university schools excellent in many respects, as I do with certain reservations, and yet realize that the way this education is given in Europe is literally impossible in the United States. Let us see what would be required to Europeanize American education. First of all, one would have to abolish all the independent liberal arts colleges (over 1000 rugged institutions —quite a job). Second, one would have to eliminate or greatly alter large areas of instruction in many universities. Third, one would have to set up a uniform examination for admission to the universities and uniform standards for degrees. Fourth, one would have to change the laws on employment of youth and the school-leaving age and correspondingly persuade labor unions and management to imitate the European practice in regard to employment of young people. And last, but by no means least, one would have to abolish local school boards and place the control of the curriculum and the employment of teachers (including their allocation to a specific school) in the hands of the government of each state.

But what would be even more difficult than all this reorganization would be a necessary reversal of the whole trend of developments in our history. One would have to persuade the people of this country to turn their backs on those characteristics of our society which are a product of our special history and which, formulated as ideals, have guided so many generations. One would have to modify profoundly the American belief in local responsibility and the American attachment to two ideals derived from our frontier history—the ideals of equality of opportunity and the equality of status of all forms of honest labor.

Anyone who wishes to take on seriously a reform movement to bring about any one of the changes I have listed is welcome to the job. To my mind, he wouldn't get to first base, nor should he. As I have already indicated, I am convinced we can develop the talents of all our youth without any basic changes in the pattern of secondary education, provided that, state by state and community by community, the citizens will do their part. Public awakening to the necessity for improvement in the light of our struggle with the Soviet Union is the first step, but alone this is not enough. Citizens in each city and town must get the facts about the local schools and then be prepared to go to work. A first-rate school board must be elected and then supported in its efforts to improve the schools. The road to better schools will be paved by the collective action of the local citizenry in thousands of communities. The responsibility for the sorely needed upgrading of our schools cannot be passed to the state legislatures or to Congress. The responsibility rests on every citizen in the land.

9
The Romantic Critics:

Paul Goodman, Edgar Z. Friedenberg, John Holt, Herbert Kohl, Jonathan Kozol, Neil Postman and Charles Weingartner, George Dennison, Allen Graubard, Ivan Illich

In the winter of 1962 the *Harvard Educational Review* published a long review of *Slums and Suburbs.* "I have grown impatient with Dr. Conant," Paul Goodman wrote. "One is struck by his technological and even economic approach, as if the pragmatic problem to be solved were the allocation of resources, rather than the psychological and political one of renewing society with each growing generation. Naturally, in the post-Sputnik delirium, our Establishment would choose a Scientist and an Administrator. Having little acquaintance with social or psychological reality, and being apparently quite complacent with the dominant goals of our Nation, Dr. Conant often expresses impatience with hair-splitting philosophers and their educational ideals. His own philosophy has been that the purpose of schooling is simply to man the Cold War and train technicians and semi-skilled apprentices for the corporations and other businesses as usual. In this new book, however, he discovers that we must also watch out for the social dynamite of accumulated frustration and resentment among those who are out-caste in the present dispensation; yet again his concern is to regularize things, rather than to improve the electorate, the proper educational aim of a democracy. I have grown impatient with Dr. Conant."

Heedless of the fact that while he was president, James Conant had *twice* "saved" the Graduate School of Education from extinction, the editors of the *Harvard Educational Review* had opened its pages to Conant's most prominent critic. A few years earlier Paul Goodman had published *Growing Up Absurd* (1960), a book that castigated and rejected the very established society Conant sought to protect. Goodman's book, after being initially rejected by nineteen different publishers, went on to sell over 100,000 copies, setting afoot a new movement in educational thought and practice.

Called "romantics," the members of this movement abjured the notion that schools must take their cues from so-called national needs. Instead, they championed human needs, insisting that schools become child- or learner-oriented. Construing education as individual growth, not socialization to a role, the romantic theorists advocated (and created) small, intimate, human-size schools controlled and often run by the community and the students. Critical (like Conant) of the "established" professional educators, they moved on (unlike Conant) to criticize and reject the established educational system itself. Seeking initially to reconstruct the existing schools, the movement ultimately came to reject all schools as appropriate vehicles for education.

✻

In many books and articles Paul Goodman reminded his readers that he was an Aristotelian. Yet few of those who read him knew what this meant. As a result, many who thought they were carrying out his Aristotelian plans for education actually corrupted them. Aristotelians insist that a basic knowable human nature exists, one and the same at all times in all places in all men. Moreover, not only man, the world itself is intelligible, not absurd; it has a nature. One understands the nature or essence of each thing by knowing its function—what it is for.

In *Growing Up Absurd* Paul Goodman writes about what it is like to grow up in a world that has lost its intelligibility. For children and adolescents, he says, "it is indispensable to have a coherent, fairly simple, viable society to grow up into; otherwise they are confused, and some are squeezed out." Thus, in Aristotelian terms, the polis, or community, functions to help a man achieve full, mature humanity—*his* function of leading "the good life." But in modern America Goodman found no community, only the organized system. And the organized system thwarts and impedes human growth; it socializes the young to a social role, a role not worthy of human nature: "Our abundant society is at present simply deficient in many of the most elementary objective opportunities and worth-while goals that could make growing up possible. It is lacking in enough man's work. It is lacking in honest public speech, and people are not taken seriously. It is lacking in the opportunity to be useful. It thwarts aptitude and creates stupidity. It corrupts ingenuous patriotism. It corrupts the fine arts. It shackles science. It dampens animal ardor. It discourages the religious convictions of Justification and Vocation and it dims the sense that there is a Creation. It has no Honor. It has no Community." *

* Paul Goodman, *Growing Up Absurd* (New York: Random House, 1960), p. 12.

Without a polis, or true community, to help them grow up, the young become either resigned or cynical. They come to construe the world, Goodman tells us, as "an apparently closed room in which there is a large rat race as the dominant center of attention." Some youth run in the race—bright fellows who do not believe in it but are afraid to stop: they become cynical. Some youths find themselves disqualified from running, but they hang around because there is nowhere else to go—the corner boys who never go to college, delinquent and not, all mesmerized by the symbols and culture of the rat race: these are the resigned and the fatalistic. Another group of resigned youth were those then called the "beat generation" (later "hippies"): they have more or less balked in the rat race, or have not had the heart to start it. Finally, a few—the radicals—vigorously attack the rat race and try to stop it.

In all these groups Goodman finds the spirit of hipsterism— the *deliberate* assumption of a convenient role in order to manipulate the system for one's own power or at least safety. He finds the hipster a lamentable human being. The hipster cannot grow. He has no faith, no support; for nothing exists, he thinks, but the rat race. He swings with the rat race, exhausting himself in actions he holds in contempt, deepening his own cynicism or resignation.

In an apparently closed room it is hard to grow up. But, although people were bemused by the organized system—pressured or coopted to live in, serve, and maintain it—Goodman believed it possible, and desirable, to create an alternative society, replete with alternatives to replace "its role playing, its competitiveness, its canned culture." There have been, Goodman claims, "missed revolutions" in modern times—in the physical environment; in our economic, social, and political arrangements; in our moral dispositions and in our educational theories—that have produced the conditions that make it hard for the young to grow up. Now we have to "work through" this unfinished past. Completing these revolutions will create a society "Where the community carries on its important adult business and the children fall in at their own pace. And where education is concerned with fostering human powers as they develop in the growing child." In such a society, Goodman explains, it will be easy to grow up: "There would be plenty of objectives, worthwhile activities for a child to observe, fall in with, do, learn, improvise on his own."

Like Aristotle and his fellow Greeks, Goodman thought that the polis was (or should be) itself educative. And what about the schools—what are they for? They are supposed to educate, and we compel the young to attend them; but, Goodman announces, they do not educate. In *Compulsory Mis-education* (1964), he decries the expansion of schooling and the aggrandizing ways of school people ("school monks," he calls them). No more money should be given to the schoolmen or the schools, he declares, because not only are they wasteful, but they also do positive damage to the young.

Because schools are the only allowable way of growing up, they have become a universal trap for American youth. Schools simply do not fit the disposition of many youths; unprepared, uninterested, they simply develop a "reactive stupidity" very different from their behavior on the street or ball field. They fall behind, play truant, and as soon as possible drop out. Those who stay in school from ages six to sixteen, or twenty, drop out internally and daydream—"their days wasted, their liberty caged and scheduled." In schools they learn, Goodman tells us, "that life is inevitably routine, depersonalized, venally graded; that it is best to toe the mark and shut up; that there is no place for spontaneity, open sexuality, free spirit." From school Goodman sees them going on to "the same quality of jobs, culture, politics." This, he concludes, is mis-education: socializing to the national norms and regimenting to the national "needs."

As Goodman sees it, schools are places where the scholastically bright are pressured and bribed, where the majority—those who are bright but not scholastic, and those who are not especially bright but have other kinds of vitality—are subdued. Inevitably, he labels the schools "concentration camps."

Throughout the book Goodman insists that we ought to spend more of our wealth on education, but not on schools; the present system of schools is just not the appropriate institution for the job. In place of schools, Goodman would have us make our whole environment more educative. He presents a number of innovative proposals:

—Have no school at all for a few classes.
—Dispense with the school building for a few classes—have teachers and students use the city itself as the school: its

streets, cafeterias, stores, movies, museums, parks, and factories.
—Use unlicensed adults of the community—the druggist, the
storekeeper, the mechanic—as the proper educators of the
young into the grown up world.
—Abolish compulsory class attendance.
—Decentralize an urban school into small units, 20 to 50, in
available storefronts or clubhouses.

In combating the mass superstition that schooling is the only
path to success, Goodman was taking an admittedly conservative
stance ("What a generation before had been the usual course, to
quit school and seek elsewhere to grow up, became a sign of
eccentricity, failure, delinquency"). But he was no elitist. "The
scholastic disposition is a beautiful and useful one," he explained;
"we are lucky that a minority of people are so inclined." But he
added, "I do not think it is the moon and the stars."

Paul Goodman's conservative notions about what (and who)
schools are for were transformed, in the latter half of the decade,
into a radical movement in American education. During this
period ordinary youthful iconoclasm and natural self-indulgence
united with the heightened idealism generated by the New Frontier
and the Great Society to create a "youth movement." The New
Frontier and the Great Society had identified victims of the
"system": the poor, the black, the Indians, the Spanish-speaking,
the old, and the infirm. Paul Goodman helped to turn the youth
movement inward, focused it on "the most oppressed minority
group in America today": youth.

As the 1960s wore on, the feelings of victimization among
youth grew more frantic. An ever escalating Vietnam war killed
more and more of them and infuriated and frightened those who
remained at home. The war drove many to attend college, some
even to study to become teachers, simply to avoid or postpone
induction into military service. Their guilt and rage about the
absurdity of the world and their own behavior led many to see Paul
Goodman as a guru who "told it like it is": "The organized system
is absurd." "Schools are concentration camps." "Students are
prisoners." "Teachers are baby sitters or policemen."

And the educators? The "school monks"? Few contradicted

Goodman, although many ignored him. A sizable number of school people agreed with him, and a few actually tried to carry out his proposals—endeavoring to convert the twentieth-century cities into a Greek polis of the fourth century B.C.

✳

There were other sensitive and sympathetic observers who decried the victimization of youth in America. One of the most influential was the sociologist Edgar Z. Friedenberg. Whereas Goodman had traced that victimization to the loss of intelligibility of the "organized system," Friedenberg discovered that American society subverted the process of growth itself: it destroyed adolescence.

In *The Vanishing Adolescent*, Friedenberg explains that adolescence is not simply a physical process, it is primarily a social one—the conflict between the individual and society. In contemporary American society he found that the American high school functioned to prohibit and eliminate all conflicts; hence, the vanishing adolescent. Thus, the school functions to Americanize the young, eliminating all differences among them. In addition, it maintains records, dossiers on a youth's intelligence, interests, medical history, and emotional stability as well as noting political interests, appraisals of the faculty, and overall promise for the future that create anxiety, dispel honesty, and coerce conformity.

A third function the school performs is to distribute status, and in doing this it threatens the self-esteem of the young by constructing the school as a lower-middle-class institution where students learn that school is primarily, if not solely, for aid in advancing to a higher status and economic level. In school students learn: (a) that they ought to want to get ahead in the world, (b) how to go about doing it, and (c) the terms on which it can be done.

The schools, of course, provide formal instruction too, but because they construe the arts as decoration and diversion and the sciences as techniques, and because they fail to establish the concept of intellectual authority, the schools never secure respect for intellectual competence; hence, they deprive most young people of any foundation for autonomy.

The high school, Friedenberg concludes, is an ungracious

institution with a shallow conception of human dignity. Lacking respect for them, it cannot promote the growth of the young. It cannot help the youngster understand himself or his relationship to other people and institutions. The school can only assess and promote adjustment or acquiescence.

With the disappearance of adolescence, we find the emergence of a new kind of adult—one who has no stable identity. Yet this is the outcome society actually expects; and under ordinary circumstances, rewards. America is producing what Ortega y Gasset called "mass man": "which sets no value on itself—good or ill—based on specific grounds, but which feels itself 'just like everybody' and nevertheless is not concerned about it."

Paul Goodman's Aristotelian criticism of what he called "the organized system" led him to anarchism; only in decentralized, polis-like organizations and institutions, he argued, could people perceive the nature of things—that schools, for example, were for education, not baby-sitting or policing or processing people into personnel. Whenever and wherever possible, Goodman would decentralize "the organized system," creating mini-schools, or storefront schools, for example. Friedenberg, while he prizes freedom as much as any anarchist, is nevertheless a disciple of Rousseau, not Aristotle. His quest is for meaning, not for truth; for personal identity, rather than for understanding of the nature of things. Like Rousseau, Friedenberg longs for a society where people will have freedom and dignity.

In *Coming of Age in America*, Friedenberg depicts how the schools victimize the young, depriving them of both freedom and dignity. First, the school victimizes the poor or, as they were now called, the "disadvantaged," the "underprivileged," the "culturally deprived." Throughout its history the school has extended concern and sympathy to the poor, but has never viewed them as having positive value or strength in their own right. The school is a friend to the poor as long as they are "properly ashamed of their poverty and their foreignness and properly anxious to get on in the world." Between the children of the poor and the staff of the school there is conflict, often enmity. The unambitious, the recalcitrant, and those striving for self-esteem rebel against the school's assaults on their privacy and dignity. Many drop out.

In addition to the poor, schools are hostile to the children of the rich. This is because they, having access to other resources, do not regard their teachers as the sole determiners of what is good, true, or proper; they challenge the teacher's moral, intellectual, and social authority. The hostile efforts teachers make to assert their authority over the children of the rich make many of them drop out, too—to enter private schools.

The third group of students against whom the school directs its animus is those who are creative. They incur hostility by refusing to do what pleases teachers, even though they know what pleases, and know, too, that this is very likely to bring success in later life. Friedenberg calls these creative students "subjective people" who "have very little use for the school and vice versa." Particularly in adolescence, they are trying to realize and clarify their identity; the school, acting as a mobility ladder, assumes instead the function of inducing them to change or alter it. "They want to discover who they are; the school wants to help them 'make something out of themselves.' They want to know where they are; the school wants to help them get somewhere. They want to learn how to live with themselves; the school wants to teach them how to get along with others. They want to learn how to tell what is right for them; the school wants to teach them to give the responses that will earn them rewards in the classroom and in social situations."

Our schools do not help the young grow up. What we need, he suggests, is a diversity of schools, "each serving a specialized, rather than a mass clientele." This means we need more and different kinds of schools—he suggests using public money to pay the fees at private and boarding schools for all who wish to attend them. What is crucial, of course, is the kind of education these diverse schools will provide. The highest function of education, Friedenberg maintains, is "to help people understand the meaning of their lives, and become more sensitive to the meaning of other peoples' lives and relate to them more fully." Each school, then, should focus on what he, in another place, calls "subjective truth." If he had his way, every child would go to a school that is relevant to his own subjective being. Schooling would become a quest for meaning, a search for personal clarity and commitment.

For schools like this to come into existence, the present total connection in the minds of both students and teachers between schooling and economic opportunity must weaken. This would constitute a complete reversal in the historical role of education in this country, something not likely to happen. Yet Friedenberg does not despair. ("Despair," he once wrote, "is not a component of the mature attitude.") True, Ortega's definition of a mass society does fit America, but not with the finality of a law of physics. Change and improvement are possible.

The teachers who followed the lead of Friedenberg and Goodman decried, like them, the present condition of American society, and, like them, held out for a utopian dream where reconstructed educational institutions could lead to a better, more humane society. And always, "better" schools meant schools that were centered on the needs of youth, not the needs of the existing society. But it was Friedenberg's construction of education as a quest for meaning, rather than Goodman's quest for truth that became the pattern for much of the educational movement that followed.* The critics who now took up the cry for better schools had in mind schools that were relevant, schools that would supply meaning to the lives of the young.

❋

The next wave of romantic critics, mostly teachers, wrote about their experiences in American schools and classrooms. On the basis of their experiences they located the true roots of what was wrong with American education in the curriculum, or in the teaching methods, or in the classroom structure and climate, or in the bureaucratic system itself. In book after book of careful scrutiny and scathing analyses they laid bare the institutionalized authoritarianism that obstructed learning and psychologically damaged the children in American schools.

One of the most penetrating books, *How Children Fail*, appeared in 1964. In it John Holt eloquently exposed what happens when teachers think it their duty and their right to tell children what they must learn. The idea of "essential knowledge everyone should know" lies behind much of what teachers do in school, Holt maintains. Thus we have a predetermined curriculum consisting of

---

* As an Aristotelian, Goodman held that meaning followed truth: if you know the nature of things, then things have meaning.

material for students to "cover," "master," and "be tested on." By construing education this way—schools and classrooms as places where children are forced to learn what we have predetermined—we make children afraid: "afraid of not doing what other people want, of not pleasing, of making mistakes, of failing, of being wrong."

Fear destroys intelligence. It affects a child's whole way of looking about and dealing with life. Dependent upon the teacher as the complete intellectual authority for what is right, true, good, and proper, the child becomes habituated to looking to authorities for correct answers. Lacking self-confidence, he may even become contemptuous of his own ability to discover the meaning of things.

> One boy, quite a good student, was working on the problem, "if you have 6 jugs, and you want to put ⅔ of a pint of lemonade into each jug, how much lemonade will you need?" His answer was 18 pints. I said, "How much in each jug?" "Two-thirds of a pint." I said, "Is that more or less than a pint?" "Less." I said, "How many jugs are there?" "Six." I said, "But that doesn't make any sense." He shrugged his shoulders and said, "Well, that's the way the system worked out." *

This boy, Holt points out, had quit expecting school to make sense. You follow the rules the way they tell you—never mind whether they have any meaning.

Anxious and fearful in a situation where teachers (even nice, kindly ones) come on as intellectual authorities, children develop strategies to survive. The logic of their situation points to strategies aimed at avoiding trouble, embarrassment, punishment, disapproval, or loss of status. Even when teachers try to make themselves and the work nonthreatening, children still view schools as prisons and teachers as absolute and final authorities whom they must please at all costs. As a result, many children become what Holt calls "producers": interested only in getting right answers, answers that will satisfy the teacher. For them the educational process is nothing more than a combination of bluffing, guessing, mind-reading, snatching at clues, and getting answers from other people."

---

* John Holt, *How Children Fail* (New York: Pitman, 1964), pp. 143–44.

Using these defensive strategies, some kids "get through" school; many do not. Almost all fail to learn how to think, how to solve problems; most important, they fail to develop confidence in themselves and end up looking for authorities to solve problems for them.

The way out of this institutionalized authoritarianism, Holt says, is to fashion child-centered courses of study. "We cannot have real learning in school if we think it is our duty and our right to tell children what they must learn. We cannot know, at any moment, what particular bit of knowledge or understanding a child needs most, will most strengthen and best fit his model of reality. Only he can do this. He may not do it very well, but he can do it a hundred times better than we can. The most we can do is try to help, by letting him know roughly what is available and where he can look for it. Choosing what he wants to learn and what he does not is something he must do for himself."

Holt would have schools and classrooms where each child, in his own way, can "satisfy his curiosity, develop his abilities and talents, pursue his interests, and from the adults and older children around him get a glimpse of the great variety and richness of life." Envisioning the school curriculum as a "great smorgasbord of intellectual, artistic, creative, and athletic activities," he wants each child to take whatever he wants—and as much as he wants, or as little.

＊

Continuing the battle against educational authoritarianism, Neil Postman and Charles Weingartner locate it in the role the teacher plays in most American schools and classrooms. Most teachers think they are in the "information dissemination business" or the "transmission of our cultural heritage business." Other critics have pointed out that the teachers' efforts to transmit the dead ideas, values, metaphors, and information of the past have turned out students who are passive, acquiescent, dogmatic, intolerant, authoritarian, and inflexible. But Postman and Weingartner go beyond this, to insist that such an approach to teaching endangers our very survival. Change, technologically wrought change, they say, "renders virtually all of our

traditional concepts (survival strategies)—and the institutions developed to conserve and transmit them—irrelevant." And if we fail
to see that these concepts are irrelevant, they further warn, "these
concepts themselves become threats to our survival."

The theme of their book *Teaching as a Subversive Activity*
(1969) is that teachers must construe their role differently, they
must switch to the right business. What business is that? The
crap-detecting business.

The way teachers can cultivate people good at crap detecting,
they tell us, is through the "inquiry method" of instruction. Here
the teacher does not tell the students what he thinks they ought to
know. His basic mode of discourse with them is questioning. Not
"What am I thinking" questions such as: "What is a noun?" or
"What were the causes of the Civil War?" or "What is the principal
river of Uruguay?" Instead of playing trivia games with students,
teachers who adopt the inquiry method concoct questions that
"open engaged minds to unsuspected possibilities." They pose such
questions as:

> What do you worry about most?
> What are the causes of your worries?
> Can any of your worries be eliminated? How?
> Which of them might you deal with first? How do you decide?
> Are there other people with the same problems? How do you
>   know? How can you find out?
> If you had an important idea that you wanted to let everyone (in
>   the world) know about, how might you go about letting them
>   know?
> When you hear or read or observe something, how do you know
>   what it means?
> Where does meaning "come from"?
> What does "meaning" mean?
> How can you tell what something "is" or whether it is?

Questions such as these elicit from students the meanings they
have stored up. Pursuing these questions subjects those meanings
to a testing and verifying, reordering and reclassifying, modifying
and extending process. In this process, Postman and Weingartner
note, the student is not a passive recipient; he becomes an active

producer of knowledge. According to their theory (based on the work of Adelbert Ames), people create knowledge; or as they put it: "Learning is meaning making." Whether he wants to or not, every teacher ends up with a student-centered curriculum simply because "subject matter" exists in the mind of the perceiver: "What each one thinks it is, is what it is."

If learning is meaning making, how does it take place? Adopting the Sapir-Whorf hypothesis—which they elaborate as the "Sapir - Whorf - Korzybski - Ames - Einstein - Heisenberg - Wittgenstein-McLuhan-et al. Hypothesis"—they claim that what we perceive, and therefore what we learn, is a function of our languaging process: "Language structures what we will see and believe; in fact, it is inseparable from what one sees and believes." For this reason the teaching process they advocate—the inquiry method—in addition to being student-centered and question-centered must also be language-centered.

As they see it, all knowledge is language: "What we call a subject is its language." Thus biology is nothing more than language; neither is history nor astronomy nor physics: "If you do not know the meanings of 'history words' or 'astronomy words' you do not know history or astronomy." So in all "subjects," they conclude, students study the relationship of language to reality, whether the "subject" is history, politics, biology, religion, or anything else. This, of course, reduces all study to linguistics, which they defined in a previous book, *Linguistics: A Revolution in Teaching* (1966), as "the use of scientific processes of inquiry into the role of language in human affairs." Ultimately, then, Postman and Weingartner want every educator to be a linguistics teacher, getting students to examine language through what they call the "scientific process of inquiry"—defining, observing, classifying, generalizing, verifying, and revising language. Teaching students how to do this will, they insist, give them the tools for survival in a world of accelerating, ubiquitous change.

If and when teachers shift their roles in this way, teaching will become a subversive activity, for it will create new learning environments that will usher in an educational revolution. The revolution will become visible, Postman and Weingartner predict, when teachers eliminate all tests, courses, requirements, full-time

administrators, and "all restrictions that confine learners to sitting
still in boxes inside of boxes."

❊

In *36 Children* (1967), Herbert
Kohl describes his own halting, groping efforts to transform the
structure and climate of his sixth-grade classroom in a Harlem
school. In looking for ways to lead children "to find a meaningful
life in school," Kohl stumbled toward what came to be called the
"open classroom." He viewed the official curriculum as dull and
lifeless, just as the children did. It did nothing to help children
"come into contact with themselves." The atmosphere, the environment of the classroom was authoritarian. In a later book, *The Open
Classroom* (1969), Kohl wrote:

> When I began teaching I felt isolated in a hostile environment.
> The structure of authority in my school was clear: the principal
> was at the top and the students were at the bottom. Somewhere
> in the middle was the teacher, whose role it was to impose orders
> from textbooks or supervisors upon the students. The teacher's
> only protection was that if students failed to obey instructions
> they could legitimately be punished or, if they were defiant,
> suspended or kicked out of school. There was no way for
> students to question the teachers' decisions or for teachers to
> question the decisions of their supervisors or authors of text-
> books and teachers' manuals.*

In time, he says, he discovered that his school in the black
ghetto was not a pathological case, for the same atmosphere and
environment existed in most schools throughout the country—
urban, suburban, black, white, integrated, segregated, elementary,
secondary. "For most American children there is essentially one
public school system in the United States, and it is authoritarian
and oppressive."

Everywhere, Kohl says, teachers consider "controlling the
children" as the one function essential for success. And if a new

---

* Herbert Kohl, *The Open Classroom* (New York: Random House, 1969),
p. 3.

teacher couldn't do this, then his colleagues and principal thought he probably wasn't suited to the job. During his first year his principal, his colleagues, and Kohl himself thought he could never become a teacher.

But with luck and advice from a friendly colleague, Kohl discovered the root of the problem in himself and in the atmosphere of the classroom—not in the students. Through trial and error—learning all the while—he slowly created an "open classroom." He learned to function in a nonauthoritarian way in an authoritarian institution.

His initial move at the outset of the school year was to ignore the school record cards of his students. Not knowing the IQ scores or achievement scores, or even who may be a source of trouble, is a way for teachers to suspend expectations and give their pupils a fresh chance to develop in new ways—"freed from the roles they may have adopted in their previous school careers." Then, allaying his fears in the process, Kohl slowly began to accept his pupils as human beings and began to present himself to them as a human being, too.

By refusing to impose routines and rules on them (calling the roll, lining up to leave the room, passing out papers and collecting them, and so on) his pupils—and he—had to find ways of functioning together without invoking arbitrary or absolute authority. He refused to assign classroom seats, allowing students to move about where they wanted. Conflicts arose, but they became an organic part of the classroom community, not something to be stifled or squelched. "Alvin's malaise or John's refusal to work were natural responses to an unpleasant environment; not merely in my class but a cumulative school environment which meant nothing more to most of the children than white-adult ignorance and authority."

Although he initially stuck to the prescribed curriculum (first social studies, then reading, then arithmetic), Kohl in time abandoned it completely. He began by "giving" his pupils a ten-minute break between lessons. But these breaks grew until, in his eyes, "the lessons were secondary." He began talking to the children about himself, what he cared about; he observed them play and live with one another; he played games and joked with them. Above all, he listened to them.

"Mr. Kohl, the junkies had a fight last night. They cut this girl up bad."

"Mr. Kohl, I couldn't sleep last night, they was shouting and screaming until four o'clock."

"I don't go down to the streets to play, it's not safe."

"Mr. Kohl, those cops are no good. They beat up on this kid for nothing last night."

What could he say to the children? His words were useless; he could do nothing about the facts. Yet listening was enough. For what the children wanted was acceptance of the truth in a classroom that had become important to them. By listening to them, accepting the facts, Kohl placed the classroom in the context of the child's real world. And by listening to them, learning about their lives, he overcame his fears, discovered their humanity. He became, he says, "more willing to respond to the children individually and less dependent on the protection of the role of teacher." I let an insult pass and discovered that the rest of the class didn't take up the insult; I learned to say nothing when Ralph returned from pacing the halls, or when Alvin refused to do arithmetic. The children did not want to be defiant, insulting, idle; nor were they any less afraid of chaos than I was. They wanted more than anything to feel they were facing it with me and not against me."

Gradually Kohl abandoned all the tactics and strategies teachers use to protect themselves—textbooks, workbooks, schedules, and lesson plans—and began to explore new things to teach the children, new areas to make the classroom more meaningful to them. He brought loads of stuff in for them: books, magazines, records, tapes, and tape recorders. The kids played checkers, chess, and jacks; they played records and danced. Most significantly, they began to write. For the first time in school, they began to write to communicate. They wrote about their block, and what they would do to change it. This led to a study of the history of man, an ambitious project Kohl undertook to discover what conditions of human existence had given rise to inequality and what could be done.

In pursuing this project Kohl had to read history, anthropology, archeology; he brought in books and pictures and maps for the children. And they, too, began to do research—discovering the library and encyclopedias. By this time the schedule was abandoned. So there were many things the children didn't "cover": days without arithmetic and weeks without spelling. But the children learned "to explore and invent, to become obsessed by things that interested them and follow them through libraries and books back into life."

As their world expanded, the children began to write. Most of *36 Children* consists of samples of this truly remarkable writing. They wrote autobiographies, stories, novels, myths, and fables. Finally they wrote, and published, a newspaper.

The publication of the newspaper brought in its wake the cold, dampening interference of the school authorities. One teacher visited the class to caution the children against writing stories about fighting and violence—the kind that had filled their newspaper; an assistant principal came round to give the class a lesson on proofreading. This bureaucratic insensitivity presaged the futility of Kohl's year of work with his class.

The following year, most of the class entered junior high school. There they again met authoritarianism, insensitivity, indifference, and scorn. When, a few years later, Kohl wrote his book about them, many of the thirty-six children had dropped out of school. As one of the children put it: "Mr. Kohl, one good year isn't enough. . . ."

✻

By the time he came to write *36 Children*, Herbert Kohl tells us he had ceased believing that the schools could be reformed from within. His friend and former Harvard roommate, Jonathan Kozol, had come to the same conclusion after *his* experiences in the Boston public schools. Kozol wrote a harrowing account of his life as a teacher in *Death at an Early Age: The Destruction of the Hearts and Minds of Negro Children in the Boston Public Schools* (1967). Both Kozol and Kohl concluded that the root of the problem lay with the bureaucratized establishment schools. They had no hope in any solution that perpetuated the existing authoritarian bureaucracy. Both, like many other educational reformers, looked to escape the institutionalized authoritarianism of public education by establishing and working in alternative, or as they were usually called, "free" schools.

One of the earliest and most moving descriptions of a free school is George Dennison's *The Lives of Children* (1969), which recounts the short life of the First Street School of New York City. The First Street School was a typical free school: small, with a low pupil-teacher ratio, relatively inexpensive to operate, and construed by teachers and pupils alike as an environment for growth. Influenced by A. S. Neill and by Tolstoy, too, but most of all by the theories of John Dewey, the relationship between the teachers and pupils was the heart of the First Street School; freedom for all was its spirit.

Here the needs of the child superseded the curriculum; not instruction, but the life of the child became paramount. Abandoning arbitrary rules of order the teachers sought to create a community, an organic community based on the natural authority of adults and the needs of children. Like Kohl (and Dewey), the teachers strove to maintain the children's continuum of experience, accepting and making part of the school the outside real world of the pupils. The teachers, Dennison explains, could not be role players, but real people who taught children, not subjects. "We made much of freedom of choice and freedom of movement; and of reality of encounter between teachers and students; and of the continuum of persons by which we understand that parents, teachers, friends, neighbors, the life of the streets, form all one substance in the experience of the child." They abolished tests and grades and lesson plans; they abolished homework, and the category of truant. They abolished all the trappings of institutionalized authoritarianism, creating what Dennison calls an "internal order"—"a structuring of activities based upon the child's innate desire to learn."

The children in the school, Dennison reports, came alive; they flourished; they grew. But the school closed at the end of the second year. And Dennison admits they could boast of very little in the way of long-range effects. Still, he persists in declaring that any hope for a new spirit in education lies outside the present establishment simply because "education is *par excellence* a human affair" and requires love—something professional educators cannot or will not give to their pupils.

> What we can give to all children is attention, forbearance, patience, care, and above all justice. This last is certainly a form of love; it is—precisely—love in a form that can be given, given without distinction to all, since just this is the anatomy of justice: it is the self-conscious, thoroughly generalized human love of humankind. This can be seen negatively in the fact that where a child (past infancy) can survive, grow, and if not flourish, do well enough in an environment that is largely without love, his development in an environment that is largely without justice will be profoundly disturbed.*

The "free school movement," as it came to be called, grew out of the realization that the institutionalized authoritarianism of the public schools is actually functional in American society. The schools *do* work: they socialize the young to fit into the existing (authoritarian) society; they encourage the kinds of values and character traits people need in this society. Therefore, the argument went, you cannot expect the public schools that support the system to eliminate this authoritarianism. It is their job to serve the interests of the status quo. Yet some in the movement argued that simply creating free schools that were not authoritarian and did not support the status quo of society was not enough. The logic of the free school movement, they argued, led beyond problems of pedagogy and school organization to the political problems of radically reforming the society itself.

But not all who joined the free school movement saw it this way. Although most opposed many of the dominant institutions and values of contemporary America, they viewed free schools as neutral or apolitical. Instead of weapons for radical political insurgence, they created schools where each child can unfold his own individuality while learning skills in a joyful, personal way. Like Kohl, in his early period, many free schoolers thought that the school—this time a *free* school—could help the young discover meaning. What they failed to see, according to those more

---

* George Dennison, *The Lives of Children* (New York: Random House, 1969), p. 116.

politically minded within the movement, was that the culture itself is meaningless. As Allen Graubard put it in *Free the Children* (1972):

> I have seen free schools all over the country and have come into contact with many young people. Most of these young people have the same confusions about meaningful ways to live that any sensitive and perceptive young person would have today. The dream that the youth will find all sorts of new ways of life that we older people can't conceive of is one of the symptoms of our current cultural malaise. The young people are scared, and they mostly do not see themselves as exuberantly finding whole new ways of living. They are at least as confused as the rest of us. That the culture provides so few meaningful ways of living is a condition we are all suffering from, the young people most of all.*

As Graubard and others saw it, the logic of the free school movement entailed moving beyond a search for meaning within a self-contained school community to a search for meaning within the society itself. We have to ask, Graubard wrote, "how the free schools as institutions can relate to the broad political and social realities of America today, what their potential effects can be as part of a development of serious educational reform, which, finally, must mean radical social change."

According to Graubard's 1972 survey, the great majority of free schools had no clear political doctrine and did not present themselves as espousing any particular political line. No one has been more scathing in denouncing those apolitical free schools than Jonathan Kozol in his book *Free Schools* (1972):

> While children starve and others walk the city streets in fear on Monday afternoon, the privileged young people in the Free Schools of Vermont shuttle their handlooms back and forth and speak of love and of "organic processes." They do "their thing." Their thing is sun and good food and fresh water and good doctors and delightful, old and battered eighteenth-century

---

* Allen Graubard, *Free the Children* (New York: Random House, 1972), p. 181.

houses, and a box of baby turtles; somebody else's thing may be starvation, broken glass, unheated rooms and rats inside the bed with newborn children. The beautiful children do not *wish* cold rooms or broken glass, starvation, rats or fear for anybody; nor will they stake their lives, or put their bodies on the line, or interrupt one hour of the sunlit morning, or sacrifice one moment of the golden afternoon, to take a hand in altering the unjust terms of a society in which these things are possible.*

In a final, emotional burst of candor, Kozol declares: "In my belief, an isolated upper-class rural Free School for the children of the white and rich within a land like the United States and in a time of torment such as 1972, is a great deal too much like a sandbox for the children of the SS Guards at Auschwitz."

❋

In 1972 there were approximately 350 free schools in the United States, enrolling about one-tenth of one percent of the schoolchildren of the country. A small movement, yet one that attracted much interest and acclaim . . . and criticism—from within and also from some with far more radical theories about education. Ivan Illich argued that free schools tend to be conservative without the redeeming traditionalism of the old. Both, he said, share "a therapeutic orientation, a utopian vision of youth and an attitude of condescension." Illich's main criticism was that "the free school movement risks reinforcing the dominant system of compulsory knowledge and public training for corporate behavior."

Appearing on the educational scene in the early 1970s, Ivan Illich carried the romantic critique of American education to its logical and apocalyptic terminus. Whereas earlier critics had located the problem in the social functions the school performed, or in the curriculum, the teaching methods, the classroom atmosphere, or in the bureaucratized school system, Illich announced that the true root of educational authoritarianism lay with the

* Jonathan Kozol, *Free Schools* (Boston: Houghton Mifflin, 1972), pp. 10–11.

schools themselves. We must, he declared, abolish schools, or, as his catch phrase put it: we must deschool society.

At first blush this sounds absurd, and many thought so. What's going to happen to the kids? As Neil Postman asked: "A world without schools? Without students? Without teachers? Without Jewish Holidays? Without summer vacation? Without diplomas? Well, it is one thing to criticize—even hate—the school establishment. But it is quite another not to have one at all." So not all the radical educational reformers would travel the road Illich was taking, thus adding to the dissension among them already created by the disagreement over apolitical free schools. Indeed it was difficult to accept Illich and still continue as an educator. Without schools, where could one work? What could one do? Yet Illich's book, *Deschooling Society* (1970), does contain the most penetrating analysis of schools in recent times.

Schools, according to Illich, are like many modern manipulative institutions: they have institutionalized values. Schools package into a graded curriculum what is to be learned; and they determine who will, who will not, receive it. But in the very act of monopolizing education, schools have created a false scarcity of education; most people have come to believe that education can occur only in schools.

The immediate consequence of this monopoly of education by the schools is the psychological impotence it causes in people. Instead of viewing work, society, and the environment as means through which one learns, people have become educationally alienated; they view education (read: "schooling") as the means to prepare them for a job, a place in the society, a life in the world. Without schooling they are "disadvantaged," "deprived," unable to fend for themselves.

The second consequence of schools is that they are socially polarizing. One of the most important functions schools perform is that of social role selection. In doing this they support and sustain the existing hierarchy of privilege in the society. It is true that people view schools as ladders upon which the aspiring can rise in the society, but this is a ritual that hides the contradictions inherent in the myth of equality of opportunity. Of course students advance on "merit." But schools define merit in accordance with the structure of the society served by the school. As Everett Reimer,

Illich's one-time mentor and associate, points out in *School is Dead* (1971), this structure "is characterized by the competitive consumption of technological products defined by institutions. Institutions define products in a way that is consistent with the maintenance of a dominant hierarchy of privilege and, in so far as possible, with the opportunity for members of the currently privileged class to retain their status in the new 'meritocracy.'" So what schools define as merit is principally the advantage of having literate parents. "Merit," Reimer concludes, "is a smoke screen for the perpetuation of privilege." By monopolizing the distribution of opportunity, the schools now determine the social divisions within the society: the unschooled are poor and they are poor because they are unschooled.

The third and most significant consequence of schools is that they lead to physical pollution. Schools do this through the "hidden curriculum" which serves as a ritual introduction into a growth-oriented consumer society. The longer one stays in school, the higher standard of living one expects. In every country, Illich points out, "the amount of consumption by the college graduate sets the standard for all others; if they would be civilized people on or off the job, they will aspire to the style of life of college graduates."

So, by expanding and increasing schooling we are polluting the environment simply because the more people attend school, the more they consume; the more they consume, the more they deplete the natural resources of the world; and the more pollution they create. Moreover, through compulsory education the school initiates the whole society into the myth of unending consumption. In the colorful and gnomic language of Ivan Illich: "School is a ritual of initiation which introduces the neophyte to the sacred race of progressive consumption, a ritual of propitiation whose academic priests mediate between the faithful and the gods of privilege and power, a ritual of expiation which sacrifices its dropouts, branding them as scapegoats of underdevelopment." Men cannot free themselves from progressive consumption, Illich says, until they free themselves from obligatory school.

Although Reimer reports that both he and Illich originally felt that the school was a lagging institution in a technological society, they later came to see schools were working quite well and "providing indispensable support for a technological society that is itself not viable." Ultimately, then, they want to destroy the existing technocratic society, and they see deschooling as the most peaceful and sanest way to bring it off.

In place of schools they would have what Illich calls "learning webs" for the autonomous assembly of resources under the personal control of each learner. As he envisages them, learning webs are networks of things and networks of people that guarantee to all the right of equal access to the tools both of learning and of sharing with others what they know or believe. In place of schools, Illich wants to build an educational world that will allow a person to gain access to any educational resource which may help him to define and order his own goals. Such a world would have skill exchanges, arrangements for peer matching, and reference services to educational objects and educators-at-large.

Whereas schools are "bureaucratic," "self-justifying," and "manipulative" institutions, learning webs will be different: they will be convivial institutions distinguished by spontaneous use (not compulsory attendance). "Student discipline, public relations, hiring, supervising, and firing teachers would have neither place nor counterpart in the networks. . . . Neither would curriculum-making, textbook-purchasing, the maintenance of grounds and facilities, or the supervision of interscholastic athletic competition. Nor would child custody, lesson-planning, and record-keeping, which now take up so much of the time of teachers, figure in the operation of educational networks."

Is such a scheme practical? Eminently so, its advocates insist. It is economically absurd to try to provide adequate schooling for everyone (Reimer reports that recent studies in the United States suggest that it would cost eighty billion *additional* dollars to meet educators' estimates of what is needed to provide adequate schooling). But it is possible to finance universal education—through educational networks, or learning webs—on the amount of money we *now* spend for schools. The scheme for carrying this out involves channeling all funds into personal educational accounts for each person and making all the educational networks and educators self-supporting. Another reason why educational net-works would be cheaper is that they would not take on the costly function of custodial care. Other arrangements would be provided to care for children—older children could look after them, for example.

There are, of course, certain necessary preconditions to deschooling: we must abolish compulsory-attendance laws; we must proscribe all discrimination on the basis of prior attendance; and we must transfer control over tax funds from benevolent institutions to the individual person. One way to initiate these changes would be a constitutional disestablishment of the monopoly of the school. Illich proposes the following as the first article of a bill of rights for a modern humanist society: "The State shall make no laws with respect to the establishment of education." Until we have such a bill of rights, however, he takes hope from the recent Supreme Court decision (*Griggs* v. *Duke Power Company*, 1971) that prohibits (logically, if not explicitly) the use of an educational pedigree as a prerequisite for employment.

The biggest obstacle to deschooling is the fact that the school is what Reimer calls a "dominating institution": it establishes advantages for one group over another. So those who have already attained the advantages conferred by the school, and those who have hopes that their children can win those advantages, will probably oppose deschooling. Yet, the deschoolers say, look at the price extracted for the advantage profferred: international, inter-class, and interpersonal competition; and progressive consumption that leads to the depletion and pollution of the environment. Finally, then, the choice becomes one of a way of life. Deschooling leads to sharing, conserving, and lowering consumption; a life relatively sparse in the kinds of products and services it provides, where people have to do things for themselves; but a life where people "have time and freedom to do what they want."

Once again, even at its most apocalyptic, the romantic educational critic perceives education as a quest for meaning.

✳

One after the other the romantic critics have uncovered layers of authoritarianism in our educational arrangements. To a man they reject imposition and advocate a child-centered or learner-centered education. The smorgasbord curriculum of John Holt, the inquiry method of Postman and

Weingartner, the open classroom of Herbert Kohl, the free school of George Dennison, the learning webs of Ivan Illich—all point to an educational process where people learn what, how, and when they like.

The trouble with this construction of education, as Arthur Pearl has noted, is that to learn what one likes is to learn prejudices. In their attempts to expunge authoritarianism from education the romantic critics actually do no more than shift its locus: we get rid of the authoritarianism of the teachers, class-rooms, and schools, but we get, in return, authoritarian students—learners who are their own final authorities for what is true, good, and worth knowing.

None of the romantic educators perceived this incipient student authoritarianism because they all were obsessed with the construction of education as a quest for meaning—not truth. Meaning *is* subjective; each one of us is the final authority for what has meaning to us and what does not. And when we apply the criterion of meaning—not truth—to what students learn, we are led to a curious epistemological subjectivism. For then knowledge appears to exist only in the mind of the knower. Thus, no one *but the knower* can be the final authority for what is known—its worth *and* its validity.

Nor is that all. An educational theory based on such epistemo-logical subjectivism inevitably ignores the social, political, cultural, and economic functions of education. Throughout history, men have construed education as the process whereby we advance knowledge, move civilization forward, and improve society; in short, people have viewed education as the key to progress. By reconstruing education in a narrow, individualistic way the roman-tic critics abandon all responsibility for the future of our civiliza-tion, our society, our knowledge. They appear ready to write off progress as a delusion and a trap.*

---

* Generalizations about such a disparate group are dangerous. It is true that Postman and Weingartner and those affiliated with the more politicized segment of the free school movement do regard schools as agents to improve society. With them my disagreement is over the ways in which schools can, in fact, improve society: their expectations of what schools can do are too great, their mode too subjective, their approach incipiently authoritarian.

Nowhere is this expressed more forcefully and more exquisitely than in the last chapter of *Deschooling Society*. Our civilization, Illich insists, has long been under the spell cast by Prometheus: we are Promethean men, bent upon improvement and progress. But in this pursuit of progress we have imposed our will on the environment, exploiting nature and manipulating other men. As we, in time, enhanced our ability to control results, expectations rose. But with rising expectations, born of our faith in our power to improve things, we experienced fading hope. Primitive man, pre-Promethean man, Illich says, had hope. Indeed, in a world governed by fate, fact, and necessity, hope was all he had: "He relied on the munificence of nature, on the handouts of gods, and on the instincts of his tribe to enable him to subsist." But Promethean man replaced hope with expectations; he turned facts into problems, called necessity into question, and defied fate.

Since appearing on the historical scene, Promethean man has engineered institutions to deal with rampant ills. Now these institutions (like schools) trap man himself. Having built a totally man-made environment, contemporary man now discovers he must constantly remake himself to fit it. "Man has become the plaything of scientists, engineers, and planners."

At last, Illich says, we begin to see that our institutions are not working—the poverty program produces more poor, technical assistance more underdevelopment, curbs on one kind of pollution increase another kind, schools produce more dropouts: "Everywhere nature becomes parsimonious, society inhumane, and the inner life is invaded and personal vocation smothered."

The only way out, he counsels, is to forsake all endeavors to progress. We must deinstitutionalize society and return to a life of hope. There, supposedly governed by facts, fate, and necessity, we can stop manipulating people and exploiting the earth; and we can learn, instead, to live with them and love them.

Illich and the other romantic critics write off education as a means of social progress because they see—correctly, I think—that all efforts to use it thus far have, in fact, led to manipulation and exploitation; in pursuit of progress, education, or schooling always seems to wind up as cultural imperialism or political socialization or personnel processing or indoctrination. Armed with this insight, the romantic critics choose to ignore all save the individualistic functions of education. For them, education becomes solely and exclusively the process of helping the young in their quest for meaning.

Yet, there is a world out there, a real world that man has created, a world of knowledge, institutions, and arrangements. It is not a perfect world, since fallible men created it—but it can be improved via education. Imposition, socialization, and manipulation are not the only ways to carry out the cultural, social, political, and economic functions of our educational institutions. Schools can serve as the mediating ground between the young and the world men have created, the place where students can critically encounter that world.

In such critical encounters the teacher neither advocates nor justifies the world he presents to the students. He encourages them to criticize it, and then he helps probe their criticisms. In short, he creates and maintains a critical dialogue between the students and the world men have created. The purpose of the critical dialogue is to improve what exists—the institutions, the arrangements, the theories. Educators and schools can have a modest yet necessary role to play in the progress of civilization; they can help people discover what's wrong with what exists—what's false, bad, or inadequate. This is the initial, necessary step to improvement. Such an education will not provide final answers; the most it can do is turn out people who have a critical approach toward all answers, who look at all knowledge, arrangements, and institutions as tentative, as experiments that can be improved through critical dialogue. Education that embodies this critical approach is an education not in pursuit of meaning, but rather a nonauthoritarian pursuit of truth and goodness. With luck it can lead to improved knowledge, a better society, an advancing civilization.

WORKS AND COMMENTARY

Paul Goodman's most important books on youth and education are *Growing Up Absurd* (New York: Random House, 1960), *Compulsory Mis-education* (New York: Random House, 1964), and *New Reformation: Notes of a Neolithic Conservative* (New York: Random House, 1970).

Edgar Z. Friedenberg has written *The Vanishing Adolescent* (Boston: Beacon, 1960), *Coming of Age in America: Growth and Acquiescence* (New York: Random House, 1963), and *The Dignity of Youth and Other Atavisms* (Boston: Beacon, 1965).

John Holt has written numerous books on education. The most famous are the first two he wrote: *How Children Fail* (New York: Pitman, 1964) and *How Children Learn* (New York: Pitman, 1967). In *Freedom and Beyond* (New York: E. P. Dutton, 1972), he aligns himself with the theories of Ivan Illich.

Herbert Kohl's books on open classrooms are *36 Children* (New York: New American Library, 1967) and *The Open Classroom* (New York: Random House, 1969).

Jonathan Kozol's account of his experiences in public school teaching is in *Death at an Early Age: The Destruction of the Hearts and Minds of Negro Children in the Boston Public Schools* (Boston: Houghton Mifflin, 1967).

Since publishing *Teaching as a Subversive Activity* (New York: Delacorte, 1969), Neil Postman and Charles Weingartner have written two additional books on education: *The Soft Revolution: A Student Handbook for Turning Schools Around* (New York: Delacorte, 1971) and *The School Book: For People Who Want to Know What All the Hollering Is About* (New York: Delacorte, 1973).

Three books that chart the course of the free school movement are: George Dennison, *The Lives of Children* (New York: Random House, 1969); Jonathan Kozol, *Free Schools* (Boston: Houghton Mifflin, 1972); and Allen Graubard, *Free the Children: Radical Reform and the Free School Movement* (New York: Random House, 1973).

The theories put forth in *Deschooling Society* (New York: Harper & Row, 1970) by Ivan Illich and in *School is Dead* (New York: Doubleday, 1971) by Everett Reimer are critically assessed in *After Deschooling, What?* (New York: Harper & Row, 1973), edited by Alan Gartner, Colin Greer, and Frank Riessman.

Excerpts from many of the romantic educational critics are anthologized in *Radical School Reform* (New York: Simon and Schuster, 1969), edited by Ronald and Beatrice Gross; and in *Innovations in Education: Reformers and their Critics* (Boston: Allyn and Bacon, 1975), edited by John Martin Rich. A collection of critiques of the movement is *Radical School Reform: Critiques and Alternatives* (Boston: Little, Brown and Co., 1973), edited by Cornelius J. Troost.

My own notions about how schools should function are sketched in *The Possibilities of Error: An Approach to Education* (New York: David McKay, 1971).

Of the two selections that follow, the one by John Holt is from *How Children Fail*, pages 23–26, 48–49, 165–81; the one by Ivan Illich is chapter 1 of *Deschooling Society*, pages 1–24.

John Holt: FROM *How Children Fail*

It has become clear over the year that these children see school almost entirely in terms of the day-to-day and hour-to-hour tasks that we impose on them. This is not at all the way the teacher thinks of it. The conscientious teacher thinks of himself as taking his students (at least part way) on a journey to some glorious destination, well worth the pains of the trip. If he teaches history, he thinks how interesting, how exciting, how useful it is to know history, and how fortunate his students will be when they begin to share his knowledge. If he teaches French, he thinks of the glories of French literature, or the beauty of spoken French, or the delights of French cooking, and how he is helping to make these joys available to his students. And so for all subjects.

Thus teachers feel, as I once did, that their interests and their students' are fundamentally the same. I used to feel that I was guiding and helping my students on a journey that they wanted to take but could not take without my help. I knew the way looked hard, but I assumed they could see the goal almost as clearly as I and that they were almost as eager to reach it. It seemed very important to give students this feeling of being on a journey to a worthwhile destination. I see now that most of my talk to this end was wasted breath. Maybe *I* thought the students were in my class because they were eager to learn what I was trying to teach, but they knew better. They were in school because they had to be, and in my class either because they had to be, or because otherwise they would have had to be in another class, which might be even worse.

Children in school are like children at the doctor's. He can talk himself blue in the face about how much good his medicine is going to do them; all they think of is how much it will hurt or how bad it will taste. Given their own way, they would have none of it.

So the valiant and resolute band of travelers I thought I was leading toward a much-hoped-for destination turned out instead to be more like convicts in a chain gang, forced under threat of punishment to move along a rough path leading nobody knew where and down which they could see hardly more than a few steps ahead. School feels like this to children: it is a place where *they* make you go and where *they* tell you to do things and where *they* try to make your life unpleasant if you don't do them or don't do them right.

For children, the central business of school is not learning, whatever this vague word means; it is getting these daily tasks done, or at least out of the way, with a minimum of effort and unpleasantness. Each task is an end in itself. The children don't care how they dispose of it. If they can get it out of the way by doing it, they will do it; if experience has taught them that this does not work very well, they will turn to other means, illegitimate means, that wholly defeat whatever purpose the task-giver may have had in mind.

They are very good at this, at getting other people to do their tasks for them. I remember the day not long ago when Ruth opened my eyes. We had been doing math, and I was pleased with myself because, instead of telling her answers and showing her how to do problems, I was "making her think" by asking her questions. It was slow work. Question after question met only silence. She said nothing, did nothing, just sat and looked at me through those glasses, and waited. Each time, I had to think of a question easier and more pointed than the last, until I finally found one so easy that she would feel safe in answering it. So we inched our way along until suddenly, looking at her as I waited for an answer to a question, I saw with a start that she was not at all puzzled by what I had asked her. In fact, she was not even thinking about it. She was coolly appraising me, weighing my patience, waiting for that next, sure-to-be-easier question. I thought, "I've been had!" The girl had learned how to make me do her work for her, just as she had learned to make all her previous teachers do the same thing. If I wouldn't tell her the answers, very well, she would just let me question her right up to them.

Schools and teachers seem generally to be as blind to children's strategies as I was. Otherwise, they would teach their courses and assign their tasks so that students who really thought about the meaning of the subject would have the best chance of succeeding, while those who tried to do the tasks by illegitimate means, without thinking or understanding, would be foiled. But the reverse seems to be the case. Schools give every encouragement to *producers,* the kids whose idea is to get "right answers" by any and all means. In a system that runs on "right answers," they can hardly help it. And these schools are often very discouraging places for *thinkers.*

Until recently it had not occurred to me that poor students thought differently about their work than good students; I assumed they thought the same way, only less skillfully. Now it begins to look as if the expectation and fear of failure, if strong enough, may lead children to act and think in a special way, to adopt strategies different from those of more confident children. Emily is a good example. She is emotionally as well as intellectually incapable of checking her work, of comparing her ideas against reality, of making any kind of judgment about the value of her thoughts. She makes me think of an animal fleeing danger—go like the wind, don't look back, remember where that danger was, and stay away from it as far as you can. Are there many other children who react to their fears in this way?

It doesn't take children long to figure out their teachers. Some of these kids already know that what pays off with us is plenty of talk, lots of ideas, even if they are wild. What can we do for the kids who may like to think but don't like to talk?

In my math classes I am on the horns of another dilemma. I want the kids to think about what they are doing. If I make the questions too hard, they begin trying to read my mind, or, as they did this morning, they throw out wild ideas, taking all too literally my statement that a wrong idea is better than none. If, on the other hand, I break the subject down into little lumps, so that when I ask a question most of the class will be able to answer with confidence, am I not doing what I found I was doing for Ruth last year, doing most of their thinking for them?

Perhaps there is no middle position, and what I must do is ask hard questions some of the time, easy questions other times. . . .

A year ago I was wondering how a child's fears might influence his strategies. This year's work has told me. The strategies of most of these kids have been consistently self-centered, self-protective, aimed above all else at avoiding trouble, embarrassment, punishment, disapproval, or loss of status. This is particularly true of the ones who have had a tough time in school. When they get a problem, I can read their thoughts on their faces, I can almost hear them, "Am I going to get this right? Probably not; what'll happen to me when I get it wrong? Will the teacher get mad? Will the other kids laugh at me? Will my mother and father hear about it? Will they keep me back this year? Why am I so dumb?" And so on.

Even in the room periods, where I did all I could to make the work non-threatening, I was continaully amazed and appalled to see the children hedging their bets, covering their losses in advance, trying to fix things so that whatever happened they could feel they had been right, or if wrong, no more wrong than anyone else. "I think it will sort of balance." They are fence-straddlers, afraid ever to commit themselves—and at the age of ten. Playing games like Twenty Questions, which one might have expected them to play for fun, many of them were concerned only to put up a good front, to look as if they knew what they were doing, whether they did or not.

These self-limiting and self-defeating strategies are dictated, above all else, by fear. For many years I have been asking myself why intelligent children act unintelligently at school. The simple answer is, "Because they're scared." I used to suspect that children's defeatism had something to do with their bad work in school, but I thought I could clear it away with hearty cries of "Onward! You can do it!" What I now see for the first time is the mechanism by which fear destroys intelligence, the way it affects a child's whole way of looking at, thinking about, and dealing with life. So we have two problems, not one: to stop children from being afraid, and then to break them of the bad thinking habits into which their fears have driven them.

What is most surprising of all is how much fear there is in school. Why is so little said about it? Perhaps most people do not recognize fear in children when they see it. They can read the grossest signs of fear; they know what the trouble is when a child clings howling to his mother; but the subtler signs of fear escape them. It is these signs, in children's faces, voices, and gestures, in their movements and ways of working, that tell me plainly that most children in school are scared most of the time, many of them very scared. Like good soldiers, they control their fears, live with them, and adjust themselves to them. But the trouble is, and here is a vital difference between school and war, that the adjustments children make to their fears are almost wholly bad, destructive of their intelligence and capacity. The scared fighter may be the best fighter, but the scared learner is always a poor learner. . . .

When we talk about intelligence, we do not mean the ability to get a good score on a certain kind of test, or even the ability to do well in school; these are at best only indicators of something larger, deeper, and far more important. By intelligence we mean a style of life, a way of behaving in various situations, and particularly in new, strange, and perplexing situations. The true test of intelligence is not how much we know how to do, but how we behave when we don't know what to do.

The intelligent person, young or old, meeting a new situation or problem, opens himself up to it; he tries to take in with mind and senses everything he can about it; he thinks about *it*, instead of about himself or what it might cause to happen to him; he grapples with it boldly, imaginatively, resourcefully, and if not confidently at least hopefully; if he fails to master it, he looks without shame or fear at his mistakes and learns what he can from them. This is intelligence. Clearly its roots lie in a certain feeling about life, and one's self with respect to life. Just as clearly, unintelligence is not what most psychologists seem to suppose, the same thing as intelligence only less of it. It is an entirely different style of behavior, arising out of an entirely different set of attitudes.

Years of watching and comparing bright children and the not-bright, or less bright, have shown that they are very different kinds of people. The bright child is curious about life and reality, eager to get in touch with it, embrace it, unite himself with it. There is no wall, no barrier between him and life. The dull child is far less curious, far less interested in what goes on and what is real, more inclined to live in worlds of fantasy. The bright child likes to experiment, to try things out. He lives by the maxim that there is more than one way to skin a cat. If he can't do something one way, he'll try another. The dull child is usually afraid to try at all. It takes a good deal of urging to get him to try even once; if that try fails, he is through.

The bright child is patient. He can tolerate uncertainty and failure, and will keep trying until he gets an answer. When all his experiments fail, he can even admit to himself and others that for the time being he is not going to get an answer. This may annoy him, but he can wait. Very often, he does not want to be told how to do the problem or solve the puzzle he has struggled with, because he does not want to be cheated out of the chance to figure it out for himself in the future. Not so the dull child. He cannot stand uncertainty or failure. To him, an unanswered question is not a challenge or an opportunity, but a threat. If he can't find the answer quickly, it must be given to him, and quickly; and he must have answers for everything. Such are the children of whom a second-grade teacher once said, "But my children *like* to have questions for which there is only one answer." They did; and by a mysterious coincidence, so did she.

The bright child is willing to go ahead on the basis of incomplete understanding and information. He will take risks, sail uncharted seas, explore when the landscape is dim, the landmarks few, the light poor. To give only one example, he will often read books he does not understand in the hope that after a while enough understanding will emerge to make it worth while to go on. In this spirit some of my fifth graders tried to read *Moby Dick*. But the dull child will go ahead only when he thinks he knows exactly where he stands and exactly what is ahead of him. If he does not feel he knows exactly what an experience will be like, and if it will not be exactly like other experiences he already knows, he wants no part of it. For while the bright child feels that the universe is, on the whole, a sensible, reasonable, and trustworthy place, the dull child feels that it is senseless, unpredictable, and treacherous. He feels that he can never tell what may happen, particularly in a new situation, except that it will probably be bad.

Nobody starts off stupid. You have only to watch babies and infants, and think seriously about what all of them learn and do, to see that, except for the most grossly retarded, they show a style of life, and a desire and ability to learn that in an older person we might well call genius. Hardly an adult in a thousand, or ten thousand, could in any three years of his life learn as much, grow as much in his understanding of the world around him, as every infant learns and grows in his first three years. But what happens, as we get older, to this extraordinary capacity for learning and intellectual growth?

What happens is that it is destroyed, and more than by any other one thing, by the process that we misname education—a process that goes on in most homes and schools. We adults destroy most of the intellectual and creative capacity of children by the things we do to them or make them do. We destroy this capacity above all by making them afraid, afraid of not doing what other people want, of not pleasing, or making mistakes, of failing, of being *wrong*. Thus we make them afraid to gamble, afraid to experiment, afraid to try the difficult and the unknown. Even when we do not create children's fears, when they come to us with fears ready-made and built-in, we use these fears as handles to manipulate them and get them to do what we want. Instead of trying to whittle down their fears, we build them up, often to monstrous size. For we like children who are a little afraid of us, docile, deferential children, though not, of course, if they are so obviously afraid that they threaten our image of ourselves as kind, lovable people whom there is no reason to fear. We find ideal the kind of "good" children who are just enough afraid of us to do everything we want, without making us feel that fear of us is what is making them do it.

We destroy the disinterested (I do *not* mean *un*interested) love of learning in children, which is so strong when they are small, by encouraging and compelling them to work for petty and contemptible rewards—gold stars, or papers marked 100 and tacked to the wall, or A's on report cards, or honor rolls, or dean's lists, or Phi Beta Kappa keys—in short, for the ignoble satisfaction of feeling that they are better than someone else. We encourage them to feel that the end and aim of all they do in school is nothing more than to get a good mark on a test, or to impress someone with what they seem to know. We kill, not only their curiosity, but their feeling that it is a good and admirable thing to be curious, so that by the age of ten most of them will not ask questions, and will show a good deal of scorn for the few who do.

In many ways, we break down children's convictions that things make sense, or their hope that things may prove to make sense. We do it, first of all, by breaking up life into arbitrary and disconnected hunks of subject matter, which we then try to "integrate" by such artificial and irrelevant devices as having children sing Swiss folk songs while they are studying the geography of Switzerland, or do arithmetic problems about rail-splitting while they are studying the boyhood of Lincoln. Furthermore, we continually confront them with what is sense-less, ambiguous, and contradictory; worse, we do it without knowing that we are doing it, so that, hearing nonsense shoved at them as if it were sense, they come to feel that the source of their confusion lies not in the material but in their own stupidity. Still further, we cut children off from their own common sense and the world of reality by requiring them to play with and shove around words and symbols that have little or no meaning to them. Thus we turn the vast majority of our students into the kind of people for whom all symbols are meaningless; who cannot use symbols as a way of learning about and dealing with reality; who cannot understand written instructions; who, even if they read books, come out knowing no more than when they went in; who may have a few new words rattling around in their heads, but whose mental models of the world remain unchanged and, indeed, impervious to change. The minority, the able and successful students, we are very likely to turn into something different but just as dangerous: the kind of people who can manipulate words and symbols fluently while keeping themselves largely divorced from the reality for which they stand; the kind of people who like to speak in large generalities but grow silent or indignant if someone asks for an example of what they are talking about; the kind of people who, in their discussions of world affairs, coin and use such words as megadeaths and megacorpses, with scarcely a thought to the blood and suffering these words imply.

We encourage children to act stupidly, not only by scaring and confusing them, but by boring them, by filling up their days with dull, repetitive tasks that make little or no claim on their attention or demands on their intelligence. Our hearts leap for joy at the sight of a roomful of children all slogging away at some imposed task, and we are all the more pleased and satisfied if someone tells us that the children don't really like what they are doing. We tell ourselves that this drudgery, this endless busywork, is good preparation for life, and we fear that without it children would be hard to "control." But why must this busywork be so dull? Why not give tasks that are interesting and demanding? Because, in schools where every task must be completed and every answer must be right, if we give children more demanding tasks they will be fearful and will instantly insist that we show them how to do the job. When you have acres of paper to fill up with pencil marks, you have no time to waste on the luxury of thinking. By such means children are firmly established in the habit of using only a small part of their thinking capacity. They feel that school is a place where they must spend most of their time doing dull tasks in a dull way. Before long they are deeply settled in a rut of unintelligent behavior from which most of them could not escape even if they wanted to.

School tends to be a dishonest as well as a nervous place. We adults are not often honest with children, least of all in school. We tell them, not what we think, but what we feel they ought to think; or what other people feel or tell us they ought to think. Pressure groups find it easy to weed out of our classrooms, texts, and libraries whatever facts, truths, and ideas they happen to find unpleasant or inconvenient. And we are not even as truthful with children as we could safely be, as the parents, politicians, and pressure groups would let us be. Even in the most non-controversial areas our teaching, the books, and the textbooks we give children present a dishonest and distorted picture of the world.

The fact is that we do not feel an obligation to be truthful to children. We are like the managers and manipulators of news in Washington, Moscow, London, Peking, and Paris, and all the other capitals of the world. We think it our right and our duty, not to tell the truth, but to say whatever will best serve our cause—in this case, the cause of making children grow up into the kind of people we want them to be, thinking whatever we want them to think. We have only to convince ourselves (and we are very easily convinced) that a lie will be "better" for the children than the truth, and we will lie. We don't always need even that excuse; we often lie only for our own convenience.

Worse yet, we are not honest about ourselves, our own fears, limitations, weaknesses, prejudices, motives. We present ourselves to children as if we were gods, all-knowing, all-powerful, always rational, always just, always right. This is worse than any lie we could tell about ourselves. I have more than once shocked teachers by telling them that when kids ask me a question to which I don't know the answer, I say, "I haven't the faintest idea"; or that when I make a mistake, as I often do, I say, "I goofed again"; or that when I am trying to do something I am no good at, like paint in water colors or play a clarinet or bugle, I do it in front of them so they can see me struggling with it, and can realize that not all adults are good at everything. If a child asks me to do something that I don't want to do, I tell him that I won't do it because I don't want to do it, instead of giving him a list of "good" reasons sounding as if they had come down from the Supreme Court. Interestingly enough, this rather open way of dealing with children works quite well. If you tell a child that you won't do something because you don't want to, he is very likely to accept that as a fact which he cannot change; if you ask him to stop doing something because it drives you crazy, there is a good chance that, without further talk, he will stop, because he knows what that is like.

We are, above all, dishonest about our feelings, and it is this sense of dishonesty of feeling that makes the atmosphere of so many schools so unpleasant. The people who write books that teachers have to read say over and over again that a teacher must love all the children in a class, all of them equally. If by this they mean that a teacher must do the best he can for every child in a class, that he has an equal responsibility for every child's welfare, an equal concern for his problems, they are right. But when they talk of love they don't mean this; they mean feelings, affection, the kind of pleasure and joy that one person can get from the existence and company of another. And this is not something that can be measured out in little spoonfuls, everyone getting the same amount.

In a discussion of this in a class of teachers, I once said that I liked some of the kids in my class much more than others and that, without saying which ones I liked best, I had told them so. After all, this is something that children know, whatever we tell them; it is futile to lie about it. Naturally, these teachers were horrified. "What a terrible thing to say!" one said. "I love all the children in my class exactly the same." Nonsense; a teacher who says this is lying, to herself or to others, and probably doesn't like any of the children very much. Not that there is anything wrong with that; plenty of adults don't like children, and there is no reason why they should. But the trouble is they feel they should, which makes them feel guilty, which makes them feel resentful, which in turn makes them try to work off their guilt with indulgence and their resentment with subtle cruelties—cruelties of a kind that can be seen in many classrooms. Above all, it makes them put on the phony, syrupy, sickening voice and manner, and the fake smiles and forced, bright laughter that children see so much of in school, and rightly resent and hate.

As we are not honest with them, so we won't let children be honest with us. To begin with, we require them to take part in the fiction that school is a wonderful place and that they love every minute of it. They learn early that not to like school or the teacher is *verboten,* not to be said, not even to be thought. I have known a child, otherwise healthy, happy, and wholly delightful, who at the age of five was being made sick with worry by the fact that she did not like her kindergarten teacher. Robert Heinemann worked for a number of years with remedial students whom ordinary schools were hopelessly unable to deal with. He found that what choked up and froze the minds of these children was above all else the fact that they could not express, they could hardly even acknowledge the fear, shame, rage, and hatred that school and their teachers had aroused in them. In a situation in which they were and felt free to express these feeling to themselves and others, they were able once again to begin learning. Why can't we say to children what I used to say to my fifth graders who got sore at me, "The law says you have to go to school; it doesn't say you have to like it, and it doesn't say you have to like me either." This might make school more bearable for many children.

Children hear all the time, "Nice people don't say such things." They learn early in life that for unknown reasons they must not talk about a large part of what they think and feel, are most interested in, and worried about. It is a rare child who, anywhere in his growing up, meets even one older person with whom he can talk openly about what most interests him, concerns him, worries him. This is what rich people are buying for their troubled kids when for $25 per hour they send them to psychiatrists. Here is someone to whom you can speak honestly about whatever is on your mind, without having to worry about his getting mad at you. But do we have to wait until a child is snowed under by his fears and troubles to give him this chance? And do we have to take the time of a highly trained professional to hear what, earlier in his life, that child might have told anybody who was willing to listen sympathetically and honestly? The workers in a project called Streetcorner Research, in Cambridge, Mass., have found that nothing more than the opportunity to talk openly and freely about themselves and their lives, to people who would listen without judging, and who were interested in them as human beings rather than as problems to be solved or disposed of, has totally remade the lives and personalities of a number of confirmed and seemingly hopeless juvenile delinquents. Can't we learn something from this? Can't we clear a space for honesty and openness and self-awareness in the lives of growing children? Do we have to make them wait until they are in a jam before giving them a chance to say what they think?

Behind much of what we do in school lie some ideas, that could be expressed roughly as follows (1) Of the vast body of human knowledge, there are certain bits and pieces that can be called essential, that everyone should know; (2) the extent to which a person can be considered educated, qualified to live intelligently in today's world and be a useful member of society, depends on the amount of this essential knowledge that he carries about with him; (3) it is the duty of schools, therefore, to get as much of this essential knowledge as possible into the minds of children. Thus we find ourselves trying to poke certain facts, recipes, and ideas down the gullets of every child in school, whether the morsel interests him or not, even if it frightens him or sickens him, and even if there are other things that he is much more interested in learning.

These ideas are absurd and harmful nonsense. We will not begin to have true education or real learning in our schools until we sweep this nonsense out of the way. Schools should be a place where children learn what they most want to know, instead of what we think they ought to know. The child who wants to know something remembers it and uses it once he has it; the child who learns something to please or appease someone else forgets it when the need for pleasing or the danger of not appeasing is past. This is why children quickly forget all but a small part of what they learn in school. It is of no use or interest to them; they do not want, or expect, or even intend to remember it. The only difference between bad and good students in this respect is that the bad students forget right away, while the good students are careful to wait until after the exam. If for no other reason, we could well afford to throw out most of what we teach in school because the children throw out almost all of it anyway.

The notion of a curriculum, an essential body of knowledge, would be absurd even if children remembered everything we "taught" them. We don't and can't agree on what knowledge is essential. The man who has trained himself in some special field of knowledge or competence thinks, naturally, that his specialty should be in the curriculum. The classical scholars want Greek and Latin taught; the historians shout for more history; the mathematicians urge more math and the scientists more science; the modern language experts want all children taught French, or Spanish, or Russian; and so on. Everyone wants to get his specialty into the act, knowing that as the demand for his special knowledge rises, so will the price that he can charge for it. Who wins this struggle and who loses depends not on the real needs of children or even of society, but on who is most skillful in public relations, who has the best educational lobbyists, who best can capitalize on events that have nothing to do with education, like the appearance of Sputnik in the night skies.

The idea of the curriculum would not be valid even if we could agree what ought to be in it. For knowledge itself changes. Much of what a child learns in school will be found, or thought, before many years, to be untrue. I studied physics at school from a fairly up-to-date text that proclaimed that the fundamental law of physics was the law of conservation of matter—matter is not created or destroyed. I had to scratch that out before I left school. In economics at college I was taught many things that were not true of our economy then, and many more that are not true now. Not for many years after I left college did I learn that the Greeks, far from being a detached and judicious people surrounded by chaste white temples, were hot-tempered, noisy, quarrelsome, and liked to cover their temples with gold leaf and bright paint; or that most of the citizens of Imperial Rome, far from living in houses in which the rooms surrounded an atrium, or central court, lived in multistory tenements, one of which was perhaps the largest building in the ancient world. The child who really remembered everything he heard in school would live his life believing many things that were not so.

Moreover, we cannot possibly judge what knowledge will be most needed forty, or twenty, or even ten years from now. At school, I studied Latin and French. Few of the teachers who claimed then that Latin was essential would make as strong a case for it now; and the French might better have been Spanish, or better yet, Russian. Today the schools are busy teaching Russian; but perhaps they should be teaching Chinese, or Hindi, or who-knows-what? Besides physics, I studied chemistry, then perhaps the most popular of all science courses; but I would probably have done better to study biology, or ecology, if such a course had been offered (it wasn't). We always find out, too late, that we don't have the experts we need, that in the past we studied the wrong things; but this is bound to remain so. Since we can't know what knowledge will be most needed in the future, it is senseless to try to teach it in advance. Instead, we should try to turn out people who love learning so much and learn so well that they will be able to learn whatever needs to be learned.

How can we say, in any case, that one piece of knowledge is more important than another, or indeed, what we really say, that some knowledge is essential and the rest, as far as school is concerned, worthless? A child who wants to learn something that the school can't and doesn't want to teach him will be told not to waste his time. But how can we say that what he wants to know is less important than what we want him to know? We must ask how much of the sum of human knowledge anyone can know at the end of his schooling. Perhaps a millionth. Are we then to believe that one of these millionths is so much more important than another? Or that our social and national problems will be solved if we can just figure out a way to turn children out of schools knowing two millionths of the total, instead of one? Our problems don't arise from the fact that we lack experts enough to tell us what needs to be done, but out of the fact that we do not and will not do what we know needs to be done now.

Learning is not everything, and certainly one piece of learning is as good as another. One of my brightest and boldest fifth graders was deeply interested in snakes. He knew more about snakes than anyone I've ever known. The school did not offer herpetology; snakes were not in the curriculum; but as far as I was concerned, any time he spent learning about snakes was better spent than in ways I could think of to spend it; not least of all because, in the process of learning about snakes, he learned a great deal more about many other things than I was ever able to "teach" those unfortunates in my class who were not interested in anything at all. In another fifth-grade class, studying Romans in Britain, I saw a boy trying to read a science book behind the cover of his desk. He was spotted, and made to put the book away, and listen to the teacher; with a heavy sigh he did so. What was gained here? She traded a chance for an hour's real learning about science for, at best, an hour's temporary learning about history—much more probably no learning at all, just an hour's worth of daydreaming and resentful thoughts about school.

It is not subject matter that makes some learning more valuable than others, but the spirit in which the work is done. If a child is doing the kind of learning that most children do in school, when they learn at all—swallowing words, to spit back at the teacher on demand—he is wasting his time, or rather, we are wasting it for him. This learning will not be permanent, or relevant, or useful. But a child who is learning naturally, following his curiosity where it leads him, adding to his mental model of reality whatever he needs and can find a place for, and rejecting without fear or guilt what he does not need, is growing—in knowledge, in the love of learning, and in the ability to learn. He is on his way to becoming the kind of person we need in our society, and that our "best" schools and colleges are *not* turning out, the kind of person who, in Whitney Griswold's words, seeks and finds meaning, truth, and enjoyment in everything he does. All his life he will go on learning. Every experience will make his mental model of reality more complete and more true to life, and thus make him more able to deal realistically, imaginatively, and constructively with whatever new experience life throws his way.

We cannot have real learning in school if we think it is our duty and our right to tell children what they must learn. We cannot know, at any moment, what particular bit of knowledge or understanding a child needs most, will most strengthen and best fit his model of reality. Only he can do this. He may not do it very well, but he can do it a hundred times better than we can. The most we can do is try to help, by letting him know roughly what is available and where he can look for it. Choosing what he wants to learn and what he does not is something he must do for himself.

There is one more reason, and the most important one, why we must reject the idea of school and classroom as places where, most of the time, children are doing what some adult tells them to do. The reason is that there is no way to coerce children without making them afraid, or more afraid. We must not try to fool ourselves into thinking that this is not so. The would-be progressives, who until recently had great influence over most American public school education, did not recognize this—and still do not. They thought, or at least talked and wrote as if they thought, that there were good ways and bad ways to coerce children (the bad ones mean, harsh, cruel, the good ones gentle, persuasive, subtle, kindly), and that if they avoided the bad and stuck to the good they would do no harm. This was one of their greatest mistakes, and the main reason why the revolution they hoped to accomplish never took hold.

The idea of painless, non-threatening coercion is an illusion. Fear is the inseparable companion of coercion, and its inescapable consequence. If you think it your duty to make children do what you want, whether they will or not, then it follows inexorably that you must make them afraid of what will happen to them if they don't do what you want. You can do this in the old-fashioned way, openly and avowedly, with the threat of harsh words, infringement of liberty, or physical punishment. Or you can do it in the modern way, subtly, smoothly, quietly, by withholding the acceptance and approval which you and others have trained the children to depend on; or by making them feel that some retribution awaits them in the future, too vague to imagine but too implacable to escape. You can, as many skilled teachers do, learn to tap with a word, a gesture, a look, even a smile, the great reservoir of fear, shame, and guilt that today's children carry around inside them. Or you can simply let your own fears, about what will happen to you if the children don't do what you want, reach out and infect them. Thus the children will feel more and more that life is full of dangers from which only the goodwill of adults like you can protect them, and that this goodwill is perishable and must be earned anew each day.

The alternative—I can see no other—is to have schools and classrooms in which each child in his own way can satisfy his curiosity, develop his abilities and talents, pursue his interests, and from the adults and older children around him get a glimpse of the great variety and richness of life. In short, the school should be a great smörgåsbord of intellectual, artistic, creative, and athletic activities, from which each child could take whatever he wanted, and as much as he wanted, or as little. When Anna was in the sixth grade, the year after she was in my class, I mentioned this idea to her. After describing very sketchily how such a school might be run, and what the children might do, I said, "Tell me, what do you think of it? Do you think it would work? Do you think the kids would learn anything?" She said, with utmost conviction, "Oh, yes, it would be wonderful!" She was silent for a minute or two, perhaps remembering her own generally unhappy schooling. Then she said thoughtfully, "You know, kids really like to learn; we just don't like being pushed around."

No, they don't; and we should be grateful for that. So let's stop pushing them around, and give them a chance.

Ivan Illich: Why We Must Disestablish School

Many students, especially those who are poor, intuitively know what the schools do for them. They school them to confuse process and substance. Once these become blurred, a new logic is assumed: the more treatment there is, the better are the results; or, escalation leads to success. The pupil is thereby "schooled" to confuse teaching with learning, grade advancement with education, a diploma with competence, and fluency with the ability to say something new. His imagination is "schooled" to accept service in place of value. Medical treatment is mistaken for health care, social work for the improvement of community life, police protection for safety, military poise for national security, the rat race for productive work. Health, learning, dignity, independence, and creative endeavor are defined as little more than the performance of the institutions which claim to serve these ends, and their improvement is made to depend on allocating more resources to the management of hospitals, schools, and other agencies in question.

In these essays, I will show that the institutionalization of values leads inevitably to physical pollution, social polarization, and psychological impotence: three dimensions in a process of global degradation and modernized misery. I will explain how this process of degradation is accelerated when nonmaterial needs are transformed into demands for commodities; when health, education, personal mobility, welfare, or psychological healing are defined as the result of services or "treatments." I do this because I believe that most of the research now going on about the future tends to advocate further increases in the institutionalization of values and that we must define conditions which would permit precisely the contrary to happen. We need research on the possible use of technology to create institutions which serve personal, creative, and autonomous interaction and the emergence of values which cannot be substantially controlled by technocrats. We need counterfoil research to current futurology.

I want to raise the general question of the mutual definition of man's nature and the nature of modern institutions which characterizes our world view and language. To do so, I have chosen the school as my paradigm, and I therefore deal only indirectly with other bureaucratic agencies of the corporate state: the consumer-family, the party, the army, the church, the media. My analysis of the hidden curriculum of school should make it evident that public education would profit from the deschooling of society, just as family life, politics, security, faith, and communication would profit from an analogous process.

I begin my analysis, in this first essay, by trying to convey what the deschooling of a schooled society might mean. In this context, it should be easier to understand my choice of the five specific aspects relevant to this process with which I deal in the subsequent chapters.

Not only education but social reality itself has become schooled. It costs roughly the same to school both rich and poor in the same dependency. The yearly expenditure per pupil in the slums and in the rich suburbs of any one of twenty U.S. cities lies in the same range—and sometimes is favorable to the poor.* Rich and poor alike depend on schools and hospitals which guide their lives, form their world view, and define for them what is legitimate and what is not. Both view doctoring oneself as irresponsible, learning on one's own as unreliable, and community organization, when not paid for by those in authority, as a form of aggression or subversion. For both groups the reliance on institutional treatment renders independent accomplishment suspect. The progressive underdevelopment of self- and community-reliance is even more typical in Westchester than it is in the northeast of Brazil. Everywhere not only education but society as a whole needs "deschooling."

Welfare bureaucracies claim a professional, political, and financial monopoly over the social imagination, setting standards of what is valuable and what is feasible. This monopoly is at the root of the modernization of poverty. Every simple need to which an institutional answer is found permits the invention of a new class of poor and a new definition of poverty. Ten years ago in Mexico it was the normal thing to be born and to die in one's own home and to be buried by one's friends. Only the soul's needs were taken care of by the institutional church. Now to begin and end life at home become signs either of poverty or of special privilege. Dying and death have come under the institutional management of doctors and undertakers.

Once basic needs have been translated by a society into demands for scientifically produced commodities, poverty is defined by standards which the technocrats can change at will. Poverty then refers to those who have fallen behind an advertised ideal of consumption in some important respect. In Mexico the poor are those who lack three years of schooling, and in New York they are those who lack twelve.

The poor have always been socially powerless. The increas-

---

* Penrose B. Jackson, *Trends in Elementary and Secondary Education Expenditures: Central City and Suburban Comparisons 1965 to 1968,* U.S. Office of Education, Office of Program and Planning Evaluation, June 1969.

ing reliance on institutional care adds a new dimension to their helplessness: psychological impotence, the inability to fend for themselves. Peasants on the high plateau of the Andes are exploited by the landlord and the merchant—once they settle in Lima they are, in addition, dependent on political bosses, and disabled by their lack of schooling. Modernized poverty combines the lack of power over circumstances with a loss of personal potency. This modernization of poverty is a worldwide phenomenon, and lies at the root of contemporary underdevelopment. Of course it appears under different guises in rich and in poor countries.

It is probably most intensely felt in U.S. cities. Nowhere else is poverty treated at greater cost. Nowhere else does the treatment of poverty produce so much dependence, anger, frustration, and further demands. And nowhere else should it be so evident that poverty—once it has become modernized— has become resistant to treatment with dollars alone and requires an institutional revolution.

Today in the United States the black and even the migrant can aspire to a level of professional treatment which would have been unthinkable two generations ago, and which seems grotesque to most people in the Third World. For instance, the U.S. poor can count on a truant officer to return their children to school until they reach seventeen, or on a doctor to assign them to a hospital bed which costs sixty dollars per day—the equivalent of three months' income for a majority of the people in the world. But such care only makes them dependent on more treatment, and renders them increasingly incapable of organizing their own lives around their own experiences and resources within their own communities.

The poor in the United States are in a unique position to speak about the predicament which threatens all the poor in a modernizing world. They are making the discovery that no amount of dollars can remove the inherent destructiveness of welfare institutions, once the professional hierarchies of these institutions have convinced society that their ministrations are morally necessary. The poor in the U.S. inner city can demonstrate from their own experience the fallacy on which social legislation in a "schooled" society is built.

Supreme Court Justice William O. Douglas observed that "the only way to establish an institution is to finance it." The corollary is also true. Only by channeling dollars away from the institutions which now treat health, education, and welfare can the further impoverishment resulting from their disabling side effects be stopped.

This must be kept in mind when we evaluate federal aid programs. As a case in point, between 1965 and 1968 over three billion dollars were spent in U.S. schools to offset the disadvantages of about six million children. The program is known as Title One. It is the most expensive compensatory program ever attempted anywhere in education, yet no significant improvement can be detected in the learning of these "disadvantaged" children. Compared with their classmates from middle-income homes, they have fallen further behind. Moreover, in the course of this program, professionals discovered an additional ten million children laboring under economic and educational handicaps. More reasons for claiming more federal funds are now at hand.

This total failure to improve the education of the poor despite more costly treatment can be explained in three ways:

1. Three billion dollars are insufficient to improve the performance of six million children by a measurable amount; or
2. The money was incompetently spent: different curricula, better administration, further concentration of the funds on the poor child, and more research are needed and would do the trick; or
3. Educational disadvantage cannot be cured by relying on education within the school.

The first is certainly true so long as the money has been spent through the school budget. The money indeed went to the schools which contained most of the disadvantaged children, but it was not spent on the poor children themselves. These children for whom the money was intended comprised only about half of those who were attending the schools that added the federal subsidies to their budgets. Thus the money was spent for custodial care, indoctrination and the selection of social roles, as well as education, all of which functions are inextricably mingled in the physical plants, curricula, teachers, administrators, and other key components of these schools, and, therefore, in their budgets.

The added funds enabled schools to cater disproportionately to the satisfaction of the relatively richer children who were "disadvantaged" by having to attend school in the company of the poor. At best a small fraction of each dollar intended to remedy a poor child's disadvantages in learning could reach the child through the school budget.

It might be equally true that the money was incompetently spent. But even unusual incompetence cannot beat that of the school system. Schools by their very structure resist the concentration of privilege on those otherwise disadvantaged. Special curricula, separate classes, or longer hours only constitute more discrimination at a higher cost.

Taxpayers are not yet accustomed to permitting three billion dollars to vanish from HEW as if it were the Pentagon. The present Administration may believe that it can afford the wrath of educators. Middle-class Americans have nothing to lose if the program is cut. Poor parents think they do, but, even more, they are demanding control of the funds meant for their children. A logical way of cutting the budget and, one hopes, of increasing benefits is a system of tuition grants such as that proposed by Milton Friedman and others. Funds would be channeled to the beneficiary, enabling him to buy his share of the schooling of his choice. If such credit were limited to purchases which fit into a school curriculum, it would tend to provide greater equality of treatment, but would not thereby increase the equality of social claims.

It should be obvious that even with schools of equal quality a poor child can seldom catch up with a rich one. Even if they attend equal schools and begin at the same age, poor children lack most of the educational opportunities which are casually available to the middle-class child. These advantages range from conversation and books in the home to vacation travel and a different sense of oneself, and apply, for the child who enjoys them, both in and out of school. So the poorer student will generally fall behind so long as he depends on school for advancement or learning. The poor need funds to enable them to learn, not to get certified for the treatment of their alleged disproportionate deficiencies.

All this is true in poor nations as well as in rich ones, but there it appears under a different guise. Modernized poverty in poor nations affects more people more visibly but also—for the moment—more superficially. Two-thirds of all children in Latin America leave school before finishing the fifth grade, but these *"desertores"* are not therefore as badly off as they would be in the United States.

Few countries today remain victims of classical poverty, which was stable and less disabling. Most countries in Latin America have reached the "take-off" point toward economic development and competitive consumption, and thereby toward modernized poverty: their citizens have learned to think rich and live poor. Their laws make six to ten years of school obligatory. Not only in Argentina but also in Mexico or Brazil the average citizen defines an adequate education by North American standards, even though the chance of getting such prolonged schooling is limited to a tiny minority. In these countries the majority is already hooked on school, that is, they are schooled in a sense of inferiority toward the better-schooled. Their fanaticism in favor of school makes it possible to exploit them doubly: it permits increasing allocation of public funds for the education of a few and increasing acceptance of social control by the many.

Paradoxically, the belief that universal schooling is absolutely necessary is most firmly held in those countries where the fewest people have been—and will be—served by schools. Yet in Latin America different paths toward education could still be taken by the majority of parents and children. Proportionately, national savings invested in schools and teachers might be higher than in rich countries, but these investments are totally insufficient to serve the majority by making even four years of school attendance possible. Fidel Castro talks as if he wanted to go in the direction of deschooling when he promises that by 1980 Cuba will be able to dissolve its university since all of life in Cuba will be an educational experience. At the grammar-school and high-school level, however, Cuba, like all other Latin-American countries, acts as though passage through a period defined as the "school age" were an unquestionable goal for all, delayed merely by a temporary shortage of resources.

The twin deceptions of increased treatment, as actually provided in the United States—and as merely promised in Latin America—complement each other. The Northern poor are being disabled by the same twelve-year treatment whose lack brands the Southern poor as hopelessly backward. Neither in North America nor in Latin America do the poor get equality from obligatory schools. But in both places the mere existence of school discourages and disables the poor from taking control of their own learning. All over the world the school has an anti-educational effect on society: school is recognized as the institution which specializes in education. The failures of school are taken by most people as a proof that education is a very costly, very complex, always arcane, and frequently almost impossible task.

School appropriates the money, men, and good will available for education and in addition discourages other institutions from assuming educational tasks. Work, leisure, politics, city living, and even family life depend on schools for the habits and knowledge they presuppose, instead of becoming themselves the means of education. Simultaneously both schools and the other institutions which depend on them are priced out of the market.

In the United States the per capita costs of schooling have risen almost as fast as the cost of medical treatment. But increased treatment by both doctors and teachers has shown steadily declining results. Medical expenses concentrated on those above forty-five have doubled several times over a period of forty years with a resulting 3 percent increase in life expectancy in men. The increase in educational expenditures has produced even stranger results; otherwise President Nixon could not have been moved this spring to promise that every child shall soon have the "Right to Read" before leaving school.

In the United States it would take eighty billion dollars per year to provide what educators regard as equal treatment for all in grammar and high school. This is well over twice the $36 billion now being spent. Independent cost projections prepared at HEW and the University of Florida indicate that by 1974 the comparable figures will be $107 billion as against the $45 billion now projected, and these figures wholly omit the enormous costs of what is called "higher education," for which demand is growing even faster. The United States, which spent nearly eighty billion dollars in 1969 for "defense" including its deployment in Vietnam, is obviously too poor to provide equal schooling. The President's committee for the study of school finance should ask not how to support or how to trim such increasing costs, but how they can be avoided.

Equal obligatory schooling must be recognized as at least economically unfeasible. In Latin America the amount of public money spent on each graduate student is between 350 and 1,500 times the amount spent on the median citizen (that is, the citizen who holds the middle ground between the poorest and the richest). In the United States the discrepancy is smaller, but the discrimination is keener. The richest parents, some 10 percent, can afford private education for their children and help them to benefit from foundation grants. But in addition they obtain ten times the per capita amount of public funds if this is compared with the per capita expenditure made on the children of the 10 percent who are poorest. The principal reasons for this are that rich children stay longer in school, that a year in a university is disproportionately more expensive than a year in high school, and that most private universities depend—at least indirectly—on tax-derived finances.

Obligatory schooling inevitably polarizes a society; it also grades the nations of the world according to an international caste system. Countries are rated like castes whose educational dignity is determined by the average years of schooling of its citizens, a rating which is closely related to per capita gross national product, and much more painful.

The paradox of the schools is evident: increased expenditure escalates their destructiveness at home and abroad. This paradox must be made a public issue. It is now generally accepted that the physical environment will soon be destroyed by biochemical pollution unless we reverse current trends in the production of physical goods. It should also be recognized that social and personal life is threatened equally by HEW pollution, the inevitable by-product of obligatory and competitive consumption of welfare.

The escalation of the schools is as destructive as the escalation of weapons but less visibly so. Everywhere in the world school costs have risen faster than enrollments and faster than the GNP; everywhere expenditures on school fall even further behind the expectations of parents, teachers, and pupils. Everywhere this situation discourages both the motivation and the financing for large-scale planning for nonschooled learning. The United States is proving to the world that no country can be rich enough to afford a school system that meets the demands this same system creates simply by existing, because a successful school system schools parents and pupils to the supreme value of a larger school system, the cost of which increases disproportionately as higher grades are in demand and become scarce.

Rather than calling equal schooling temporarily unfeasible, we must recognize that it is, in principle, economically absurd, and that to attempt it is intellectually emasculating, socially polarizing, and destructive of the credibility of the political system which promotes it. The ideology of obligatory schooling admits of no logical limits. The White House recently provided a good example. Dr. Hutschnecker, the "psychiatrist" who treated Mr. Nixon before he was qualified as a candidate, recommended to the President that all children between six and eight be professionally examined to ferret out those who have destructive tendencies, and that obligatory treatment be provided for them. If necessary, their re-education in special institutions should be required. This memorandum from his doctor the President sent for evaluation to HEW. Indeed, preventive concentration camps for predelinquents would be a logical improvement over the school system.

Equal educational opportunity is, indeed, both a desirable and a feasible goal, but to equate this with obligatory schooling is to confuse salvation with the Church. School has become the world religion of a modernized proletariat, and makes futile promises of salvation to the poor of the technological age. The nation-state has adopted it, drafting all citizens into a graded curriculum leading to sequential diplomas not unlike the initiation rituals and hieratic promotions of former times. The modern state has assumed the duty of enforcing the judgment of its educators through well-meant truant officers and job requirements, much as did the Spanish kings who enforced the judgments of their theologians through the conquistadors and the Inquisition.

Two centuries ago the United States led the world in a movement to disestablish the monopoly of a single church. Now we need the constitutional disestablishment of the monopoly of the school, and thereby of a system which legally combines prejudice with discrimination. The first article of a bill of rights for a modern, humanist society would correspond to the First Amendment to the U.S. Constitution: "The State shall make no law with respect to the establishment of education." There shall be no ritual obligatory for all.

To make this disestablishment effective, we need a law forbidding discrimination in hiring, voting, or admission to centers of learning based on previous attendance at some curriculum. This guarantee would not exclude performance tests of competence for a function or role, but would remove the present absurd discrimination in favor of the person who learns a given skill with the largest expenditure of public funds or—what is equally likely—has been able to obtain a diploma which has no relation to any useful skill or job. Only by protecting the citizen from being disqualified by anything in his career in school can a constitutional disestablishment of school become psychologically effective.

Neither learning nor justice is promoted by schooling because educators insist on packaging instruction with certification. Learning and the assignment of social roles are melted into schooling. Yet to learn means to acquire a new skill or insight, while promotion depends on an opinion which others have formed. Learning frequently is the result of instruction, but selection for a role or category in the job market increasingly depends on mere length of attendance.

Instruction is the choice of circumstances which facilitate learning. Roles are assigned by setting a curriculum of conditions which the candidate must meet if he is to make the grade. School links instruction—but not learning—to these roles. This is neither reasonable nor liberating. It is not reasonable because it does not link relevant qualities or competences to roles, but rather the process by which such qualities are supposed to be acquired. It is not liberating or educational because school reserves instruction to those whose every step in learning fits previously approved measures of social control.

Curriculum has always been used to assign social rank. At times it could be prenatal: karma ascribes you to a caste and lineage to the aristocracy. Curriculum could take the form of a ritual, of sequential sacred ordinations, or it could consist of a succession of feats in war or hunting, or further advancement could be made to depend on a series of previous princely favors. Universal schooling was meant to detach role assignment from personal life history: it was meant to give everybody an equal chance to any office. Even now many people wrongly believe that school ensures the dependence of public trust on relevant learning achievements. However, instead of equalizing chances, the school system has monopolized their distribution.

To detach competence from curriculum, inquiries into a man's learning history must be made taboo, like inquiries into his political affiliation, church attendance, lineage, sex habits, or racial background. Laws forbidding discrimination on the basis of prior schooling must be enacted. Laws, of course, cannot stop prejudice against the unschooled—nor are they meant to force anyone to intermarry with an autodidact—but they can discourage unjustified discrimination.

A second major illusion on which the school system rests is that most learning is the result of teaching. Teaching, it is true, may contribute to certain kinds of learning under certain circumstances. But most people acquire most of their knowledge outside school, and in school only insofar as school, in a few rich countries, has become their place of confinement during an increasing part of their lives.

Most learning happens casually, and even most intentional learning is not the result of programmed instruction. Normal children learn their first language casually, although faster if their parents pay attention to them. Most people who learn a second language well do so as a result of odd circumstances and not of sequential teaching. They go to live with their grandparents, they travel, or they fall in love with a foreigner. Fluency in reading is also more often than not a result of such extracurricular activities. Most people who read widely, and with pleasure, merely believe that they learned to do so in school; when challenged, they easily discard this illusion.

But the fact that a great deal of learning even now seems to happen casually and as a by-product of some other activity defined as work or leisure does not mean that planned learning does not benefit from planned instruction and that both do not stand in need of improvement. The strongly motivated student who is faced with the task of acquiring a new and complex skill may benefit greatly from the discipline now associated with the old-fashioned schoolmaster who taught reading, Hebrew, catechism, or multiplication by rote. School has now made this kind of drill teaching rare and disreputable, yet there are many skills which a motivated student with normal aptitude can master in a matter of a few months if taught in this traditional way. This is as true of codes as of their encipherment; of second and third languages as of reading and writing; and equally of special languages such as algebra, computer programming, chemical analysis, or of manual skills like typing, watchmaking, plumbing, wiring, TV repair; or for that matter dancing, driving, and diving.

In certain cases acceptance into a learning program aimed at a specific skill might presuppose competence in some other skill, but it should certainly not be made to depend upon the process by which such prerequisite skills were acquired. TV repair presupposes literacy and some math; diving, good swimming; and driving, very little of either.

Progress in learning skills is measurable. The optimum resources in time and materials needed by an average motivated adult can be easily estimated. The cost of teaching a second Western European language to a high level of fluency ranges between four and six hundred dollars in the United States, and for an Oriental tongue the time needed for instruction might be doubled. This would still be very little compared with the cost of twelve years of schooling in New York City (a condition for acceptance of a worker into the

Sanitation Department)—almost fifteen thousand dollars. No doubt not only the teacher but also the printer and the pharmacist protect their trades through the public illusion that training for them is very expensive.

At present schools pre-empt most educational funds. Drill instruction which costs less than comparable schooling is now a privilege of those rich enough to bypass the schools, and those whom either the army or big business sends through in-service training. In a program of progressive deschooling of U.S. education, at first the resources available for drill training would be limited. But ultimately there should be no obstacle for anyone at any time of his life to be able to choose instruction among hundreds of definable skills at public expense.

Right now educational credit good at any skill center could be provided in limited amounts for people of all ages, and not just to the poor. I envisage such credit in the form of an educational passport or an "edu-credit card" provided to each citizen at birth. In order to favor the poor, who probably would not use their yearly grants early in life, a provision could be made that interest accrued to later users of cumulated "entitle-ments." Such credits would permit most people to acquire the skills most in demand, at their convenience, better, faster, cheaper, and with fewer undesirable side effects than in school.

Potential skill teachers are never scarce for long because, on the one hand, demand for a skill grows only with its performance within a community and, on the other, a man exercising a skill could also teach it. But, at present, those using skills which are in demand and do require a human teacher are discouraged from sharing these skills with others. This is done either by teachers who monopolize the licenses or by unions which protect their trade interests. Skill centers which would be judged by customers on their results, and not on the personnel they employ or the process they use, would open unsuspected working opportunities, frequently even for those who are now considered unemployable. Indeed, there is no reason why such skill centers should not be at the work place itself, with the employer and his work force supplying instruction as well as jobs to those who choose to use their educational credits in this way.

In 1956 there arose a need to teach Spanish quickly to several hundred teachers, social workers, and ministers from the New York Archdiocese so that they could communicate with Puerto Ricans. My friend Gerry Morris announced over a Spanish radio station that he needed native speakers from Harlem. Next day some two hundred teen-agers lined up in front of his office, and he selected four dozen of them—many of them school dropouts. He trained them in the use of the U.S. Foreign Service Institute (FSI) Spanish manual, designed for use by linguists with graduate training, and within a week his teachers were on their own—each in charge of four New Yorkers who wanted to speak the language. Within six months the mission was accomplished. Cardinal Spellman could claim that he had 127 parishes in which at least three staff members could communicate in Spanish. No school program could have matched these results.

Skill teachers are made scarce by the belief in the value of licenses. Certification constitutes a form of market manipulation and is plausible only to a schooled mind. Most teachers of arts and trades are less skillful, less inventive, and less communicative than the best craftsmen and tradesmen. Most high-school teachers of Spanish or French do not speak the language as correctly as their pupils might after half a year of competent drills. Experiments conducted by Angel Quintero in Puerto Rico suggest that many young teen-agers, if given the proper incentives, programs, and access to tools, are better than most schoolteachers at introducing their peers to the scientific exploration of plants, stars, and matter, and to the discovery of how and why a motor or a radio functions.

Opportunities for skill-learning can be vastly multiplied if we open the "market." This depends on matching the right teacher with the right student when he is highly motivated in an intelligent program, without the constraint of curriculum.

Free and competing drill instruction is a subversive blasphemy to the orthodox educator. It dissociates the acquisition of skills from "humane" education, which schools package together, and thus it promotes unlicensed learning no less than unlicensed teaching for unpredictable purposes.

There is currently a proposal on record which seems at first to make a great deal of sense. It has been prepared by Christopher Jencks of the Center for the Study of Public Policy and is sponsored by the Office of Economic Opportunity. It proposes to put educational "entitlements" or tuition grants into the hands of parents and students for expenditure in the schools of their choice. Such individual entitlements could indeed be an important step in the right direction. We need a guarantee of the right of each citizen to an equal share of tax-derived educational resources, the right to verify this share, and the right to sue for it if denied. It is one form of a guarantee against regressive taxation.

The Jencks proposal, however, begins with the ominous statement that "conservatives, liberals, and radicals have all complained at one time or another that the American educational system gives professional educators too little incentive to provide high quality education to most children." The proposal condemns itself by proposing tuition grants which would have to be spent on schooling.

This is like giving a lame man a pair of crutches and stipulating that he use them only if the ends are tied together. As the proposal for tuition grants now stands, it plays into the hands not only of the professional educators but of racists, promoters of religious schools, and others whose interests are socially divisive. Above all, educational entitlements restricted to use within schools play into the hands of all those who want to continue to live in a society in which social advancement is tied not to proven knowledge but to the learning pedigree by which it is supposedly acquired. This discrimination in favor of schools which dominates Jencks's discussion on refinancing education could discredit one of the most critically needed principles for educational reform: the return of initiative and accountability for learning to the learner or his most immediate tutor.

The deschooling of society implies a recognition of the two-faced nature of learning. An insistence on skill drill alone could be a disaster; equal emphasis must be placed on other kinds of learning. But if schools are the wrong places for learning a skill, they are even worse places for getting an education. School does both tasks badly, partly because it does not distinguish between them. School is inefficient in skill instruction especially because it is curricular. In most schools a program which is meant to improve one skill is chained always to another irrelevant task. History is tied to advancement in math, and class attendance to the right to use the playground.

Schools are even less efficient in the arrangement of the circumstances which encourage the open-ended, exploratory use of acquired skills, for which I will reserve the term "liberal education." The main reason for this is that school is obligatory and becomes schooling for schooling's sake: an enforced stay in the company of teachers, which pays off in the doubtful privilege of more such company. Just as skill instruction must be freed from curricular restraints, so must liberal education be dissociated from obligatory attendance. Both skill-learning and education for inventive and creative behavior can be aided by institutional arrangement, but they are of a different, frequently opposed nature.

Most skills can be acquired and improved by drills, because skill implies the mastery of definable and predictable behavior. Skill instruction can rely, therefore, on the simulation of circumstances in which the skill will be used. Education in the exploratory and creative use of skills, however, cannot rely on drills. Education can be the outcome of instruction, though instruction of a kind fundamentally opposed to drill. It relies on the relationship between partners who already have some of the keys which give access to memories stored in and by the community. It relies on the critical intent of all those who use memories creatively. It relies on the surprise of the unexpected question which opens new doors for the inquirer and his partner.

The skill instructor relies on the arrangement of set circumstances which permit the learner to develop standard responses. The educational guide or master is concerned with helping matching partners to meet so that learning can take place. He matches individuals starting from their own, unresolved questions. At the most he helps the pupil to formulate his puzzlement since only a clear statement will give him the power to find his match, moved like him, at the moment, to explore the same issue in the same context.

Matching partners for educational purposes initially seems more difficult to imagine than finding skill instructors and partners for a game. One reason is the deep fear which school has implanted in us, a fear which makes us censorious. The unlicensed exchange of skills—even undesirable skills—is more predictable and therefore seems less dangerous than the unlimited opportunity for meeting among people who share an issue which for them, at the moment, is socially, intellectually, and emotionally important.

The Brazilian teacher Paulo Freire knows this from experience. He discovered that any adult can begin to read in a matter of forty hours if the first words he deciphers are charged with political meaning. Freire trains his teachers to move into a village and to discover the words which designate current important issues, such as the access to a well or the compound interest on the debts owed to the *patron*. In the evening the villagers meet for the discussion of these key words. They begin to realize that each word stays on the blackboard even after its sound has faded. The letters continue to unlock reality and to make it manageable as a problem. I have frequently witnessed how discussants grow in social awareness and how they are impelled to take political action as fast as they learn to read. They seem to take reality into their hands as they write it down.

I remember the man who complained about the weight of pencils: they were difficult to handle because they did not weigh as much as a shovel; and I remember another who on his way to work stopped with his companions and wrote the word they were discussing with his hoe on the ground: *"agua."* Since 1962 my friend Freire has moved from exile to exile, mainly because he refuses to conduct his sessions around words which are preselected by approved educators, rather than those which his discussants bring to the class.

The educational matchmaking among people who have been successfully schooled is a different task. Those who do not need such assistance are a minority, even among the readers of serious journals. The majority cannot and should not be rallied for discussion around a slogan, a word, or a picture. But the idea remains the same: they should be able to meet around a problem chosen and defined by their own initiative. Creative, exploratory learning requires peers currently puzzled about the same terms or problems. Large universities make the futile attempt to match them by multiplying their courses, and they generally fail since they are bound to curriculum, course structure, and bureaucratic administration. In schools, including universities, most resources are spent to purchase the time and motivation of a limited number of people to take up predetermined problems in a ritually defined setting. The most radical alternative to school would be a network or service which gave each man the same opportunity to share his current concern with others motivated by the same concern.

Let me give, as an example of what I mean, a description of how an intellectual match might work in New York City. Each man, at any given moment and at a minimum price, could identify himself to a computer with his address and telephone number, indicating the book, article, film, or recording on which he seeks a partner for discussion. Within days he could receive by mail the list of others who recently had taken the same initiative. This list would enable him by telephone to arrange for a meeting with persons who initially would be known exclusively by the fact that they requested a dialogue about the same subject.

Matching people according to their interest in a particular title is radically simple. It permits identification only on the basis of a mutual desire to discuss a statement recorded by a third person, and it leaves the initiative of arranging the meeting to the individual. Three objections are usually raised against this skeletal purity. I take them up not only to clarify the theory that I want to illustrate by my proposal—for they highlight the deep-seated resistance to deschooling education, to separating learning from social control—but also because they may help to suggest existing resources which are not now used for learning purposes.

The first objection is: Why cannot self-identification be based also on an *idea* or an issue? Certainly such subjective terms could also be used in a computer system. Political parties, churches, unions, clubs, neighborhood centers, and professional societies already organize their educational activities in this way and in effect they act as schools. They all match people in order to explore certain "themes"; and these are dealt with in courses, seminars, and curricula in which presumed "common interests" are prepackaged. Such theme-matching is by definition teacher-centered: it requires an authoritarian presence to define for the participants the starting point for their discussion.

By contrast, matching by the title of a book, film, etc., in its pure form leaves it to the author to define the special language, the terms, and the framework within which a given problem or fact is stated; and it enables those who accept this starting point to identify themselves to one another. For instance, matching people around the idea of "cultural revolution" usually leads either to confusion or to demagoguery. On the other hand, matching those interested in helping each other understand a specific article by Mao, Marcuse, Freud, or Goodman stands in the great tradition of liberal learning from Plato's Dialogues, which are built around presumed statements by Socrates, to Aquinas's commentaries on Peter the Lombard. The idea of matching by title is thus radically different from the theory on which the "Great Books" clubs, for example, were built: instead of relying on the selection by some Chicago professors, any two partners can choose any book for further analysis.

The second objection asks: Why not let the identification of match seekers include information on age, background, world view, competence, experience, or other defining characteristics? Again, there is no reason why such discriminatory restrictions could not and should not be built into some of the many universities—with or without walls—which could use title-matching as their basic organizational device. I could conceive of a system designed to encourage meetings of interested persons at which the author of the book chosen would be present or represented; or a system which guaranteed the presence of a competent adviser; or one to which only students registered in a department or school had access; or one which permitted meetings only between people who defined their special approach to the title under discussion. Advantages for achieving specific goals of learning could be found for each of these restrictions. But I fear that, more often than not, the real reason for proposing such restrictions is contempt arising from the presumption that people are ignorant: educators want to avoid the ignorant meeting the ignorant around a text which they may not understand and which they read *only* because they are interested in it.

The third objection: Why not provide match seekers with incidental assistance that will facilitate their meetings—with space, schedules, screening, and protection? This is now done by schools with all the inefficiency characterizing large bureaucracies. If we left the initiative for meetings to the match seekers themselves, organizations which nobody now classifies as educational would probably do the job much better. I think of restaurant owners, publishers, telephone-answering services, department store managers, and even commuter train executives who could promote their services by rendering them attractive for educational meetings.

At a first meeting in a coffee shop, say, the partners might establish their identities by placing the book under discussion next to their cups. People who took the initiative to arrange for such meetings would soon learn what items to quote to meet the people they sought. The risk that the self-chosen discussion with one or several strangers might lead to a loss of time, disappointment, or even unpleasantness is certainly smaller than the same risk taken by a college applicant. A computer-arranged meeting to discuss an article in a national magazine, held in a coffee shop off Fourth Avenue, would obligate none of the participants to stay in the company of his new acquaintances for longer than it took to drink a cup of coffee, nor would he have to meet any of them ever again. The chance that it would help to pierce the opaqueness of life in a modern city and further new friendship, self-chosen work, and critical reading is high. (The fact that a record of personal readings and meetings could be obtained thus by the FBI is undeniable; that this should still worry anybody in 1970 is only amusing to a free man, who willy-nilly contributes his share in order to drown snoopers in the irrelevancies they gather.)

Both the exchange of skills and matching of partners are based on the assumption that education for all means education by all. Not the draft into a specialized institution but only the mobilization of the whole population can lead to popular culture. The equal right of each man to exercise his competence to learn and to instruct is now pre-empted by certified teachers. The teachers' competence, in turn, is restricted to what may be done in school. And, further, work and leisure are alienated from each other as a result: the spectator and the worker alike are supposed to arrive at the work place all ready to fit into a routine prepared for them. Adaptation in the form of a product's design, instruction, and publicity shapes them for their role as much as formal education by schooling. A radical alternative to a schooled society requires not only new formal mechanisms for the formal acquisition of skills and their educational use. A deschooled society implies a new approach to incidental or informal education.

Incidental education cannot any longer return to the forms which learning took in the village or the medieval town. Traditional society was more like a set of concentric circles of meaningful structures, while modern man must learn how to find meaning in many structures to which he is only marginally related. In the village, language and architecture and work and religion and family customs were consistent with one another, mutually explanatory and reinforcing. To grow into one implied a growth into the others. Even specialized apprenticeship was a by-product of specialized activities, such as shoemaking or the singing of psalms. If an apprentice never became a master or a scholar, he still contributed to making shoes or to making church services solemn. Education did not compete for time with either work or leisure. Almost all education was complex, lifelong, and unplanned.

Contemporary society is the result of conscious designs, and educational opportunities must be designed into them. Our reliance on specialized, full-time instruction through school will now decrease, and we must find more ways to learn and teach: the educational quality of all institutions must increase again. But this is a very ambiguous forecast. It could mean that men in the modern city will be increasingly the victims of an effective process of total instruction and manipulation once they are deprived of even the tenuous pretense of critical independence which liberal schools now provide for at least some of their pupils.

It could also mean that men will shield themselves less

behind certificates acquired in school and thus gain in courage to "talk back" and thereby control and instruct the institutions in which they participate. To ensure the latter we must learn to estimate the social value of work and leisure by the educational give-and-take for which they offer opportunity. Effective participation in the politics of a street, a work place, the library, a news program, or a hospital is therefore the best measuring stick to evaluate their level as educational institutions.

I recently spoke to a group of junior-high-school students in the process of organizing a resistance movement to their obligatory draft into the next class. Their slogan was "participation—not simulation." They were disappointed that this was understood as a demand for less rather than for more education, and reminded me of the resistance which Karl Marx put up against a passage in the Gotha program which—one hundred years ago—wanted to outlaw child labor. He opposed the proposal in the interest of the education of the young, which could happen only at work. If the greatest fruit of man's labor should be the education he receives from it and the opportunity which work gives him to initiate the education of others, then the alienation of modern society in a pedagogical sense is even worse than its economic alienation.

The major obstacle on the way to a society that truly educates was well defined by a black friend of mine in Chicago, who told me that our imagination was "all schooled up." We permit the state to ascertain the universal educational deficiencies of its citizens and establish one specialized agency to treat them. We thus share in the delusion that we can distinguish between what is necessary education for others and what is not, just as former generations established laws which defined what was sacred and what was profane.

Durkheim recognized that this ability to divide social reality into two realms was the very essence of formal religion. There are, he reasoned, religions without the supernatural and religions without gods, but none which does not subdivide the world into things and times and persons that are sacred and others that as a consequence are profane. Durkheim's insight can be applied to the sociology of education, for school is radically divisive in a similar way.

The very existence of obligatory schools divides any society into two realms: some time spans and processes and treatments and professions are "academic" or "pedagogic," and others are not. The power of school thus to divide social reality has no boundaries: education becomes unworldly and the world becomes noneducational.

Since Bonhoeffer contemporary theologians have pointed to the confusions now reigning between the Biblical message and institutionalized religion. They point to the experience that Christian freedom and faith usually gain from secularization. Inevitably their statements sound blasphemous to many churchmen. Unquestionably, the educational process will gain from the deschooling of society even though this demand sounds to many schoolmen like treason to the enlightenment. But it is enlightenment itself that is now being snuffed out in the schools.

The secularization of the Christian faith depends on the dedication to it on the part of Christians rooted in the Church. In much the same way, the deschooling of education depends on the leadership of those brought up in the schools. Their curriculum cannot serve them as an alibi for the task: each of us remains responsible for what has been made of him, even though he may be able to do no more than accept this responsibility and serve as a warning to others.

Index of Names

Plato, 105, 115, 130, 162, 348
Pliny, 27
Pope, Alexander, 87–89
Postman, Neil, 293–95, 304, 307, 311
Priestley, Joseph, 46

Rantoul, Robert, 71
Reimer, Everett, 305–7, 311
Richards, Theodore, 238
Riessman, Frank, 311
Rollin, Charles, 18–20, 26, 30, 34, 38
Roosevelt, Theodore, 189
Rousseau, J.-J., 221, 222, 289
Ruffner, Viola, 174–78
Rush, Benjamin, 47
Rusk, Ralph Leslie, 119

Schlipp, Paul A., 219
Shakespeare, William, 115
Smith, William, 13
Smyth, Albert Henry, 16
Socrates, 348
Spiller, Robert E., 119

Stiles, Ezra, 2
Swedenborg, 115, 120

Tocqueville, Alexis de, 69
Tolstoy, Leo, 300
Troost, Cornelius J., 311
Turnbull, George, 18, 22, 26, 29, 32, 37–40

Van Doren, Carl, 3
Veysey, Lawrence, 161
Vico, Giambattista, 113

Walker, Obadiah, 18, 23, 33
Washington, Booker T., 173–99
Washington, George, 44
Webster, Daniel, 63, 70
Weingartner, Charles, 293–95, 308, 311
Welter, Rush, 80
Whicher, Stephen E., 119
White, Morton, 119, 204
Williams, Wallace E., 119
Wirth, Arthur G., 219
Woody, Thomas, 16
Wordsworth, William, 107

Index of Subjects

361